The Big Band Almanac

REVISED EDITION

Leo Walker

A DA CAPO PAPERBACK

Library of Congress Cataloging in Publication Data

Walker, Leo.
  The big band almanac.

  (A Da Capo paperback)
  1. Big bands – Dictionaries. 2. Jazz musicians – Bio-
graphy – Dictionaries. I. Title.
[ML102.B5W34 1989]   785′.092′2   [B]   88-33463
ISBN 0-306-80345-3

First paperback printing – March, 1989

This Da Capo Press paperback edition of *The Big Band Almanac*
is an unabridged republication of the edition published in
Hollywood, California in 1978, here updated with author
corrections and additions.

Published by Da Capo Press, Inc.
A Subsidiary of Plenum Publishing Corporation
233 Spring Street, New York, N.Y. 10013

The Big Band Almanac

Leo Walker

Preface

The era of the great dance bands embraces a period that began to develop just before the 1920s, reached its peak in the early forties, and declined into relative obscurity by the late fifties. Periodic revival attempts have met with only limited success, despite the fact the music from this period has outlived most of what resulted from the musical forms and styles that followed.

Before the passage of time dims it beyond recall, I believe the memory of the bandleaders who made up this era should be preserved. In the pages that follow, an attempt is made, through a combination of text and photographs, to provide the reader with information about each individual, how he got started, what he accomplished, and to a limited degree, what he was like. Currently the generation that did not get to dance to the original big bands is indicating a strong interest in knowing about them and I hope satisfactory answers are provided here. For those who were there when it was happening, this book should refresh some old memories.

If you are in the latter group, and find one of your own favorites missing, it's because sufficient material was not available to give him detailed coverage. At the peak of the great dance band era, a trade journal regularly listed itineraries of over 600 name, semi-name, and territory bands. My objective was to profile here, in some depth, those who were best known, made some unusual contribution, or were particularly newsworthy for one reason or another. Little or no opinion of the musical value of their playing style will be found, as I believe that this is a matter of individual likes and dislikes.

The listings of the band personnel rely on individual memories, discographies, and other reference sources, which even collectively are in most cases less than complete. Apologies are offered to those who may not be included.

To the many bandleaders, musicians, and personal managers who cooperated in providing material, I want to publicly express my appreciation—with special thanks for pictorial material to Barney McDevitt, Ralph Portnor, Wally Heider, Jack Lomas, Frank Driggs, Bill Wilson, and Paul Mertz.

And a very special note of appreciation to my wife Peg, without whose tireless efforts on the typewriter the project could never have been accomplished.

Introduction

by Les Brown

Naturally those of us who have spent our lives in the band business are pleased when someone writes a book about that business, particularly when it gives each bandleader individual coverage.

Leo Walker's *Big Band Almanac* tells our story in simple, easy to read language, illustrated with pictures, many of which are collectors' items. Out of the many filing cabinets where he has stored all this big band era memorabilia, he has come up with many things which we should have collected for our own scrap books and didn't. The book makes a big contribution to the history of a wonderful era, a time when the guy took the gal in his arms to dance with her and when participation in the music business necessitated the ability to read notes.

The Big Band Almanac is written by a guy who knows what he's writing about, and if you lived through the big band era or are curious to know what happened, then it's a book you should have.

Introduction

by Harry James

The band business has been my life and it's been a good life. It's taken me all over the world and through it I have met many important and interesting people.

Most people think of the "big band era" as a period which began about 1935 and ended sometime in the 1950s. Actually, the band business hasn't died at all, even though it has undergone many changes. Some of these came about as a result of the changing times, some through the effects on the whole entertainment industry of such things as television. Those changes began shortly after World War II and progressed through the 1950s. Theaters which had featured dance bands as headline entertainment discontinued them and many even closed their doors. So, too, did a lot of the ballrooms. And hotels which had featured dancing with name bands changed their policies; many simply because night-time television killed remote pickups from these hotels, which had been a very important means of advertising. The ranks of the bandleaders were thinned out as many decided not to compete in a changing and declining market. For those of us who did adapt to the new market for our music, the business has always been good and still is. My own band has all the work it can handle and the same is true with fellow bandleaders Woody Herman, Count Basie, and Les Brown. The Duke Ellington band is still active under the leadership of Duke's son, Mercer, so, too, is the

Lombardo band, and there's still a Dorsey and Glenn Miller band on the road.

It's true most of the jobs we're playing are different from those we played twenty-five years ago. Many are concert dates and a lot are private parties, but there is still a good mix of ballroom and promotion dates included. The hotel/casinos in Nevada still offer opportunities to occasionally set down for a longer stay. But we're the same people who were booked steadily during the big band era. Everywhere we go it's indicated there's a bigger market for our music than there are bands to supply it. There's a crying need to develop new and younger bands to take over the business when we eventually retire. It's a mistake to believe that the younger generation has no interest in the music from the big band era—some of the concert dates we play are in high schools. More and more younger people are being seen in our audiences and all over the country young musicians are forming bands to play our kind of music, even though many of them accomplish little beyond the kick of playing together. However, the ability to launch one of these new bands into a suc-cessful venture without an interest on the part of the major recording companies and without band remotes is almost impossible.

In Leo Walker's first book, *The Great Dance Bands*, he traced the history of the big band era from its development to its decline, including the various segments of the band business. During that wonderful era there were hundreds of active bands, ranging from local attractions to territory, semi-name, and name bands. Their ranks were decimated as many of them dropped out to pursue other careers, some simply retired, and far too many are no longer with us. In his new book, *The Big Band Almanac*, Leo secures a place in history for these band-leaders by telling their individual stories and making a permanent record of the era. Excellent photographs also give you a chance to see the bandleaders then and now and the size of the bands which they fronted. I'm also glad this type of book is being written by a man so well-qualified through his many years of close association with those people who made up the wonderful big band era.

The Big Band Almanac

IRVING AARONSON

Started First Band   Mid-twenties
Where   New York City
Sidemen With Band Included   An impressive list of the greats of the twenties and thirties, including Mickey Bloom, Red Stanley, Harold Saliers, Herman Hyde, Phil Saxe, Sal Cibelli, Ralph Napoli, Stanley Johnson, Frank Cornwell, Mack Walker, Artie Quenzer, Nat Shilkret, Charlie Trotta, Artie Shaw, Tony Pastor, Jack Armstrong, Harry McKeown, Red Jessup, Ernie Mathias, Joe Gillespie, Sam Rubenowitch, Morty Friedman, Horace Diaz, Dick Dixon, Gene Krupa, George Green, Reggie Merrill, Skippy Carlstrom, Mike Renzulli.
Vocalists With Band Included   Betty Cannon, Lois Still
Tag Line   "Irving Aaronson And His Commanders"
Theme Song   "Commanderism"
Recording Affiliations   Edison, Victor, Vocalion, Columbia

Aaronson and his Commanders was rated as one of the top dance orchestras of the twenties and early thirties. In addition to employing some of the best musicians of that period, his band was the training ground for such future great bandleaders as Artie Shaw, Tony Pastor, and Gene Krupa. Although they initially concentrated in the New York and East Coast area, they did engage in nationwide tours, travelling in private automobiles, with a large truck carting the instruments, and other props. They were very popular in ballrooms and theaters. Their first trip to the West Coast was made in 1934, at which time they played the Avalon Ballroom in Catalina. Aaronson was the first name band to play the spot, setting off a name band policy which was in effect on a full-time basis until World War II interrupted it. Some time after the mid-thirties Aaronson gave up the band and in the early forties became the musical director for MGM Studios in Hollywood. At one time he was an associate producer with Joe Pasternak. He was still associated with the studio as a musical director when he died in March 1963, at the age of sixty-eight.

The Irving Aaronson Orchestra in the mid 1920s.

The Irving Aaronson Orchestra, on Catalina, 1934. Band personnel: George Green, Julie Losch, Horace Diaz, Dick Dickson, Ernie Mathias, Morty Friedman, Joe Gillespie, Skippy Carlstrom, Harry McKehan, "Chin Chin" Braciante, Sam Rubenowitch, Phil Saxe, Mike Renzulli, Reggie Merrill, vocalists Betty Cannon, Lois Still.

CHARLIE AGNEW

Started First Band 1924
Where Chicago
Previous Band Affiliations Harry Yerkes, Charlie Strickland, Vincent Lopez, Del Lampe
Vocalists With Band Included Harlan Hassburg, Irene Taylor, Jeanne Carroll
Sponsored Radio Shows "The Yeast Foam Program," "The Armandes Face Cream Program," "The Lucky Strike Magic Carpet"
Longest Engagement Two years at the Stevens Hotel, one-and-one-half years at the Edgewater Beach Hotel
Theme Song "Slow But Sure"
Songs Written "Slow But Sure," "Fools In Love," "Too Many On My Mind"
Recording Affiliations RCA, Columbia

Charlie Agnew.

Agnew's first engagement with his own band was at the Trianon Ballroom. The reputation which he built there permitted him to move into Chicago hotel locations, and with good air time he soon built up a strong following throughout the Midwest. During the next years he continued to make Chicago his base of operations, from which point he moved out to play coast-to-coast one-nighters and in such key locations as the Baker Hotel in Dallas, the Rice in Houston, the Peabody in Memphis, the Schroeder in Milwaukee, the Netherland Plaza in Cincinnati, the Muehlebach in Kansas City, the St. Paul Hotel in St. Paul, Minnesota, Lakeside Park in Denver, the Graystone Ballroom in Detroit, and Bill Green's Casino in Pittsburgh. He was also very popular in theater appearances. Stylewise he was basically a smooth band aimed at providing good tempos for dancing. In the mid-forties he had an extended run at the El Rancho in Las Vegas and was one of the early dance bands to play Las Vegas locations. In the late forties he concentrated on radio staff assignments in the Chicago area, often with a smaller group rather than a full-sized band. He remained active into the early fifties, at which time he retired from the music business to pursue other interests. He passed away in Chicago on October 22, 1978.

Jeanne Carroll, Charlie Agnew Band.

3

VAN ALEXANDER

Started First Band 1938
Where New York City
Previous Band Affiliations None as a musician but arranged for Chick Webb, Benny Goodman, Paul Whiteman
Sidemen With Band Included Si Zentner, Ted Nash, Shelly Manne, Irv Cottler, "Butch" Stone, Ray Barr, Neal Hefti, Alvin Stoller, "Slam" Stewart, Charlie Shavers, Don Lamond, Arnold Fishkind, Bill Schallen, Dick Raymond
Vocalists With Band Included David Allen, Butch Stone, Phyllis Kenny
Sponsored Radio Shows "The Callihans," repeat appearances on "Fitch Bandwagon"
Longest Engagement Roseland Ballroom, New York City
Theme Song "Alexander's Rag Time Band"
Songs Written "A Tisket, A Tasket" (co-authored with Ella Fitzgerald), "Got A Pebble In My Shoe," "I Close My Eyes," "Hot Dog Joe"
Recording Affiliations Bluebird, Victor, Varsity

Van Alexander with his orchestra, at Loew's State Theater, New York, 1940.

Alexander gave up his career as a bandleader in 1944. The next year he moved to California, where he became active as a writer and conductor for motion pictures and television. He piled up an imposing list of credits in pictures and was three times nominated for an Emmy for his television work. He also turned out some LPs for Capitol Records with studio bands. He is a member of the music branch of the Motion Picture Academy and is past president of the Los Angeles Chapter of N.A.R.A.S.

BERT AMBROSE

Started First Band Early twenties
Where London, England
Previous Band Affiliations Theater bands
Sidemen With Band Included Eddie Calvert, George Melachrino, Stanley Black, Kenny Baker, George Shearing, Ted Heath, Lew Stone, Danny Polo, Tommy McQuater, Bill Amstell, Bert Barnes, Max Bacon, Lew Davis
Vocalists With Band Included Vera Lynn
Recording Affiliations HMV, Decca

During the thirties and forties Bert Ambrose, billing himself as Ambrose and His Orchestra, was one of the top bands in England and very popular in the United States on records. He studied music in New York City and played violin in theater and symphony orchestras there. He returned to England to start his own band, opening with it at Luigi's Embassy Club in London, where he remained for six years. He had another six-year run at the New Mayfair Hotel, and by that time he was established as one of England's best bands, becoming extremely popular on English radio. His early musical style was primarily sweet music, ideal for hotel dance rooms. When swing took over in the mid-thirties, he altered his style to go along with it, and somewhat later borrowed some of the Glenn Miller style. The band was featured in several British movies, the best known of which was "Soft Lights and Sweet Music." Throughout his years as a leader Ambrose featured nothing but the best musicians available. The peak of his popularity was in the forties during which time he was extremely active in night clubs, theaters, on radio, and particularly on records. In the early fifties he diminished his activity and fronted a smaller band playing primarily club dates. He died in 1973.

RAY ANTHONY

Started First Band 1946
Where New York City
Previous Band Affiliations Al Donahue, Glenn Miller, Jimmy Dorsey
Vocalists With Band Included Dee Keating, Marcie Miller, Tommy Mercer, The Skyliners
Sponsored Radio Shows Mutual Broadcasting System Band Shows
Television With Band "The Chesterfield Show," two years
Theme Song "Young Man With A Horn"
Recording Affiliations Sonora, Capitol

Anthony, who was often described as looking like movie star Cary Grant, left his home town of Cleveland while still a teenager, for his first major band assignment with Al Donahue. In 1941 Glenn Miller offered him an opportunity to play in his trumpet section, where he spent several months, a period which was probably terminated because of repeated clashes between Anthony and Miller. He then joined the Jimmy Dorsey band, which was riding the crest of popularity generated by a string of hit records, and remained there until he entered the navy soon after the start of World War II. Eventually he became the leader of what was reputedly one of the best service bands headquartered in the Pacific area.

Ray Anthony.

Once the war was over he decided it was time to realize his own ambition to be a bandleader. The crew he put together was a well-disciplined organization of young men whose neat appearance on the bandstand made a substantial contribution to their suc-

Anthony and the service band he fronted during World War II.

At the Pennsylvania Hotel in the mid 1950s.

In the mid 1950s Anthony was featured on Chesterfield's TV show and was billed as the Chesterfield Orchestra on personal appearances.

cess. Although his trumpet was played in the style of Harry James, the arrangements leaned heavily in the direction of the Miller style, with an occasional James version thrown in. In the postwar years his was one of the fastest-rising new dance bands, despite the fact that the overall band business was declining. A record contract with Sonora and a couple of movie shorts made for Columbia contributed to his success. By 1951 he was a strong contender for the mythical title of "Band of the Year." By that time television had become the major entertainment medium and even though Anthony at first had said he wanted no part of it, he was quick to respond when a cigarette sponsor offered him a program, a show which lasted a couple of seasons. In the late fifties Anthony gave up his big band and organized a small musical combo featuring a group of female vocalists and for the next several years appeared regularly with them, doing repeat appearances in the lounges of Las Vegas, Lake Tahoe, and the other few remaining spots around the nation still booking live entertainment. In the early seventies he put together a show titled "Directions '71," which incorporated some of the best sounds from the great dance bands into a program balanced with current pop stylings. This was a small group of musicians who did the instrumentals and backed his vocalists. Offering both nostalgic memories for those who sought them and the type of music the younger set related to bridged the generation gap which others had overlooked. Thus he soon began enjoying a new wave of popularity, which is still going strong.

LOUIS ARMSTRONG

Started First Band   1929, although he had taken brief flings at fronting a band under his own name prior to that date

Where   New York City

Previous Band Affiliations   King Oliver, Kid Ory, Fletcher Henderson, Erskine Tate, Carrol Dickerson, Clarence Jones

Sidemen With Band Included   Those in the bands of Luis Russell and Les Hite, which he fronted for brief periods under his own name. Other bands included at various times Earl Hines, Henry "Red" Allen, J. C. Higginbotham, Barney Bigard, Dick Carey, Sid Catlett, Arvell Shaw, Jack Teagarden, Billy Kyle, Edmund Howe, Trummy Young, Joe Bushkin, Cozy Cole

Theme Song   Best identified with "Sleepy Time Down South," although he first used "On the Sunny Side of the Street"

Recording Affiliations   The list is endless and on a variety of labels including Decca, Columbia, Victor, Verve, Riverside

Armstrong, affectionately known as "Louie" or "Satchmo," is doubtless the best known of all America's great jazz musicians. Born in New Orleans in 1900, he was placed in a waif home when he had barely reached his teens. It was there that he began to study the cornet and got the training which made it possible for him to play in local bands with some of the great jazz men of the Crescent City. These included King Oliver who later, in 1922, invited Armstrong to come to Chicago to join his own band, which was doing well in that city. Armstrong's fame as a musician grew so rapidly that he was soon able to move in and out of any of the top black bands both in the Chicago area and in New York.

As a bandleader in his own right he fronted a large organization of no less than fifteen musicians throughout the thirties and into the mid-forties. Although this was the period of peak popularity for the big

Without "my horn" he wouldn't really have been Louis Armstrong.

At the Regal Theater in Chicago, 1938. *Left to right:* trumpet — Henry "Red" Allen; trombone — J. C. Higginbotham; trumpet — Louis Bacon; trombone — George Washington; trumpet — Shelton Hemphill; trombone — Jimmy Archey; piano/arranger — Luis Russell; drums — Paul Barbarin; trumpet — Louis Armstrong; tenor sax — Albert Nicholas; guitar — Lee Blair; alto sax — Charlie Holmes; bass — Pops Foster; alto sax — Pete Clark; clarinet, tenor sax — Bingie Madison.

In 1931 Armstrong and his band visited the boys' home in New Orleans, where he spent time as a teenager. Band members (*left to right*): bass—Johnny Lindsay; alto sax—George James; trumpet— Z. T. Randolph; banjo—Mike McKendrick; drums—Fred "Tubby" Hall; Louis Armstrong; piano—Charlie Alexander; tenor sax—Al Washington; trombone—Preston Jackson; alto sax—Lester Boone.

swinging bands, it is doubtful that Armstrong prospered during those years in direct proportion to his personal reputation and the musicianship of the organization he fronted. But his fame continued to spread, not only in the United States but on the European continent where he was repeatedly invited to go for continental tours, sometimes fronting bands which were assembled for him there. Shortly after the end of World War II, he dropped the big band in favor of a small all-star group, usually six or seven in number including himself. His success with this group was almost instantaneous, giving him the financial success which had probably eluded him before. With it he toured the United States, playing all the top locations, and with additional tours abroad. Eventually the sound of his trumpet, his big smile, and the ever-present white handkerchief, were known round the world. His reception in foreign countries earned for him the title "America's Ambassador of Jazz." During his long career he was featured in many motion pictures, including several made with Bing Crosby, one of his greatest friends and admirers. The first of the Crosby pictures was made in 1936, "Pennies From Heaven." Some of the better known pictures in which he appeared were "The Glenn Miller Story," "The Five Pennies," and "High Society."

Louis Armstrong in 1954.

Despite the fact that he was America's most famous jazz man, he was very often quoted as expressing a strong like for the smooth music played by Guy Lombardo. There are rumors that in the late twenties it was Armstrong's trumpet which Chicago labelled "The Sweetest Music This Side Of Heaven," a tag line that was later permanently adopted by Lombardo. Armstrong was active as a performer almost to the very end of his life. On July 4, 1970, he was given a mammoth seventieth birthday celebration in Los Angeles, followed by similar tributes in Newport and New York. The following March he was hospitalized with a heart ailment but by early summer he was talking of making personal appearances again. But it was not to be. Two days after his seventy-first birthday, he died quietly in his New York home. Perhaps his old friend Bing Crosby best expressed what was in the hearts of the millions who mourned his passing: "He was the only musician who ever lived who can't be replaced by someone."

GUS ARNHEIM

Started First Band   1926
Where   Cocoanut Grove, Ambassador Hotel, Los Angeles, California
Previous Band Affiliations   Was pianist with Abe Lyman
Sidemen With Band Included   Jimmie Grier, Fred MacMurray, Henry Jaworski, Sterling Young, Manny Stein, Stan Kenton, Bob Ballard, Irving Fazola, Andy Russell
Vocalists With Band Included   The Rhythm Boys (Bing Crosby, Al Rinker, Harry Barris), Russ Columbo, Loyce Whiteman, Joy Hodges, Shirley Ross, Donald Novis, Ruth Lloyd, the Sportsmen, and Andy Russell
Musical Style   Concentrated on smooth dance tempos, ideally styled for hotels and ballrooms
Sponsored Radio Shows   "This Is The Cocoanut Grove," a two-hour coast-to-coast broadcast originating from the Grove in the early thirties
Longest Engagement   The Cocoanut Grove
Theme Song   "Sweet And Lovely," "I Cried For You," "It Must Be True," and others
Recording Affiliations   Most of his recording was done for Victor

Gus Arnheim.

During Arnheim's early years at the Cocoanut Grove, a singing job with his orchestra was considered a probable stepping stone to greater success in motion pictures or radio. In a book of his own, Bing Crosby credited his exposure at the Grove with Arnheim as being the major contributor to his success. Russ Columbo became a recording star in his own right as a result of the same exposure, singing in a style which so closely resembled Crosby's that when Crosby failed to appear for the broadcasts Arnheim had Columbo fill in. Joy Hodges, Shirley Ross, and Donald Novis went on to motion pictures and radio success and The Sportsmen were later to be featured on the Jack Benny show.

The Arnheim band, usually fourteen including a female vocalist, frequently toured the forty-eight states, playing ballrooms, hotels, and theaters. Arnheim made at least two European tours, the first in 1929. Shortly after World War II he gave up the band to concentrate on writing for the picture studios. He died in his Beverly Hills home in January 1955, victim of a heart attack at age fifty-six.

The Arnheim band at the Ambassador, Los Angeles. Bing Crosby standing by the piano.

Gus Arnheim's orchestra playing a Chicago theater date in 1935.

The Gus Arnheim Orchestra in 1942. In the front row, third from the left, is Andy Russell, who was playing drums as well as singing.

The Bob Astor Band in the early 1940s. Drummer is Shelley Mann; Les Elgart is in the trumpet section; Larry Elgart is in the sax section.

PAUL ASH

Started First Band Early twenties
Where Springfield, Illinois
Previous Band Affiliations Vaudeville groups
Sidemen With Band Included John Linn, John Valentine, Roscoe Lantz, Herbert Nettles, Phil Wing, Howard Grantham, Harry Barris, Julian Davidson, Danny Polo, Hank Winston, Seger Ellis, Irving Kaufman, Don Lindley, Vernon Hayes, Harry Hoffman, Harry Struble, Maurice Feiler, Arthur Layfield, Pierre Olker
Vocalists With Band Included Milton Watson
Songs Written "Thinking Of You," "What Do We Care If It's One O'Clock," "That's Why I Love You," "Just Once Again," "Who's Your Sweetheart"
Recording Affiliations Brunswick, Columbia

Ash was born in Germany but while still an infant was brought to the United States by his family who made their home in Milwaukee, Wisconsin. His work in vaudeville bands was interrupted for military service in World War I, following which he started a dance band of his own and before long was returning out recordings. By the mid-twenties his was one of the very popular bands in the Chicago area but by the late twenties he began to de-emphasize dance engagements in favor of working theaters. He had a long run at Chicago's Oriental Theater, then went to New York to play the Paramount and it was during that engagement that he gave then unknown singer Helen Kane a boost on the way to stardom by featuring her in his Paramount appearances. During the 1933 World's Fair in Chicago he was one of its featured bands returning to New York in the mid-thirties to become musical director at the Paramount. He led the band at the Roxy Theater from late 1936 until about 1945. He later retired from the music business and died in New York City in July 1958.

BOB ASTOR

Started First Band Early forties
Where Los Angeles
Previous Band Affiliations Small combos in the New Orleans and East Texas area
Sidemen With Band Included Shelley Manne, Zoot Sims, Les Elgart, Larry Elgart, George Williams, Illinois Jacquet, Dave Pell, Marty Napoleon, Neal Hefti, Irv Levin, Tommy Allison, Tony Faso, Irv Kluger, Ernie Figueroa
Vocalists With Band Included Jo Napoleon, Neal Hefti, Irv Levin, Tommy Allison, Tony Faso, Irv Kluger, Ernie Figueroa
Theme Song "Blue Lights"
Songs Written "If You Don't Believe I'm Leaving, Count The Days I'm Gone," "Fat Sam," "Here Comes The Judge," "I Remember Harlem," "In The Cool Of The Evening," "There Ain't No Flies On Me," "You're My Baby You," "I'm The Butcher Boy"

Astor's bandleading career was rather brief. He launched it at Hermosa Beach in Southern California in 1940 and was perhaps the first West Coast band to feature black musicians. Although the band got its start on the West Coast, it did tour the Midwest and East, playing such spots as the Elms Ballroom in Youngstown, Ohio, and the William Penn Hotel in Pittsburgh, Pennsylvania, with extended runs in each location. Astor's popularity was given a boost by appearances on the Fitch Bandwagon and by remotes from his locations. Although he did a substantial amount of composing, the band did not put its efforts on wax. About the time Astor's recording deal with Decca was about to jell, Petrillo (head of the musician's union) called the first of his recording bans and the contract was never signed. Eventually Astor gave up bandleading to become a disc jockey.

GEORGIE AULD

Started First Band   Early forties
Where   New York City
Previous Band Affiliations   Bunny Berigan, Artie Shaw, Jan Savitt, Benny Goodman
Sidemen With Band Included   Bernie Privin, Nelson Shellady, Chuck Peterson, Les Jenkins, Harry Rodgers, George Arus, Henry Freeman, Les Robinson, Ron Perry, Bob Kitsis, Al Avola, Dick Horvath, Ralph Hawkins, Johnny Best, Harry Geller, Dave Barbour, Henry Adler
Theme Song   "I've Got A Right To Know"
Recording Affiliations   Varsity

Auld was one of the great tenor sax men of the big band era. He had started out on alto sax, on which instrument he had been a child prodigy, and had studied saxophone with Rudy Wiedoeft. He was a featured soloist with many name bands, and had intermittently led small combos, before finally taking a fling at leading a big band of his own. His bandleading career was brief. It was interrupted for military service in 1943, but that too was of short duration. In the early postwar period he led several groups of his own, most of them small combos, with intermittent attempts to lead a big band. The

Georgie Auld.

last of these was made in the early forties. In 1976 he once again distinguished himself by playing the tenor saxophone sound tracks in the motion picture "New York, New York," which starred Liza Minelli. By that time he was making his home in Palm Springs, with only occasional activity as a musician. He died in January 1990.

MITCHELL AYRES

Started First Band   Mid-thirties
Previous Band Affiliations Little Jack Little
Sidemen With Band Included   Marty Olsen, John d'Agostino, James Milazzo, William Beeby, Harry Terrell, Ernie Diven, Phil Zolkind, Ludwig Flato, George Cuomo, Aaron Goldmark, Joe Dale, Dean Kincaid, Dick Dale, Johnny Bonn, Babe Russin, Warren Covington, Armand Anelli, Lou Regiero, Milt Laufer, Phil Laufer, George Popa, Maurie Roy, Lew Korb, Harry Pelsinger, John Bonafede, Gene Lorello, Don Brassfield

Vocalists With Band Included   Ruth Gaylor, Mary Ann Mercer, Joe Dale, Tommy Taylor
Theme Song   "You Go To My Head"
Recording Affiliations   Vocalion, Bluebird

For several years the Mitchell Ayres band toured the country playing good solid dance music designed for dancing. During the early forties Ayres was on the road with the Andrews Sisters and worked with them in one or more movies. Motion pictures in which the band appeared included "Lady, Let's Dance" and "Moonlight And Cactus."

Georgie Auld and his orchestra.

Mitchell Ayres.

In addition the Ayres orchestra was featured on the Andy Russell show in 1944-45. Shortly after that, Ayres disbanded his orchestra, and became musical director for Perry Como, first on radio and later on television. This association continued into the mid-sixties. In the mid-sixties he became musical director for "The Hollywood Palace," also making occasional appearances in Las Vegas. He was fatally injured when hit by a car in Las Vegas in September 1969.

SMITH BALLEW

Started First Band   Early twenties
Where   Dallas, Texas
Previous Band Affiliations   College bands
Sidemen With Band Included   Babe Russin, Bruce Yantis, Bobby Van Eps, Carl Kress, Ward Lay, Stan King, Pete Pumiglio, Mickey Bloom, Jack Purvis, Dee Orr, Wally Curtis, Richard Swanker, Rex Gavitte, Manny Klein, Glenn Miller, Tommy Gott, Jimmy Dorsey, Joe Venuti, Frank Guarente, Bunny Berigan, Charlie Butterfield, Chester Hazlett, Lou Kosloff, Harry Hoffman, Joe Meresco, Perry Botkin, Artie Bernstein, Larry Gomar, Victor Young, Chummy MacGregor, Jimmy McPartland, Harry Goodman, Ray McKinley, Stew Pletcher, Skeets Herfurt, Roc Hillman
Vocalists With Band Included   Smith Ballew, Kay Weber
Theme Song   "Tonight There Is Music In The Air," signed off with "Home"
Recording Affiliations   Paramount, Okeh, Banner, Crown, Columbia

Ballew's personal claim to fame was as a vocalist who could handle all types of lyrics and adapt to practically any key. Even after having led a band of his own for several years, he disbanded for awhile to sing briefly for such bandleaders as Ben Pollack, Ted Fio Rito, Meyer Davis, George Olsen, Hal Kemp, and Sam Lanin. He formed a band of his own again in 1929 in New York City, to play at Whyte's Restaurant. In the early thirties he once more put together a larger band, with which he was quite successful on the hotel circuit. The personnel of this band was somewhat transient and at various times included some of the country's best sidemen. With it he was also extremely active on records, some of them made as "Smith Ballew and His Orchestra," and occasionally as "Buddy Blue and His Texans." He gave up bandleading in the mid-thirties to become the singing host of the "Shell Chateau" on radio, a program on which Victor Young had the orchestra. He also worked in a motion picture and during the rest of the thirties starred in several low budget movies. During World War II he was in defense work. In the early fifties he left show business, to pursue a business career in Fort Worth, Texas.

WALTER BARNES

Started Band Mid-twenties
Where Detroit
Sidemen With Band Included Ted Burke, Leon Scott, George Thigpen, Urbie Gage, Leon Washington, Lucius Wilson, William Bradley, Otis Bates, Bill Winston, Paul Johnson, Bill Thompson, William All, Charles Harkless, Quinn Wilson, Lawrence Thomas, Wilson Underwood, Robert Turner, Claude Alexander, Leon Gray, Augustine Deluce, John Frazier, Ralph Barrett, Bob White, Ernest Smith, Henry Palmer, Fred Edwards, Zinky Cohn, Harry Gray, Tom Watkins, Otis Williams, Richard Dunlap, Chick Gordon, Joe Gauff, Jim Coles, Don Pullen, Harry Walker, Bud Washington, Jack Johnson, John Fryer, Jim Cox, Les Cadwell, Wally Mercer, Edgar Brown, Paul Scott, Calvin Roberts, John Reed, John Henderson, Jesse Washington, Clarence Porter, Arthur Edwards, Oscar Brown
Tag Line "Walter Barnes and His Royal Creolians"
Recording Affiliations Brunswick

Walter Barnes was born in Vicksburg, Mississippi in 1907. In the early twenties he moved to Chicago, where he completed his high school education and studied music. During the early twenties he played saxophone and clarinet with several bands in Chicago and Detroit before becoming a bandleader himself. The band which Barnes put together was usually described as a "hot band" but its fame was not in keeping with its musicianship. Initially he concentrated in the Detroit and Chicago areas, with nearly a two-year stand at the Cotton Club in Cicero, Illinois, a club owned by Al Capone's brother Ralph. During that period they were on the air nightly and this earned them a New York engagement. Shortly after that Barnes moved to Florida to make his home, and from there toured the South, playing an extended string of one-nighters. In the late thirties he returned to Chicago to make a brief appearance at the Savoy Ballroom. In the spring of 1940 one of the band's one-nighters took them into Natchez, Mississippi to play the Rhythm Club, an old garage converted into a night club. During the performance a fire broke out, spreading quickly through the old frame building and permitting only a few to escape through the front door, the only exit. Barnes and his entire band perished in the fire.

Walter Barnes and his Royal Creolians, a Chicago band which was one of the first Midwest orchestras to make regular, annual tours of the South. *Front row:* Ed Burke, Leon Scott, George Thigpen, Walter Barnes (*standing, center*), Urbie Gage, Leon Washington, Lucius "Chaps" Wilson. *Back row:* William Bradley, Otis Bates, Bill Winston (drums), Paul Johnson, Bill Thompson. (Identifications by Ed Burke.)

CHARLIE BARNET

Started First Band 1933
Where Paramount Grill, Hotel Paramount, New York City
Previous Band Affiliations Frank Winegar, Beasley Smith, Hank Biagini, Huston Ray, the California Ramblers
Sidemen With Band Included Gordon Griffin, Eddie Myers, Toots Camarata, George Bohn, Les Cooper, Don Morres, Jack Henderson, Billy Miller, Buford Turner, Pete Peterson, Rudy De Julius, Eddie Sauter, Red Norvo, Kermit Simmons, Joe Hostetter, Frank Amaral, George Vaughn, Willard Brady, Bob Parks, Horace Diaz, Frank Klinger, Sid Weiss, George Kennedy, Irving Goodman, Sonny Lee, Murray Williams, Henry Galtman, Kurt Bloom, John Nicolini, Tom Morgan, Buddy Schutz, Frank Newton, Jimmy Milazzo, Harry Carrel, Ernie Diven, Ludwig Flato, George Cuomo, Bob Burnet, Bill Robertson, Nat Jaffe, Charlie Shavers, Billy May, Phil Moore, Spud Murphy, Skip Martin, Bill Miller, Cliff Leeman, Noni Bernardi, Bernie Privin, Sam Skolnick, Lyman Vunk, Ford Leary, Leo White, Conn Humphries, Bob Price, Bob Dawes, Mickey Bloom, James Cathcart, Neal Hefti, Wally Barron, Jack Mills, Irv Berger, Joe Ferrante, Charlie Zimmerman, Russell Brown, Doc Severinson, Jack Jarvis, and many others
Vocalists With Band Included Del Casino, Mary Ann McCall, Larry Taylor, Harriet Clark, Bob Carroll, Lena Horne, Al Lane, The Modernaires, Kay Starr, Frances Wayne
Musical Style Always a good solid swing band with a little bit of Ellington influence showing
Sponsored Radio Shows "Saturday Night Swing Session," "The Coca Cola Spotlight Bands," "Fitch Bandwagon"
Television With Band Mostly specials, "Cavalcade of Bands," "The Tonight Show," the "Edie Adams Show"
Longest Engagement Lincoln Hotel, New York City
Theme Song "Redskin Rhumba"

Charlie Barnet.

Songs Written "Skyliner," "Redskin Rhumba," "Myna," "Knockin' At The Famous Door," "In A Mizz," "Tappin' At The Tappa"
Recording Affiliations Bluebird, Victor, Decca, Columbia, Capitol, Everest, Verve, Clef, Mercury

As a bandleader Barnet was in the enviable position of not having the financial problems which plagued many of his contemporaries. He came from a well-to-do family and through an inheritance was financially secure. This doubtless contributed to his ability to put together the kind of musical organization he wanted, both in terms of musical style and the men who worked for him. He consistently maintained a fine musical organization, with a book of arrangements that were classified as "hard to cut" but the caliber of sidemen he employed were usually up to it. The result was consistently a great sound, sometimes styled more for listening than for dancing, and often reflecting his admiration for Duke Ellington. He was a sax man himself, playing tenor, alto, and soprano, and

Charlie Barnet and his orchestra at the Palomar in September 1939. On October 2 the ballroom burned to the ground, destroying the band's instruments and library.

At the Strand Theater, New York, in 1942.

The Barnet Orchestra in 1949. By this time many bands were diminishing in size, but Barnet was maintaining an organization with maximum strength in all sections.

1956, at Catalina Island. Barnet, now in semiretirement, worked with a small combo of seven including himself.

Harriet Clark, one of vocalists who worked with Barnet orchestra.

getting a tone on each of them that was distinctly Barnet.   He was born in New York City and spent his early boyhood there. When he was fourteen the family moved to Winnetka, Illinois where he attended high school. The gift of a C-Melody saxophone started him on a musical career and ultimate mastery of all the reed instruments. His decision to make music his profession was disappointing to his family, who had looked forward to his becoming a corporation lawyer.

While still a teenager, he worked with a band on the *S. S. Republic*, making transatlantic cruises. He then went on to play professionally with the series of name bands listed earlier. By 1933 he felt that he could be a bandleader himself and launched his first orchestra at the Paramount Grill in New York City. The Barnet organization enjoyed moderate success from the very beginning and by the end of the thirties he had one of the finest swing outfits in the business. In its early stages a great deal of its arranging was done by Paul Weirick, and later by Barnet himself, with Billy May making a substantial contribution in the late thirties. In the fall of 1939 the band made a trip to the West Coast to play the Palomar in Los Angeles. Two nights before the end of their engagement a fire broke out on the bandstand during an intermission. It spread so rapidly that the musicians were not able to recover either their instruments or the band library. These losses caused a setback that would have put most bandleaders out of business. But Barnet survived the catastrophe with the help of other bandleaders, who loaned him arrangements until he could have a new library written.

In the early forties he moved into the top brackets and throughout the decade was active in the nation's best ballrooms and theaters, with a crew usually made up of the best sidemen available. He was among the first white leaders to feature Negro stars. In addition to instrumentalists, he featured Lena Horne as vocalist, giving her a major stepping stone in her career. In the early fifties he was one of the first name bands to be booked into the gambling casinos in Las Vegas. Towards the end of the fifties, Barnet's activities as a bandleader diminished and he eventually entered personal management in the Hollywood area. This was a brief venture after which he retired to Palm Springs, emerging occasionally to put together a full-sized band for a weekend at Hollywood Palladium, or to play with a small combo in a Palm Springs club, or in the Avalon Ballroom in Catalina. His undiminished love for the big bands was expressed in the mid-sixties when he engaged the Duke Ellington orchestra to play for his birthday at a private party. In 1984 his autobiography, *Those Swinging Years,* was published. He passed away in San Diego on September 4th, 1991.

BLUE BARRON

Started First Band Mid-thirties
Where Cleveland, Ohio
Previous Band Affiliations Minor participation with local bands
Vocalists With Band Included Russ Carlyle, Tommy Ryan, Clyde Burke, The Clark Sisters, Pat Laird
Longest Engagement The Edison Hotel in New York City
Theme Song "Sometimes I'm Happy"
Musical Style A "sweet" band patterned somewhat after the style of Sammy Kaye and Kay Kyser
Recording Affiliations Bluebird, MGM. His biggest record was "Cruising Down The River" backed by "Powder Your Face With Sunshine," which rode high on the charts in the early months of 1949

Blue Barron.

The Blue Barron Orchestra on the stand, Pennsylvania Hotel, New York City.

Barron's biggest area of popularity was on the East Coast, in the Midwest and the Southwest, although he made at least one trip to the West Coast to play the Palladium. He drew well in top-rated theaters, ballrooms, and the college prom circuit. Though there were many sweet bands in the business at the time, he managed to produce a sound sufficiently different to be distinctive, and billed himself with the tag line, "Music of Yesterday and Today—Styled the Blue Barron Way." Like many other leaders he interrupted his career for military service, going into the army in September of 1943. An attempt to keep the band going during his absence was made with moderate success, first under the leadership of vocalist Tommy Ryan and then with Jimmy McDonald at the helm. Released from the service in early 1946, Barron took up where he had left off, including his annual appearances at the Edison Hotel. The new band was reviewed at the Edison by Billboard in February 1947, and was rated up to its prewar standards. The momentum given his career by his 1949 record hit ("Cruising Down The River") carried him well into the fifties. Eventually the big band slump caused a curtailment of his activities along with the rest. The size of Barron's band was usually twelve musicians plus vocalists.

TONY BARRON

Started First Band 1967
Where South Bend, Indiana
Previous Band Affiliations School bands
Vocalists With Band Included Tony Barron, Steve Bice
Theme Song "How I Miss You When The Summer Is Gone" (Previously Hal Kemp's theme)

Despite the degree to which rock and roll dominated the sounds of the sixties, there was a great deal of evidence around the country that musicians in their teens and early twenties were interested in listening to and playing the music of the big band era. All across the country, bands of young musicians were formed to play the arrangements of Glenn Miller, the Dorseys, Artie Shaw, Goodman, and others. Unfortunately most of them were playing it for their own enjoyment and accomplished little beyond periodic rehearsals, for their ability to find employment was limited. One young bandleader who accomplished more than that was Tony Barron. The band which he put together when just out of high school was styled in the Jan Garber-Guy Lombardo mold and was strictly for dancing. First playing nothing but local jobs, mostly on weekends, Barron built sufficient following to branch out from his home base in South Bend for other weekend dates and occasional tours of one-nighters through the Midwestern ballroom chains, including the famous Coliseum Ballroom in Davenport, Iowa. The band members pooled their resources to cut a record which they offered for sale in ballrooms where they appeared. Ten years after his 1967 start Barron was still enthusiastically fronting a young band of high school and Notre Dame students and looking for the break that might make him a "name" bandleader, a break which will be hard to come by without the support of the record industry and remote air time.

The Tony Barron Orchestra.

COUNT BASIE

Started First Band   1935
Where   Kansas City, Missouri
Previous Band Affiliations   Walter Paige's Blue Devils, Benny Moten
Sidemen With Band Included   Lester Young, Herschel Evans, Earl Warren, Harry Edison, Buck Clayton, Dick Wells, Benny Morton, Freddy Green, Jo Jones, Walter Page, Don Byas, Buddy Tate, Lucky Thompson, Illinois Jacquet, Paul Gonsalves, Emmett Berry, Al Killian, Joe Newman, Vic Dickenson, J. J. Johnson, Buddy De Franco, Clark Terry, Wardell Gray, Thad Jones, Frank Wess, Frank Foster, Marshall Royal and others
Vocalists With Band Included   Jimmy Rushing, Earl Warren, Joe Williams, Helen Humes, Billie Holiday
Sponsored Radio Shows   "The Kate Smith Show"
Television With Band   Many specials
Theme Song   "One O'Clock Jump"
Songs Written   "One O'Clock Jump," "Jumpin's At The Woodside," "Basie Boogie," "John's Idea," "Swingin' The Blues," "Tunetown Shuffle," and "Feather Merchant"

Count Basie.

Recording Affiliations   Decca, Okeh, Vocalion, Columbia, Victor, Verve, Roulette, Reprise

Basie's bandleading career began at the Reno Club in Kansas City, where the band worked long hours for very little money, seven days a week. He soon had the best of Benny Moten's men working with him. A local station picked them up for broadcasts, a break which brought them to the attention of jazz critic John Hammond. He was so impressed that he prevailed upon Music Corporation of America to sign them, bringing them into New York late in 1936. At that time Basie was probably the only black band on the MCA roster, an association which he later became unhappy with and terminated in 1940. John Hammond also was instrumental in getting Decca to sign the band to a recording contract.

By the end of the thirties the combination of airtime and records had made the Basie band known from coast to coast. Basie's first West Coast trip was made in late 1939 to play the San Francisco World's Fair and the Palomar Ballroom. They were to have been the Palomar's first black band, but two nights before their opening the place burned to the ground. His popularity continued on an upward trend throughout the forties, enhanced by good record sales and appearances in several motion pictures.

By the early fifties, with the band business deteriorating Basie fronted a small group for nearly two years, but then resumed with a big band, achieving new success while others dropped out. In 1954 he made the first of several European tours. On one tour he played a Command Performance for the Queen of England. At home, his triumphs included being the first black band to play the Waldorf Astoria, where he appeared for thirteen weeks in 1957.

Throughout the sixties his career continued on unabated, even though many were proclaiming the band business officially dead. He made several tours of Europe, and at least one to Japan and the Orient. He made regular appearances in Las Vegas and was in big demand for concerts throughout the nation. Most of the annual jazz festivals

Earl Warren.

featured the Basie band, and although some jazz critics were complaining that his music was not up to earlier standards, most writers were rating him the nation's number one band. During the sixties he made several TV guest appearances with the band on Frank Sinatra Specials and did similar stints for Andy Williams, Fred Astaire, Tony Bennett, Sammy Davis, and appeared on the Bell Telephone Hour and the Ed Sullivan Show. The band is still very active, with Basie fronting it despite a serious heart attack. Throughout the years the Basie band has been made up of top instrumentalists, playing a musical library written by an imposing list of well-qualified arrangers. This list includes Eddie Durham, who recorded in the early days of the band, Benny Carter, Neal Hefti, Ernie Wilkins, and Johnny Mandel.

His long career came to an end in April, 1984, a victim of cancer.

Basie in action, 1944.

The Basie Band in the early 1940s.

At Catalina Island in the late 1960s.

RAY BAUDUC

Started First Band 1945
Where Los Angeles
Previous Band Affiliations Freddy Rich, Ben Pollack, Dorsey Brothers, Bob Crosby
Sidemen With Band Included George Nowlan, Johnny Plonsky, Curly Broyls, Paul Montgomery, Bill Harrison, Dan Pooley, Steve Strohman, Bill Aynesworth, Bill Kribs, Joe Lenza, Joe Reisman, Gil Rodin, Hal Dean, Ward Erwin, Dwight Travis
Vocalists With Band Included Johnny Allen

In the postwar years, veteran sidemen who had gained worthwhile reputations with other name bands were all taking a shot at putting bands of their own together. Bauduc had been the featured drummer with several bands, most notably Ben Pollack and Bob Crosby. "Big Noise From Winnetka," which Pauduc had made with Bob Haggart in the Crosby band, had made both of them semi-stars in their own right. Bauduc was assisted in putting his band together by Gil Rodin,

another veteran of the Crosby and Pollack bands. Both of them were returning to civilian life after being in the service, and they elected to try the band venture rather than return to the Crosby band. Rodin stayed in the background and played his tenor sax, and also handled the business arrangements, thus permitting Bauduc to be the front man. Arrangements were done by Tommy Todd, Joe Reisman, and Billy May. Most of the sidemen were young musicians, eager to make a place for themselves in the business. The sound which was produced was somewhat reminiscent of the old Crosby band, yet distinctive enough to stand on its own. Although the band was based in Los Angeles, it toured from coast to coast working major locations, including Frank Dailey's Meadowbrook. It was not able to make it, however, in the post-war decline and by 1947 Bauduc was playing with Jimmy Dorsey, and then later joined Jack Teagarden. He passed away in Los Angeles in 1988.

The Ray Bauduc Orchestra in the mid 1940s.

TEX BENEKE

Started First Band 1946 (Became the official leader of the Glenn Miller band)
Where New York City. First engagement at Capitol Theater
Previous Band Affiliations Territory bands, and the Glenn Miller Orchestra
Vocalists With Band Included Edye Gorme, Greg Lawrence, The Moonlight Serenaders; Beneke also featured himself on vocals
Sponsored Radio Shows "The Chesterfield Supper Club"
Television With Band "Calvacade of Bands"
Theme Song "Moonlight Serenade"
Recording Affiliations RCA Victor

The biggest day in Tex Beneke's career was whenhe joined the Glenn Miller orchestra in 1938, having been hired on the recommendation of Gene Krupa. Prior to that time he had been playing in territory orchestras in Texas and Oklahoma. His home town was Fort Worth. Beneke quickly became a key figure in the Miller band, with his tenor sax featured on both broadcasts and records. He finally became a star vocalist, with the recording of "Chattanooga Choo Choo." He remained with the Miller orchestra until Miller broke it up to go into the service in the fall of 1942. Beneke then played very briefly with Horace Heidt before going into the navy with the rating of chief petty officer. He spent the war in Norman, Oklahoma directing a Navy dance orchestra. After the war's end, Miller's widow selected Beneke as the logical man to keep the Miller band going, and he became its leader in January 1946. With Miller a fallen hero, demand for the Miller sound was bigger than ever, and the band played to capacity audiences everywhere. A record-breaking 6,750 dancers crowded the floor when they opened at the Hollywood Palladium in 1947. During the years he fronted the Miller band, its key personnel were the same sidemen who had been in the band prior to the war. As Beneke's own reputation grew he became increasing-

Tex Beneke.

ly discontented with his arrangement and it was terminated by mutual consent in the early fifties.

Beneke continued on as a bandleader in his own right, still playing the Miller sound, but billing himself as "Tex Beneke and His Orchestra, Playing the Music Made Famous by Glenn Miller." Eventually the declining band business forced him to discontinue maintaining a band on a permanent basis, but he still remained active. From his home in St. Louis he moved around the country for special engagements hiring qualified musicians in the various cities to play the musical library he carried with him. For West Coast appearances many of the old Miller sidemen would be found working with him and often the current version of the Modernaires would appear on the program with him. In the early '80s he moved to Southern California to make his home and from there he was usually "on tour" playing "The Music Made Famous by Glenn Miller."

On stage at the Paramount Theater in the late 1940s.

The Tex Beneke Orchestra on the stand in the early 1950s, at the Pennsylvania Hotel, New York.

Tex fronts a band, many of whom are ex-Miller sidemen, to play "The Music Made Famous By Glenn Miller" in the early 1970s.

Tex Beneke and Orchestra at Disneyland, mid 1970s.

37

BUNNY BERIGAN

Started First Band 1937
Where New York City
Previous Band Affiliations Hal Kemp, Rudy Vallee, Freddy Rich, Abe Lyman, Paul Whiteman, Benny Goodman, Tommy Dorsey
Sidemen With Band Included Edgar Sampson, Joe Marsala, Bud Freeman, Joe Bushkin, Dave Barbour, Dave Tough, Paul Ricci, Forest Crawford, Cozy Cole, Red Jessup, Toots Mondello, Babe Russin, Henry Greenwald, Ford Leary, Mattie Matlock, Hymie Schertzer, Henry Freeman, Georgie Auld, George Wettling, Irving Goodman, Al George, Sonny Lee, Mike Doty, Nat Loborsky, Ray Conniff, Gus Bivona, Buddy Rich, Murray Williams, Joe Lippman, Don Lodice, Allan Reuss, Al Jennings, Jack Sperling, Vido Musso
Vocalists With Band Included Chick Bullock, Art Gentry, Gail Reese, Ruth Gaylor, Jayne Dover, Kathleen Lane, Lynne Richards, Nita Sharon
Theme Song "I Can't Get Started With You"
Recording Affiliations Brunswick, Vocalion, Victor, and Decca

Bunny Berigan.

Berigan was not destined for big success on his own as a bandleader and his bandleading attempts were highlighted by periodic breakups and reorganizations. During the in-between periods he worked as a sideman, usually returning to the Tommy Dorsey band but occasionally working with Goodman. At least one of his band ventures ended with a bankruptcy application, but he always came back to try again and, fortunately, to record with each organization. Berigan could be described as a person who had no enemy in the world but himself. Sidemen recall that when he had a good week financially he was quick to cut them in, with bonuses added to regular salaries. But self-discipline was not one of his virtues, and this lack contributed to his financial problems and eventually the complete loss of his health. He had been in and out of the hospital for months, suffering from cirrhosis of the liver and even a brief bout with pneumonia. He died on June 2, 1942. An unsuccessful attempt to keep the band going under the leadership of sax man Vido Musso was soon abandoned. Perhaps the public was not yet ready to accept a band whose leader had departed. Twenty years later it would become common practice. The round open tone of Berigan's trumpet will never be forgotten by those fortunate enough to hear him in person during his all too short career. Fortunately some of his best efforts were recorded and are still available.

The Berigan band in action, 1939.

MEMO BERNABEI

Started First Band 1958
Where Los Angeles
Previous Band Affiliations Ray Pearl, Don Reid, Arvin Dale, Jan Garber
Theme Song "Memories Of You"
Songs Written "Bernabei's Bounce"
Recording Affiliations Windsor

Memo Bernabei.

Bernabei's entrance into the band business as a leader came after the opportunities for building a national reputation had substantially diminished. Consequently he confined his activities to the Southern California area where he did quite well. He was a veteran of many years on the road with other bands, the longest period having been spent with Jan Garber. His musical style reflected the Garber influence. It was aimed at the dancers, and ideal for hotels and ballrooms. His first major engagement was at the Chateau Ballroom in downtown Los Angeles, where he spent a couple of seasons. In the mid-sixties he went into the Golden West Ballroom in Norwalk, and eventually became the house band and ballroom manager. He was still there in the mid-seventies, dispensing a style of dance music that kept capacity crowds coming back for more.

The Memo Bernabei Orchestra.

BEN BERNIE

Started First Band 1921

Where New York City

Previous Band Affiliations None of note, had played violin in a vaudeville act with Phil Baker

Sidemen With Band Included Don Bryan, Harry Henson, Ken Sisson, Sam Fink, E. M. Caffrey, Hymie Farberman, Harold Rehrig, Mickey McCullough, Len Kavash, Jack Pettis, Al Goering, Frank Sarlo, Bill Moore, Norman Ronemous, Nick Gerlach, Oscar Levant, Max Rosen, Phil Hart, Paul Weigan, Dick Stabile, Clay Bryson, Merrill Kline, Dillon Ober, Manny Prager, Bruce Hudson, Ray Woods, Gill Grall, Eddie Oliver, Julian Davidson, Ward Archer, Johnny Blowers, Lou McGarrity, Nick Brodeur, Bunny Snyder, Joe Bauer, Charles Huffine

Vocalists With Band Included Irving Kaufman, Jack Kaufman, Lester O'Keefe, Arthur Fields, Jack Pettis, Scrappy Lambert, Frank Luther, Eddy Thomas, Dick Robertson, Ray Hendricks, The Bailey Sisters, Donal Saxon, Johnny Ryan

Sponsored Radio Shows "The Pabst Blue Ribbon Show"

Theme Song Opened with "Lonesome Old Town" and closed with "Au Revoir"

Recording Affiliations Decca

Although he was primarily a showman, Bernie usually fronted a musical organization which was top caliber. During the late twenties he, along with a few other leaders, enjoyed the distinction of having what was described in the business as a "musician's band." He was one of the earliest bandleaders to become active in radio and it was there he found his biggest success. There are many who credited him with being the first to use a radio theme song; but whether or not this can be substantiated he is quite likely the first to use one song for bringing the show on the air and a different one for signing off. Part of his popularity on radio developed when he and Walter Winchell teamed up for an air waves feud in the early thirties, which went on for a year or two and got both of them tremendous publicity. In addition to radio, Bernie played in the best ballrooms, hotels, theaters, and nightclubs throughout the country. In 1943, at the age of 52, his career was cut short by a sudden fatal illness just after he had completed a successful engagement on the West Coast.

Ben Bernie and his orchestra in the mid 1920s, New York City.

During the 1933 World's Fair, Bernie was at Chicago's College Inn. That's Dick Stabile in the sax section on Bernie's right.

For several years Bernie was featured on the Pabst Blue Ribbon radio show.

Bernie with Dick Stabile at the Paramount Pictures studio, 1934.

FRANK BETTENCOURT

Started Band   1962
Where   Dallas, Texas
Previous Band Affiliations   Nick Stewart, Phil Levant, Jan Garber
Vocalists With Band Included   Julie Vernon; Bettencourt does male vocals himself
Theme Song   "Dreams Of You"
Songs Written   "Clodhopper," "Pflugerville Pflip," "Blue Room Bounce," "Call To The Post Cha-Cha," "The Magic Fire Of Love"

Bettencourt is a veteran sideman of the big band years who did not go on his own until the period identified as "the big band era" was long over. His experience included twenty years with Jan Garber, where he not only played trombone but did a great deal of the arranging and often conducted the band during shows. The launching of his own band was beset with various difficulties, but eventually he began to book it into the Shamrock in Houston, and branched out from there to other Midwest locations. The entire year of 1968 was spent at the Boulevard Room of the Conrad Hilton in Chicago, the last band to work the room before its closing. Eventually he became a regular at the Roseland in New York, playing an average eight-week stand there each year. Other locations which present his music include the Willowbrook in Chicago and the St. Anthony in San Antonio, Texas. He also plays several horse shows in the South and Southwest, a string of engagements which he inherited from his former boss, Jan Garber. Bettencourt is still busy as a bandleader, with the size of his band tailored to fit the individual engagement.

Houston, Texas, 1973, at the Pin Oak Horse Show.

BILLY BISHOP

Started First Band 1931
Where Toronto, Canada
Previous Band Affiliations The Bissett-McLean Orchestra
Vocalists With Band Included Alice Mann, Denny Dennis
Sponsored Radio Shows "The Rinso Radio Revue," "Waltz Time" (both in London, England)
Theme Song "Billy"
Songs Written "Hoping"
Recording Affiliations HMV, and Victor — a great deal of recording done in London.

Born Billy Bissett, he did not change his name to Bishop until he came to the United States in the early forties. Prior to that he had been active as a sideman and leader in his native Canada, dating back to the mid-twenties. From 1926 to 1930 he was co-leader of the Bissett-MacLean Orchestra, moving into the Silver Slipper in Toronto with a band under his own name in 1931. For the next five years he played the hotels and resort areas in Montreal, Quebec, and Toronto, and was heard regularly over the Canadian Radio Commission network and NBC. Early in 1936 he went into the International Sporting Club in Monte Carlo. London engagements followed, with success interrupted only by the start of World War II in September 1939. In January 1940 he organized a new band in California. But after playing key West Coast spots, Bishop established headquarters in Chicago. He quickly became a Midwest favorite in such important locations as the Aragon and Trianon Ballrooms, the Blackhawk Restaurant, and the Shroeder Peabody, and Roosevelt Hotels (New Orleans). He remained active in that area until 1953, when he gave up his bandleading career to become a stockbroker. In 1969 he retired and with his wife Alice Mann, who had been his band vocalist, moved to San Diego.

Billy Bishop and his orchestra.

WILL BRADLEY

Started First Band 1939
Where New York City
Previous Band Affiliations Red Nichols, Ray Noble, Benny Goodman
Sidemen With Band Included Ray McKinley, (co-leader), Freddie Slack, Nick Ciazza, Jo-Jo Huffman, Doc Goldberg, Herbie Bell, Joe Wiedman, Steve Lipkins, Jim Emert, Bill Corti, Arti Mendelsohn, Peanuts Hucko, Sam Sachelle, Delmar Kaplan, Bill Barford, Steve Jordan, Felix Giobee, Hal Mitchell, Alec Fila, Lee Castle, Mahlon Clark, John van Eps, John Mays, Ralph Muzillo, Les Robinson, Pete Mondello, Art Rollini, Larry Molinelli, Billy Maxted, Jimmy Grimes, Don Ruppersberg, George Koenig, Ralph Snyder, Pete Candoli
Vocalists With Band Included Ray McKinley, Carlotta Dale, Larry Southern, Jimmy Valentine, Louise Tobin, Phyllis Myles, Lynn Gardner, Terry Allen
Theme Song "Think"
Recording Affiliations Vocalion, Columbia

Will Bradley.

Will Bradley (born Wilbur Schwichtenberger) was established as a successful bandleader largely through the efforts of Willard Alexander. At that time (1939) Alexander was an executive of the William Morris Agency, and the man who had played a big part in Benny Goodman's success. Alexander put the Bradley band together as a William Morris property. Before the band ever appeared in public, Alexander arranged for it to make some records in order to give it some public exposure to the juke boxes and the disc jockeys. The band's first public appearance was at the Roseland State Ballroom in Boston in the fall of 1939. Next the agency put together a very thorough and expensive promotional campaign to publicize the band. Seven months after the band was launched, it went into the Famous Door in New York City, at that time one of the top spots on 52nd Street. Within a year after its first personal appearance the band was on the stage of New York's Paramount Theater for a four-week stand, and was then booked into the New York Biltmore Hotel. With arrangements written by Leonard Whitney, the band developed a style which featured boogie-woogie piano rhythms. Titles of the band's recording reflect this, including "Rumboogie," "Rock A Bye The Boogie," "Scrub Me Mama With the Boogie Beat," "I Boogied When I Should Have Woogied," "Chicken Gumboogie," "Boogie Woogie Conga," "Boogly Woogly Piggie," "Basin Street Boogie," and the band's biggest hit "Beat Me Daddy Eight To The Bar." The vocal chores on all these selections went to Ray McKinley, who was also the band's co-leader. Since he was the drummer, he surrendered the leading chores to Bradley, who was a capable front man playing fine trombone. Apparently, however, friction developed between the two and McKinley left in 1942 to start a band of his own. During World War II the Bradley band broke up and was never reorganized. He died in 1989.

TINY BRADSHAW

Started First Band 1934
Where New York City
Previous Band Affiliations Horace Henderson's Collegians, The Alabamians, The Savoy Bear Cats, Mills Blue Rhythm Band, Luis Russell
Sidemen With Band Included George Mathews, Eugene Green, Lincoln Mills, Lester Collins, Max Maddox, Russell Procope, Bobby Holmes, Happy Caldwell, Edgar Courance, Clarence Johnson, Ernest Williamson, Bob Lessey, Charlie Shavers, Carl Warwick, Eddie Morant, Sonny Leavy, Ronald Hayes, Fred Williams, John Williams, Bill Johnson, Billy Kyle, Oscar Smith, John McLean, Nelson William, Roger Jones, Henderson Chambers, Joe Allston, George Dorsey, Chink Williams, Charley Fowlkes, Albert Allston, Paul Randle, Willis Nelson, Robert Plater, Jimmy Johnson, Winston Jeffrey, Lowell Hastings, Tack Teaberg, Joe Brown, Ross Wilson, James Warwick, Fred Radcliffe, Gil Fuller, Alfonso King, Sammy Yates, Sonny Stitt, Donald Hill, George Nicholas, Duke Anderson, Earl Walker, and many others.
Vocalists With Band Included Bradshaw handled vocals himself
Recording Affiliations Decca

Bradshaw was born in Youngstown, Ohio in 1905. His first break came when he joined Horace Henderson's Collegians as the band's vocalist, and moved with them to New York City. He later worked with various bands in New York City (as listed above), the last of which was Luis Russell. His opening engagement with his own band was at the Renaissance Ballroom in New York in the summer of 1934. During the next ten years Bradshaw fronted a big band with a pleasing musical style. He gained some national popularity but most of his activity was concentrated in the New York area, the East Coast, and the Midwest. Veteran band manager Eddie MacHarg tells about making

Tiny Bradshaw and his orchestra, Apollo Theater, 1939.

a trip with the Bradshaw band through the Midwest and into the South, with only moderate success. Particularly in the South they ran into problems with poorly promoted engagements and promoters who sometimes were not able to, or not inclined to, pay off. The personnel of the Bradshaw band was constantly changing, which may have contributed to (or was the result of) Bradshaw's inability to break through into the comfortable income brackets being enjoyed by some other black bandleaders at that time. The band recorded a substantial number of sides for Decca. Most of these records featured Bradshaw's vocal efforts more prominently than the instrumentalists. During World War II Bradshaw was commissioned a major in the army, and fronted a large band with which he made overseas trips to entertain the troops. After the war he gave up the big band to front smaller groups, eventually moving into the rhythm and blues field. In the late fifties he suffered a series of strokes and died in Cincinnati, Ohio in 1959.

NAT BRANDWYNNE

Started First Band   Early thirties
Where   New York City
Previous Band Affiliations   Leo Reisman, Eddy Duchin
Vocalists With Band Included   Buddy Clark, Bernice Parks, Jerry Wayne, Lois Wynne, Diane Courtney, Art Gentry, Dick Stone
Sponsored Radio Shows   The "Kate Smith Show"
Theme Song   "If Stars Could Talk"
Songs Written   "Peacock Alley," "Stars Over Bahia," "If Stars Could Talk," "Little Rock Rag"
Recording Affiliations   ARC, Brunswick, Decca

Brandwynne's was basically a hotel band featuring good danceable music built around his own piano playing. His first engagement was at New York's Waldorf-Astoria, where he remained for several years. Throughout most of his bandleading career he remained in New York, with only occasional transcontinental tours. In the late 1950s he moved to

Nat Brandwynne.

Las Vegas, and became the house band conductor at Caesar's Palace. He died on March 7, 1978, after a heart attack, at the age of sixty-seven.

LOU BREESE

Started First Band   Mid-thirties
Where   Chicago
Previous Band Affiliations   Bert Lown, Paul Specht, also theater bands
Theme Song   "Breezing Along With The Breeze"
Recording Affiliations   Decca

Lou Breese (born Lou Calabreese) concentrated his activities in the Chicago area, and primarily in night clubs, although he did take occasional brief Midwestern tours. His longest engagement was at Chicago's Chez Paree, where he had nightly air time that made him well known throughout the entire Middle West. His musical style was occasionally somewhat reminiscent of Henry Busse's shuffle rhythm. In 1942 after he disbanded briefly, he and his band returned to the Chez Paree for a four-year run. In 1946

Lou Breese.

he took the house band in the Chicago Theater. He remained active as a bandleader in the Chicago area through the fifties.

ACE BRIGODE

Started First Band   Early twenties
Where   Charleston, West Virginia
Sidemen With Band Included   Billy Hayes, Fred Brohez, Penn Fay, Happy Masefield, Gene Fogarty, Lucien, Criner, Johnny Poston, Jimmy Freshour, Eddie Allen, Nick Cortez, Teddy King, Abe Lincoln, Al Delaney, Don Juille, Dillon Ober, Bud Lincoln, Frank Skinner, Al Tresize, Cliff Gamet, Ray Welch, Charlie Sexton, Ignaz Berber, Max Pitt, Bob Kinsley, and others
Sponsored Radio Shows   "White Rose Gasoline Show," "Jersey Cereal Show"
Longest Engagement   Four years at New York City's Monte Carlo
Theme Song   "Carry Me Back To Old Virginny"
Recording Affiliations   Edison, Columbia, Okeh, Harmony

The size of Brigode's "Virginians" ranged from ten to fourteen musicians and a vocalist. Brigode's instrument was alto sax, doubling on clarinet. After developing an East Coast following, he gradually branched out to coast-to-coast coverage. Most of this increased activity happened after he signed with MCA in the late twenties. He played practically every major location in the country at one time or another. His last tour was made in 1945, and he played his last job in Salt Lake City. He then gave up the band to become publicity and promotion manager for Chippewa Lake Park in Cleveland, where he remained for several years. He died in 1959.

Ace Brigode and his Virginians.

RANDY BROOKS

Started First Band   1945
Where   New York City
Previous Band Affiliations   Rudy Vallee,
Hal Kemp, Claude Thornhill, Les Brown
Theme Song   "Harlem Nocturne"
Recording Affiliations   Decca

The Randy Brooks trumpet had been featured in several fine bands before he launched his own in February 1945. Under the management of General Amusement Corporation, he opened at the Howard Theater in Washington, D.C. and was soon playing major ballrooms and other key locations, primarily on the East Coast. The band which he fronted was made up of twelve musicians and two vocalists, and was styled to produce good solid dance music. Reviews in such trade journals as *Billboard* were consistently favorable. In 1949 Brooks was married to bandleader Ina Ray Hutton, a marriage which lasted for seven years, ending in divorce in 1957. In 1950, at the height of his career, he suffered a stroke which put an end to his bandleading, and left him partially paralyzed. On March 3, 1967, the apartment house in which he was residing in Springdale, Maine caught fire, and he died from smoke inhalation at the age of 49. Brooks was probably best known for his recording of "Tenderly."

Randy Brooks and his orchestra, New York City, in the late 1940s.

LES BROWN

Started First Band 1938, although he had previously been the leader of a Duke University campus orchestra called "The Duke Blue Devils" which he took over in 1934
Where New York City
Previous Band Affiliations As an arranger for the bands of Ruby Newman, Isham Jones, Jimmy Dorsey, Larry Clinton, and Red Nichols
Sidemen With Band Included John Atkins, Bill Irwin, Bob Thorne, Joe Pillatto, Gus Brannon, Joe Grando, Dutch McMillan, Herb Muse, Coon Pyar, Stacy McKee, Kenny Dutton, Don Kramer, Corky Cornelius, Earl Kirk, Jimmy Blake, Max Herman, Les Kritz, Fred Ohms, Steve Madrick, Wolfe Taninbaum, Stewart McKay, John Pepper, Glenn Osser, Allan Reuss, Bassie Deters, Lewis Mann, John Martel, Mel Hurwitz, Bob Fishel, Eddie Julian, Don Hammond, Carl Rand, Joe Petroni, Warren Brown, Ray Noonan, Hal Wallace, Herb Thompkins, Ed Bailey, Paul Fredericks, Si Zentner, Ronnie Chase, John Knepper, Abe Most, Charlie Green, Joe Bogart, Nat Polen, Don Jacoby, Nick Dimaio, Gerald Brooks, Billy Butterfield, Butch Stone, Arnold Fishkin, Les Jenkins, Ray Linn, Harry Di Vito, Gus Bivona, Shelley Manne, Frank Comstock, Hank D'Amico, Jimmy Zito, Paul Montgomery, Bob Scarda, Dick Noel, Chuck Maxon, Hal McKusick, Barney Kessel, Harold Hahn, Randy Brooks, Ted Nash, Teddy Walters, Evan Aiken, Jeff Clarkson, Stumpy Brown, Mark Douglas, Warren Covington, Dick Gould, Al Muller, Don Boyd, Ray Klein, Dale Pierce, Jimmy Rowles, Tony Rizzi, Joe Mondragin, Jackie Mills, Buddy Childers, Bob Fowler, Ray Asche, Ray Leatherwood, Dave Pell, Al Curtis, Wes Hensel, Jack Sperling, Abe Aaron, Rolly Bundock, Milt Bernhart, Sol Libero, and others
Vocalists With Band Included Miriam Shaw, Betty Bonney, Ralph Young, Doris Day, Eileen Wilson, Ray Kellogg, Lucy Ann Polk, Jo Ann Greer, Butch Stone
Tag Line "Les Brown and the Band of Renown"
Sponsored Radio Shows The "Bob Hope Show," many repeat appearances on "Spotlight Bands," and "Fitch Bandwagon"
Television With Band The "Bob Hope Show," the "Dean Martin Show," the first "Rowan and Martin Show," plus many special programs
Theme Song "Dance Of The Blue Devils," "Shangri La," "Leap Frog," the latter adopted in 1943
Recording Affiliations Decca, Bluebird, Okeh, Columbia, Coral

It all began at Duke University. This 1935 shot shows the "Duke Blue Devils" on the campus; young Les is in the center, drummer Don Kramer, far right.

The Brown Band on the stand, 1941.

Doris Day at the mike in the mid 1940s.

Eileen Wilson, featured with Les Brown.

Jo Ann Greer, with Les Brown and the Band of Renown.

Butch Stone, who did comedy numbers and played saxophone, joined the band late in 1941.

Jimmy Zito takes a trumpet chorus in this action shot made in New York in the late 1940s. Burch Stone is on sax directly in front of Zito.

These expressions in front of the bandstand reflect interest, envy, and enjoyment as Lucy Ann Polk entertains.

Throughout his bandleading career Les Brown has consistently fronted a top caliber organization with fine arrangements played by capable musicians and producing a sound always clean, crisp and driving. Success did not come easily to Brown although he did move steadily forward from his October 1938 opening for a three-month stand in New York's Edison Hotel. Under the guidance of Joe Glaser, the important theaters and dance locations opened up to them one by one, first in the New York and New England areas and later in the Midwest. A 1940 stand in Chicago's Blackhawk Restaurant gave them heavy air time on WGN's 50,000-watt coverage of the Midwest. Their first West Coast trip was made in the summer of 1942 to play the Hollywood Palladium and work in a motion picture called "Seven Days Leave."

The band had been active on records with sales good but not sensational. Best sellers had been "Mexican Hat Dance," "Tis Autumn," and "Bizet Has His Day," all done for Okeh, the latter in 1941. In late 1944 they recorded "Sentimental Journey," a song on which Les collaborated, with Doris Day featured on the vocal. Doris had first joined the band in 1939, staying a year and returning in 1943. By early summer of 1945 every juke box in the nation was "sentimental" and "The Band of Renown" was off on a journey which hasn't ended yet. Doris Day left the band in September of 1946 to launch a motion picture career. Later that fall Les broke up the band in New York in order to take a rest, and to spend some time in his new Southern California home. He reorganized in the spring of 1947 with all his former key sidemen. Eileen Wilson came in to replace the departed Doris Day and Ray Kellogg, formerly with Sonny Dunham, came in to do the male vocal chores. The new band was broken in on a tour of the Pacific Northwest before going into the Palladium and eastern locations.

During the summer of 1948 Bob Hope was looking for new people for his top-rated

Les Brown and the Band of Renown with Bob Hope in Long Binh, December 25, 1971. This was one of the many annual Christmas tours made with Hope to entertain the service men.

Les duets on clarinet with the King of Siam, 1971.

At the Hollywood Palladium, 1950; the vocalist is Lucy Ann Polk.

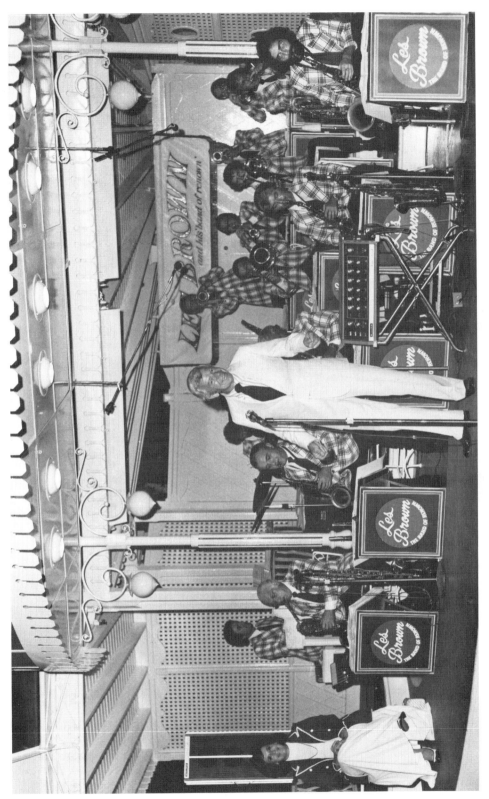

Les Brown and his band at Disneyland in the 1970s.

radio show and was auditioning both bands and vocalists. Someone brought him some Les Brown records, primarily to interest him in Doris Day as the show's replacement for Frances Langford. Doris never joined the show, but Hope became so intrigued with the sound of the band that he insisted on having it. That was the beginning of an association which survived the transition from radio to television, and included Les Brown in every Bob Hope tour which required the use of music. All of Hope's annual Christmas tours included the Les Brown band.

Throughout the fifties Brown was very active, enjoying a popularity which appeared to have no diminishing point. In 1958 he won the *Downbeat* "best dance band" poll for the fifth consecutive year, was voted Number One by Metronome, and by the National Ballroom Operators of America, and "favorite band of 1958" in *Billboard's* poll of the nation's disc jockeys. In the early sixties he settled down in the Hollywood area to concentrate on television activity with only occasional personal appearance tours.

Today there appears to be a surge of renewed interest in the big bands, and Brown's music is still in demand. During a recent luncheon, his long-time manager, Don Kramer, stated that a recent Midwestern and Eastern tour had been the most successful they had seen in years with indications the younger generation had suddenly discovered the big band sound. With a couple of his steady television shows having left the air, Brown was planning additional tours and was being kept busy on the West Coast for both private and public engagements. In the summer of 1977 the recording industry was experimenting with "direct-to-disc," using modern electronic techniques to improve on what was the basic method of recording prior to the introduction of magnetic tape. A leader in this field was the Great American Gramophone Company, a subsidiary of Keysor-Century Records and Les Brown was one of the bands selected by them. In March 1989 the Big Band Academy of America saluted Les for his fifty active years as a bandleader.

SONNY BURKE

Started First Band 1938
Where New York City
Previous Band Affiliations College bands, Xavier Cugat, Buddy Rogers, Joe Venuti, all these primarily as an arranger
Sidemen With Band Included (Many on recording sessions only) . . . Harry Gozzard, Eddie Webb, Charlie Shavers, Ken Haughey, Kenny Miesel, John Forys, Bill Nichols, Paul Fetrilla, Al Carosell, Wayne Herdell, Pete De Mill, Walt Sherman, Harold Hahn, Bernie Mitchell, Louis La Rosa, Mitch Paul, Sam Donahue, Johnny Best, Conrad Gozzo, Frank Beach, Red Benson, Si Zentner, Ray Conniff, Mahlon Clark, Clint Neagley, Frank Carlson, Pete Candoli, Milt Bernhart, Milt Raskin, Paul Tanner

Vocalists With Band Included Don Burke, Jo Ann Greer
Recording Affiliations Vocalion, Okeh, Decca

Burke is much better known as an arranger, but had a number of bandleading ventures, the longest of which lasted some two-and-a-half years. Born in Scranton, Pennsylvania, he began the study of violin and piano at a very early age. Later, at Duke University, he was one of the campus bandleaders along with Les Brown and Johnny Long. During his final summer vacation from college he took a fifteen-piece band on an ocean liner, playing for passengers on a European cruise. After graduation he dropped out of music

The Sonny Burke Orchestra at the Palladium.

briefly, then did arranging chores for a series of bandleaders before starting a band of his own in 1938. He disbanded in 1940 to do the arranging for Charlie Spivak's newly formed band, leaving Spivak in 1942 for a summer assignment with Jimmy Dorsey. In the mid-forties he moved to Hollywood, where he later became recording director of Decca Records in the early fifties. He also made recordings with a band under his own name. They intermittently appeared at the Hollywood Palladium and played other engagements in the Southern California area. One of Burke's records — "Mambo Jambo" — was a big hit, prompting others similarly styled. Eventually Burke devoted his full time to writing and arranging music. In the early seventies he started a recording company of his own under the name of Daybreak Records. He died in June, 1980, a victim of cancer at age 66.

EARL BURTNETT

Started First Band Early twenties
Where Los Angeles
Previous Band Affiliations Art Hickman
Vocalists With Band Included Those sidemen qualified to do so doubled as vocalists
Longest Engagement Biltmore Hotel, approximately three years
Recording Affiliations Columbia, Brunswick

Basically Burtnett was a West Coast band. Except for one tour to Miami and another through the Middle West, his musical career was spent on the West Coast, most of it in Los Angeles. He did a great deal of recording. In addition, banjoist Ray Hobach, still living in Southern California, recalls that the band played a lot of air time, some of which was sponsored by the Paul G. Hoffman Studebaker Agency. The band's instrumentation was three saxophones, two trumpets, one trombone, four rhythm, and two strings. Burtnett gave up his bandleading career in the late twenties and sometime later was running a restaurant in Bremerton, Washington.

The Earl Burtnett Biltmore Hotel Orchestra, 1927.

HENRY BUSSE

Started First Band 1931
Where Castle Farm in Cincinnati
Previous Band Affiliations Paul Whiteman
Sidemen With Band Included Travers Wooster, George Zybanek, Axel Monroe, Sandy Runyon, Victor Bowen, Bob Baker, Ted Kennedy, Jack Grace, Don Borden, Hal Hoffer, Seymour Drugan, Jerry Wheeler, Ted Tillman, Steve Bowers, Carl Grayson, Larry Duran, Murray Williams, Phil Gray
Vocalists With Band Included "The Four Recorders," "The Three Strikes," Carl Grayson, Bob Hannon, Skip Morr, Tom Huston, Dick Wharton, Billy Sherman, Roberta Lynn
Sponsored Radio Shows Repeat appearances on "Fitch Band Wagon" and Coca Cola's "Spotlight Bands"
Theme Song Opened with "Hot Lips" and signed off with "When Day Is Done"
Songs Written "Hot Lips" and "Wang Wang Blues"
Recording Affiliations Victor, Columbia, Decca

Henry Busse.

At the College Inn, Chicago, in the early 1930s.

Betty Brownell.

Roberta.

Although Busse had been one of the most featured and highly paid instrumentalists in the Whiteman band, he never quite achieved, with his own band, the same degree of success enjoyed by some of the other Whiteman graduates with whom he had played. Nonetheless his was a good dance band which appeared at one time or another in all of the best hotels, ballrooms and theaters in the country, breaking attendance records in some of them. In the swing era of the late thirties and early forties his instrumentation was usually five reeds, six brass, and four rhythm, plus a vocalist. During World War II, when the trend was to larger bands, Busse expanded his to nineteen musicians. Busse's strongholds, where he appeared regularly, included the Edgewater Beach Hotel and Chez Paree in Chicago, the Hotel New Yorker in New York, the Roosevelt in New Orleans, the Rice Hotel in Houston, the Peabody in Memphis, Lakeside Park in Denver, and the Trianon Ballroom in Southgate, California. During the war he spent a great deal of time at the Palace Hotel in San Francisco with what was announced in early 1943 as a "for the duration" booking but he left before the war was over. In the postwar years he reduced the size of his band to fourteen musicians and finally, when the band recession of the early fifties made survival difficult, he fronted a band of only ten musicians with vocalists. Little resemblance to the early Busse full sound remained. By that time the West Coast, where he was making his home, had little employment to offer him. He spent most of his time in the Midwest and South playing one-nighters in the few locations that remained. One of those one-nighters took him into Memphis in April of 1955 to play the National Undertakers Convention. During the evening's engagement he was stricken with a heart attack and died in his hotel room at the Peabody Hotel.

The Henry Busse Orchestra at the Circle Theater in Indianapolis, 1939.

At Catalina Island in 1954 with the King Sisters.

BILLY BUTTERFIELD

Started First Band 1945
Previous Band Affiliations Austin Wylie,
Bob Crosby, Artie Shaw, Benny Goodman,
Les Brown
Theme Song "Moonlight In Vermont"
Recording Affiliations Capitol

Butterfield is much better known as the
trumpet star of a long list of name bands
than as a bandleader in his own right. He
was born in Ohio in 1917 and attended college in Lexington, Kentucky. He left school
to take his first big band job, a trumpet
chair in the Austin Wylie band. The next
year he joined the Bob Crosby band, remaining with them until 1940. Then he went with
Artie Shaw, initially to work in the movie
"Second Chorus," but then stayed on to hold
down a regular chair in the band for the
next couple of years. He then moved on to
work with Benny Goodman and Les Brown
before taking a New York radio studio job,
which he held until he went into the military service. Immediately after he was released from the service he started a group
of his own, a good solid swinging band with
which he made personal appearances and
turned out some very fine recordings. With
the business in a decline, however, he found
the going too difficult and gave up the band

Billy Butterfield.

after a couple of years to do free lance studio
work and lead small combos. In the mid-
sixties he became a member of "The World's
Greatest Jazz Band," led by Yank Lawson
and Bob Haggart. He died in Palm Beach,
Florida on March 18, 1988, at age 71.

BOBBY BYRNE

Started First Band 1939
Where New York City
Previous Band Affiliations The Dorsey
Brothers Orchestra, Jimmy Dorsey Orches-
tra
Vocalists With Band Included Dorothy
Claire, Jimmy Palmer
Television With Band The "Steve Allen
Show" but with a Dixieland style group rath-
er than a big band
Theme Song "Danny Boy"
Songs Written "My Colleen"
Recording Affiliations Decca

Byrne was an excellent trombonist—almost
a child prodigy. As a bandleader he was a
musical perfectionist who leaned hard on his
sidemen to get what he wanted. When he did
not achieve it the resulting frustration which
he displayed often created an atmosphere of
tension within the band, which probably contributed to its never attaining the success it
deserved. Backed by Jimmy Dorsey for his
initial band venture, Byrne was fortunate
enough to be booked into the Glen Island Casino in the summer of 1941. Thus, with the
help of his Decca Records contract, he was

on his way to making a place for himself in the rarified world of bandleaders which existed at that time. For the next couple of years things seemed to be coming his way until he interrupted his career for World War II military service. Returning in the fall of 1945, he reorganized his band and continued for a few years, but then gave it up to devote his time to free lance work in the New York area.

Bobby Byrne, trombone playing leader who started with the Dorsey Brothers when he was still a teenager.

C

CHUCK CABOT

Started First Band   1939
Where   Los Angeles
Previous Band Affiliations   College bands
Sidemen With Band Included   Rudy Gangie, Bud Greene, Ryland Weston, Cliff Olson, Chuck Butler, Joe Meyer, Paul McCoy, James Talbert, Zeke Ellis, Babe Bowman, Doc Zenor, Jack Cascales, Pat McCarthy, Stan Wrightsman, Bill Schumacher, Gerry Noble, Jim Peck, Vernon Brown, Buzz Brauner, Larry Royster, Bill Quenzler, Arnie Monroe, Joe Cabot, Jimmy Foy, Paul Selden, Nat Pierce, Eugene Tackett, John Davenport
Vocalists With Band Included   Beth Harmon, Cabot did male vocals himself
Recording Affiliations   de Ville

Cabot (born Charles Cascales) was born in San Fernando, California, attended high school there, and started a musical career at the University of Southern California. When he organized his first band he was given a substantial break: through the help of Kay Kyser, he landed an appearance on the "Fitch Bandwagon," a weekly showcase for dance bands. Cabot played coast-to-coast with regularity, appearing at such places as the Roosevelt Hotel in New Orleans, the Peabody in Memphis, and the Roseland Dance City in New York. Basically his music was smooth and styled for dancing, with an occasional touch of Dixieland thrown in, and now and then a few Latin rhythms.

The Chuck Cabot Orchestra.

THE CALIFORNIA RAMBLERS

Started First Band   Early twenties, probably 1921
Where   Los Angeles
Sidemen With Band Included   The original band contained Arthur Hand (leader), Irving Brodsky, William Moore, Frank Cush, Arnold Brillhart, Robert Davis, Ray Ketchingham, Lloyd Nelson, Adrian Rollini, Stanley King. Later members who came and went were Jimmy Dorsey, Tommy Dorsey, Fud Livingston, Chelsea Quealey, Spencer Clark, Fred Cusick, Bunny Brown, Ray Johnston, Abe Lincoln, Red Nichols, Jack Russin, Sam Ruby; Glenn Miller was used on a few recording dates.
Theme Song   "California, Here I Come"
Recording Affiliations   Edison, Embassy, Pathe, Paramount, Silvertone, Vocalion, Columbia, Cameo, Harmony

This band was one of those which in the early twenties was often described as a "musician's band" because of the all-stars of the day who intermittently played with it. Put together in California by Arthur Hand, the band soon moved to the East Coast, playing its first engagement in Atlantic City. Then after playing Rector's, the Keith circuit, and the Palais Royale, it ended up at the California Rambler's Inn for a long run. The operator of the Inn was Ed Kirkeby, who became the band's manager and later even directed it on some recording dates. Because of its popularity at the Inn, the band was soon one of the busiest in the New York area on record dates and for a variety of labels. To avoid complications they also recorded under several pseudonyms—The Golden Gate Orchestra, The New York Casino Orchestra, The New Jersey Dance Orchestra, the Cairo Ramblers. Recording as "The California Ramblers" continued into the mid-thirties, but by that time there was little or no regular band personnel. Some recordings under that name were also done by Tommy Dorsey with his full orchestra (1935) and Charlie Barnet (1937).

The California Ramblers, 1923: trumpet—Arthur Hand, Irving Brodsky, William Moore; trumpet, saxophone—Arnold Brillhart; saxophone, clarinet—Robert Davis; banjo, trombone—R. F. Kitchingham; trombone, saxophone, cello—Lloyd Olsen; saxophone, piano, xylophone—Adrian Rollini; drums—Stanley King.

CAB CALLOWAY

Started First Band   About 1928
Where   Chicago—took over leadership of the Alabamians
Previous Band Affiliations   Featured vocalist with the Alabamians
Sidemen With Band Included   Both the Alabamians and the Missourians, the latter the second band Calloway fronted, were groups of the best black musicians of the period. In the early forties his band included such stars as Jonah Jones, Russell Smith, Dizzy Gillespie, Lammar Wright, Cozy Cole, "Foots" Thomas, Tyree Glenn, Quentin Jackson. Later bands included Ben Webster and Chu Berry
Sponsored Radio Shows   In the early forties he was on a sponsored radio show featuring himself and his "Hepster's Dictionary of Jive Talk"
Motion Picture Work   He was prominently featured in the "Big Broadcast" motion picture series which began in 1932, also appeared in a Jolson picture, "The Singing Kid," and a prominent part in "Stormy Weather" and in "Sensations of 1945"

Cab Calloway.

Theme Song   "Minnie The Moocher"
Recording Affiliations   Brunswick, Victor, Vocalion, Okeh, Columbia, and Epic

The Cab Calloway Orchestra in the early 1940s, including: Shad Collins, Jonah Jones, Russell Smith, L. Wright, Teddy McRae, Jimmy Blake, Andy Brown, Milt Hinton, Benny Pzine, Foots Thomas, Ky Johnson, Tyree Glenn.

Calloway's long suit was showmanship rather than musicianship. He usually backed up that showmanship with a good band. Probably the song "Minnie The Moocher," recorded in 1931, did the most to make him a national attraction. Known as the "Hi-De-Ho" man, he did very well in nightclubs, ballrooms, and theaters. He gave up his bandleading career in the early fifties to concentrate on musicals, with occasional appearances on television. In the mid-forties he had a feature role in "Porgy And Bess" and toured both the United States and Europe with the show. His career was kept alive through the sixties with similar intermittent activities.

FRANKIE CARLE

Started First Band 1944 (had one brief fling at bandleading ten years earlier and had led a school band as a teenager)
Where New York—The Pennsylvania Hotel
Previous Band Affiliations Mal Hallett, Horace Heidt (eventually became the co-leader of the Heidt band)
Vocalists With Band Included Phyllis Lynn, Marjorie Hughes, Paul Allen, Greg Lawrence
Sponsored Radio Shows The "Chesterfield Supper Club"
Theme Song "Sunrise Serenade"
Songs Written "Sunrise Serenade," "Oh What It Seemed To Be," "Roses In The Rain," "Falling Leaves," "Lover's Lullaby," "Carle Boogie," "Don't You Remember Me?" and "Estelle"
Recording Affiliations Columbia, RCA Victor

Frankie Carle.

Carle was far from an unknown in the world of music when he finally launched his own successful band in 1944. His piano had been featured with the Mal Hallett orchestra, where he played alongside such famous musicians as Jack Teagarden, Jack Jenney, and Gene Krupa. In the Horace Heidt organization he was heavily featured and had made several piano albums for Columbia which were very successful. The band which he fronted was always a fine, full-sounding musical organization ideally styled for hotel and ballroom dancing. It was also very popular in theaters. In the mid-fifties he dropped the big band in favor of working with a smaller group called "Frankie Carle and His Girl Friends" with which he played night clubs and the Nevada lounges. He eventually retired from activity as a leader to make his home in Southern California with royalties from a long string of hit songs to maintain him. In 1972 he came out of retirement to make a three months tour with a show put together by Freddy Martin and called "The Big Band Cavalcade."

The Frankie Carle Orchestra, 1944: vocalists Phyliss Lynn and Paul Allen.

Frankie Carle and daughter Marjorie Hughes in mid-forties motion picture shot.

RUSS CARLYLE

Started First Band   1940
Where   New York City
Previous Band Affiliations   Blue Barron,
was featured vocalist
Vocalists With Band Included   Patty Clay-
ton
Tag Line   "The Romantic Style of Russ
Carlyle"
Theme Song   At various times used three
—"You Call It Madness," "If I Ever Love
Again," and "The Chapel In The Moonlight"
Recording Affiliations   Paramount

Patty Clayton and Russ Carlyle.

Carlyle's bandleading career was interrupted in 1943 for military service. His sister
Louise attempted to keep the band together
until he returned, but eventually she gave it
up. After the war Carlyle reorganized his
band and for the next several years featured
a Hal Kemp style of music arranged by an
ex-Kemp arranger. Eventually he dropped
this but continued to offer good smooth
dance tempos for dancers in New York's
Roseland Dance City, the Peabody Hotel in
Memphis, the Roosevelt in New Orleans and
the other popular dancing spots in the Midwest and South. In 1956 his was voted the
best new sweet band by the National Ballroom Operators Association, a title which
seemed somewhat inappropriate for a leader
who started in 1940. Carlyle is still active,
playing the Midwestern one-nighter circuit
and two or three long-term engagements
annually at the Dunes Hotel in Las Vegas.

Russ Carlyle and his ABC Paramount Recording Orchestra, 1960.

BENNY CARTER

Started First Band 1933
Where New York City
Previous Band Affiliations Horace Henderson, Duke Ellington, Fletcher Henderson, McKinney's Cotton Pickers
Sidemen With Band Included Chu Berry, Sid Catlett, Teddy Wilson, Wilbur De Paris, Eddie Heywood, Jonah Jones, Tyree Glenn, Vic Dickenson, J. J. Johnson, Buddy Rich
Vocalists With Band Included Savannah Churchill
Theme Song First was "Melancholy Lullaby," later he adopted "Malibu"
Recording Affiliations Columbia, Vocalion, Okeh, Decca, Bluebird, Capitol, Deluxe, Verve

Carter played both saxophone and trumpet, and recorded on both instruments. Jazz authority Leonard Feather rated Carter's alto sax work along with that of Johnny Hodges, who was unsurpassed as a tone man. Feather played a part in the Carter success story by getting him a position as staff arranger for the British Broadcasting Corporation and the radio band of Henry Hall. This was in the late thirties. During the World War II years Carter had a big band which got considerable excellent air time from various locations where they played. During that period he was headquartering in the Hollywood area. After several reorganizations of his band he gave it up to concentrate on writing and arranging for motion pictures and television. He became one of Hollywood's best known and respected writers, with a long list of outstanding credits. Among those film credits which dealt with the music business were "The Gene Krupa Story," and "The Five Pennies." Aside from occasional brief appearances with a musical organization he is still busily engaged with his Hollywood writing.

The Carter sax section, 1943. *Left to right:* George Irish, Bill White, Carter, George Dorsey, Fred Mitchell.

Benny Carter and his orchestra, Loew's State Theater, 1945.

LEE CASTLE

Started First Band   1940
Previous Band Affiliations   Joe Haymes,
Dick Stabile, Artie Shaw, Red Norvo, Tommy
Dorsey, Jack Teagarden
Recording Affiliations   Musicraft, Epic

Lee Castle (born Lee Castaldo) was a trumpet player who started his professional career at age eighteen. He distinguished himself as a featured soloist in all the bands
with which he worked. His career as a bandleader in his own right consisted of three or
four brief ventures, the first of which began
in 1940. The next year he was with the Will
Bradley band, and transfered to the Artie
Shaw organization late in the year. The next
year he again fronted his own band for
awhile, giving it up that time to join Benny
Goodman for a stay of approximately a year.
In the mid-forties he once again fronted his
own band for a couple of years. In the early
fifties he was with Artie Shaw but when the
Dorsey Brothers reunited in 1953 he joined
them to become the band's featured trumpet
soloist. When Tommy died in 1956, Lee be-

Lee Castle.

came the assistant bandleader, taking over
the band completely when Jimmy passed
away the following year. From that time on
the band was billed as "The Jimmy Dorsey
Band Directed by Lee Castle." Lee died of a
heart condition in November 1990.

CATO'S VAGABONDS

Started First Band   1921
Where   Des Moines, Iowa

Although information on personnel, etc., is not available, this was a very popular Midwestern band in the twenties and early thirties. Lawrence Welk, reminiscing about his own experience barnstorming Nebraska and Iowa in the mid-twenties, recalls that his toughest competition came from Cato. Cato Mann was the band's manager and it was usually directed by Lester Rhode. Soon after its start in Des Moines the band became sufficiently well known to play with regularity in the Twin Cities and surrounding area, including several summer seasons at Interlaken Park in Fairmont, Minnesota. In those days a territory band depended almost entirely on its personal appearances to build its popularity, for radio was in its in-fancy and had not yet begun to feature on-location band broadcasts. Then a 1926 engagement at the Kelpine Ballroom in Omaha gave them air time on station WOAW and a substantial boost in their following. By this time the original six-piece orchestra had grown to ten musicians and a vocalist. During the next ten years they continued to be extremely active in Iowa and the surrounding states, with occasional appearances in the southern states of Georgia and Florida. They made at least one appearance in New York's Roseland Ballroom (1928) and played extended engagements at the Syracuse Hotel and the Marigold Restaurant in Rochester, New York in 1931 and 1932. Cato Mann retired from the music business in 1936 to become involved with other interests in the Des Moines area.

JOHNNY CATRON

Started First Band   1939
Where   Boston, Massachusetts
Previous Band Affiliations   Ben Pollack
Sponsored Radio Shows   The "Union Oil Company Show" over KFI in Los Angeles
Theme Song   "Just A Memory," "Love Day"
Songs Written   "There's a Time and a Place for Everything," "Love Day," "Valerie," "A Little Affection," "The Volkswagen Song Polka," "This Old Place," "Big D"
Recording Affiliations   Nortac Records

Catron probably deserves a bronze plaque for durability if not for outstanding success. His days as a musician go back to the Kansas City period, which spawned such great musicians as Jay McShann and Count Basie. During that time Catron was playing in local clubs with various groups, including one under his own name. After World War II he established himself in a Volkswagen dealership in Pomona, California. This was a very successful venture and one which permitted him to finance his true love, a big band. With it he played local engagements and occasionally took the band on tour. For the most part, however, he devoted his bandleading activities to the weekends. As big band activity declined, some of the best sidemen in the business were available to work with him because they preferred not to go on the road with the few bands who were still travelling. One or more summer engagements were played at Catalina Island. Eventually Catron took over a ballroom-restaurant in Glendora, California, which became his permanent base of operations. Catron's arrangements are top drawer, resulting in a full big band sound, pleasing to both listeners and dancers. He is still active in the Southern California area.

The Vagabonds at the Syracuse Hotel, 1932.

The Vagabonds at Green Gables, Hazleton, Pennsylvania, 1932.

Johnny Catron and his orchestra: "25 Years of Swing," Avalon, California.

CARMEN CAVALLARO

Carmen Cavallero.

Started First Band   1939
Where   St. Louis, opened at Statler Hotel
Previous Band Affiliations   Frank La Marr
Al Kavelin, Rudy Vallee, Abe Lyman, Meyer
Davis, Jimmy Lanin
Tag Line   "The Poet of the Piano"
Sponsored Radio Shows   "Shaeffer Parade,"
and repeat appearances on the "Kraft Music
Hall," the Fitch Band Wagon," and "Spot
light Bands"
Television With Band   Guest appearances
Theme Song   "Polonaise," "My Sentimen
tal Heart"
Recording Affiliations   Decca

Cavallaro's was a hotel-styled band and with
it he worked the circuit of hotels which featured sweet, danceable tempos from the
Mark Hopkins in San Francisco to the
Waldorf-Astoria in New York. He was a
strong box office draw at all locations and
in addition to his hotel assignments did very
well at Frank Dailey's Meadowbrook and at
the Paramount Theater in New York. The
band was usually a group of no more than
ten or twelve musicians, with his own piano

heavily featured, usually from a conspicuous
position up front. He turned out a steady
string of records on the Decca label, most of
which sold consistently well. He also worked
in many motion pictures, including "Hollywood Canteen," "Out Of This World," "Diamond Horseshoe," "The Time, The Place,
and the Girl," and did the piano sound track
for "The Eddy Duchin Story." Sometime
during the fifties he gave up the band to
front a smaller group and appear as a single
attraction. He passed away in 1989.

The Carmen Cavallero Orchestra.

BOB CHESTER

Started First Band Mid-thirties
Where Detroit
Previous Band Affiliations Arnold Johnson, Irving Aaronson, Paul Specht, Ben Bernie, Ben Pollack, Russ Morgan
Sidemen With Band Included Al Stuart, Alec Fila, Sid Brantley, Herbie Dell, Si Shaffer, Eddie Scalzi, Manny Gershman, Harry Schumann, George Brodsky, Buddy Brennan, Bob Dominick, Lew Mann, George Yorke, Garner Clark, Al Sherman, Ray Leatherwood, Ray Cameron, Jesse James, Cody Sandifer, Bob Bass, Al Mastren, Bob Peck, Mario Mariano, Rocque Domenick, Max Katz, John Reynolds, Louis Mucci, Conrad Gozzo, Sammy Stearns, Lionel Prouting, Mack Pierce, Chick Robertson, Paul Cohen, Herb Spitalny, Chuck Parsons, Red McGarvey, Hank Wayland, Cy Baker, Clarence Willard, Paul Geil, Peanuts Hucko, Wilton Hitton, Donald Miller, Ernie Strickler, Jim Sands, Ted Nash, Dick Spangler, Mel Lopez, Paul Jordan, Bobby Gibbons, Morey Samuel, George Yokum, Charles Grant, Joe Vernon, Joe Harris, Johnny Bothwell, Bill Harris, Herbie Steward, and John La Porta
Vocalists With Band Included Kathleen Lane, Dolores O'Neill, Al Stuart, Betty Bradley, Bill Darnell, Bill Reynolds, Gene Howard, the Rhythmaires
Theme Song "Sunburst"
Songs Written "Sunburst," "The Octave Jump"
Recording Affiliations Bluebird

77

The band which Bob Chester fronted in the late thirties and early forties was styled so much like that of Glenn Miller's that on one of Miller's tours, in an area which he had not yet explored but in which Chester was already popular, Miller was asked why he was copying the Chester sound. In later years Chester changed the band's style to emphasize swing, with musicians recruited from other swing bands. He always delivered good dance music sparked by his own tenor saxophone, and with arrangements occasionally written by David Rose and Gray Raines. Chester came from a wealthy Detroit family, who was prepared to underwrite his bandleading venture and see it through to success. He did quite well during the late thirties and early forties, but disbanded for awhile in the mid-forties. He came back to lead a band until the early fifties, at which time he gave it up for a Detroit business career.

Bob Chester, who had a fine band during the mid 1940s.

BILL CLIFFORD

Started First Band   1941
Where   San Francisco
Previous Band Affiliations   Anson Weeks, Griff Williams, Gary Nottingham
Vocalists With Band Included   Mary Marshall, Betty Holt, Louise Vienna, Johnny Cochran
Longest Engagement   Riverside Hotel, Reno, Nevada
Theme Song   "My Bill"

Clifford was born in Hollywood and majored in music at USC. He got his professional start in San Francisco playing violin with Anson Weeks, then playing both violin and trombone with the bands of Griff Williams and Gary Nottingham, and doing a creditable job as the Nottingham band's vocalist. His first job with his own band was at the Bal Tabarin in 1941 and the next year he was chosen to open El Rancho, Las Vegas' first entertainment strip hotel. He spent World

Bill Clifford.

Bill Clifford and his orchestra at San Francisco's Edgewater Ballroom, 1948.

Bill Clifford and his orchestra at the Claremont Hotel, Berkeley, California, 1949.

War II in the navy, directing the band for Admiral Nimitz. On his return from the service he picked up again with his dance band, going into the Bal Tabarin in 1946 and spending the next three years there and in the Fairmont Hotel. In 1949 he became the musical director of the Flamingo Hotel in Las Vegas. In the early fifties he toured the Midwest, with successful engagements at Chicago's Aragon Ballroom. He returned the next year to play the Aragon and then take his band into the Waldorf-Astoria in New York. Following that tour he was booked into the Riverside Hotel, where he served the next six years as musical director. He returned to San Francisco following the Reno engagement to spend two years in Bombo's 365 Club. In 1960 he gave up bandleading to become president and general manager of radio station KUPD in Phoenix, Arizona. In the early seventies he returned to the music business as musical director for impressionist Jim Bailey, then took over the band at the Fairmont Hotel in New Orleans. He passed away in 1984 at the age of 67.

LARRY CLINTON

Started First Band 1938
Where New York City
Previous Band Affiliations Dorsey Brothers, Isham Jones, Glen Gray and the Casa Loma orchestra; did arranging for many other bands including Tommy Dorsey and Bunny Berigan
Sidemen With Band Included Ralph Muzillo, Skeets Herfurt, Babe Russin, Irving Brodsky, Jack Chesleigh, Chauncey Morehouse, Ford Leary, Hugo Winterhalter, John Van Eps, Arthur Ryerson, "Butch" Stone, George Esposito
Vocalists With Band Included Bea Wain (biggest record hits featured her), Carol Bruce, Dick Todd, Ford Leary, Mary Dugan, Terry Allen, Peggy Mann
Theme Song Used several—"Dipsy Doodle," "Study In Brown," "My Reverie"
Songs Written "Dipsy Doodle," "My Reverie," "Satan Takes A Holiday," "Our Love," "Study In Brown"
Recording Affiliations Victor, Bluebird

Clinton's skill as an arranger and composer built for him a reputation which made it easy for him to launch his own band. When "Dipsy Doodle" became one of Tommy Dorsey's big hits in 1938, Clinton decided it was time to make the move and had little difficulty in establishing himself. The success of "My Reverie" a year later, with Bea Wain on

Larry Clinton.

the vocal, did a great deal to put the band in the big money bracket. Several additional Clinton-Wain hits followed in rapid succession. Clinton did an occasional vocal himself, and was one of the few instrumentalists who doubled successfully on both trumpet and trombone. For several years Clinton played top hotels, ballrooms and theaters, with periodic long engagements at the Hotel New Yorker. He remained active throughout the forties, retiring in the early fifties. He passed away in May 1985, a victim of cancer at age 75.

The Larry Clinton Orchestra in action, with Clinton playing trombone instead of the trumpet, with which he was most identified.

The Coon-Sanders "Nighthawks," ready to do a WGN broadcast in Chicago, in the late 1920s: Carleton Coon at the drums, Joe Sanders at the piano.

COON-SANDERS
(THE KANSAS CITY NIGHTHAWKS)

Started First Band   1919
Where   Kansas City
Previous Band Affiliations   None for either coleader (Carleton Coon and Joe Sanders)
Sidemen With Band Included   Bob Norfleet, Harry Silverstone, Clyde Hendrick, Swede Molberg, Harold Thiell, Hal McLean, John Thiell, Nick Mussolina, Orville Knapp, Rex Downing, Floyd Estep, Bob Pope, Joe Ricolson, Elmer Krebs
Vocalists With Band Included   Carleton Coon, Joe Sanders
Sponsored Radio Shows   The "Florsheim Frolic"
Longest Engagement   Blackhawk Restaurant
Theme Song   "Nighthawk Blues"
Songs Written   (by Sanders) "Nighthawk Blues," "Hallucinations," "What A Girl, What A Night," "Got A Great Big Date," "Beloved." Carleton Coon was the co-composer on "Hi Diddle Diddle," which became a big hit during the twenties
Recording Affiliations   Victor

This was one of the first bands to discover the potency of radio and to cash in on it. Their first trial broadcast was made in 1921 for a Kansas City newspaper. Soon after that they went into the Muehlebach Hotel in Kansas City for an extended engagement, and before long were broadcasting nightly over WDAF, a station which blanketed the Middle West and the east slope of the Rockies, and was occasionally even heard on the East Coast. Because they came on so late at night they dubbed themselves the "Nighthawks." They soon formed what was doubtless the first radio fan club, which they called the "Nighthawk Club." (Some years later when they had moved into New York they changed this to the "Nightriders' Club".) While other bands also claimed to have done the first radio broadcast, the Nighthawks

were definitely the first band to be on the air every night of the week and that publicity made them a big attraction in a short period of time.

They made their first trip into Chicago in May 1924 to play the Lincoln Tavern, a roadhouse in the Evanston area. Then after three months there followed by a successful six-week MCA road trip, they went into the Congress Hotel in October. Following that engagement, they returned to the Muehlebach Hotel. In 1926 Jules Stein, president of MCA, convinced Otto Roth, owner of the Blackhawk Restaurant in Chicago, that what he needed was a dance policy and a name orchestra. When Roth finally agreed, they brought in the Coon-Sanders Nighthawks and simultaneously put a wire into the place for nightly pickups by WGN, the strongest radio station in the Middle West. After a very successful Blackhawk season, MCA took the band on another extended one-nighter tour. The band played to capacity crowds wherever they went, proving that nothing could do so much to insure heavy one-nighter business for a band than remote broadcasts from a key location. The radio broadcasting pattern which they established was adopted by every band in the business, and many of these other bands benefited later from similar bookings into Roth's famous restaurant.

After six extended engagements at the Blackhawk, the band went into New York in the fall of 1931, for an engagement in the Terrace Room of the Hotel New Yorker. By that time they were as big on records as they were on the radio. They were also featured constantly on the Lucky Strike NBC coast-to-coast show emceed by Walter Winchell. In the spring of 1932 they returned to Chicago, this time to go into the College Inn of the Hotel Sherman. Soon after their College Inn opening, Carleton Coon developed a jaw infection which resulted in his death on May 4, 1932. His funeral was held in Kansas City with all the band members attending. Old friend Ben Bernie filled in for them on the College Inn bandstand while they were away.

Joe Sanders kept the band going, now billed as "Joe Sanders Original Nighthawks,"

but disbanded during the Depression. Later he put the band together again and did quite well with it for a number of years, although he never again enjoyed the level of success which he and Coon had experienced as co-leaders. He finally retired to live in Kansas City where he died in May 1965 at the age of 68.

DEL COURTNEY

Started First Band   1933
Where   Claremont Hotel, Berkeley, California
Previous Band Affiliations   Al Hill
Vocalists With Band Included   Dotty Dotson, Judith Blair, Gil Vester
Sponsored Radio Shows   The "Kodak Camera Program"
Television With Band   "The Sylvania Program," a West Coast show originating from San Francisco
Longest Engagement   Blackhawk Restaurant in Chicago, thirty-two weeks
Theme Song   "Good Evening"
Songs Written   "Good Evening"

Recording Affiliations   Columbia, Okeh, Brunswick, Capitol

Courtney's was a band ideally styled for hotels, as characterized by his billing, "The Old Smoothie." With it he played the country's leading hotels such as the New Yorker and Ambassador in New York, Edgewater and Stevens in Chicago, the Roosevelt in New Orleans, the Baker and Adolphus in Dallas, the Royal Hawaiian in Honolulu, and the Ambassador's Cocoanut Grove in Los Angeles. In the early fifties Courtney returned to his original home, the San Francisco Bay area, both to live and to be featured on one of the first West Coast tele-

Del Courtney.

Dotty Dotson, one of Del Courtney's best known female vocalists.

83

vision shows for Sylvania. After this show was dropped, he gave up bandleading to operate a television dealership in the East Bay. Then he became one of the most popular disc jockeys on radio station KSFO, and while working at this assignment, he once again formed a dance band to play local engagements and to occasionally appear at Lake Tahoe. He eventually left KSFO to buy an interest in another local station and to direct a band for the Oakland Raiders Football Team. During the run of the "King Family Television Show" in the mid-sixties, he was a regular member of that cast.

"The Old Smoothie" and his orchestra, New York City, the late 1940s.

GENE COY

Started First Band Mid-twenties
Where Amarillo, Texas
Sidemen With Band Included Ann Coy (Mrs. Gene Coy), Red Thompson, Alton Moore, Ted Manning, Clyde Durham, Ben Webster, Allen Durham, Isiah Young, Oscar Cobb, Dick Wilson, Eddie Walker, Lester Taylor, Junior Raglin, Otto Sampson, Henry Powell, Charlie Lewis, Andre Duryea, "Bat" Johnson, Tyree Johnson
Tag Line "Gene Coy and His Harlem Swing"

A good share of Coy's bandleading career was spent in the Southwest and Midwest, playing a continuous string of one-nighters. Like most black bands of that period, he found the better spots were not open to him, although he did play theater dates. In the early forties he made a West Coast swing of some duration, headquartering in San Francisco. Booked by an advance man, he played up and down the coast, working the Pacific Northwest and even venturing into Canada. In the summer of 1940 the band played a one-nighter for me in Grants Pass, Oregon, at which time Coy was fronting a fine fourteen-piece organization styled for both dancing and stage presentation. They arrived from Portland in a beaten-up old bus to play to a capacity crowd, who went away highly appreciative of the band's efforts. Unfortunately the Coy music was never captured on records. He died in California in the mid-sixties.

FRANCIS CRAIG

Started First Band   Mid-twenties
Where   Nashville, Tennessee
Sidemen With Band Included   George Thomas, Malcolm Crain, James Melton, Kenny Sargent, Cecil Bailey, Newton Richards, Ray McNeary, Ken Binford, Herb Hill, Powell Adams, Phil Harris, Clarence Morrison
Theme Song   "Red Rose," "Near You"
Songs Written   "Red Rose," "Near You," "Beg Your Pardon," "Tennessee Tango," "A Broken Heart Must Cry," "Foolin'," "Do Me A Favor"
Recording Affiliations   Columbia, Bullet, MGM, Decca

Craig was a very popular bandleader in the South and Midwest for many years and was consistently heard on radio from a Nashville Hotel called The Hermitage. A pianist himself, he fronted a band which featured good dance music and relied on strong vocalists such as Kenny Sargent and James Melton, the latter having worked with the band for a time in the late twenties. Craig had been in the business a long time, but he finally attained national prominence in 1947 when his his own song, "Near You," became a sensational hit. He followed that up the next year

Francis Craig.

with "Beg Your Pardon," which did almost as well. He remained active in the music business into the early sixties.

JACK CRAWFORD

Started First Band   Late twenties
Where   Midwest
Sidemen With Band Included   Bob Huff, Jerry Miller, Ted Willis, Joe Snyder, Carroll Willis, Harry Sosnik, Joe Bucher, Earl Center, Paul McKnight, Manny Stein
Tag Line   "The Clown Prince of Jazz"
Recording Affiliations   Gennett, Victor

Crawford's tag line "The Clown Prince of Jazz" was given him because of his antics in front of the band. Nonetheless, in addition to being a comedian, he was an accomplished musician, playing all the saxophones, and

was one of the few exponents of the C Melody sax, an instrument usually disdained by professionals. Starting as a leader in the late twenties, Crawford had become a big Midwest favorite by the mid-thirties, with a band which usually did not exceed ten musicians and a vocalist. Consistent air time from Midwest locations built his reputation sufficiently to permit his agency (Fredericks Brothers) to set up tours which took him coast-to-coast. During the World War II years (about 1942), he dropped the big band and formed a cocktail lounge combo of four people.

Jack Crawford and his orchestra, Hotel Lowry, St. Paul, Minnesota, 1933.

BOB CROSBY

Bob Crosby.

Started First Band   1935
Where   New York City
Previous Band Affiliations   Vocalist with Anson Weeks, the Dorsey Brothers
Sidemen With Band Included   The stars of the Ben Pollack orchestra, including Gil Rodin, Matty Matlock, Nappy La Mare, Ray Bauduc, Yank Lawson, and Eddie Miller. The band later included Charlie Spivak, Bob Haggart, Ward Smith, Billy Butterfield, Bob Zurke, Joe Sullivan, Jess Stacy, Mugsy Spanier, and arranging was done by such artists as Deane Kincaide, Paul Weston, as well as Ray Conniff and Henry Mancini
Vocalists With Band Included   Kay Weber, Doris Day, Anita O'Day
Sponsored Radio Shows   With own band, guest appearances on "Fitch Bandwagon." Later (the late forties) was MC of a radio show called Club 15, on which the band of Jerry Gray was featured
Theme Song   "Summertime"
Recording Affiliations   Decca, Coral, Dot

Bob Haggart and Ray Bauduc about to play "Big Noise From Winnetka," 1938.

Whether being the brother of Bing Crosby was an asset or a liability to Bob is unknown, but the chances are it was a little of both. Certainly it made the way easier for him to break into the music business, but it was probably also a handicap later because of the public's natural tendency to make comparisons between the two.

Not a musician himself, he confined his activities to being a front man, at which he became quite capable. His opportunity to be a bandleader came when the key members of the Ben Pollack orchestra parted com-

pany with Pollack on the West Coast and returned east without him. Being extremely anxious to keep together what they felt was a great band, they looked about for a front man. It was Cork O'Keefe of the Rockwell-O'Keefe Agency who sold them on the idea of Crosby and worked out the arrangements. Crosby took his place in front of the band in the summer of 1935. Both the band and he became big successes, despite the fact that the trend at that time was towards front men who were skilled instrumentalists and had gained a reputation of their own playing

The Crosby Band on the stand at Catalina in 1940.

in the big bands of the twenties and early thirties. His affable personality, combined with the strength of the musical organization behind him, contributed to this success, which was given a big lift when Bob Haggart and Ray Bauduc recorded "Big Noise From Winnetka" as a fill-in for the "B" side on a recording session and it became one of the biggest hits of the day. Appearances in one or more motion pictures contributed to the band's success and added substantially to its income.

Soon after the start of World War II, Crosby joined the marines where he became a lieutenant in the Special Services Division, participating in the organization of entertainment for the leathernecks in the Pacific. He came out of the service in December 1945, and resumed as a bandleader with a band waiting for him which had been organized by Eddie Miller. Miller had already shaken it down on a West Coast tour. With Crosby in front of it, the band went into the Hollywood Palladium in the early part of

1946 and was well on the way to resuming its prewar success. After a couple of years, Crosby began to reduce his activity as a bandleader in favor of becoming a radio and television personality. By the end of the fifties he was almost entirely engaged in other activities, with only occasional returns to the music business. After several years in Hawaii, he made his home in La Jolla near San Diego.

In the early seventies a revival of big band interest brought him out of retirement to play annual engagements at Disneyland, with a band usually made up of many of the sidemen who had been with him during the thirties and forties. Always very popular in the Middle West, he once again found himself in demand for one-nighters in that area, usually flying into Chicago to put together a band in that area to handle Midwestern dates. Early in 1977 I had several conversations with him. At that time he was still busily engaged on the one-nighter trail and apparently doing very well at it.

Crosby's postwar band, 1946.

At Disneyland, 1975.

XAVIER CUGAT

Started First Band Early thirties
Where West Coast
Previous Band Affiliations Anson Weeks
Sidemen With Band Included Miguelito Valdes (who came out of the band to be a leader himself)
Vocalists With Band Included Lina Romay, Lorraine, Abbe Lane
Sponsored Radio Shows "Camel Cigarette Show," the "Drene Show" starring Rudy Vallee, "Spotlight Bands," (on this, during its last year, he was on once a week as one of three regular bands)
Theme Song "My Shawl"
Recording Affiliations Columbia

In the early thirties Cugat made the surprising announcement that Latin rhythms would be the next musical style to sweep the nation, and immediately put together a band to cash in on it. With that style he did very well, proving that, at least for him, it was the way to go. By the early forties he was undisputed "Rhumba King," playing major hotels and theaters coast to coast. A 1942 *Billboard* story credited him with ten annual stands at the swank Waldorf-Astoria, a string which he extended substantially beyond that point. As the number of places using bands on a full-time basis steadily diminished during the fifties and sixties, Cugat reduced the size of his organization to a small combo. small enough to play Nevada lounges. It was about this time that he began to place heavy emphasis on a sexy female vocalist, with his show built to a large degree around her. It was this emphasis which launched Abbe Lane into a night club star in her own right, and eventually did the same thing in the early seventies for Charo. For those who like Latin rhythms there is a lot of Cugat music preserved on Columbia discs. He passed away at age 90 in a Barcelona, Spain hospital on October 26, 1990.

Cugat, "The Rhumba King."

Lina Romay.

Cugat and his orchestra at the peak of his popularity.

BERNIE CUMMINS

Started First Band   1919
Where   Indiana (Toadstool Inn)
Sidemen With Band Included   Carl Radlach, Paul Miller, Walter Cummins, Paul Roberts, Bernard Rohenstien, Eddie Lane, Charlie Callas, Paul Blakely, Ernie Mathias, Wally Smith, Bill Diehl, Bob Gebhart, Jimmy McMillen, Dippy Johnson, Ford Cansfield, Chuck Campbell, Thurman Sheeler, Chet Jones, Winston Leach, Don McLure, Paul Thatcher, Fred Benson
Sponsored Radio Shows   Repeat appearances on the "Coca Cola Spotlight Bands Program" and "Fitch Bandwagon"
Vocalists With Band Included   Walter Cummins, Belle Mann, Dorothy Crane, Frank Munn, Connie Barleau, Jerry Lang, The Sophisticates
Theme Song   "Dark Eyes"
Recording Affiliations   Gennett, Brunswick, Columbia, Victor, Vocalion, Bluebird, Decca

Bernie Cummins, 1930.

Cummins was a drummer who started out with a small combo which soon became a full-size dance band. One of his first important engagements was at the Biltmore Hotel in New York. His longest was at the Hotel New Yorker but there were other locations where he also had extended runs. The smoothly styled Cummins band was ideal for hotels and ballrooms and he played the length and breadth of America during his forty years in the business. In Chicago he played both the Aragon and Trianon ballrooms, the Blackstone, Congress, and Edgewater Beach Hotel. He did repeat appearances at the Raddisson in St. Paul, Minnesota, the Meuhlbach in Kansas City, the Roosevelt in New Orleans, and the Baker in Dallas, with sixteen appearances at the latter. In San Francisco he played both the Palace and St. Francis and such popular amusement parks

as Elitch's Gardens in Denver. He had consistent remote air time from all those locations which contributed to the sale of his records, made on every major label. The peak of Cummins' career was during the thirties and early forties. During the fifties he worked such Las Vegas locations as the Last Frontier, El Rancho, and the Flamingo. He retired from bandleading activity in 1959 to make his home in Florida.

Bernie Cummins, Palace Hotel, San Francisco.

Bernie Cummins and his Hotel Roosevelt Orchestra in 1935, including Paul Miller, Bill Diehl, Wally Smith, Don McGovern, Paul Blakely, Jimmy McMullen, Walter Cummins, Bob Gebhardt.

FRANK DAILEY

Started First Band   Early twenties
Where   East Coast
Sidemen With Band Included   Phil Baird,
William Burger, Louis Martin, William
Wachsman, Henry Muller, Jack Margolin, Al
Weber, Fred Eckert, Al Fish, Jack Shilkret,
Michael Jay, Charles Amsterdam, Michael
Treetino, Cliff Dailey, Frank Hope, Harry
Berman, Gene Hammond, Louis Alpert,
George Odell, Birt Apikian, Curly Barron,
Phil Baird, Arnold Ross
Vocalists With Band Included   Howard
Dulany, Curly Barron, Ann Seton, Barbara
Bush
Theme Song   "Gypsy Violin"
Recording Affiliations   Embassy, Bluebird,
Variety, Vocalion

Dailey's sphere of influence as a bandleader
was limited to the eastern seaboard. He
gave it up to become much more famous as
a ballroom and night club operator operating Frank Dailey's Meadowbrook in Cedar
Grove, New Jersey. The night spot became
so famous that a song (Pompton Turnpike)
was written about the highway on which it
was located. The Meadowbrook became one
of the most popular name band locations in
the United States, and a target for all those
leaders who were on their way up or had
already arrived. Its nightly remote broadcasts were beamed across the nation, as well
as a special Saturday show called "Matinee
At Meadowbrook." In later years attempts
were made to adapt this show to television
with only moderate success. In the postwar
years the popularity of the place declined
and Dailey eventually filed for bankruptcy.
He died in late 1956.

JOHNNY "SCAT" DAVIS

Started First Band Mid-thirties (had several brief bandleading ventures)
Previous Band Affiliations Fred Waring, Jimmy Joy, Red Nichols, Will Osborne, Smith Ballew, Glen Gray
Theme Song "Hooray For Hollywood"
Recording Affiliations Decca

Davis is much better known for his work with other bands and in motion pictures than he was as a bandleader. He was a trumpet player of moderate talent, but developed a raspy-toned singing style which became his trademark. In the bands listed above he both played trumpet and did featured vocal work. Probably his greatest popularlity came on the Fred Waring Show in the early thirties. During the period 1935 through 1937 he intermittently led a dance band of his own. In 1937 he appeared in a motion picture with Dick Powell acquitting himself well as both a comedian and a singer. Other movies followed, including "Hollywood Hotel." In the late thirties he toured with a big band and played a very successful engagement at the Blackhawk Restaurant in Chicago. Perhaps the best band from the standpoint of musicianship was one which he put together in the mid-forties and which is pictured here. Its existence was also short, despite good reviews and successful appearances. Later Davis confined his musical activity to smaller groups. He passed away in Texas on November 25, 1983 at age 73.

The Johnny "Scat" Davis Orchestra, Claridge Hotel, Memphis, 1946: saxophones — Pete Johnson, Buzzy Ellis, Bob Wall, Garth Andrews, Joe Reisman; trumpets — Art Davis, Dick Dalrymple, Mario Dentino, George Bruton; trombones — Kenny Trimble, Sam Woodgate; bass — Bob Baldwin; drums — Jimmy Matzer.

HAL DERWIN

Started First Band 1940
Where Chicago
Previous Band Affiliations Boyd Raeburn, Louie Panico, Shep Fields, Les Brown
Longest Engagement Biltmore Bowl, Los Angeles — six years
Theme Song "Derwin's Melody"
Recording Affiliations Capitol

Derwin's start in the music business was with a vocal trio which included Lee Gillette, who was later one of Capitol Records' top artists and repetoire men. He then moved on to work with several name bands until he started his own organization in 1940. For the next several years he toured the country, with primary concentration in the Middle West. Eventually he settled down on the West Coast, going into the Biltmore Bowl in the early fifties. His band featured former Jan Garber sax man Freddie Large. Eventually he gave up the band for other activities in the music business.

AL DONAHUE

Started First Band 1925
Where Boston area
Previous Band Affiliations Campus and local bands, also with steamship bands aboard the Eastern Steamship line
Vocalists With Band Included Paula Kelly, Dee Keating, Lynne Stevens, Phil Brito, and Snooky Lanson
Theme Song "Lowdown Rhythm in a Top Hat"
Record Affiliations Vocalion

With his first band Donahue opened at the Weber Duck Inn in Boston, where he gained enough public acclaim and popularity to be invited to take a larger band into the Hollywood Beach Hotel in Florida, for the first of five annual engagements. Later he took his band into the Bermudiana Hotel, an arrangement which ultimately developed into Donahue's providing bands for the entire hotel chain and several steamship lines. At one time he had thirty-seven units working and was one of the largest contractor of steamship orchestras in the world. In the mid-thirties he filled in briefly for Ray Noble at the Rainbow Room in Rockefeller Center, then went back annually for the next six years. Stylewise his was a "society" orchestra until the early forties at which time he revamped his library to become a swing band and play such places as Frank Dailey's Meadowbrook, the Hollywood Palladium, and top theaters coast to coast. It was at the Palladium in 1941 that he lost vocalist Paula Kelly to Glenn Miller, who preceded Donahue at the popular ballroom. In the postwar years he converted back towards the sweet side, although for awhile he used a combination made up of five saxes, five brass, four violins, and three rhythm, large enough to play any type of engagement. He moved to the West Coast, and continued to tour successfully throughout the forties. He worked in a motion picture "Sweet Genevieve," and in the early fifties was featured in a short-lived television show emanating from the West Coast. He then returned to the Furness Bermuda Line as musical and cruise director. With his long-time band manager, Frank Walsh, Donahue also opened a music and record store in Bermuda, which was later taken over by the government, forcing them to sell and leave the country. Together they bought Ponzi's House of Music in Oceanside, California, operating it until the mid-'70s. Donahue passed away February 20, 1983, at age 80.

Lynne Stevens.

Al Donahue and vocalist Paula Kelly, who left him in 1941 to join Glenn Miller and the Modernaires.

Al Donahue and his orchestra, working in a picture at Universal in 1947.

SAM DONAHUE

Started First Band   Mid-thirties
Where   Detroit
Sidemen With Band Included   Bud Davis, Mitchell Paull, Harry Gozzard, Ken Houghey, Ken Meisel, Bill Nichol, John Forsythe, Max Kriseman, Wayne Herdell, Paul Petrilla, John Jordan, Walter Sherman, Hal Hahn, Tack Vorian, Andy Blaine, Dick Le Fave, Pete Abramo, Harry Peterson, Nick Manley, Billy Marshall, Freddie Guerra, Dick Richardson, Leo Mazza, George Perry, "Tippy" Morgan, Joe Reisman, Bob Burgess, O. B. Masingill, Ed Fromm, Ed Cunningham, Doc Severinsen, Bill Faffley, Fern Caron, Don Faffley, Clyde Reasinger, Larry Brooks, Ernie Bernhardt, Ralph Craig, Nick Cavas, Charlie Givens, Dick Clay, Earle Griffiths, Pat Chartrand, Murray Romanoff, Lou Carrafiello, Adelaide Robins, Bill Turner, Bud Stayton, Ronny Bedford, and others
Vocalists With Band Included   Frances Wayne, Irene Day, Bob Matthews, Shirley Lloyd, Bill Lockwood
Theme Song   "Minor Deluxe," "Lonesome"
Songs Written   "Lonesome," "I Never Purposely Hurt You," "Sax-A-Boogie," "It Counts a Lot," "Six Mile Stretch," "Skotter"
Recording Affiliations   Okeh, Bluebird, Capitol

Sam Donahue.

Donahue had several ventures as a bandleader, each of which found him fronting a band that was musically strong. The first band which he put together in Detroit was a young group which was later taken over by Sonny Burke. At that time Donahue, an accomplished tenor sax man himself, joined

The Sam Donahue Orchestra backing Jo Stafford at the Paramount, New York, 1948: piano—Ray Rossi; saxophones—George Perry, Harry Peterson, Bill Nichols, Tom Morgan, Joe Reisman; trombones—Bob Burgess, O. B. Massingill, Ed Fromm; bass — Ed Cunningham; drums — Harold Hahn; trumpets — Doc Severinsen, Bill Faffley, Fern Caron, Don Faffley.

the Gene Krupa band for a two-year stay. In 1940 he worked for both Harry James and Benny Goodman, and then once again resumed as a bandleader, with a band which was primarily the same as the one which he put together in Detroit. With it he played key eastern locations, including the Glen Island Casino and Frank Dailey's Meadowbrook. During the war he was in the navy, where he worked with Artie Shaw's navy band and took over its leadership upon Shaw's leaving the service. Once out of the service himself, he organized a new band in 1946 with a strong sax section of five men in addition to himself. When the band appeared at the Paramount Theater in 1948, backing headliner Jo Stafford, its trumpet section included Doc Severinsen and the arrangements were being done by Joe Reisman, who was also playing baritone sax. It was a fine, solid, swinging band. But just when the fu-

ture looked brightest for Donahue he was called back into service in 1951 for the Korean War. This time when he came out of the service he went to work for Tommy Dorsey, leaving him in 1953 for another band venture of his own. The next year Ray Anthony bought the Billy May band when May decided to call it quits, and made a deal with Donahue to be its front man. That band stayed on the road for several years, but was dissolved in the late fifties. Donahue then spent a couple of years with Stan Kenton. In late 1961 he was asked to front the Tommy Dorsey orchestra, which at that time was touring with Frank Sinatra, Jr. He remained with the Dorsey organization until the late sixties, when he left to become musical director of John Ascuagua's Nugget in Sparks, Nevada. He died in a Reno hospital in March of 1974, a victim of cancer.

JIMMY DORSEY

Started First Band   1935, but had previously had a band with brother Tommy, known as the Dorsey Brothers Orchestra
Where   New York City
Previous Band Affiliations   Scranton Sirens, The California Ramblers, Red Nichols, Jean Goldkette, Ben Pollack, Paul Whiteman
Sidemen With Band Included   His 1935 band included Roc Hillman, Bobby Byrne, Don Matteson, George Thow, Bobby Van Epps, Jack Stacy, Skeets Herfurt, Ray McKinley. Subsequently sidemen included Tutti Camarata, Fud Livingston, Freddie Slack, Shorty Sherock, Dave Matthews, Davey Tough, Milt Yaner, Sam Rubinowich, Charlie Frazier, Herbie Haymer, Buddy Schutz, Nate Kazebier, Sonny Lee, Joe Lippman, Ray Bauduc, Charlie Teagarden
Vocalists With Band Included   Bob Eberly, Phil Washburn, June Richmond, Helen

Jimmy Dorsey

Bob Eberly

Helen O'Connell.

O'Connell, Kitty Kallen, Kay Weber, Martha Tilton. Frances Langord also recorded with the band in the mid-thirties

Sponsored Radio Shows   "The Bing Crosby Show"

Television With Band   Co-leader with brother Tommy on "Stage Show," a Jackie Gleason production

Theme Song   "Contrasts"

Recording Affiliations   Decca, Brunswick

Jimmy's musical training began about the time he entered grade school. He was only seventeen years old when his first big professional break came, a job with the Scranton Sirens. In this and succeeding bands in which he worked he was not long in finding a place for younger brother Tommy and his trombone, and the balance of the twenties found him paving the way for both of them into all of the biggest name bands of the period. While both were still with Whiteman, they cut a number of records with all-star groups from Whiteman's and other bands, under the billing "The Dorsey Brothers Orchestra." This continued through the early thirties with the Dorsey Brothers Orchestra becoming a full-time unit in 1934. It broke up in 1935, primarily because of a

dispute between the brothers over how the band should be run.

Jimmy was not so quick to find success with his own band as was Tommy. A 1936 Palomar weekly bulletin announced his coming engagement, but described him as a capable clarinetist not to be compared with Benny Goodman, who had so greatly excited Palomar dancers the year before. Throughout the balance of the thirties, Jimmy was just another bandleader, despite a stint on the Bing Crosby Show which originated from the West Coast. His records sold well but not in hit numbers. But as the forties got under way it was apparent that his momentum was increasing, and early in 1941 his records of "Amapola" and "Green Eyes," featuring the fine vocal efforts of Helen O'Connell and Bob Eberly, jumped to the top of the charts to make Jimmy the biggest success story of the year. Other top-selling records and a series of motion pictures followed, establishing him firmly in the top brackets. O'Connell and Eberly played an important part in the band's success, both on records and in personal appearances. When O'Connell left the band she was replaced by Kitty Kallen, who also worked very well with Eberly. The band was a good, solid, entertaining dance band, in demand in all the best spots in the nation.

During the early fifties Jimmy was still a top name in a business which was in a steady decline. Early in 1953 he and Tommy surprised the musical world by once more merging into a single band, with Tommy taking top billing and Jimmy identified as the featured attraction and co-leader. Those who saw and heard the band in person were quick to point out that not much had changed since the old days of the original Dorsey Brothers Orchestra—Tommy called the shots and Jimmy went along with it. The only thing that had apparently changed was their ability to get along with one another. Their success with this new band venture was given a big boost when Jackie Gleason put them on a weekly television show in 1954. For the next two years this was the biggest television show in existence that was built around a dance band, and encour-

aged other bandleaders to hope that there might be a place in television for them as well. Tommy's death in 1956 left Jimmy to carry on, but his own health was failing rapidly. He deserted the band in Houston, Texas to return to New York and a hospital bed in March of 1957. He died there in June of that year, a victim of throat cancer. As he lay on his deathbed one of his own records, "So Rare," was riding the top of all the nation's popularity charts, the first big band record to accomplish this distinction in years. It seemed a fitting final touch in making his position among the all-time greats completely secure.

As a leader Jimmy was generally easy going, relaxed, and had a reputation as a good guy to work for. Nonetheless he insisted on having the best men available in his band and the best vocalists as well. Luckily he left us a great deal of recorded material as evidence of his high standards.

The Jimmy Dorsey Orchestra in the early 1940s. Vocalists Bob Eberly and Helen O'Connell in the background.

The orchestra in 1949: trombone—Herb Winfield; saxophone—Art Lyons; bass—Bill Lolatte; clarinet—Jimmy Dorsey; trumpet—Charlie Teagarden; drums—Ray Bauduc.

At Catalina Island, 1951.

TOMMY DORSEY

Started First Band 1935 but had been co-leader with brother Jimmy of the Dorsey Brothers Orchestra
Where New York City
Previous Band Affiliations Scranton Sirens, California Ramblers, Jean Goldkette, Paul Whiteman, plus recording with many all-star groups
Sidemen Who With Band Included Andy Ferretti, Sterling Bose, Dave Jacobs, Noni Bernardi, John Van Eps, Sam Weiss, Paul Weston, Max Kaminsky, Johnny Mince, Freddy Stulce, Skeets Herfurt, Bud Freeman, Lee Castle, Pee Wee Irwin, Maurice Purtill, Carmen Mastren, Gene Traxler, Dave Tass, Earle Hagen, Hymie Schertzer, Deane Kincaide, Buddy Morrow, Charlie Spivak, Babe Russin, Yank Lawson, Mickey Bloom, Cliff Leeman, Zeke Zarchy, Buddy Rich, Ray Linn, Don Lodice, Joe Bushkin, Clyde Hurley, Ziggy Elman, Heinie Beau, Shorty Sherock, Manny Klein, Milt Raskin, Abe Most, Sam Most, Buddy Childers, Bobby Nichols, Charlie Shavers, Sam Donahue, Terry Gibbs
Vocalists With Band Included Frank Sinatra, Dick Haymes, The Pied Pipers, Edythe Wright, Jack Leonard, Connie Haines, Anita Boyer, Jo Stafford, Frances Irvin, Barbara Canvin, Stuart Foster
Sponsored Radio Shows "Raleigh Cigarettes," repeat appearances on "Fitch Bandwagon" and Coca Cola's "Spotlight Bands Show"
Television With Band "Stage Show," a Jackie Gleason-sponsored production
Theme Song "I'm Getting Sentimental Over You"
Recording Affiliations Victor, Decca, Capitol, Bell

During the slightly more than twenty years of his bandleading career, Tommy Dorsey was one of the most dominant factors in the business. It was he who had the first big success with a style combining both sweet and swing. It was he who first made vocal

Tommy Dorsey.

Connie Haines, vocalist with the Dorsey band for two years in the early 1940s.

103

Joe Bauer, Les Jenkins, Axel Stordahl, Steve Lipkins, Max Kaminsky, Red Bone, Tommy Dorsey, Dave Tough, Joe Dixon, Fred Stulce, Carmen Mastren, Bud Freeman, Gene Traxler, Bob Bunch, Dick Jones, Edythe Wright, Jack Leonard.

groups a really important part of the dance orchestra. He even did a great deal to popularize the trombone and bring it out of the brass section to make it a lead instrument.

When he and Jimmy broke up the Dorsey Brothers Orchestra in 1935, Tommy took over the Joe Haymes band and quickly started to shape it into his own style. He had no trouble getting a recording contract, but not much happened with his records until 1937. Then his recording of "Marie" became a big hit, followed quickly by "Song Of India." From that time on his records sold steadily and consistently made the popularity charts in *Billboard* and other trade publications. The listing at that time consisted of "the top 10." The end of 1937 found him competing with Benny Goodman for the title of "Number One Band in the Land, and when he got a sponsored radio show the next year he never again retreated from the top brackets.

As a bandleader Tommy was considered to be a perfectionist and hard taskmaster.

The results which he obtained reflected this and were definitely brought about by his maintaining a well-disciplined organization. Few people had his ability to whip a band into shape in minimum time. Throughout the years the roster of his band, both instrumentalists and vocalists, were made up of the best people in the business, many of whom went on to become stars in their own rights.

When Jack Leonard left the Dorsey band in late 1939, Tommy quickly brought in Frank Sinatra, hiring him away from the Harry James band. Sinatra was a major contributor to the success of Dorsey records in the next several months, including the top-rated "I'll Never Smile Again," on which he was featured with the Pied Pipers. By the time Sinatra left the band in late 1942 to launch his own career as a single, he had won the *Downbeat* poll as the Number One Male Band Vocalist two years in a row, and had left his imprint on a lot of fine Dorsey

The Pied Pipers: When the Pied Pipers first joined the Dorsey band in 1939 there were eight members. Tommy soon reduced it to four with Jo Stafford, John Huddleston, Chuck Lowry, and Allen Storr staying on. Dick Whitting-hill, shown at far left, went into radio and became one of Hollywood's best known and most popular disc jockeys.

records. His contribution to the Dorsey band was substantial but on balance probably each made an equal contribution to the other. For a replacement Dorsey once again went to the Harry James band and brought in Dick Haymes.

During the early forties Dorsey was in demand wherever big bands appeared. He was brought to the West Coast in the fall of 1940 to open the new million-dollar Palladium Ballroom, and came back for many repeat performances. Later, unhappy with the money the Palladium was paying, he went into a ballroom venture of his own, buying the Casino Gardens in Santa Monica, where

he not only made his own Southern California appearances but competed with the Palladium for the services of all the other important names. During the war years he augmented the size of his band substantially, despite the fact that the draft continually thinned out the ranks of available sidemen. He brought in a string section of twenty, all of them girls, a section somewhat larger than his whole band had been in the late thirties. Shortly after the war ended the big string section disappeared.

The competition between Tommy and Jimmy was a very real thing and not totally confined to the bandstand. It occasionally

The Hollywood Palladium opened for business October 29, 1940, featuring the Dorsey Band.

One of the last action shots of the two Dorseys, made in the mid 1950s. That's Lee Castle on the trumpet.

This motion picture studio shot in the early 1940s includes the Pied Pipers, Connie Haines, Frank Sinatra, Buddy Rich on drums, Ziggy Elman in the trumpet section, Dave Jacobs in the trombone section, and Joe Bushkin at the piano.

erupted into violence, with fists flying, usually sparked by Tommy's quick Irish temper. Nonetheless, in the spring of 1953 they resolved their long and highly publicized differences to once more form a single band, which was usually billed as "The Tommy Dorsey Orchestra Featuring Coleader Jimmy Dorsey." They appeared to be on their way to new success when Fate intervened, to take both of them within a six-month period. Tommy was the first to go. Death came in his Connecticut home in November 1956, when he apparently choked to death in his sleep. After Jimmy died in June of the following year the band was kept alive by a series of front men. Most of them had been identified with the Dorsey band, now billed as "The Tommy Dorsey Orchestra Under the Direction of — —." During his bandleading career Tommy made many motion pictures with his orchestra. In the early fifties a movie based on the life of both brothers was made which purported to tell the story of their careers and was titled "The Fabulous Dorseys."

EDDY DUCHIN

Started First Band   1931
Where   New Jersey—first engagement at the Ross-Fenton Farm
Previous Band Affiliations   Pianist with Leo Reisman Orchestra
Sidemen With Band Included   Lew Sherwood, Andrew Wiswell, John Geller, Aaron Voloshin, Fred Morrow, Milt Shaw, Lester Morris, Bruce Anderson, M. Leibrook, Harry Campbell, Charles Trotta, Frank Saracco, Horace Diaz, Gene Baumgarden, Al Kunze, Buddy Morrow, Al Carroll, Stan Worth, Johnny McAfee, Bill Heathcock, Joe Bogart, James Troutman, Martin Oscard, Stew McKay, John Drake, Leonard Gellers, Al Giroux, Winston Bogart, Sid Rhein, Murray Williams, Elmer Hardwick
Vocalists With Band Included   Frank Munn, The De Marco Sisters, Jimmy Newell, Buddy Clark, Patricia Norman, The Charioteers, Carolyn Horton, The Three Earbenders, June Robbins, Tony Leonard, Jimmy Blair, Phil Brito
Tag Line   "The Ten Magic Fingers Of Radio"
Sponsored Radio Shows   Cadillac Motor Cars, Pall Mall Cigarettes, Elizabeth Arden Cosmetics, Texaco
Longest Engagement   The Waldorf-Astoria, where he played annual return engagements averaging six months in duration for a period of ten years
Theme Song   "My Twilight Dream"

Eddy Duchin.

Recording Affiliations   Brunswick, Columbia. Was a pioneer in the introduction of ten-inch album sets consisting of four or more discs

Duchin was born in Boston, studied pharmacy in college, but gave it up when Leo Reisman offered him a job as pianist in 1927.

When he left Reisman in 1931 to organize an orchestra of his own the musical style which he put together caught on quickly at the Waldorf-Astoria and soon made him one of the most accepted society bandleaders in the business. His society following made him a favorite of the leading composers of the day, and such writers as George Gershwin, Richard Rogers, and Cole Porter called upon him to introduce new songs. It was not just his music which the social set accepted, they loved Duchin as well. Among the socially prominent people he met at the Waldorf was Marjorie Oelrichs whom he married in 1933. Four years later she died giving birth to their son Peter. He interrupted his career for World War II service, entering the navy in 1942, where he saw a great deal of combat duty. At the time of his discharge in 1946 he had risen to the rank of lieutenant commander, senior grade. He quickly resumed his activities, with an orchestra patterned identically after his pre-war organization. With it he was still enjoying a popularity which appeared to have no time limits when leukemia took his life on February 9, 1951. He was forty-one years of age. Somewhat later his life was depicted in a motion picture with Tyrone Power playing the title role. The piano music on the sound track was played by Carmen Cavallaro.

Eddy Duchin, at the Steel Pier, Atlantic City, 1935.

PETER DUCHIN

Started First Band   1962
Where   New York City, St. Regis Hotel
longest Engagement   Three years at the
St. Regis
Theme Song   "My Twilight Dream"
Recording Affiliations   Decca

Peter Duchin.

At a time when the music world would have
given you long odds that a new dance band
could not be successfully launched, young
Peter Duchin embarked on a new career as
an orchestra leader, without regard for the
gloomy predictions of the old pros. The band
which he took into the St. Regis was styled
after that of his famous father, Eddy, and
just as his father had done thirty years
earlier, he quickly became the toast of the
social set. While his father's reputation may
have contributed to the rapidity of his success, Peter himself had talent and knew
what to do with it. From the St. Regis he
went to the Fontainebleu Hotel in Miami
and then to the Cocoanut Grove in Los Angeles. By this time the magic Duchin name
together with the reputation he had built at
the St. Regis for playing danceable rhythms
had created a lively demand for his music
to which he decided to respond. To do this he
organized Peter Duchin's Orchestras, a service that provided musical units of any size
for important functions throughout the
country. Duchin units became regulars for
White House functions and the inaugural
balls, beginning with the ball for President
Johnson in January, 1965. He turned out a
series of successful albums for Decca and,
during his Cocoanut Grove appearance in
1965, signed a contract with Universal Pictures which called for the making of one
movie annually for the next five years. The
subsequent decline of the motion picture industry, however, did not justify the production of all the movies involved in the contract. At present Duchin and his orchestras
are enjoying a success which shows no sign
of declining.

SONNY DUNHAM

Started First Band   June 1940
Where   Hollywood, California
Previous Band Affiliations   Paul Tremaine,
Ben Bernie, Glen Gray and the Casa Loma
Orchestra
Sidemen With Band Included   Nick Buono,
Corky Corcoran, Hal Mooney, Pete Candoli,
Kai Winding
Vocalists With Band Included   Harriet
Clark, Dorothy Claire, Ray Kellogg

Sponsored Radio Shows   Repeat appear-
ances on Coca Cola's "Spotlight Bands" and
Frank Dailey's "Matinee Meadowbrook"
Television With Band   Early "Steve Allen
Show," "Robert Q. Lewis Show"
Longest Engagement   Hotel New Yorker,
two 13-week and one 16-week run
Theme Song   "Memories Of You"
Songs Written   "Come And Git It"
Recording Affiliations   Bluebird, Hit, Vogue

Peter Duchin and his orchestra, New York, June 1964.

Dunham was one of the featured trumpet players with the Casa Loma Orchestra and can be heard on a great deal of the fine recordings which that organization turned out for Decca. Perhaps one of his best known selections played with Casa Loma was "Memories Of You." He became so well identified with it that when he struck out with a band of his own it was understandable that he would take it for his theme song. At least one recording of the number was done with his own band. As a front man Dunham had a great deal going for him. He was a very versatile musician and one of the few trumpet men who could double on trombone with equal skill. Throughout the forties he was featured in the nation's best dance spots coast to coast. During one of his West Coast appearances at the Hollywood Palladium, he was tagged for a motion picture and, with the full band, did a full length feature with the Ritz Brothers at Universal, followed

Sonny Dunham.

later by several musical shorts for both Universal and Warner Brothers. In the early 1950s he disbanded briefly but reorganized in 1952. He remained active until the decline in the band business forced him to give up the battle for the limited bookings still available. When I contacted him in the mid-sixties, he was leading a steamship band out of New York and booking other units for similar excursions.

The Sonny Dunham Orchestra in its early days, about 1941.

E

BILLY ECKSTINE

Started First Band 1944
Previous Band Affiliations Earl "Fatha" Hines
Sidemen With Band Included Dizzy Gillespie, Gene Ammons, Lucky Thompson, Charlie Parker, Leo Parker, Dexter Gordon, Art Blakey, Howard McGhee, Fats Navarro, Kenny Dorham, Miles Davis, Jerry Valentine, and others
Vocalists With Band Included Eckstine himself, Sarah Vaughan
Recording Affiliations Bluebird

Eckstine was best known as a singer, a career which began while he was still in school. Afer a two-year association with Earl Hines, he had enough reputation and self-confidence to leave the band and work briefly as a single. Then in 1944 with the help of Budd Johnson, Eckstine put together a big band. Many of the band's arrangements were done by Dizzy Gillespie and the Eckstine band did a great deal to introduce "bop." As a front man Eckstine had an opportunity to showcase his vocal abilities and also to occasionally play good trombone. During a three-year period the band toured the nation, playing a few good location jobs and lots of one-nighters. Usually they did good business but needed a good hit record to put them into the winner's circle. Early in 1947 the band venture was abandoned, and Eckstine continued his career as a single with much greater success.

LES ELGART

Started First Band 1945
Where Brooklyn, New York, first job at Pelham Heath Inn
Previous Band Affiliations Bunny Berigan, Woody Herman, Charlie Spivak, Raymond Scott
Theme Song "Heart Of My Heart," "Sophisticated Swing"

Songs Written "Bandstand Boogie"
Recording Affiliations Columbia

Les Elgart entered the band business just as a long downward trend made it difficult for new musicians to survive. Nonetheless, Elgart did survive, and remained active after some of the big names of the mid-forties

113

Les Elgart.

had hung up their instruments. Elgart's own instrument was the trumpet, and his brother Larry played lead alto sax in the band. The sound which Les developed was distinctly his own. Its unique sound was partially due to the fact that no piano was used. It was good dance music, but to some listeners the sound pattern from one number to the next was so consistent that it became somewhat tiresome. Although the radio remotes featuring dance bands disappeared from the air waves during the fifties and the recording companies gradually turned their interest to other sound, Elgart continued to build his popularity and to play the still-remaining band spots on a coast-to-coast basis. He and his band are still on the road, operating from a base in Dallas, Texas.

The Les Elgart Orchestra at the Pennsylvania Hotel, New York.

DUKE ELLINGTON

Started First Band In early twenties, but had small combo of his own while still in high school

Where Washington, D.C. but quickly moved into New York City

Previous Band Affiliations A brief period spent with Wilbur Sweatman

Sidemen With Band Included A long list of greats, some of whom worked most of their careers with him, including Sonny Greer, Johnny Hodges, Elmer Snowden, Ben Webster, Fred Guy, Bubber Miley, Joe Nanton, Harry Carney, Barney Bigard, Ray Nance, Juan Tizol, Cootie Williams, Lawrence Brown, Toby Hardwicke, Rex Stewart, Jimmie Hamilton, Oscar Pettiford, Willie Smith, Louie Bellson, Billy Strayhorn, Russell Procope, Mercer Ellington

Vocalists With Band Included Herb Jeffries, Al Hibbler, Ivy Anderson, Kay Davis, Joya Sherrill, Maria Ellington (Mrs. Nat Cole)

Television With Band Several specials and guest appearances

Theme Song He used several during his career—"East St. Louis Toodle-oo," "Solitude," "Take The 'A' Train"

Songs Written Well over a thousand. Some of the best known were "Mood Indigo," "Sophisticated Lady," "Solitude," "In A Sentimental Mood," "Creole Love Call," "Sentimental Lady," "Just Squeeze Me," "Cottontail," "Satin Doll," and "I Let A Song Go Out Of My Heart"

Recording Affiliations Gennett, Brunswick, Vocalion, Harmony, Regal, Victor, Okeh, Columbia, Musicraft

Duke Ellington's music has withstood the test of time and the efforts of innumerable writer critics to tell him what he had played, what he intended to play, and what he should have played. Actually his music was rated highly by all contemporary musicians, and was above review by any laymen. As a composer of popular music and jazz he has had no peer. From his ever-active mind there

A closeup of the Duke in the late 1950s.

flowed a continuous stream of hits. Many of them were said to have been recorded before they were ever written down. Not content to excel in the popular and jazz field, Ellington also ventured successfully into the area of religious music, as both composer and conductor.

Born in Washington, D.C. on April 29, 1899, he was studying piano by the time he was seven years old, due to the encouragement of his mother. By the time he graduated from high school he was earning a living from music, and very quickly became an entrepreneur, supplying small bands for private and public dances in the manner of Meyer Davis. Other people were in the same business in the Washington area, but Ellington attracted the most attention by buying a telephone directory ad larger than those of his competitors.

His first trip to New York, to play with the Wilbur Sweatman band, was not particularly successful and he returned to Washington. In 1923 he took his own group called

At the Kentucky Club in New York, 1926.

"Duke Ellington and the Washingtonians" back to New York, where they went to the Kentucky Club for an engagement that lasted four years. During that period they began to record, made their first radio broadcasts, and adopted their first theme song — "East St. Louis Toodle-oo."

By the end of another four-year run at the Cotton Club, where they started playing in 1927, Ellington's now ten-piece band had become one of the most popular in America. His popularity was not limited to the United States. Europe was clamoring to see and hear the band in person. He made his first European tour in 1933, and the many appearances included the London Palladium. The second tour was made in 1939. In be-

tween he travelled the States, made countless recordings, and penned immortal music.

During the early forties the band was in several motion pictures and a stage review in Los Angeles called "Jump For Joy." The latter was scheduled to be taken to New York but closed at the end of the Los Angeles run. In 1943 they went into Carnegie Hall for a jazz concert, the first to be given there since Benny Goodman's unprecedented appearance a few years earlier. This concert was particularly noteworthy, it featured Ellington's presentation of his "Black, Brown and Beige," which ran nearly an hour and was received with enthusiastic acclaim. By that time Ellington had become an American institution known round the

Oriental Theatre, Chicago, 1932. *Left to right:* trumpet—Freddy Jenkins; bass—Wellman Brand; trumpet—Cootie Williams; baritone sax—Harry Carney; trumpet—Arthur Whetsol; alto sax—Johnny Hodges; valve trombone—Juan Tizol; trombone—Joe Nanton; clarinet—Barney Bigard; drums—Sonny Greer; guitar—Fred Guy; leader/piano—Duke Ellington.

world, without doubt the most prolific band-leading composer in the business. In August 1943 a *Saturday Evening Post* article by Maurice Zolotow credited him with having composed 950 tunes, many of them retained in his head until he was forced by his publisher to put them on paper. His recording sessions were described as scenes of wild confusion, with the orchestra blowing notes aimlessly and the Duke doodling on the piano to produce the theme he was searching for. After an hour or so of this, each man would have found his own version of the theme. Then, with the unity they al-

ways presented on the bandstand, the group would record another great Ellington original. If Ellington had 950 compositions to his credit in 1943, it would be difficult to estimate the total for his entire career. His song writing continued, although there were those who felt the quality of his later compositions was somewhat below those turned out in the early part of his career.

Ellington's band was often described as an instrument, on which he played as his own mood dictated. That impression was the result of the orchestra's consistent unison, an apparently complete understanding of

117

1949, *left to right*: trombone – Lawrence Brown; drums – Sonny Greer; trombone – Quentin Jackson; bass – Wendell Marshall; trombone – Tyree Glenn; piano – Duke Ellington; clarinet – Jimmy Hamilton; alto sax – Johnny Hodges; tenor sax – Ben Webster; trumpet – Al Killian; trumpet – Harold Baker; alto sax – Russell Procope; trumpet – Francis Williams; trumpet – Shelton Hemphill; baritone sax – Harry Carney; cornet, violin – Ray Nance.

what the Duke wanted and what every other instrumentalist was going to do. Most of them had been playing together for several years, for key men seldom left Ellington. When it did happen it made news. In 1941 much publicity was given to Benny Goodman's hiring Cootie Williams away from Ellington at a salary of $200 weekly—a great deal of money at that time considering that the total Ellington payroll was reported to be $2400 weekly for fourteen musicians plus vocalists and band boy. Unlike other bands, featured sidemen were not given to stepping out on their own to be leaders. A few tried but most of them came back including Johnny Hodges. When Hodges died suddenly in a New York dentist's office in 1970, the greatest tone ever produced from an alto saxophone was stilled. It was a great loss to the Ellington band.

Probably the music of Duke Ellington had a greater influence on others in the business than that of any other bandleader. Yet, un-like the sound created by Glenn Miller, it was never completely imitated. Probably Charlie Barnet came closest, and echoes of the style can be found in many of the records turned out by both Harry James and Les Brown.

During the downward trend of big band popularity, which had put most others on the sidelines by the mid-fifties, Ellington's was one of the few who survived and remained active on a full-time basis. But it became an entirely different business. Gone were the theaters in which his band had been showcased so well. There were virtually no top night clubs or hotels where he could play, and very few ballrooms. Staying busy meant concerts and an endless series of one-nighters. He kept busy with these and occasional tours, meanwhile finding time to write, produce, and conduct several ambitious stage productions and concerts.

In 1969 President Nixon invited him to the White House for a party, honoring a

Ellington prepares to record, in the late 1950s.

great jazz man on his seventieth birthday and paying tribute to the monumental contribution he had made to America's music. No one could have been more deserving of the honor.

In May of 1974 close friends of Ellington received Christmas cards from him. Some of them realized that the message in those cards was more than a Christmas greeting and they were right. On May 24 in a New York hospital he died, a victim of cancer and pneumonia, at the age of seventy-five. His son Mercer carried on with the band which his father had made so famous.

Ellington celebrates his seventieth birthday at the White House in 1969.

ZIGGY ELMAN

Started First Band   Late forties
Where   Hollywood
Previous Band Affiliations   Benny Goodman, Tommy Dorsey
Theme Song   "And The Angels Sing"
Songs Written   "And The Angels Sing"
Recording Affiliations   MGM

Elman's bandleading career was limited to a brief fling in the post-war years. Before that he had a long career as a sideman playing brilliant trumpet. Actually he had first started out to study the trombone, switching later to the trumpet. On that instrument he was heavily featured in both the Benny

Ziggy Elman.

Goodman and Tommy Dorsey orchestras. It was his trumpet work that made his own composition, "And The Angels Sing," a big hit for Benny Goodman. His musical career was interrupted for military service from 1943 to 1946. When he returned to civilian life he rejoined the Tommy Dorsey band, then put together a band of his own. Most of its appearances were made on the West Coast, including the Hollywood Palladium, but he did make one or more midwestern tours. After giving up the band, he worked in several motion pictures, including *The Benny Goodman Story.* Television work kept him busy for several years but in the early sixties he dropped out of sight temporarily and was hospitalized for a nervous breakdown. He died in Van Nuys, California on June 25, 1968 at the age of 54.

SKINNAY ENNIS

Started First Band   1938
Where   Los Angeles
Previous Band Affiliations   Hal Kemp
Vocalists With Band Included   Carmine. Ennis did male vocals himself
Sponsored Radio Shows   "The Bob Hope Show," "The Abbott and Costello Camel Show"
Theme Song   "I've Got A Date With An Angel"
Recording Affiliations   Victor, Signature, Phillips

Ennis started his musical career while attending the University of North Carolina by playing on the campus with the Hal Kemp orchestra. He played the drums with the group and, partially as a gag, he also began handling the vocals. Surprisingly his slightly-out-of-breath style caught on, and he soon became the band's featured attraction. When the Kemp band left the campus to

Skinnay Ennis.

achieve nationwide popularity, Ennis stayed with them for thirteen years, until he finally left to be a leader. He was not long in getting the one big break that eluded so many leaders—a spot on a sponsored radio show. Bob Hope was changing bands on the "Pepsodent Show" and gave Ennis the job. There he shared the spotlight with Hope, who gave him many important comedy lines on every show. With this kind of buildup he had no difficulty in booking his band into the top dance spots in the nation during the summer season when the radio show was not on. He interrupted his career for military service during World War II, returning to take up his batoning in 1946. He also resumed his spot on the Hope radio show, but left it in 1948. He then did a brief stint on the "Abbott and Costello Show." During the next several years he toured the nation, playing the leading hotels but maintaining his home in the Hollywood area, where he had substantial real estate holdings. During

Skinnay entertains the servicemen, 1946.

The postwar band of Skinnay Ennis.

the mid-fifties he confined his activities largely to the Southern California area, and was chosen to open the Los Angeles Statler Hilton Hotel in downtown Los Angeles in 1958. He remained there for the next five years. He died in June 1963, because of choking on food particles while dining in a plush Hollywood restaurant. Just before his death he recorded an LP on the Phillips label titled, "Skinn'ay Ennis Salutes Hal Kemp," using some of the musicians who had been in the original Kemp band.

Ennis and the orchestra with Frances Langford, while working in a picture at Universal in 1941.

JACK EVERETTE

Started First Band 1926
Where Cedar Rapids, Iowa
Sidemen With Band Included Eddie Rommers, Vern Scollon, Bill Williams, Earl Hulen, Lock Lohman, Kelly Christensen, George Mull, Skeets Evans, Al Knorr

His real name was Jack Everette Jackson but he billed himself as Jack Everette and His Orchestra because another popular Midwest orchestra was billed as Jack Jackson and His Orchestra. He was born in Cedar Rapids, Iowa, where he started his first band. With the help of a weekly feature on radio station KWCR, he was able to build his prestige throughout Iowa and the surrounding area. By the mid-thirties he had become a very popular midwest territory band, with a long run at the Mayfair Club in Des Moines. He also occasionally took the band into Chicago and into the Kansas City area, where he played the Kansas City Pla-Mor Ballroom with regularity. With the ranks of his band depleted by the draft, Everette disbanded during World War II and opened a restaurant in Springfield, Missouri. Later he took a turn at operating a large dance hall. When the war was over, he resumed his bandleading career, with his prewar band personnel practically intact. He remained active as a bandleader until 1956. In the early sixties he and his son David opened a booking office in Kansas City, called Jakson Artist Corporation.

Jack Everette and his orchestra. *Top row includes:* Eddie Rommers, Verne Scollon, Bill Williams, Earl Hulen, Lock Lohman, Kelly Christensen. *Bottom row:* George Mull, Jack Everette, Skeet Evans, Al Knorr.

MAYNARD FERGUSON

Started First Band Mid-fifties (Had previously had small band of his own in Canada in early forties)

Previous Band Affiliations Boyd Raeburn, Jimmy Dorsey, Charlie Barnet, Stan Kenton

Sidemen With Band Included Chico Alvarez, Al Porcino, Shorty Rogers, Milt Bernhart, Bud Shank, Art Pepper, Conte Candoli, Herb Geller, Bill Holman, Ian Bernard, Don Payne, Jerry Frommer, Bob Gordon, Red Mitchell, Buddy Childress, Ray Linn, Bob Burgess, Georgie Auld, Alvin Stoller, Joe Ferrante, Nick Travis, Ernie Wilkins, Ernie Royal, Al Stewart, Jimmy Cleveland, Joe Burnette, Tony Ortega, Bill Chase, Jimmy Ford, Don Ellis, Joe Farrell, Don Rader, Slide Hampton, Gene Coe, Frank Hittner, Rufus Jones, John Bello, Jimmy Nottingham, Urbie Green, John Messner, Bill Watrous, and many others who came and went

Recording Affilations Capitol, Mercury, Emarcy, Roulette, Cameo

Maynard Ferguson.

Ferguson was a master of many instruments, including the trumpet, the valve trombone, the alto sax, the clarinet, the oboe, French horn, and baritone horn. He was best known for his high register trumpet work, which was featured in every band with which he appeared. He was identified for the longest period with the Kenton band, where he felt right at home with the Kenton progressive jazz arrangements. His initial ventures into bandleading were sporadic, beginning in the mid-fifties after free-lancing in the Los Angeles area for several years, working with various types of musical combinations. In 1956 he led the Birdland Dream Band, and shortly afterward put together a permanent band which usually averaged thirteen pieces. The band's initial popularity was achieved in the East, where Ferguson appeared regularly at Birdland and other jazz locations. Occasional tours were also made into his home province of Quebec, Canada. Ferguson kept the band going throughout the fifties and into the mid-sixties, at which time he reduced its size to a sextette. He is still active and still considered one of the best trumpet soloists in the business.

SHEP FIELDS

Started First Band   About 1929
Where   New York City
Vocalists With Band Included Sonny Washburn, Dorothy Allen, Clare Nunn, Thelma Gracen
Sponsored Radio Shows "The Woodbury Show"
Theme Song   "Rippling Rhythm"
Recording Affiliations   Decca, Bluebird

Shep Fields.

In order to give themselves and their music a personality which was distinctive, each bandleader searched for a different sound or gimmick for identification. By standing near the microphone and blowing through a straw into a glass of water Shep Fields identified his music with a sound he called "Rippling Rhythm." A press agent insisted that he accidentally discovered it while sucking Coca Cola through a straw, but there were others who suspected that it wasn't Coca Cola which was coming through the straw at the time the idea was born. Nonetheless Fields and his band caught on in the mid-thirties and by the end of 1936 every jukebox in the country was playing his record of "Plenty Of Money And You." Other hit records followed. The early forties Fields still a big attraction, with his orchestra featured on commercial radio on "The Woodbury Show." In 1941 he reorganized. Having already proven that orthodox methods were not for him, he abandoned conventional instrumentation and put together an orchestra made up completely of reed instruments. The resulting sound was unique and somewhat intriguing, although many listeners found it rather monotonous if listened to in overlong sessions. Fields retained this format during most of World War II, but finally gave it up to front a conventional organization, which included a brass section and the other standard instruments. In the early fifties Fields moved to Houston, Texas where he remained active in the music business for the next several years, with frequent engagements at the Shamrock Hotel. In 1963 he brought his career as a bandleader to a close by joining up with his brother Freddy to operate a Hollywood talent agency, called Creative Artists, an agency which they later sold. In the mid-seventies Fields was still in the personal management business. In addition to the long list of records Fields turned out, his orchestra was featured in at least one motion picture on the Paramount lot. In declining health for several years he passed away in a Hollywood hospital on February 23rd, 1981, at age 70.

The all-reed orchestra of Shep Fields, organized in 1941, was abandoned in the postwar years in favor of conventional instrumentation.

JACK FINA

Started First Band   1946
Where   West Coat, first job at Claremont Hotel in Berkeley, California
Previous Band Affiliations   Clyde McCoy, Freddy Martin
Sidemen With Band Included   Al King, Jerry Kadovitz, Peppie Landeros, Jimmy Morris, Bob Bates, Le Roy Crouch, John Kirchies, Lenny Leyson, Tony Leonard, Irving Geller, Paul Desmond, Ricky Marino, Bob Morrison, Tiny Magardo, Eddie Gangale, Joe Maita
Vocalists With Band Included   Harry Prime, Gil Lewis

Theme Song   "Dream Sonata"
Songs Written   "Bumble Boogie," "Dream Sonata," "Piano Portrait"
Recording Affiliations   MGM

Introduced on radio remotes as "The Ten Most Talented Fingers In Radio" Fina's musical background was strong before he made the attempt with his own band. During his ten years with Freddy Martin, he had been heavily featured and it was Martin's recording of "Bumble Boogie," with Fina on the piano, that gave him the status necessary to become a leader in his own right. His first orchestra was a sixteen-piece organization. His Claremont Hotel opening in the fall of 1946 was the beginning of a series of annual return engagements for the next six or seven years. The combination of good air time and his recordings made him a national figure, and his band was heard repeatedly in such spots as Elitch's Gardens in Denver, The Chase Hotel in St. Lous, the Aragon Ballroom in Chicago, the Balinese Room in Galveston, Texas, and the Waldorf-Astoria in New York. He also appeared in a number of motion pictures made at Columbia. Sometime in the fifties he reduced the size of his band and settled in San Francisco. In addition to playing local engagements with his band, he operated a talent agency called the "Concerto Music & Entertainment Agency," in partnership with his personal manager, Al King. Early in 1960 he was booked into the Beverly Hills Hotel, where he fronted a very small but danceable group and where he remained for a successful eight-year engagement. During that same period he was also featured (as a single) on a nationally syndicated television show with Dick Sinclair. In the spring of 1970, he returned once more to the Beverly Hills Hotel, where he

Jack Fina.

had established a very strong following. During this engagement he suffered a heart attack and died on May 14, 1970 in his Sherman Oaks home.

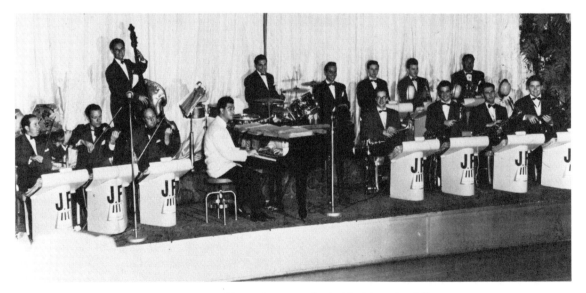

Jack Fina and his orchestra at the Waldorf-Astoria, 1949.

CHARLIE FISK

Started First Band   Early forties
Where   Midwest

Fisk was a graduate of the University of Missouri. The band which he launched in the early forties created a great deal of attention in the midwestern area. Featuring his own Harry James-styled trumpet, Fisk fronted a group of capable musicians. The vocals were handled by Ginny Coon, Fisk's wife and the daughter of Carleton Coon of Coon-Saunders fame. MCA picked the band up for bookings and placed them in such midwestern landmarks as the Tunetown Ballroom in St. Louis; the Pla-Mor in Kansas City; Riverview Park in Des Moines; the Pleasure Pier in Port Arthur, Texas; the New Casino in Fort Worth; the Indiana Roof in Indianapolis; and the Nu-Elm Ballroom in Youngstown, Ohio. A 1942 *Billboard* ad touted the band as "the band of tomorrow that's a tremendous hit today." A review in the same issue of *Billboard* described the Fisk band as a "band to watch," which would soon be expanding its influence from the Midwest to become a nationally famous band. Fisk prospered in the midwestern area throughout the forties, and was still active in the early fifties; but as the overall band business declined he faded from sight.

TED FIO RITO

Started First Band   1928
Where   Chicago
Previous Band Affiliations   Danny Russo (It later became the Russo-Fio Rito Orchestra)
Sidemen With Band Included   Dusty Rhodes, Paul Weirick, Al King, "Candy" Candido, Charlie Price, Muzzy Marcellino, Donald Rhea, Ray Hendricks, Harold Loynd, Walter Mauver, Harry Daugherty, Woody Taylor, Paul James, Clyde Hylton, J.C. Caballero, Norman Botnick, Vic Garber, Bill Ross, Vito Mumolo, Frank Flynn
Vocalists With Band Included   The Debutantes (Betty Noyes, Dorothy Compton, Marjorie Briggs), Betty Grable, Maureen O'Connor, June Haver, "Candy" Candido, Stanley Hickman, Muzzy Marcellino, Del Casino, Bob Carroll
Sponsored Radio Shows   "The Skelly Gasoline Show"
Theme Song   "Rio Rita"
Songs Written   "King For A Day," "No, No, Nora," "Charley, My Boy," "I Never Knew," "Sometime," "I'm Sorry, Sally," "Three On A Match," "Laugh, Clown, Laugh," "Lily Of Laguna," "Toot Toot Tootsie Goodbye," "When Lights Are Low,"

Fio Rito and his most famous vocalist, Betty Grable.

"Drifting Apart," "You've Never Been Blue," "Now That You're Gone," "Alone At A Table For Two," "Roll Along, Prairie Moon," "Soft Green Seas," "Kalua Lullaby"
Recording Affiliations   Victor, Brunswick, Decca

At the St. Francis Hotel, 1934.

As the song credits above indicate, Fio Rito was a prolific composer, with at least 100 titles to his credit. Yet, unlike most songwriting bandleaders, he was not given to overemphasizing his own compositions and sometimes even had to be urged to play them. Seldom did a bandleader who was a songwriter fail to use one of his own tunes for a theme song. But Fio Rito adopted "Rio Rita," probably because of the similarity to his name, a hit song from the motion picture of the same name written by two other composers.

His career in the music business began in the St. Louis-Chicago area in the early twenties. He joined the Danny Russo orchestra as featured pianist, and became its co-leader when they were booked into the Oriole Terrace in Detroit in 1922. Given heavy publicity by the owner of the club, they soon became a middlewestern favorite. Returning to Chicago, their reputation continued to grow, with a considerable assist from the fact that Fio Rito continued to dash off hit songs. They were the orchestra chosen to open the Aragon Ballroom for the Karzas Brothers in 1926. Eventually Russo and Fio Rito went their separate ways and Ted

Muzzy Marcellino and the Debutantes, Chicago, 1936.

started his own band, using his prestige as a songwriter for momentum.

Initially he concentrated in the Chicago and St. Louis areas. Then in 1929 he made

At the Coconut Grove, 1934.

a trip to the West Coast, to play the Mark Hopkins Hotel in San Francisco during a brief period when Anson Weeks was taking time off from the assignment for a tour of his own. That engagement was not too successful, but he returned to the West Coast in 1931 to work in one of the first motion pictures featuring a dance orchestra and to play an extended engagement at the Plantation Ballroom. The next year he went into the St. Francis Hotel in San Francisco for the first of several successful appearances in that location. It was during that time that Muzzy Marcellino joined him as guitarist and vocalist. Somewhat later he hired Betty Grable, who had been singing with a local San Francisco band. During the balance of the thirties, Fio Rito concentrated on the West Coast, playing the Cocoanut Grove, Topsy's, the Beverly Wilshire Hotel, the St. Francis, and several return engagements to the Palomar. He also continued to make periodic national tours, with Chicago appearances at the Morrison, the Congress, and Edgewater Beach Hotel, and occasional trips into New York.

During World War II, Fio Rito altered his style somewhat in an attempt to go along with the trend towards larger organizations playing swing music. Toward the war's end, soon-to-be-movie star June Haver sang briefly with the band. In the postwar period Fio Rito went back to his original style, and continued to be featured in choice locations although many were rapidly dropping out of the business. In the early fifties he was booked into Las Vegas for an engagement which continued on for more than five years. There were rumors in music circles that the longevity of this engagement was due, at least in part, to Fio Rito's inability to pick up his gambling markers.

In 1959 he opened a private club in Scottsdale, Arizona, called the Black Sheep Club, which he operated for the next three years with little or no participation in the music business. The club was unsuccessful and in 1962 he gave it up. He then formed a small band of five or six men and they played the California-Nevada circuit until his death from a heart attack in 1971. During his better than forty years as a bandleader, Fio Rito played every conceivable type of location and was featured in many motion pictures.

131

RALPH FLANAGAN

Started First Band 1949
Where New York City
Previous Band Affiliations Sammy Kaye
Vocalists With Band Included Harry Prime, The Young Sisters
Sponsored Radio Shows Chesterfield's "ABC's of Music," "Air Force Recruiting "Let's Go Show"
Television With Band "Kreisler Bandstand," "Arthur Murray Show," "Cavalcade of Bands"
Theme Song "Singing Wind"
Recording Affiliations Victor

Ralph Flanagan.

In addition to playing piano, Flanagan was an accomplished arranger. After playing several years with the Sammy Kaye band, he took time out during World War II to serve in the maritime service. After the war he became Perry Como's staff arranger. His career as a bandleader was launched somewhat reluctantly, a fact which he liked to bring up in later years when events were not going to his satisfaction. In addition to his arranging chores for Perry Como, he worked as a studio musician for RCA Victor. When some of their big artists started leaving them for other labels, RCA decided to build names of their own and chose Flanagan to be their test bandleader. Throughout late 1949 they gave him such heavy promotion on records that he had been built to big-name status even before he took the band on the road early in 1950. Soon Victor had proven their point. In the early fifties Flanagan was one of the top orchestras in the business. In a *Billboard* ad in July 1951, his personal managers, Herb Hendler and Bernie Woods, proclaimed that during a period between March 15, 1950 and March 15, 1951 he had grossed over $500,000 and played to over two million people. Over a period of 594 days he had been booked 574. He had been proclaimed the number one band in the Martin Block poll, *Billboard's* college poll, the *Motion Picture Daily* poll, and had taken most of the honors in *Billboard's* annual disc jockey poll.

The Young Sisters.

All this success could not overcome his apparent dislike for being a public figure. Ballroom operators were enthusiastic about his music but often critical of his attitude

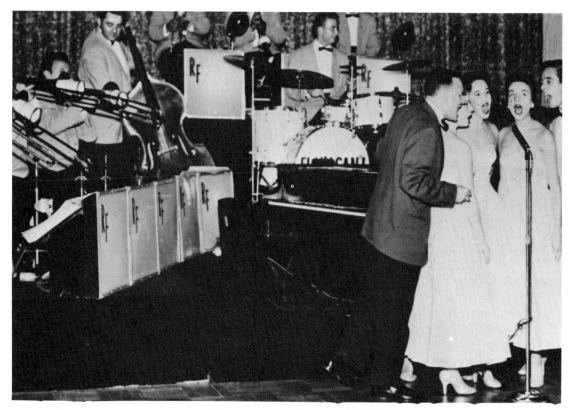

The Flanagan Band in the early 1950s.

The Flanagan Band on tour.

of indifference. A good share of the time he was uncooperative with the press, and the resulting coverage was not to his advantage. Never did he get so much press coverage as that which resulted from his taking an early morning stroll in the nude along an East Coast beach in the mid-fifties. Twenty years later he might have had to step over other nude bathers on the same beach, but the morning he tried it he was somewhat ahead of his time.

Flanagan's musical style was patterned after Glenn Miller, so much so that some of his earliest recordings might have been mistaken for Miller's. He and the band played most of the nation's top locations which were still operating during the fifties. Wherever possible he made the trips in his own private plane. Towards the end of the fifties he gave up the big band, except for occasional tours, and most of his personal appearances were made with a small combination of five or six people.

BASIL FOMEEN

Started First Band 1933
Where New York City
Previous Band Affiliations Joe Moss, Meyer Davis
Theme Song "Manhattan Gypsy"
Recording Affiliations Victor, Brunswick, Columbia, Decca

He was born Wasily Fomin. He played his accordion with Joe Moss and in Meyer Davis units before starting his own orchestra at New York's Savoy Plaza in 1933. Fomeen's musicians became an internationally famous society band. His initial engagement at the

Savoy Plaza lasted two years. Then he spent two years at the St. Moritz. Eventually he went into the Waldorf-Astoria, where he played many return engagements. His orchestra was also a favorite at the Carlton in Washington, D.C. When he finally came to the West Coast, playing at Ciro's in Hollywood, he became very popular with the movie crowd. He toured Europe, Africa, India, and China as a USO unit, and also had a long engagement at the Copacabana Casino in Rio de Janeiro. Fomeen was also an accomplished composer with a long list of credits.

CHUCK FOSTER

Started First Band 1938
Where Los Angeles, opened at the Biltmore Bowl
Previous Band Affiliations Played reed instruments in the house band at Topsy's Restaurant in South Gate, California
Sidemen With Band Included Probably best known was Hal Pruden, pianist who later became the leader of his own band
Vocalists With Band Included Dorothy Brandon, Jean Gordon, Dotty Dotson, Jimmy Castle
Sponsored Radio Shows Several repeat appearances on the "Coca Cola Parade of Spotlight Bands"

Longest Engagement Myron's Ballroom, Los Angeles
Theme Song "Oh, You Beautiful Doll"
Songs Written "I've Been Drafted, Now I'm Drafting You"
Recording Affiliations Okeh, Mercury, Phillips

Foster's was basically a hotel band offering a "sweet" brand of music which incorporated a little bit of the styles of many other leaders. A reviewer in the early forties described it as a bit of Sammy Kaye, Kay Kyser, Russ Morgan, and Jan Garber. At one time Foster even included the use of

Basil Fomeen in Rio de Janeiro, 1941.

Chuck Foster and his orchestra, Peabody Hotel, Memphis, in the early 1950s.

singing song titles, in the style made so popular by Kay Kyser on his "Lucky Strike Show." The band was launched at the Biltmore Bowl in Los Angeles, a location which had very good air time, including a good deal of coast-to-coast coverage. When Foster left there he had built up sufficient name value to make one-nighters productive and to create a demand for him in other hotels across the country. For the next several years he toured from a West Coast base. When the West Coast dance band picture declined, he made his headquarters in the Midwest, where he became a strong favorite at such spots as the Peabody Hotel in Memphis, the Roosevelt in New Orleans, the Blackhawk Restaurant and the Aragon Ballroom in Chicago. He also periodically invaded New York, where he usually played at the New Yorker Hotel, and also appeared at the Roseland Ballroom. In the mid-sixties he returned to the West Coast to make his home in the San Fernando Valley and to play a long engagement at Myron's Ballroom in downtown Los Angeles. When that

Chuck Foster.

engagement finally came to an end, he returned to the road to make four or five midwestern tours annually, most of them one-nighters. He is still actively engaged in these band tours.

Chuck Foster, Muehlbach Hotel, Kansas City.

JAN GARBER

Started First Band 1918
Where In the New York area
Sidemen With Band Included Chelsea Quealey, Harry Goldfield, Harold Peppie, Benny Davis, Paul Weirick, Joe Rhodes, Freddie Large, Fritz Heilbron, Norman Donahue, Jerry Large, Rudy Rudisill, Don Shoup, Charlie Ford, Lew Palmer, Doug Roe, Russ Brown, Bill Kleeb, Jack Barrow, Frank MacCauley, Tony Briglia, Al Powers, Memo Bernabei, Vince Di Bari, Ernie Mathias, Frank Bettencourt, Jack Motch, Ted Bowman, Bill Oblak, Billy Hearn, Don Korinek, Walter Moore
Vocalists With Band Included Virginia Hamilton, Lee Bennett, Judy Randall, Tony Allen, Dorothy Cordray, Fritz Heilbron, Bob Allen, Debby Claire, Liz Tilton, Tim Reardon, Alan Copeland, and the Twin Tones, Tommy Traynor, Janis Garber, Bob Grabeau, Thelma Gracen, Roy Cordell, Larry Dean, Deanna St. Clair, Marv Nielsen
Sponsored Radio Shows Briefly on the "Burns and Allen Show"
Theme Song "My Dear"
Songs Written Collaborated on "My Dear" with Freddie Large
Recording Affiliations Columbia, Brunswick, Victor, Decca, Okeh, Hit, Black & White, Capitol, and Dot

Picture of a man enjoying his work, 1952.

Although the style of his music did not meet the approval of some dedicated critics, Garber has to be rated as one of the leaders who helped elevate the dance band business to the "big business" status which it once enjoyed. He began his bandleading career many years before the "big band era," and was still active long after most of his fellow leaders had given up because of the declining business. When he retired in the early '70s, very few people could equal his record of successful continuity in a highly competitive business.

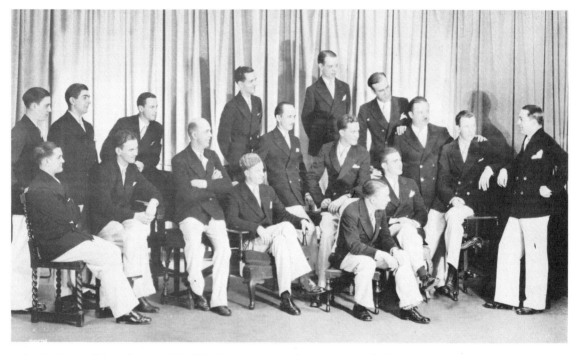

Jan Garber and his orchestra, 1926. This fifteen-piece band was substantially larger than most others of this period, and larger than the bands Garber would later be identified with.

1940: vocals — Lee Bennet; bass — Charley Ford; trumpet *(right)* — Fritz Heilbron; saxophone *(right)* — Freddie Large.

Memphis, 1949: bass—Frank McCauley; trumpets—Ernie Mathias, Bill Kleeb, Vince Di Bari; trombones—Jack Barrow, Frank Bettencourt; piano—Jack Motch; saxophones—Memo Bernabei, Freddie Large, Al Powers, Jo Jo Huffman; vocalists—Bob Grabeau and Janis Garber.

In the Blue Room of the Roosevelt Hotel, New Orleans, 1957.

The small group which he first organized in 1918 was a four-piece combination featuring Jan on violin. He gave that up to briefly front one of the many Meyer Davis units. In the early twenties he merged with Milton Davis (no relation to Meyer) to form an orchestra of six men, which eventually grew to fifteen, substantially larger than most bands of that period. This Garber-Davis orchestra headquartered in Atlanta and concentrated their activities in the South and Southeast, where they became extremely popular. A few old reviews still available indicate that they were regarded as one of the best jazz bands in that part of the country. In 1927 Garber bought the interest of his partner Davis, and moved the band to Chicago, which had become one of the nation's best band organizing cities. There he met Freddie Large, who had recently come down from Canada with a band of his own and was having difficulty getting under way in the states. Garber gave up his own band, and worked out a deal to take over Large's band. With Garber as the front man and Large as the key musician, they soon made themselves a very firm place in both the Chicago scene and the entire Midwest. When they played at the Trianon, the air time from that ballroom quickly boosted them into national prominence. It was during the Trianon engagement that an announcer dubbed Jan "The Idol of the Airlanes", a tag line which caught on and which he used for many years.

Garber always maintained that it was he who originated the practice of playing one-night stands. Whether or not this was completely correct, he certainly was one of the first, and one of those who did the most to further the practice. Soon after he had moved to Chicago, the rapidly growing Music Corporation of America signed him. Under their guidance he toured the Midwest, reaping the benefit of his heavy Trianon air time by playing to packed houses. His first West Coast trip was made in 1934 to play Catalina Island's Avalon Ballroom, and the West Coast received him so cordially that he eventually moved there to make his home. Probably no other band played Catalina as often as Jan, and he did equally well at the Palomar Ballroom until it burned down in 1939. Despite his well-established identification with a Lombardo-styled sweet band, he gave it up in mid-1942 to go with what appeared to be the trend of the times and organized a large swing band. That venture was very expensive for him. Despite the fact that he hired some of the best musicians in the business, he did not do well with the swing band, perhaps because too many of the public were unwilling to accept his change of musical style. In the spring of 1945 he disbanded the swing band and retired for six months. In the fall of 1945 he resumed, with a band once again built around saxophonist Freddie Large (who had worked in a defense plant during the war), and with the arrangements written by Larry Owen, Lombardo's arranger. Owen joined the Garber band on a full-time basis, staying with them for several years. Soon Garber was back in the swing of things, with his activities ranging from coast to coast. In the early fifties he decided to move to Shreveport, Louisiana, the home town of his wife Dorothy. From his Shreveport headquarters he continued to be booked solidly, usually spending the winter months at the Roosevelt Hotel in New Orleans. The balance of the year was devoted to playing fairs, one-nighters, and an occasional horse show throughout the Midwest. In 1959 the Ballroom Operators of America expressed their approval of the veteran bandleader and his style of music by voting him the Number One All-Around Dance Band.

Quite likely it was the death of his longtime friend and associate, Freddie Large, that prompted him to go into retirement in the early seventies. During a career which spanned more than fifty years of fronting a dance band "Genial Jan" had probably played every major hotel, ballroom, and theater in the United States. After several years of declining health he died in a Shreveport hospital on October 5, 1977, a month before his eighty-third birthday.

DIZZY GILLESPIE

Started First Band   About 1945
Previous Band Affiliations   Eddie Hill, Earl Hines, Benny Carter, Les Hite, Lucky Millinder, Cab Calloway, Billy Eckstine; arranged for many bands including Woody Herman, Jimmy Dorsey, Charlie Barnet
Songs Written   "Groovin' High," "Swing Low Sweet Cadillac," "Something Old, Something New," "Cool World," "Blue Boogie," "Interlude," "Blue Mood," "Cool Breeze"
Recording Affiliations   Musicraft, Victor, Verve, Dee Gee

Gillespie is rated as one of the jazz greats and the one who did the most to establish the musical style known as "bop." Along with the style of music which he played he will be remembered for the unusual trumpet which he played, made especially for him, with the bell extending upward from the middle of the horn at a sharp angle of 45 degrees. He insisted that gave it some special sound which could not otherwise be attained. Both the trumpet and the musical style were developed while he was free lancing in the New York area in the late thirties. It was further developed with the help of Charlie Parker with whom he worked in the Earl Hines band in 1942 and 1943. For approximately a year starting in late 1943 Gillespie and Oscar Pettiford had a combo together which was quite popular which was given up to go with Billy Eckstine's band but in late 1944 he was back working with Charlie Parker in a combo which was totally dedicated to the bop sound. In 1945 Gillespie put together a big band which he kept busy for approximately a five-year period, during which time it not only played the States but made several European tours. Following the breakup with this big band he toured with Jazz At The Philharmonic. In the mid-fifties he put together a big band for overseas tours under the sponsorship of the United States Government, following which he once again confined his musical activities to work with smaller groups.

DON GLASSER

Started First Band   1938
Where   Derry, Pennsylvania
Previous Band Affiliations   Jerry Grey, Ray Pearl, Art Kassell
Vocalists With Band Included   Lois Costello (Mrs. Glasser), Roger Lopez
Longest Engagement   Twenty-six weeks at the Vogue in Chicago
Theme Song   "You Call It Madness, I Call It Love"
Songs Written   "Hey, Pretty Legs," "I Saw Both Ends Of A Rainbow"
Recording Affiliations   Stephanie, Cha Cha

Although Glasser started in the Pennsylvania area, he eventually made Chicago his headquarters. From there he toured the Midwest. His "Music Smooth As Glass" was one of the Midwest's favorites for many

Don Glasser.

years. Stylewise the band was often compared to Lombardo, Sammy Kaye, and Jan Garber. He survived the big band decline to remain active through the sixties and into the seventies, primarily playing the one-nighter circuit with occasional time out at such locations as the Roseland in New York City and the Willowbrook in Chicago.

JEAN GOLDKETTE

Started First Band   Early twenties
Where   Detroit
Sidemen With Band Included   Paul Mertz, Fuzzy Farrar, Ray Lodwig, Joe Venuti, Doc Ryker, Alan Wilber, Bill Rank, Jimmy Dorsey, Tommy Dorsey, Don Murray, Howdy Quicksell, Dewey Bergman, Bix Beiderbecke, Chauncey Morehouse, Russ Morgan, Duke Sellers, Spiegel Wilcox, Frank Trumbauer, Eddie Lang, Bill Challis, Danny Polo, Itzy Riskin, Steve Brown, Andy Secrest, Sterling Bose, Harold Stokes, Hoagy Carmichael, Pee Wee Hunt, Vernon Brown, Bob Strong, Victor Young, Artie Shaw, Charlie Spivak, Glenn Miller
Vocalists With Band Included   Seymour Simons, Frank Bessinger, Walter Preston, Billie Murray, Harold Stokes (sometimes used a vocal trio on recordings)
Sponsored Radio Shows   "The Studebaker Champion Program" (late twenties)
Theme Song   Used more than one; "Sweetheart Time," "I Know That You Know," "The Old Refrain"
Recording Affiliations   Victor

Jean Goldkette, concert pianist.

There are those in the music world who declare that Jean Goldkette was a myth who never existed. Discussions with musicians who worked for him developed very contradictory impressions of the man, his accomplishments and what occurred during his active years. The only area of agreement is that during the twenties one of the greatest dance orchestras of the period bore his name, and provided employment for most of those who would become important leaders a few years later.

Basically Goldkette was a concert pianist. Born in France, he came to the United States in 1911 and was a professional musician by the age of sixteen. He had a burning ambition to be the leader of a dance band and organized his first group in 1921 in Detroit. It was a small, semiconcert style band, with which he played for about a year at the Detroit Athletic Club. In 1922 he took a larger band into the Graystone Ballroom. In 1923 (quoting Goldkette) his real break came when the Graystone could not meet the band payroll and turned the place over to him to run. He immediately changed the policy of the place and set about to hire the best musicians in the business. The list of names above will indicate how successful he was in getting the musicians. Somehow he shaped them together to obtain not one but two or three bands, all bearing the Gold-

The Jean Goldkette Orchestra in Detroit, 1926, under the direction of Russ Morgan.

The Goldkette Victor Orchestra, 1927. *Back row:* Riskin, Brown, Quicksell. *Front row:* Ludwig, Farrar, Beiderbecke, Morehouse, Murray, Ryker, Willcox, Rank.

kette name. In addition he became an entrepreneur, booking other bands which he built into prominence, among them McKinney's Cotton Pickers, Don Redman's orchestra, and the Orange Blossom Band, which later became the Casa Loma Band.

His principal interest was in the Graystone Ballroom band and the band which worked consistently at the Book Cadillac Hotel, both booked under the Goldkette name. Strictly speaking, Goldkette was not a bandleader at all. He did not front the band, never came to rehearsals, and was once threatened with mayhem by an arranger for making a minor change in a number. To quote Goldkette himself: "I wanted to leave the men alone to express themselves in their own way without my telling them what to do. That was the secret of our success." Perhaps it was. In retrospect it seems almost incredible that such an approach could produce what was perhaps the greatest white band of the twenties, but it did. The only thing constant about the Goldkette band was change. Since he was not a front man himself, a number of his featured sidemen had their turns being the "standup" leader, with no record existing as to how most of them were selected. Joe Venuti, Russ Morgan, and Frankie Trumbauer all had their turns as did several others. In later years the problem of putting the Goldkette story together was complicated by the interviews these front men had given to various members of the press in the interim. Each of the leaders had a different version, usually related to his own importance in the band's success, and most stories were substantially different, from the one Goldkette told personally.

Perhaps the best information source from the band itself is Paul Mertz who, from his piano bench, had a better view than any of them. He joined the band when it was barely six months old, and except for a brief period, was with it almost to the breakup. His recollections and voluminous scrapbooks of dated clippings are the source of much of the material used here. He credits drummer Charlie

Horvath with being both the driving force within the band and the steadying influence which kept it together. He also recalls that although they were regarded as an "arrangement band," only two full-time arrangers were ever on the payroll, and not simultaneously. One of them was Bill Challis, who came in about 1926. Most of their best numbers were first "head arrangements," placed on paper after they had been worked out by separate rehearsals of the brass, reed, and rhythm sections.

Since the band at the Book-Cadillac Hotel had the advantage of more radio broadcast time than the band at the Graystone Ballroom, Goldkette made the most of that air time to sell both bands. It got them an invitation to play New York's Roseland Ballroom early in 1926 There they played alternating sets with the great Fletcher Henderson orchestra and earned raves from the New York press. On the first Roseland engagement the band was fronted by Russ Morgan. When they went back later in the same year, Frankie Trumbauer had taken over as leader. It was Trumbauer who had brought Bix Beiderbecke into the band. Bix read little or no music and memorized his parts on most arrangements after listening to someone else play them through. Although Bix participated in many recording sessions with the band, the Victor people were somehow not favorably impressed, and many of the records which featured him were never released. Goldkette's last big success was with the Studebaker Program in 1925. That band was initially fronted by Harold Stokes who was replaced by Victor Young, hired in New York by Goldkette himself for the assignment. Soon after this, Goldkette disbanded all his bands. He made several attempts to reenter the field during the thirties and the mid-forties. None of them was successful and he once more became a concert pianist, continuing to make appearances until the mid-1950s.

I first met Goldkette in 1961 when I was working on another book. We had several telephone conversations before we actually

The Goldkette Studebaker Orchestra, directed by Harold Stokes, 1929.

got together, but in the months that followed I saw him many times. He was extremely anxious to give me his story, and concerned that his place in America's musical scene would not be thoroughly recorded. He was also a very bitter man, apparently feeling that most of those he had helped along the way to success had all turned their backs on him later. I felt that he was angry with himself, perhaps subconsciously, for having turned away from the music business when he had so much going for him. He died in a Santa Barbara hospital in March 1962 while on a fund-raising trip for the National Artists Foundation, a nonprofit organization he had founded to promote amateur talent. His funeral was attended by only a handful of music people but the newsreels acknowledged his importance by covering the story at the mortuary. I was an honorary pallbearer, and was also pressed into service at the cemetery to help carry him to his final resting place. Two of the active pallbearers, both well known bandleaders, had left the mortuary the moment the newsreels finished shooting their pictures.

BENNY GOODMAN

Started First Band 1934
Where New York City, first engagement was played at Billy Rose Music Hall
Previous Band Affiliations Jules Herbuveaux, Ted Lewis, Ben Pollack, Benny Krueger, Isham Jones, Red Nichols
Sidemen With Band Included Arthur Bernstein, Nick Fatool, Fletcher Henderson, Ziggy Elman, Red Ballard, Corky Cornelius, Lionel Hampton, Gene Krupa, Harry James, Nate Kazebier, Pee Wee Irwin, Johnny Guarnieri, Chris Griffin, Murray McEachern, Hymie Schertzer, George Koenig, Art Rollini, Vido Musso, Harry Goodman, Vernon Brown, Dave Mathews, Noni Bernardi, Bud Freeman, Jess Stacy, Ben Heller, Dave Tough, Jerry Jerome, Buddy Schutz, Charlie Christian, Teddy Wilson, Roy Eldridge, Billy Butterfield, Dave Barbour, Georgie Auld, Joe Bushkin, Red Norvo, Joe Rushton, Cootie Williams, Louie Bellson, Milt Bernhart, Terry Gibbs, Lee Castle, and many others who came and went
Vocalists With Band Included Martha Tilton, Helen Ward, Helen Forrest, Peggy Lee, Patti Page, Art Lund, Dick Haymes
Tag Line "The King of Swing"
Musical Style Although he could not take credit for originating it, it was Goodman who made "swing" nationally popular
Success Formula Goodman's initial success resulted from remote broadcasts originating from the Palomar Ballroom in Los Angeles. This followed a year of disappointing response from East Coast audiences, who heard the band both in person and on radio
Sponsored Radio Shows The "Let's Dance" program for National Biscuit Company, the "Camel Caravan," the "Victor Borge Show"

Benny Goodman

Perhaps the first picture made of the Goodman band, 1935.

Television With Band Periodic specials, several of them for Texaco and many guest appearances

Theme Song Opening theme was "Let's Dance" and closing signature was "Goodbye"

Recording Affiliations Victor, Columbia, Capitol, and Decca. The Goodman clarinet was heard on a variety of labels as a sideman prior to starting his own band

Goodman's sensational rise to prominence following his Palomar date in 1935 is considered by most people in the music business to have been the single event which did the most for the band business and started what has been described as the "big band era." Prior to that the business had been in

the doldrums, attempting to recover from the great depression. For the next eight or ten years at least one new band followed the trail blazed by Goodman to become "the band of the year." It was a long uphill road to the Palomar success. Goodman was born in Chicago, in 1909, to a family which knew what it was to struggle for a living. He began taking clarinet lessons at the age of ten, and a year later was playing in a local theater pit band. He gave that up to play with a five-piece orchestra on a Lake Michigan steamer, and next joined Jules Herbuveaux, who had one of the better known bands in the Chicago area in the early twenties.

In the mid-twenties he went to the West Coast to join Ben Pollack and his newly formed orchestra playing at the Venice Ball-

The Goodman Band about 1938, shortly before Harry James left to go on his own.

room. His first stay with the Pollack band was about two years. When the band broke up briefly in Chicago, Benny worked for a short time with Benny Kreuger at the Uptown Theater, then rejoined Pollack. He left him again to go with Isham Jones. But when Pollack went to New York to play the Park Central Hotel Goodman went along, remaining in the band until the fall of 1929. He then joined Red Nichols until late 1931, after which he kept busy with free-lance work in the various New York radio stations.

In the fall of 1934, with a library built around some of Fletcher Henderson's best arrangements, Goodman organized his own orchestra, playing his first engagement at Billy Rose's Music Hall in New York City. A booking into the Roosevelt Hotel followed, but despite the band's buildup on the NBC "Let's Dance" program the Roosevelt dancers were not ready for the Goodman style. Neither were most of those he played for on a coast-to-coast tour in the summer of 1935. At Elitch's Gardens in Denver they competed with Kay Kyser, playing nearby Lakeside Park, and were no match for him in drawing the dancing crowd.

Disheartened, Goodman continued on to the West Coast to make the Palomar appearance. Many sources claim that he was reconciled to giving up the band at the end of the Palomar engagement. But suddenly the whole picture changed—the Palomar crowds literally went wild in expressing their approval of the Goodman style, and "The King of Swing" was finally on his way. For the next five years he dominated the world of dance music with the style he had made popular, becoming the driving force which inspired many others to success. He turned out hundreds of records, appeared in motion pictures, and had a popular radio show. At the Paramount Theater in New York the fans were uncontrollable. The orchestra was a smash hit in the nation's top hotels, at the San Francisco World's Fair, the Hollywood Bowl, and even in Carnegie Hall.

In the spring of 1940 Goodman disbanded to take a rest and to treat a back ailment. He reorganized several months later and had little trouble in once again becoming one of the top bands in the business. But some of the feeling that had sparked the

The Goodman Sextet at Catalina, 1940.

band of the thirties was never recaptured, in spite of several reorganizations. Writers lamented that Benny had become temperamental, hard to work for, and the "Goodman ray" was supposed to be all the notice its recipient needed to tell him he should look for another job. He was a perfectionist himself, so his difficulty in finding the patience to rebuild the orchestra he had worked so hard to put together in the thirties is understandable. Unhappy with his relationship with MCA, and unable to break his contract, he disbanded in 1944, electing to be inactive until the contract expired. In 1945 he came back with an organization closely resembling that with which he had left off. Throughout the balance of the decade he fronted a big band, but in the early fifties he dropped it for a small group. Not too much later he went into semiretirement, emerging periodically to play carefully selected engagements, usually with a small unit.

In 1955 his life was depicted on film in *The Benny Goodman Story*, a not-too-accurate version, with the title role played by Steve Allen and with Goodman recording the sound track. Following the release of the film he stepped up his own activity for a time and even made a trip to the Far East. Other overseas trips were made throughout the sixties, including a much-publicized tour of Soviet Russia. By the end of the sixties his state-side appearances had become pretty much limited to performances as a soloist. During the early and mid-seventies his activity consisted of occasional concert tours and television appearances. In January 1978 he returned to the scene of one of his triumphant engagements of forty years earlier, a concert in Carnegie Hall. The concert reportedly sold out the first day tickets were on sale.

Goodman's record as an innovator was not restricted to his popularization of "swing." More than anyone else he established the clarinet as a respectable instrument for a front man. He was the first white leader to break down the color line and use black musicians, first with Teddy Wilson, then with Lionel Hampton, Charlie Christian, Roy Eldridge, and Cootie Williams. He was still semi-active to the time of his death of a heart attack in his New York apartment on June 13, 1986.

At the Hollywood Palladium, 1943: trumpets—Lee Castle, Bob Guyer, Ray Linn; trombones—Miff Mole, Charles Castaldo, John Walton; saxophones—Lennie Kaye, Hymie Schertzer, Bob Taylor, Joe Rushton; piano—Jess Stacy; bass—Gus Van Camp; guitar—Bart Roults; drums—Louie Bellson; vocals—Peggy Lee (not shown).

At the University of Oregon in 1940. That's Johnny Guarneri at the piano, and Helen Forrest is seated beside him.

Goodman with a smaller band in 1949.

CLAUDE GORDON

Started First Band   Late fifties
Where   Los Angeles
Previous Band Affiliations   Matty Malneck, Ronnie Kemper, Frankie Masters
Vocalists With Band Included   Darts Alexander
Recording Affiliations   Alma Records

In the late fifties the dance band business had declined so far that the American Federation of Musicians tried to stage a revival. In 1959 a series of regional "best new band" contests was sponsored, climaxed by a national event in New York's Roseland Ballroom. Claude Gordon was the winner of the national title, with a thirteen-piece band he had organized in Los Angeles. Trumpet player Gordon had been very active in the Hollywood musical scene since the late forties and had many years' experience as a staff musician at CBS. He had also taught trumpet and accordion at the Los Angeles Conservatory of Music. During the early

Claude Gordon.

forties he had been on the road with travelling bands. As the winner of the national contest, the Gordon band was given a new set of instruments, an appearance on a network TV show, and a record contract. A coast-to-coast tour of one-nighters was arranged. The band was under the personal management of Frank Monte, who had long managed Harry James, and before him the Benny Goodman band. It seemed that all the ingredients for success were present. But the odds at the time were too great, despite the fact that it was a first-rate dance band with some great arrangements by Billy May. Gordon attempted to keep the band on the road during the early sixties, but with diminishing success. Eventually he returned to teaching music and the band appeared only on a part-time basis.

The Claude Gordon Orchestra in the early 1960s.

GRAY GORDON

Started First Band   Mid-thirties
Sidemen With Band Included   Chet Roble, Bill North, Lew Ashbrook, Carl Carelli, Larry McManus, Bobby Blair, Floyd Lauck, Curt Grass, Lionel Segur, Emmett Carles, Frank Adams, Johnny Johnson, Chet Bruce, Glen Rolfing, Roy Mace, Sil Raskind, Joe Dale, Herb Curbelo, Frank Linali, Babe Fresk, Alex Goldstein, Harry Levenson, Eugene Ferraro, Bob Fishel, Bob Negron, Joe Andreozzi, Hal Tennyson
Vocalists With Band Included   Betty Lane, Shirley Lane, Betty Bradley, Rita Ray, Johnny Victor, Art Berry, Meredith Blake
Theme Song   "One Minute To One"
Recording Affiliations   Bluebird, Victor

"Gray Gordon and His Tic Toc Rhythm" toured the nation during the late thirties and forties playing hotels, theaters, ballrooms, and amusement parks. Gordon's musical style was aimed at the dancers and provided by an organization which usually averaged twelve musicians plus vocalists.

The Gray Gordon Orchestra, 1942.

GLEN GRAY and
THE CASA LOMA ORCHESTRA

Started First Band 1929 (Most of the same band had been together as the "Orange Blossom Band" since 1924)

Where Detroit

Previous Band Affiliations Jean Goldkette

Sidemen With Band Included Pat Davis, Les Arquette, Larry Sloat, Chink Dougherty, Billy Rausch, Pee Wee Hunt, Joe Hall, Gene Gifford, Harold George, Walter Urban, Jack Richman, Mel Jenssen, Tony Briglia, Grady Watts, Clarence Hutchenrider, Sonny Dunham, Denny Dennis, Kenny Sargent, Dan D'Andrea, Art Ralston, Fritz Hummell, Frankie Zullo, Murray McEachern, Jacques Blanchette, Jack Burdette, Joe Reisman, Bobby Jones

Vocalists With Band Included Jack Richman, Kenny Sargent, Pee Wee Hunt, Eugenie Baird

Sponsored Radio Shows "The Camel Caravan"

Theme Song "Smoke Rings"

Recording Affiliations Okeh, Paramount, Brunswick, Decca (In the late fifties, several years after his retirement as a bandleader,

Glen Gray.

Glen Gray recorded a series of LPs for Capitol, using studio musicians and re-creating the sounds of most of the big bands, using each band's original arrangement.)

154

The Casa Loma Band started out as a cooperative band and remained that way during the years of its greatest popularity. Its first leader was Henry Biagini, who was replaced a year later by violinist Mel Jenssen. The band was incorporated in April 1930 and Jenssen remained its leader for the next several years. In 1937 Gray became the leader by popular vote of the corporate members of the orchestra, and there were some stories which indicated he did so reluctantly. Nonetheless he was a capable front man and one whose handsome appearance did much to enhance the band's musical efforts. He continued to play saxophone when the arrangement dictated, augmenting the regular sax section.

The band moved out of Detroit soon after incorporation, to establish headquarters on the East Coast. In the fall of 1930 they were in the Lido Venice in Boston and spent most of that winter and the following spring playing one-nighters. In the late summer of 1931 they went to the Steel Pier in Atlantic City, following which they once again went on the road for an extensive tour of the Middle west. In the summer of 1933 they were in the Glen Island Casino in New Rochelle, with regular air time which greatly enhanced their popularity. In the fall of that year they went into the Essex House in New York City, for the first of many stands in that location. It was during the Essex House engagement that they landed the "Camel Caravan" show, remaining on the show for the next three years. It was also during that time that Larry Clinton came in as arranger and Eddie MacHarg joined the band as its manager.

They made their first appearance on the stage of the Paramount Theater and had a long run at the Rainbow Room. Several ap-

Glen Gray, now the leader, and the Casa Loma brass section, about 1937. *Top row:* Billy Rauch, Pee Wee Hunt, Fritz Hummel. *Bottom row:* Walter Smith, Grady Watts, Frankie Gullo.

155

pearances were also made at the Congress Hotel in Chicago. Early in 1937 they left New York on a long westward tour which took them to the Palomar in Los Angeles in July. This was the first of two appearances in this major West Coast location and while the band was there they were signed for the "Burns and Allen Show." By the time they celebrated their tenth anniversary in April 1939 they were one of the nation's leading dance bands. In addition to their success on personal appearances they had been enjoying a very steady sale of their recordings on the Decca label. Perhaps the best known of these were "Casa Loma Stomp," "No Name Jive," and the band's never-to-be-forgotten theme "Smoke Rings."

Their momentum was unabated as they moved into the early forties, with the band now strongly identified as "Glen Gray and the Casa Loma Orchestra." During the war years the demand for bands exceeded the supply and the Casa Lomans still rode the crest of the wave, although there were mur-

murings that the band was not what it used to be. In the early postwar years these murmurs increased in volume, with critics in the trade journals saying that the band had slipped a long way and that companionship had apparently replaced musicianship. Slowly the original members had dropped out, several of them to become bandleaders themselves. Those who did well at it were Sonny Dunham and Pee Wee Hunt. Gray kept the organization active until the early fifties, at which time it was broken up and he went into retirement on the East Coast. He never resumed activity as a bandleader, except to come to Hollywood in the late fifties to record the first of a series of highly successful albums for Capitol, on which he recreated the sounds of most of the big bands of the swing era. He was still actively engaged with this project in the early sixties, but by the end of 1962 his close friends knew that he was a very sick man, a victim of cancer. He died in his Massachusetts home in August 1963.

Glen Gray and the Casa Loma Orchestra, in the late 1930s. *Left to right:* Glen Gray, Pat Davis, Grady Watts, Pee Wee Hunt, Frank Zullo, Clarence Hutchenrider, Bill Rauch, Sonny Dunham, Murray Mc Eachern, Art Ralston, Tony Briglia, Jack Blanchette, Dan d'Andrea, Stan Dennis, Kenny Sargent, Joe Hall.

The Casa Loma Orchestra, 1941.

The Glen Gray Orchestra at the Shamrock Hotel, Houston, 1949.

JERRY GRAY

Started First Band 1945
Where Los Angeles
Previous Band Affiliations Artie Shaw, Glenn Miller — primarily as arranger
Vocalists With Band Included Tommy Traynor, Linda Lee
Sponsored Radio Shows "The Philip Morris Frolics," "The Margaret Whiting Show," and "Club 15," the latter emceed by Bob Crosby
Longest Engagement Fairmont Hotel in Dallas
Theme Song "Desert Serenade"
Songs Written "String Of Pearls," "Pennsylvania 6-5000," "Here We Go Again," "Sun Valley Jump," "I Dreamt I Dwelt In Harlem"
Recording Affiliations Capitol, Majestic, and Mercury

Jerry Gray's versatility as an arranger contributed much to the success of at least two other bandleaders before he became a leader himself. It was his arrangement for Artie

Jerry Gray.

On the Hollywood Palladium bandstand.

Shaw's recording of "Begin The Beguine," which started Shaw on the way. He also did the arranging of "In The Mood," which was Glenn Miller's first big hit. When the Miller orchestra was broken up in the fall of 1942, Gray briefly joined Andre Kostelanetz, and then went into the service himself, joining Miller's service band for the duration of the war. He was with Miller the night before Miller's disappearance, and played a big part in keeping the Miller service band going until the war's end. For these efforts he was awarded a Bronze Star. His own career as a bandleader was not launched early enough to cash in on the peak years

of the band business, which deteriorated steadily in the postwar years. Nonetheless he did enjoy a few years of success with a band styled in the Miller tradition and his activities on commercial radio reduced the necessity of consistent travelling. During the late fifties he gave up his large orchestra to concentrate on arranging in the Hollywood area, with occasional returns to bandleading with a small group. In the late sixties he reorganized a band for an engagement at the Fairmont Hotel in Dallas, and there found a permanent home. He was still playing there when he died of a heart attack in August 1976.

HAL GRAYSON

Started First Band   1932
Where   West Coast
Sidemen With Band Included   Information on personnel limited. At one time Stan Kenton worked with the band
Vocalists With Band Included   Betty Grable, Martha Tilton, Shirley Ross

Grayson's band played sweet music, and was often described as a "society band." However, he did play the ballroom circuits as well, including such spots as Jantzen Beach in Portland and the Avalon in Catalina. He also played such hotels as the St. Francis and Ambassador, and toured coast-to-coast

The Hal Grayson Orchestra.

to play the Waldorf-Astoria. Appearances in one or more Warners Brothers pictures were made with the band. Grayson's bandleading career extended from 1932 to 1944, when he gave it up. During the next several years he remained active in other phases of the music business. In the early 1950s a nervous breakdown hospitalized him at the Camarillo State Hospital, where he remained until late 1958. In the fall of 1959 he was found dead in his room in a Hollywood hotel, with death attributed to natural causes. He was fifty-one years of age.

JOHNNY GREEN

Started First Band 1933
Where New York City
Previous Band Affiliations Pianist in Buddy Rogers' orchestra, arranger for Guy Lombardo, Paul Whiteman, Victor Young, and Buddy Rogers
Sidemen With Band Included Dave Terry, Perry Botkin, Jimmy Lytell, Pee Wee Irwin, Angie Ratiner, Phil Jiardina, Charles Dale, Murray Cohan, Ernest White, Leo Krucezck, Lou Kosloff, Joe Baum, Kaspar Markowitz, Al Lapin, and others. Also working with Green on recordings were Mannie Klein, Benny Goodman, and Artie Shaw
Vocalists With Band Included Jimmy Farrell, Marjorie Logan
Sponsored Radio Shows The "Ruth Etting Show" for Oldsmobile, the "Socony Sketch Book," the "Packard Hour" with Fred Astaire, the Jello program with Jack Benny, the "Phillip Morris" program
Longest Engagement Hotel St. Regis Roof, New York City, one-and-one-half years
Theme Song "Body And Soul"
Songs Written "Coquette," "I'm Yours," "Out Of Nowhere," "I Wanna Be Loved," "I Cover The Waterfront," "The Song Of Raintree County," "Body And Soul," "Easy Come, Easy Go," "You're Mine, You," "The Same Time, The Same Place," "Tomorrow Night," "Hello My Lover Goodbye"
Recording Affiliations Columbia, Royale, Brunswick, Decca

Green was born in New York City and attended Harvard. His composing and arranging began while he was in college. Immediately after leaving college he worked for awhile in a Wall Street brokerage firm, but gave it up in the late twenties to concentrate on his music. One of the first of his songs was "Coquette," which was made a hit by Guy Lombardo, for whom Green was doing arranging at that time. He was given further stature as a composer when his "Body And Soul" was featured by Libby Holman in the Broadway show *Three's A Crowd*. After working with Buddy Rogers as pianist and arranger for awhile, he started his own band in 1933, with personal appearances concentrated primarily in the New York area. He quickly made a place for himself in radio, becoming the featured bandleader on the "Ruth Etting Show" in 1934, the "Jack Benny Show" in 1935, and the "Fred Astaire Show" in1936. In the late thirties and early forties he was on the "Phillip Morris Show," and then moved west to concentrate his activities in the motion picture studios about 1942. For all practical purposes he gave up his activities with the dance band in 1941. In the late forties he became musical director of MGM, a position which he held into the mid-sixties. During those years he wrote for a long string of important motion pictures and conducted the music for several of them. In addition he was busy in television and was chosen to conduct the orchestra for several Academy Award telecasts. He also made appearances as guest conductor of various symphony orchestras. He passed away in 1989 at age 80 after a lingering illness.

JIMMIE GRIER

Started First band 1932
Where Los Angeles, first engagement at Cocoanut Grove
Previous Band Affiliations Abe Lyman, Georgie Stoll, Gus Arnheim
Sidemen With Band Included Stanley Green, Cliff Barber, Jimmy Briggs, Art Grier, Gordon Green, Dick Webster, Henry Jaworski, Frank Schumacher, Eddy Campbell, Hal Chanslor, Paul King, Jack Ordean, Everet McLaughlin, Jack Mootz, Clyde Ridge, Bill Hamilton, Vince Dibari, Wally Roth
Vocalists With Band Included Donald Novis, Ray Hendrix, Joy Hodges, Pinky Tomlin, Red Harper, Trudy Wood, Julie Gibson, Ed Morley, Armide Whipple, Jean Taylor.
Sponsored Radio Shows The "Joe Penner Show," the "Jack Benny Show"
Longest Engagement Biltmore Bowl (five years)
Theme Song "Music In The Moonlight" and "Bon Voyage, Ship Of Dreams"
Songs Written "Music In The Moonlight" "Bon Voyage, Ship of Dreams," "It's Somebody's Birthday"
Recording Affiliations Brunswick, Columbia, Decca

Grier's tag line identified him as "The Musical Host of the Coast," but though he did maintain his headquarters on the West Coast he was nationally known because of his periodic tours through the Middle West and South to play leading hotels and ballrooms. During the mid-thirties he was the busiest bandleader in the Los Angeles area, playing nightly at the Biltmore Bowl, writing and arranging for motion pictures, recording not only with his own band but as background music for Bing Crosby, Russ Colombo, and the Boswell Sisters, and at one time was working on two radio shows. On a midwestern tour, he discovered Pinky Tomlin, at that time a college student in Norman, Oklahoma, and invited him to come to the

The Musical Host of the Coast, Jimmie Grier.

Ed Morley.

162

West Coast when he was out of school. When Tomlin arrived, he brought with him some original compositions, including "The Object Of My Affections," which Grier recorded with the Tomlin vocal and made it into one of the biggest hits of 1934. Other Tomlin hits recorded with Grier's band were "Don't Be Afraid To Tell Your Mother" and "What's The Reason I'm Not Pleasin' You?" Altogether they gave Tomlin enough impetus to launch his own band. After nearly five years in the Biltmore, Grier's became more of a touring band, with periodic Biltmore engagements of shorter duration. Late in 1942 he volunteered for military service, entering the Coast Guard, where he became Rudy Vallee's assistant bandleader with the Coast Guard Band. When Vallee left the service, Lieutenant Junior Grade Grier took over, carrying on as leader until the war ended. He then attempted to resume his bandleading career, once more going into the Biltmore for a stay of nearly a year. With the overall band business declining his postwar efforts were only moderately successful. In the late forties he gave up attempting to maintain a large band to remain in the Hollywood area working with a small combo, doing arranging and trying his hand briefly

Armide Whipple.

at being a disc jockey. Eventually he gave up the music business entirely to enter real estate. He was still engaged in the real estate business when he was stricken with a serious illness, which caused his death in June 1959 at age fifty-seven.

At the Biltmore Bowl, 1932. The vocalists are Larry Cotton and Joy Hodges.

GEORGE HALL

Started First Band Early twenties
Where New York City
Sidemen With Band Included George Knapp, Frank Comisky, Mike Martini, Sam Horowitz, Ben Rapfogel, Charles Ruoff, Moe Spivak, Rudy Reinhart, Jack Linton, Sam Rore, Phil Silverman, Howard Carlson, John Sterling, Abe Markowitz, William Sorrentino, Charles Romano, Frank Klinger, Fred Duro, Bernie Miller, Johnny Doyle, Jack Shilkret, George Paxton, Michael Bruce, Johnny Guarnieri, Doc Goldberg, Joe Ferrante, Charles Zimmerman, Bud Lacombe, Carmen Mastren
Vocalists With Band Included Scrappy Lambert, Irving Kaufman, Loretta Lee, Barry Wells, Allen Church, Johnny McKeever, Dolly Dawn
Theme Song "Love Letters In The Sand"
Recording Affiliations Pathe, Banner, Cameo, Bluebird, Variety, Vocalion, Okeh

Hall's, whose tag line was "Dance With Romance," was primarily a New York band. He played eight consecutive seasons at the Hotel Taft, and repeat performances at the Paramount and Loew's State theaters in New York. Tours were primarily concentrated in the Middle West and South, where he played amusement parks and such popular hotels as the Claridge in Memphis, the Baker in Dallas, and the Roosevelt in New Orleans. He was one of the first travelling bands to play Elitch's Gardens in Denver, brought there by MCA, who booked him throughout his bandleading career. When Dolly Dawn joined the band as featured vocalist in the mid-thirties, Hall began to promote her, and occasionally recorded the band under the name of "Dolly Dawn and Her Dawn Patrol." Eventually Hall believed the band under her leadership had more potential than under his. In a well-publicized ceremony at New York's Roseland Ballroom, on July 4, 1941, he turned the band over to her, staying on as its manager. This arrangement lasted slightly less than a year, when Dolly gave up fronting the band to become a single attraction. Hall never resumed with the band himself.

MAL HALLETT

Started Band   Early twenties
Where   Boston
Sidemen With Band Included   Toots Mondello, Andy Russo, Carl Swearingen, Bill Carlin, Nelson Arguesso, Sam Sherman, Ollie Ahearn, Frank Guilfoyle, Larry de Laurence, Frank Friselle, Brad Gowans, Chet Gonier, Joe Holmes, Joe Carbonaro, Frank Ryerson, Clark Yocum, Jim Johnson, Turk Murphy, Stewart Anderson, Frankie Carle, Gene Krupa, Jack Jenney, Jack Teagarden, and others
Vocalists With Band Included   Buddy Welcome, Jerry Perkins, Teddy Grace, Charlie Blake, Clark Yocum
Theme Song   "The Boston Tea Party"
Recording Affiliations   Okeh, Harmony, Paramount, Perfect, Columbia, Vocalion, Decca

Mal Hallett.

Hallett's was basically a New England band working from a base in Boston. During

The Mal Hallett Orchestra, in the mid 1920s.

World War I he played in a band entertaining U.S. troops in France. After the war he worked as a violinist in theaters and hotels in the Boston area until he started his own band. His first band engagement was at the American House in Boston. The Hallett band became one of the most popular on the East Coast, playing New York hotels and the Arcadia and Roseland Ballrooms. He was also a regular at Atlantic City and toured the whole Eastern Seaboard, with occasional ventures into the Middle West. The peak of his popularity was reached in the thirties and forties but he continued to be active as a bandleader until the early fifties. He died in Boston in December 1952.

HENRY HALSTEAD

Started First Band   Early twenties
Where   San Francisco
Sidemen With Band Included   Ted Schilling, Glen Hopkins, Ross Dugat, Ernie Reed, Chuck Moll, Abe Maule, Hal Chanslor, Zebe Mann, Craig Leach, Phil Harris, Red Nichols, Dick Hart, Don Hopkins, Harold Peppie
Recording Affiliations   Victor

The first Halstead band spent three years at the St. Francis Hotel in San Francisco, but most of the personnel listed above were not with it. Nightly hour-long broadcasts over station KGO in San Francisco made Halstead's name well known both up and down the West Coast and in Hawaii. When he left the St. Francis in 1925 he reorganized, bringing into his own group the major portion of a Los Angeles band which had lost its leader. This reorganized band included the sidemen listed above. Halstead had this new group meet him in Seattle, where he had leased a ballroom, intending to become an entrepreneur himself. Because he was well known in the Pacific Northwest, he did a good business in the new location, until trouble developed with the Seattle union because the union president's daughter was interested

Plantation Ballroom, Los Angeles, in the late 1920s.

in one of the band members. They left Seattle, played briefly in Tacoma and Spokane; then one-nighted their way back to San Francisco to play at Tait's Pompeiian Room. In the spring of 1926 Halstead moved to Los Angeles to play the Lafayette Hotel. It was during this time that Red Nichols was featured in the band. The band's next location was at the Edgewater Beach Club in Santa Monica, followed by a booking into the Plantation Ballroom for a lengthy stay. About that time talking pictures were developing and Halstead's is credited by many as having been the first dance band to make a movie short. Eventually Halstead gave up the band to enter the real estate business in Phoenix.

LIONEL HAMPTON

Started First Band 1940 (Had previously put together his own band for a brief West Coast tour in 1935)
Where West Coast
Previous Band Affiliations Paul Howard, Les Hite, Benny Goodman
Sidemen With Band Included Personnel fairly transient—included Jack McVea, Arnett Cobb, Illinois Jacquet, Dexter Gordon, Marshall Royal, Earl Bostic, Milt Buckner, Al Grey, Benny Bailey, Jimmy Nottingham, Leo Sheppard
Theme Song "Flying Home"
Songs Written "Hamp's Boggie," "Central Avenue Breakdown," "Flying Home," "Midnight Sun"
Recording Affiliations Victor, Columbia, Decca, Verve

Hampton's big break undoubtedly occurred the night that Benny Goodman, then working at the Palomar, went to a small local club, the Paradise Inn, to hear Hampton, who was appearing there with his own small combo. Goodman liked what he heard so much that he persuaded Hampton to record with his band, and then go on the road with them as part of the Benny Goodman Sextet. That was in 1936. Later, in 1940, it was the temporary disbanding of the Goodman orchestra that prompted Hampton to launch his own big band. The 1940 venture was not Hampton's first attempt. In the late summer of 1935 in an Oregon resort town, I danced to a Lionel Hampton orchestra which was billed as "Lionel Hampton, The World's Fastest Drummer, And His Orchestra." The

Lionel Hampton.

band was musically professional, and at the end of the evening's dancing program, Hampton brought his drums down on the floor and presented an exhibition which had the audience dazzled. But that band's activities were limited to the one West Coast tour.

Soon after launching his 1940 band, Hampton signed a contract with Victor to turn out a series of records which sold with mod-

The Hampton orchestra on the stand in New York in the late 1940s.

At its peak the Hampton band was a big, brassy powerhouse organization.

erate success. He did very well in the wave of band prosperity which existed from early 1942 through 1946. His style could probably best be described as "powerhouse big band jazz." He did some compromising with style in the immediate postwar years, when the public was indicating it wanted something more danceable. For a time he featured a glee club, doing numbers which some reviewers described as almost "saccharine," but that period was of short duration.

In the decline of the fifties he fared much better than most of his fellow bandleaders. Hampton was one of the few able to stay on the road with a large organization, through the fifties and into the early sixties. By this time a great deal of his time was being spent overseas with several European tours and, in 1963, a tour of Japan and other countries in the Orient. By the mid-sixties the market for big bands was at such a low ebb that he gave up to organize a sextet, with which he worked for the next several years. In addition, Hampton intermittently put together tours with a full-sized unit, which included appearances at Disneyland on its itinerary. He is still semiactive in the music business.

PHIL HARRIS

Started First Band 1932 (Had previously been co-leader of the Lofner-Harris Orchestra)
Where Los Angeles—first engagement at Cocoanut Grove
Previous Band Affiliations Walter Krausgrill's Strand Theater Orchestra, Glen Oswald, Henry Halstead, Herb Wiedoft
Sidemen With Band Included Irving Verret, Floyd O'Brien, Jack Holmes, Bill Fletcher, Joe Huffman, Skippy Anderson, Frank Remley, Sid Jacobs, Nappy Lamare, Nick Fatool, Joe Huffman
Vocalists With Band Included Leah Ray, Judy Janis, Ruth Robin
Sponsored Radio Shows "The Jack Benny Show," the "Rexall Drug Show," "Fitch Bandwagon," and repeat appearances on "Coca Cola Spotlight Bands"
Theme Song Opened with "That's What I Like About The South," closed with "Rose Room"
Recording Affiliations Columbia, Vocalion, Decca, Victor, ARA

Phil Harris.

Harris will probably be best remembered as a radio-TV-nightclub personality; but his heart was always in the music business and for some fifteen years he was a very successful bandleader. Without doubt he was one of the strongest personalities to ever front a dance band, coming on stronger than the Indians attacking Custer at the Little Big Horn. Because of his reputation as a wisecracking front man it might well have been forgotten that he was an accomplished drummer, although his secret ambition was to play trombone.

Judy Janis, vocalist with the Harris band in the mid
1930s.

Ruth Robin.

The Harris Orchestra at the Wilshire Bowl, 1936.

In 1928 he teamed up with Carol Lofner to form an orchestra. Under their co-leadership it became famous, with a three-year run at the St. Francis Hotel in San Francisco. At the end of this engagement Lofner and Harris went their separate ways, with Phil forming a band of his own in Los Angeles to go into the Cocoanut Grove. By the time he left there he was firmly established as a top name and went on an extended tour of the East Coast, returning in 1936 for repeated engagements at the Los Angeles Palomar Ballroom. He soon became one of the Palomar's most popular attractions.

It was during a Palomar appearance that he was chosen by Jack Benny to be the bandleader on the Jello radio show. The degree to which Benny made him an important part of the show did much to establish Harris as a comedian in his own right. Meanwhile, during the summer months, Harris made annual tours with the band, with his prominence on the Benny show contributing to his drawing power. During the early forties he was rated by Music Corporation of America as one of the most consistent and strongest box office attractions in the band business. During the winter season when the radio show tied him to the Los Angeles area, he usually worked at the Wilshire Bowl, a spot which benefited strongly from his and Benny's constant reference to it on the radio show.

When he married Alice Faye in 1941 he gave up travelling with the band. His association with Benny continued on for several years. In 1946 he and Alice teamed up for a popular radio show of their own, which ran on NBC until 1955. As his activities with the radio show began to take more and more of his time, he finally dropped the band entirely. In the mid-fifties he moved to Palm Springs, where he could be found almost daily playing golf at the Thunderbird Country Club. Since that time he has kept busy with guest appearances on many TV shows as a comedian and singer, and even with some meaty dramatic parts. Las Vegas clubs regularly invited him there to be a headliner. Well into the seventies he was still busy with an average of three annual appearances at the Desert Inn, and more recently moving to the Frontier, for repeat appearances as a headliner on a show which usually co-billed Harry James and his Orchestra.

COLEMAN HAWKINS

Started First Band Late thirties
Where New York City
Previous Band Affiliations The Jazz Hounds, Fletcher Henderson
Theme Song "Body and Soul," "Honeysuckle Rose"
Recording Affiliations Bluebird, Apollo, Decca, Savoy

Although he was a giant on his instrument, the tenor sax, and enjoyed a long career as a jazz man, his career as the leader of a big band was short. Starting in late 1939, he toured with a sixteen-piece band throughout 1940 and part of 1941. During that time the band also recorded. But he abandoned the big band effort to work with smaller combos, where his incomparable tenor sax work was better showcased. Hawkins made many all-star recordings, some under his own name, and some with other groups. During the sixties and early seventies he and his saxophone were featured on many television programs. Hawkins was actively engaged in music until shortly before his death in May, 1969 at the age of sixty-four.

Coleman Hawkins and his orchestra.

ERSKINE HAWKINS

Started First Band Mid-thirties
Where Alabama
Tag Line "The Twentieth-Century Gabriel"
Theme Song "Swing Out," "Tuxedo Junction"
Songs Written "Swing Out," "Raid The Joint," "Tuxedo Junction," "Gabriel Meets The Duke," "Hot Platter," "Weddin' Blues," "Strictly Swing," "You Can't Escape From Me," "Gin Mill Special"
Recording Affiliations Vocalion, Bluebird, Victor

As Hawkins's tag line would indicate, he was a trumpet player and one noted for hitting all the high notes. His bandleading career began in college with a group called the 'Bama State Collegians. Once out of school, he took the band into New York in mid-1936 to record and to play such important spots as the Harlem Opera House and the Savoy Ballroom. In 1939 the band's hit, "Tuxedo Junction," made them a top attraction. The fact that the song was also recorded quite successfully by other bandleaders added to Hawkins' personal status. He was a prolific composer and wrote a great deal of the material the band recorded. The band's chief arrangers were Avery Parrish, Sammy Lowe, and William Johnson. Throughout its existence, this band had a number of good instrumental soloists, such as Wilbur Bascomb. Bascomb did the trumpet work on "Tuxedo Junction," although most people who purchased the record thought it was Hawkins. The band worked steadily all through the forties and into the fifties, with their time fairly evenly divided between Harlem clubs, theaters, and one-nighter tours. In the mid-forties the band was given a new boost by its hit record, "Tippin' In." In the late fifties Hawkins gave up the big band to front smaller combos, remaining active in the music world into the early seventies.

Erskine Hawkins and his orchestra.

JOE HAYMES

Started First Band   Early thirties
Where   Midwest
Previous Band Affiliations   Arranger with the Ted Weems orchestra
Sidemen With Band Included   Ward Silloway, Pee Wee Erwin, Roy Wager, Dan D'Andrea, Toots Mondello, Mike Doty, Paul Ricci, Chris Fletcher, Larry Murphy, Jimmy Underwood, Charlie Bush, John Scott, Paul Mitchell, Gene Traxler, Mac Cheikes, Dave Jacobs, Cliff Weston, Andy Ferretti, Bud Freeman, Sterling Bose, Joe Ortolano, Sid Stoneburn, Noni Bernardi, Clyde Rounds, John Van Eps, Gordon Griffin, Zeke Zarchy, Mike Michaels, Freddie Fellensby, Bill Miller, Brick Fleagle, Charlie Zimmerman, Dave Frankel, Hank Haupt, John Langford, Clyde Rogers, Hawk Kogan, Max Goodman
Vocalists With Band Included   Phil Dooley, Skeeter Palmer, Rose Blane, Jane Dover, The Headliners
Theme Song   "Midnight"
Recording Affiliations   Victor, Banner, Columbia, Bluebird, The American Recording Company

The style of the Haymes orchestra was built around both the sax section and some fine arranging. Although it did not become as well known as some of the others, it was one of the early swing bands. As indicated above in the list of sidemen, it had a lot of talent which had either already appeared in top bands or was destined to later. Haymes's own instruments were the clarinet and alto sax, and he also did some of the vocals. The band's usual base of operations was Oklahoma. Haymes was very busy in the recording studios. Some of his records became collector's items. In addition to recording as the Joe Haymes Orchestra, he recorded under a variety of other names including the Radio Rascals, Karl Snyder and his Orchestra, Roy Wager and his Orchestra, Jimmy Underwood and his Orchestra, Mike Doty and his Orchestra, Dick Clark and his Orchestra, the Williams Cotton Club Orchestra, Elliot Everett and his Orchestra, and the Mad Hatters.

When the Dorsey Brothers broke up in 1935, Tommy worked out a deal with Haymes to take over his band practically intact, and Haymes then dropped out of the business.

LENNIE HAYTON

Started First Band About 1937 (Had previously led bands on the "Bing Crosby" and "Burns and Allen" radio shows)
Previous Band Affiliations Frankie Trumbauer, Red Nichols, Joe Venuti, Paul Whiteman
Sidemen With Band Included Bill Graham, Walter Mercurio, Wendell De Lory, George Jaffe, John Dillard, John Saola, Willard Brady, Slats Long, Mike Doty, Dave Barbour, Bernie Friedland, Bunny Shawker, and others
Vocalists With Band Included Paul Barry, Linda Keene
Theme Song "Times Square Scuttle"
Recording Affiliations Decca, Vocalion

Hayton was widely known as a jazz pianist, and his venture as a leader of a big band represented only a small percentage of his career. It began in 1937 and ended in 1940. During that time, booked by Mills Artists Incorporated, New York City, he toured coast-to-coast, playing one-nighters and locations with a band ranging from twelve to as many as twenty musicians. He gave up the band in the early forties to become musical director at MGM Studios in California, remaining there until about 1953. In 1949 his scoring of *On The Town* won an Oscar. He picked up another in 1970 for scoring *Hello Dolly*. In the late forties he married singer Lena Horne and eventually gave up his position at MGM to travel with her as musical director. He died of a heart attack in Palm Springs in April 1971.

TED HEATH

Started First Band About 1944
Where London, England
Previous Band Affiliations Bert Firman, Jack Hylton, Ambrose, Sid Lipton
Vocalists With Band Included Dickie Valentine, Lita Roza
Theme Song "Listen To My Music"
Recording Affiliations London

The Ted Heath band was originally put together in a BBC studio for a series of radio broadcasts. They began playing concerts at the London Palladium, eventually on a weekly basis. These concerts, combined with the radio broadcasts and hit records, made Heath's one of the biggest band attractions in both England and the European

The Joe Haymes Orchestra at the Steel Pier, Atlantic City, 1934.

Lennie Hayton and his orchestra.

continent. In the mid-sixties Heath brought his band to the United States for a tour of both concert and dance dates. It was very successful, and was followed by several similar tours. With the help of some fine arrangements, Heath always produced a very solid big band sound. Instrumentally his band usually consisted of four trumpets, four trombones, five saxophones, two pianos, string bass, and drums. His recordings always found a ready market with American big band fans. One of his last recording engagements was a series on which he recreated, note for note, the sounds of other famous bands. He died in November 1969 at the age of 67.

Ted Heath and his orchestra.

ERNIE HECKSHER

Started First Band Late thirties
Where San Francisco
Previous Band Affiliations College bands
Recording Affiliations MGV

Hecksher was born in England, but raised in San Francisco, and attended Stanford University. He took up the banjo at a very early age, and by the time he was fifteen was a professional on the RKO circuit. Later he switched to piano. He started his band while he was a student at Stanford University, and it became quite popular playing campus events. Once out of school he took the band into the Palace Hotel, which until then had been reserved for name bands, and surprised the management by doing a capacity business. During the early forties he toured the Midwest and South, with the band playing hotels in St. Louis, Memphis, and San Antonio. He was drafted into the army in 1943. When he got his service discharge in 1945, he once again put together a band. It was booked into the Blackstone Hotel in Chicago for an engagement which lasted a year. He then returned to the San Francisco area to make his base and play the Mark Hopkins Hotel. He went into the Fairmount in 1948, to settle down there for a long run which is still going on, except for occasional brief interruptions.

NEAL HEFTI

Neal Hefti.

Started First Band   1951
Previous Band Affiliations   Bobby Byrne, Charlie Barnet, Charlie Spivak, Woody Herman, Charlie Ventura; also arranged for Buddy Rich, Georgie Auld, Harry James, Art Mooney, Count Basie
Theme Song   "Coral Reef"
Songs Written   "Coral Reef," "Plymouth Rock," "Two For The Blues," "Oh What A Night For Love," "The Kid From Red Bank," "Sunday Morning," "Wildroot," "Girl Talk," "Fawncy Meeting You," "Falling In Love All Over Again," "Softly With Feeling," "Time For The Blues," "Cute," "Countdown," and many others
Recording Affiliations   Coral

Hefti made his mark in the music world both as a trumpet player and as a composer-arranger. He spent a great deal more time as a sideman and arranger with other name bands than he did as a bandleader. The band which he put together in 1951 featured his wife, Frances Wayne, on vocals. She too had prior experience with name bands, having been with the Woody Herman band when Neal was working with it in the mid-forties. The band played location dates and toured intermittently for a couple of years during the early fifties and was then broken up. Hefti then concentrated on scoring and conducting record sessions and television shows for such people as Kate Smith, Arthur Godfrey, and others. He wrote the background music for several movies and several of his many compositions were written especially for the Count Basie band.

The Ernie Hecksher Orchestra plays to a capacity San Francisco audience.

177

HORACE HEIDT

Started First Band   1923
Where   Oakland, California—his first engagement at the nearby Claremont Hotel
Previous Band Affiliations   None
Sidemen With Band Included   Jerry Bowne, Warren Lewis, Art Thorsen, Harold Plummer, Paul Know, Dave Phennig, Clarence Moore, Harold Moore, Lee Lykins, Charles Midgley, Charles Bradshaw, Lee Fleming, Norman Kingsley, Wayne Webb, Bob Riedel, Frankie Carle, Alvino Rey, Warren Covington, "Shorty" Sherock, Joe Rushton, Bobby Hackett, Ronnie Kemper
Vocalists With Band Included   The King Sisters, Larry Cotton, Charles Goodwin, Red Farrington, Frank De Vol, the Heidt-Lights, Art Carney, the Le Ahn Sisters, Ruth Davis, Ollie O'Toole, Donna and her Don Juans, Ronnie Kemper, Gordon MacRae
Tag Line   "Horace Heidt and his Musical Knights"
Sponsored Radio Shows   "Horace Heidt For Alemite," The "Pot Of Gold," "Stop Me If You've Heard This One," "The Phillip Morris Youth Opportunity Show"
Television With Band   The "Youth Opportunity Program"
Theme Song   "I'll Love You In My Dreams"
Recording Affiliations   Victor, Brunswick, Columbia

Horace Heidt.

Had it not been for a serious back injury sustained in a football game, Heidt might have been a career athlete instead of a bandleader. This injury occurred while he was a member of the University of California football team in the early twenties (he graduated in the class of 1924). His mother had forced him to study piano, at which he developed a degree of proficiency, although he seldom displayed it in later years. His first bandleading job at the Claremont was with a small band which, in addition to its musical ability, featured the antics of the band's mascot, a trained German shepherd dog named Lobo. Perhaps that was a forecast of

the course Heidt would pursue, for throughout his career as a bandleader he often featured something which was a little offbeat. Some of his ideas may have been considered corny by his contemporaries, but most of them were extremely successful.

From the Claremont he moved into the Athens Athletic Club, to play for dancing and participate in a local radio program. Next he went into the Grand Lake Theater, where Fanchon and Marco picked the band to be one of their travelling show units. With them he made it into New York in the early thirties. At the Palace Theater in New York, his orchestra was such a sensation that they were kept on for sixteen consecutive weeks. This earned him a three-month engagement in Monte Carlo, after which they came back to the Palace for a return engagement. Because this was not too successful, Heidt packed up the band and returned to the West Coast.

The band and artists who did the Alemite Show, 1936. Featured were Alvino Rey and the King Sisters.

With a newly organized band he got a job at the Golden Gate Theater in San Francisco, backing the vaudeville acts from the pit and later moving the band on to the stage. During that engagement the Fred Waring orchestra came in for a booking, with Heidt opening the show from the pit. He incurred Waring's lasting wrath by quickly duplicating some of the Waring numbers and presenting them from the pit before Waring could play them from the stage.

His next major assignment was at the Drake Hotel in Chicago, for a two-week engagement which stretched into six years. In 1936 he got the first of his sponsored radio shows and was well on his way to becoming one of the biggest names in the music business. This was the Alemite Show and on it Heidt's band included fourteen musicians and a glee club, and featured the singing guitar of Alvino Rey and the vocals of the King Sisters. From the Drake he went to the Biltmore in New York for another six-year run, during which time he developed his second popular radio show, "Pot Of Gold," one of the first radio giveaway shows. It

became so popular that it inspired a motion picture, which also featured the band and all of its stars. The program used a spinning dial, a telephone directory, and the phone call to the number selected by the dial. The person who answered the phone received a prize of $1,000, which was a lot of money in 1939.

With his popularity unabated during the forties, Heidt followed the trend towards swing, hiring some of the best musicians available, including members of the Glenn Miller band when Miller went into the service in late 1942. When the draft began to thin out his ranks and limit the number of available replacements, Heidt, never orthodox in his methods, kept an ad running in *Billboard* magazine offering top pay to any qualified musician who was free to join his unit.

Like Benny Goodman, he became unhappy with the handling of his affairs by Music Corporation of America and engaged in a long-drawn-out battle to have his contract voided. When this was not successful he retired in late 1943, and for the next few years

Ronnie Kemper, Donna (of the Don Juans), Ollie O'Toole, and Horace Heidt on stage in the early 1940s.

his only contact with the music business was through his operation of the Trianon Ballroom in South Gate, California. He also kept busy looking after his other holdings, which included a hotel in Palm Springs and a successful restaurant in Santa Monica.

In the fall of 1946 he put together what he called "The Youth Opportunity Show," breaking it in with a week's engagement at a theater in Fresno, California. It was during that first engagement that he picked up Dick Contino, who became a featured star of the show and famous later in his own right. Heidt quickly demonstrated that his Midas touch was still working, for the show became very popular. It toured the nation, playing to packed houses wherever it went, and utilized amateur talent in a manner which made Major Bowes look like a small town promoter. Although there were skeptics who thought the applause meter by which the winners were selected might be subject to the whims of its master, a number

of people did make their entrée into show business through this show. The winners quickly became members of satellite units, also booked by Heidt. When television replaced live radio programming, Heidt made an unsuccessful attempt to convert this show to the new medium, but gave it up after a couple of seasons, retiring from the music business with his own private pot of gold. He built himself a deluxe condominium unit in the Van Nuys area of the San Fernando Valley, and soon had his units rented to other members of the world of show business. Although throughout most of his career his band continued to play dance engagements, Heidt's organization from the start could better be described as a show unit than as a dance orchestra. He himself was more of a front man than a musician. But he did consistently lead a band of qualified musicians, with occasional periods when the band was outstanding. He died on December 1, 1986, at the age of 85.

The Heidt organization in the NBC Studios for their weekly Hires Root Beer Show, 1943.

South Gate, California, 1944: on the stand at the Trianon Ballroom, owned at the time by Heidt himself.

FLETCHER HENDERSON

Started First Band About 1923
Where New York City
Previous Band Affiliations None, had toured with Ethel Waters show
Sidemen With Band Included Consistently an all-star cast—along with his brother Horace Henderson, such names as Louis Armstrong, Rex Stewart, Bobby Stark, Tommy Ladnier, Red Allen, Roy Eldridge, Joe Thomas, Emmett Berry, Jimmy Harrison, Charlie Green, Don Redman, Benny Carter, Coleman Hawkins, Buster Bailey, Kaiser Marshall, J. C. Higginbotham, Benny Morton, Edgar Sampson, Dickie Wells, Claude Jones, Russell Procope, Ben Webster, Chu Berry, Clarence Holiday, John Kirby, Walter Johnson, Sid Catlett, Israel Crosby
Theme Song "Christopher Columbus"
Recording Affiliations Columbia, Vocalion. Some of Henderson's material was also released on Victor, Riverside, and Decca

Henderson, through his musical style, his compositions and his arrangements, may well have been the greatest single influence in creating what is described as the "Big Band Era." That style, developed by Henderson during the twenties, became the framework for "swing," made popular by Benny Goodman in the mid-thirties, and adopted to one degree or another by almost every successful bandleader of the thirties and forties. But little of that success was shared by Henderson himself. From the time he organized his first orchestra in 1923 until he disbanded his last one in the early fifties, he never enjoyed, except intermittently, success commensurate either with his own musicianship and that of his orchestra or the lasting impact which he left on American popular music.

Frank Driggs, formerly a producer for Columbia Records, accurately describes Henderson's life as "a study in frustration." The great compositions which he wrote and recorded during the twenties enjoyed only mediocre sales at that time. The same tunes with the same arrangements were recorded by Goodman a few years later and became big hits. Perhaps during the twenties Henderson's was an idea whose time had not yet arrived. The orchestra which he organized under his own name in 1923 first played at the Club Alabam. The next year it was booked into the Roseland Ballroom. Here they remained for five years, during which time Henderson introduced and featured such future greats as Louis Armstrong, Coleman Hawkins, Rex Stewart, Buster Bailey, Don Redman, Jimmy Harrison, John Kirby, Joe Smith, Benny Carter, Benny Moten, and others. Not only was the Henderson band of that period the showcase for every important black musician of the time, but it was also the envy of every white musician in New York. Why then, did lasting success elude him?

Probably jazz critic John Hammond, who knew Henderson well, sums it up most accurately. He describes Henderson as a poor businessman who should have placed himself under capable management, but never did; and who was so easygoing that the band was virtually without discipline. Hammond's comments came from personal experience. During a brief fling as a downtown New York theatre operator in the early thirties, he booked the Henderson band for a week's engagement, but found less than half the members on hand ready for the opening show. He had a similar experience later as the producer of a Fletcher Henderson recording session. The last musician arrived over two hours after the three-hour session was scheduled to begin.

Henderson was born in Georgia in December 1898, and arrived in New York in 1920. He had been studying music since the age of seven, and although he came to New York to earn a master's degree in chemistry at Columbia University, he ended up in music instead. He spent some time as a commercial song demonstrator for a music publish-

The Fletcher Henderson Orchestra in Atlantic City in the early 1930s.

Another Atlantic City photo.

ing firm, and then made a theatre tour with Ethel Waters: he was director of the band. That tour lasted six months and gave quite a boost to Henderson's reputation. Back in New York, he recorded steadily with his newly formed band, which included Coleman Hawkins and the young Don Redman. It was

these recordings which led to an audition for the Club Alabam job, which began in mid-1923. It ended a year later when the whole band walked out over the manager's insistence that Coleman Hawkins be fired.

They were not long in moving into the Roseland Ballroom and it was there that

Henderson hit his stride. Soon a job in his band was the objective for every black musician on the way up. Louis Armstrong signed on in late 1924, to become the band's most featured soloist. He remained for a year, leaving in late 1925. By that time the Henderson orchestra, with its great arrangements and all-star roster, was jamming the Roseland with happy dancers and was the talk of New York. In addition to their activities on the Roseland stand, they were busy with recording sessions and with occasional one-nighter tours scheduled during the summer months when they were not at Roseland. The Roseland engagement ended in late 1929 and now, the best years of Henderson's career were behind him.

Perhaps the turning point for Henderson came in 1928, when he was involved in a very serious automobile accident. From that time on Lady Luck seemed to elude him, and although the Henderson band continued to feature great musical talent, its fortunes rather continuously went downhill. In 1935 he gave it up to join Benny Goodman's orchestra as arranger. The Henderson influence could be clearly perceived in the Goodman style, an influence which was not restricted to the Henderson originals, such as "King Porter Stomp," which Goodman recorded. In 1936 he left Goodman and again formed an orchestra under his own name. This group was considered by some as one of the best he had ever had and, like his others, it turned out a lot of fine recordings, including a hit number, "Christopher Columbus." This band had a new crop of all-stars, but even though its musicianship was excellent it could not compete with other bands of the day and was broken up in 1939. At that time Henderson again joined the Goodman orchestra.

His next attempt at leading a band under his own name was made in 1941, and with it he again opened at the Roseland Ballroom. He was no longer able to get top musicians, so this venture was not successful and in 1945 he was once again arranging for the Goodman band. He made several later attempts to reenter the business. Most of them were with small groups, but he formed a big band in 1950. Later that year he suffered a stroke, and died in December 1952, leaving a musical legacy far greater than the acclaim it brought him while he was living.

RAY HERBECK

Started First Band   1935
Where   Los Angeles
Previous Band Affiliations   Leighton Noble
Sidemen With Band Included   George Van, George Winslow, Whitney Boyd, Benny Stabler, Bob McReynolds, Jay Stanley, James Baker, Jim Hefti, Bunny Rang, Art Skolnick, Louis Math, Tom Clark, Al Ciola, Chi Chi Crozza, Bob Hartzell, Leo Benson, and others
Vocalists With Band Included   Betty Benson, Hal Munbar, Kirby Brooks, Ray Olson, Lorraine Benson, Roy Cordell, Irene Wilson
Tag Line   "Ray Herbeck and His Music With Romance"

Ray Herbeck

Longest Engagement Edgewater Beach, Chicago; St. Francis Hotel
Theme Song "Romance"
Songs Written "Time Stood Still"
Recording Affiliations Columbia, Okeh, Vocalion, Bullet, Four Star, Alvin. Also on Langworth Transcriptions

Herbeck's was definitely a commercial band, styled for dancing. Although he organized it on the West Coast, he moved to the Chicago area in the late thirties, where he concentrated on Midwest engagements until the late forties. Those engagements included, in addition to the Edgewater Beach and St. Francis, such hotels as the New Yorker, the Schroeder, the Peabody, the Edison, the Muehlebach, the Claridge, the Lowry, the Brown Palace, and most of the best ballrooms in the nation. The band was also popular in theaters and the college prom circuit. During World War II Herbeck made over 300 USO camp show appearances, and appeared several times on the Coca Cola Company's "Spotlight Bands" radio show, picked up from service camps and defense installations. In the late forties he returned to the

Lorraine Benson.

West Coast, to play for a year at the Riverside Hotel in Reno, followed by two years at the Last Frontier in Las vegas. In the early fifties he gave up the band business to enter the real estate business, first in California and later in the Phoenix, Arizona area, where he died of cancer in 1989.

The Ray Herbeck Orchestra, 1941.

LENNY HERMAN

Started First Band Early fifties
Where New York City
Tag Line "The Mightiest Little Band in the Land"
Theme Song "No Foolin'"

For approximately fifteen years, Herman was a very popular bandleader in the New York area, playing music styled for dancing in the Hotel Astor, Edison, Roosevelt, Waldorf-Astoria, the New Yorker, the Warwick in Philadelphia, the Straymore in Atlantic City, the Cavalier in Virginia Beach, and the Baker in Dallas. Never was his band larger than ten men, and he featured himself on accordion. In the mid-sixties he moved west to concentrate his activities in the resort hotels in the Lake Tahoe-Reno area. By that time he had reduced the size of his band to five or six, to fit the available market in that area. At last report, he is still there.

Lenny Herman.

WOODY HERMAN

Started First Band 1936, took over leadership of the Isham Jones band
Where New York
Previous Band Affiliations Tom Gerun, Harry Sosnik, Gus Arnheim, Isham Jones
Sidemen With Band Included Steady Nelson, Cappy Lewis, Toby Tyler, Neal Reid, Joe Bishop, Frank Carlson, Tommy Linehan, Hy White, Walter Yoder, Saxey Mansfield, Nick Ciazza, Herb Tompkins, Ray Hofner, Deane Kincaide, Bob Price, Murray Williams, Clarence Willard, Sam Rubinowich, Mickey Folus, Billie Rogers, Bill Harris, Flip Philips, Dave Tough, Red Norvo, Stan Getz, Terry Gibbs, Milt Jackson, Al Cohn, Zoot Sims, Red Mitchell, Urbie Green, Vince Guaraldi, Bill Chase, Jake Hanna, Milt Bernhart, and a host of others
Vocalists With Band Included Sharri Kaye, Mary Ann McCall, Carol Kaye, Dillagene Plumb, Kitty Lane, Muriel Lane, Carolyn Grey, Anita O'Day, Frances Wayne. Woody usually handled male vocals himself

Sponsored Radio Shows The "Wildroot Show"
Theme Song "Blue Prelude," "Blue Flame"
Recording Affiliations Decca, Columbia, Capitol, MGM, Verve

Woody Herman was born in Milwaukee in 1913 and in 1919, at the age of six, he was reportedly tap dancing and singing in theaters and clubs in that city. That was the beginning of his show business career, which took a more definitive direction when he began to study saxophone at the age of nine. About 1930 he joined the band of Tom Gerun and left Milwaukee with them for the West Coast. When he left Gerun he played with the bands of Harry Sosnik and Gus Arnheim, then joined the great Isham Jones orchestra about 1935. In the fall of 1936, plagued by ill health, Jones decided to give up the orchestra and its last job was played in Memphis, Tennessee. Key members of that band wanted to keep it going so they put together,

The Herman sax section, 1940. *Left to right:* Mickey Folus, Bill Vitale, Herb Tompkins, Saxey Mansfield.

in New York, the Woody Herman orchestra as a cooperative unit in which they all owned stock. In that corporate structure Woody was president, Joe Bishop was first vice president, Walt Yoder was second vice president, and Neil Reid was treasurer. A special vote of thanks goes to Walt Yoder for the voluminous scrap books which he kept during that period and which were made available to me as a reference source.

The first job of any substance which the band had was at the Roseland in Brooklyn, where they had good air time over the Mutual Broadcasting System. From there they moved to the New York Roseland where, again with good air time, the band's popularity began to pick up momentum. By mid-1937, under the direction of Rockwell-O'Keefe,

bookings in the best locations were opening up to them, including a triumphant return to Herman's home town of Milwaukee, for an appearance at the Schroeder Hotel. Decca had been quick to sign them for recordings and began to turn these records out with regularity. Their best record of 1937 was "Doctor Jazz," which was also rated as one of the best records of the year. It was not until two years later, however, that they really began to click on records, when their recording of "Woodchopper's Ball," made a tremendous contribution toward boosting them into the ranks of the nation's top bands.

In the interim, what seemed to be steady progress had been interspersed with moments when the struggle appeared almost

At the Panther Room, in the Sherman Hotel, Chicago, 1940. Personnel: trumpets—Bob Price, Steady Nelson, Cappy Lewis; trombones—Toby Tyler, Neal Reid; fluegelhorn—Joe Bishop; drums—Frank Carlson; piano—Tommy Linehan; guitar—Hy White; bass—Walter Yoder; tenor saxes—Saxy Mansfield, Nick Ciazza; alto saxes—Herb Tompkins, Ray Hofner; vocals—Carl Kay; clarinet and alto sax—Woody Herman.

Trumpet section, 1940. *Left to right:* Bob Price, Steady Nelson, Cappy Lewis.

At the Hotel New Yorker, 1942, Woody displays congratulatory wires.

too big for the cooperative organization. In 1938 *Metronome's* band poll listed them as twenty-third in the sweet category, fourteenth in the swing category, and sixteenth in the best band category. A year later the same poll rated them twelfth in the sweet category, seventh in the swing category, and seventh in the best band category. Despite their high rating as a sweet as well as a swing band, they struck out at Chicago's Trianon Ballroom in 1939, where the management described them as "too loud and too fast" and gave them their notice on opening night, ignoring the fact that they had drawn a very large crowd. Late that year trade journal stories were hinting that Woody was discouraged with the band's income and was seriously considering giving up the whole idea.

Early in 1940, however, the picture began to brighten, partially from the impetus from "Woodchopper's Ball," followed by other recordings which also sold well. In April, following a February appearance in the Sherman Hotel in Chicago, they went into Frank Dailey's Meadowbrook. The May 18, 1940 issue of *Billboard* headlined "Herman, The Coming Band," followed with a story which rated him as the top contender to take over the title "King of Swing," which had previously been the sole possession of Benny Goodman. In August the band went into the Hotel New Yorker for a sixty-day stand, with the hotel publicizing it as Herman's first appearance in a hotel in the New York area. During that stand the band was selected to play the Harvest Moon Ball at Madison Square Garden, and followed

In 1943 the Herman Band had added Elizabeth Rogers to its trumpet section. The vocalist was Carolyn Grey.

the New Yorker engagement with an appearance at the Strand Theater. It was also during the New Yorker engagement that Woody introduced his new theme song, "Blue Flame," which he had written to replace the old "Blue Prelude," by Joe Bishop, which had been their theme since the band was started. The 1940 *Downbeat* poll rated the band as sixth in the sweet category and the No. 3 swing band in the nation.

As 1941 got under way it was quite apparent the Woody Herman band had arrived. They were doing heavy business wherever they appeared. In summer of that year they worked their way to the West Coast for a mid-July opening at the Hollywood Palladium, originally scheduled for six weeks.

A story in *Billboard* credits Herman with an opening night draw of 4800, second only to Glenn Miller's 5200, and his became the first band to draw a holdover at the new ballroom, which had opened the previous October. At the end of their stay, stories indicated he had broken every attendance record at the Palladium except those of Miller and Tommy Dorsey. Shortly after his Palladium engagement Herman surprised the musical world by bringing into his trumpet section Elizabeth Rogers, a sharp-looking gal who not only added to the appearance of the section but did a very good job musically.

When the war broke out it took its toll of sidemen from the Herman band just as it did from all the others. During the war years

The Herman Herd in New York City, 1952.

the band personnel changed completely and so did its musical style. The "Band That Played the Blues" gradually became submerged in something else. By the war's end the band's style had become louder, more and more dependent on a screaming brass section. Few of Herman's original members remained, Bill Harris was in on trombone, Chubby Jackson on bass, and Red Norvo was there with his vibes. That year they were No. 1 in the *Downbeat*, *Metronome*, and *Esquire* polls. In mid-1947 Woody surprised everyone by dropping the band for a brief period and becoming a disc jockey on KLAC in Hollywood. This was of short duration and he was soon back in front of the band again.

For the next several years he appeared to be vying with Stan Kenton to have the loudest, most brassy band in the business. There followed, one on the other, a series of "Herman's Herds," each style slightly differ-ent than the other. In early 1949 he switched to Capitol Records for his recordings, after many years with Decca, and some time spent on the Columbia label. For a time during the fifties he, like many other band-leaders, gave up the large band to front a small group. During the sixties, seventies, and well into the eighties he was one of the few big band leaders who remained steadily active but playing nothing but one-nighters, most of them concerts. A renewed big band interest in the late seventies made bookings easier to come by but the financial returns were not adequate to keep the I.R.S. off his back for an old tax liability. Heart failure and pneumonia took his life in Los Angeles on October 29, 1987, at age 74. Herman has to be rated as one of the big band era's musical giants and deserves a special award for durability.

ART HICKMAN

Started First Band　About 1913
Where　San Francisco
Sidemen With Band Included　Fred Coffman, Walt Rosener, Bert Ralton, Clyde Doerr, Vic King, Ben Black, Mark Mojica, Steve Douglas, Bela Spiller, Frank Ellis, Jess Fitzpatrick, Juan Ramos, Roy Fox, Forrest Ray, Ed Fitzpatrick, Dick Winfree, Earl Burtnett, Dick Noolan, Hank Miller, Lou Marcasie, Ray Hoback
Theme Song　"Rose Room"
Songs Written　"Rose Room"
Recording Affiliations　Columbia, His Majesty's Voice, Victor

Although it's a point that is certainly debatable, many music buffs credit Hickman with having assembled the first organized dance band. Prior to the formation of Hickman's band, dance engagements had been somewhat impromptu affairs, with a group of musicians whipped together to play a single engagement, usually on weekends. Hickman organized his band to entertain the San Francisco Seals baseball team at their spring training camp, and then took it into the St. Francis Hotel on a six-night-a-week basis. His initial group was a six-piece organization, which was augmented later as their popularity grew. The San Francisco World's Fair of 1915 and the influx of people it brought to San Francisco created a great demand for entertainment, which Hickman helped to provide. This exposure substantially helped to publicize his band. One of those who visited the St. Francis and heard the Hickman band was Florenz Ziegfeld, who invited them to New York in 1919, where they first played an engagement at the Biltmore Hotel Roof, followed by one at the Ziegfeld Roof. That New York stay lasted approximately six months. The following year the Hickman band was hired for the entire run of the 1920 Ziegfeld Follies and then stayed on to play the Amsterdam Theater and the Amsterdam Roof. They returned to the West Coast and the St. Francis Hotel late in 1920. In 1921 Hickman's band was chosen to open the Cocoanut Grove of the Ambassador Hotel in Los Angeles. After that engagement ended, it was followed by another at the Biltmore. Then Hickman tired of the band business and turned the orchestra over to Frank Ellis, who kept it intact until the late twenties. Hickman died in San Francisco in the mid-thirties.

Biltmore Hotel, 1924. The personnel: Jess Kirkpatrick, Juan Ramos, Roy Fox, Forrest Ray, Harlan "Red" Sparrow, Ed Fitzpatrick, Dick Winfree, Earl Burtnett, Dick Noolan, Hank Miller, Lou Marcasie, Ray Hoback.

TINY HILL

Started First Band About 1933
Where Illinois
Previous Band Affiliations College bands
Sidemen With Band Included Jack Alexander, Sterling Bose, Bob Anderson, Ralph Richards, Dick Coffeen, Russ Phillips, Bob Kramer, Nick Schreier, Bob Walters, Norman Maxwell, Pat Patterson, Lloyd McCahn, Monte Mountjoy, Rolly Carpenter, Al Larsen, Leroy Hendricks, and others
Vocalists With Band Included Allen De Witt, Al Larsen, Bob Freeman, Irwin Bendel, and Hill himself
Sponsored Radio Shows "All-Time Hit Parade" (early forties)
Theme Song "Angry"
Recording Affiliations Vocalion, Okeh, Mercury

Whether or not his music justified it, Tiny Hill could lay claim to being one of the biggest bandleaders in the business, for he

"Tiny" Hill.

The "Tiny" Hill Orchestra.

193

weighed just under 400 pounds. He started his musical career with a trio while attending Illinois State Normal College. He was a drummer and enjoyed considerable success playing local jobs with his trio. Then he put together a larger band, to play the Midwest dance circuit. Hill quickly made his band a favorite in such places as Tom Archer's string of ballrooms throughout Iowa, Nebraska, and Missouri. That popularity continued through the forties and into the early fifties, when the big band decline put many bands off the road. Hill remained a heavy Midwest favorite through the fifties and into the sixties. He died in 1972.

RICHARD HIMBER

Started First Band Early thirties
Where New York City
Previous Band Affiliations Rudy Vallee (was manager for Buddy Rogers' band)
Sidemen With Band Included Jerry Colonna, Joey Nash, Johnny McGee, Ruby Weinstein, Sam Persoff, Dave Levy, Ernie Capozzi, Jack Kimmel, Nat Levine, Jimmy Roselli, Pete Pumiglio, Jess Carneol, Sam Amoroso, Jack Lacey, Lloyd Turner, Lyle Bowen, Paul Ricci, Lou Raderman, Eddie Steinberg, Harry Patton, Charlie Margulis, Russ Case, Will Bradley, Sam Weiss, George Mazza, Rolly Dupont, Milt Yaner, Al Evans, Frank Victor, John Cusumano, Mel Solomon, Wally Barron, Sid Stoneburn, Jimmy Smith, Haig Stevens, John Dilliard, Ruby Waltzer, Bill Graham, Hank d'Amico, Milt Schutz, Jim Blake. Adrian Rollini, Bunny Berigan, and Artie Shaw also recorded with the Himber band
Vocalists With Band Included Guy Russell, Joey Nash, Stuart Allen, and a vocal group made up of Dolores Gray, Johnny Johnston, Harry Stanton, and Joseph Lilley. Johnny Mercer also cut one or more records with the Himber band
Sponsored Radio Shows "The Eddie Peabody Show," "Studebaker Champion Show," the "Melody Puzzle Show" (Lucky Strike)
Theme Song "It Isn't Fair"
Songs Written "It Isn't Fair," "Moments In The Moonlight," "Haunting Memories," "Day After Day," "After The Rain," "Time Will Tell," "Am I Asking Too Much?," "Today," "I'm Getting Nowhere Fast With You," and others

Richard Himber.

Recording Affiliations Vocalion, Bluebird, Victor, Decca

The Himber band was quite popular during the thirties and forties. One of its earliest bookings was at the Essex House in New York. They later played the Hotel Pierre and the Ritz-Carlton. Stylewise Himber's music was a combination of sweet and swing, played by capable musicians as the personnel list above indicates. Perhaps because he had already been in show business with such

194

people as Sophie Tucker and Rudy Vallee, his career as a bandleader was not very old before he landed a spot on a good sponsored show with Eddie Peabody. This broadcasting was followed by several others. Perhaps he was best known for his appearances on the Studebaker Show, when he billed himself as Richard Himber and his Studebaker Champions. Somewhat later he introduced a style change and briefly called the band his "Rhythmic Pyramids Orchestra." In the early forties he featured a sizable string section. He disbanded briefly in the mid-forties, but was back with a new band by the end of 1945. He remained active as a bandleader well into the early fifties. Throughout his career Himber recorded regularly and enjoyed record sales that were moderate to good. Part of his early career had included vaudeville, during which time he had developed a talent as an amateur magician. In later years he delighted his audiences with his feats of magic, and appeared to enjoy that almost as much as he enjoyed leading the band. He died in December 1966 at the age of 59.

EARL "FATHA" HINES

Started First Band A brief bandleading venture in 1924, followed by a more successful group in 1928
Where Chicago
Previous Band Affiliations Lois Deppe, Carroll Dickerson, Sammy Stewart, Jimmie Noone, Louis Armstrong
Sidemen With Band Included Walter Fuller, Freddie Webster, Omar Simeon, Darnell Howard, Jimmie Mundy, Budd Johnson, Trummy Young, Ray Nance, Alvin Burroughs, Dizzy Gillespie, Charlie Parker, Wardell Gray, Willie Cook, Dickie Wells, Jonah Jones, Benny Green, Jerome Richardson, Osie Johnson
Vocalists With Band Included Ivy Anderson, Herb Jeffries, Arthur Lee Simpkins, Billy Eckstine, Sarah Vaughan
Theme Song "Cavernism," "Deep Forest"
Songs Written "Rosetta," "Everything Depends On You," "Deep Forest"
Recording Affiliations Vocalion, Brunswick, Victor, Columbia, Capitol, and Fantasy

Hines is credited by many with having exerted the greatest single influence on jazz piano. He knew what it took to make a piano produce the right kind of jazz sounds. He must also have discovered some secret formula for youth, because seventy years after his birth he still looked like a young man.

Earl "Fatha" Hines.

Born in Duquesne, a suburb of Pittsburg, Pennsylvania, in December 1905, he began to study piano at the age of nine, with the intention of becoming a concert pianist. However, early in his high school years he discovered jazz at a Pittsburgh night club, and formed his own trio with a violinist and drummer. At the age of fifteen he was

The Hines Orchestra in 1935: trombone—Trummy Young *(fifth left)*; saxophone/arranger—Jimmy Mundy *(sixth right)*.

playing with Lois Deppe in the Pittsburgh area, leaving high school to accept this as a permanent assignment at $15.00 a week. Later he went on tour with this band and it was with him that he made his first records. In 1923 Deppe and the band moved into Chicago and very quickly sent for Hines to join them. For the next year and a half he worked both with the Deppe orchestra and as a single entertainer in the Elite Club.

His first and not too successful bandleading venture was launched in 1924, but did not last the year out. Hines then joined the Carroll Dickerson orchestra for a forty-two week tour of the Pantages Theater circuit, which took them to the West Coast and then back to Chicago in the spring of 1926, where they opened up at the Sunset Cafe. In 1927 Dickerson stepped out of the band, turning it over to Louis Armstrong, who made Hines his musical director. The Armstrong band became one of the most popular black bands in Chicago. It was also greatly admired by the young white Chicago musicians who developed what was later known as "Chicago style." Several recordings were made by this group on the Vocalion label. After a brief but unsuccessful attempt at operating a ballroom with Louis Armstrong and Zutty Singleton as partners, Hines joined Jimmie Noone's band at the Apex Club, and spent the better part of a year with him.

By December 1928 Hines was ready to try it again as a bandleader in his own right. He opened with a full-size band at the Grand Terrace Ballroom, a location reportedly controlled by the Capone mob. Although they had gone in for a short-term booking, the engagement stretched on and on, and the

The Hines "big band" of the mid 1940s.

Terrace became their home for the next ten years. With the help of nightly broadcasts, Hines became known from coast to coast. It was during this engagement that he became "Fatha" Hines, a name given him by a radio announcer who had overtrained at the bar. Unfortunately, due to the nature of his contract with the Grand Terrace management, his income during this period did not keep pace either with his reputation or his outward signs of success. Nonetheless Hines could not terminate the contract until the union finally stepped in and ruled that it was unfair and illegal.

During the early forties Hines' music style changed to what was later recognized as a forerunner of bop. In his band many of the most successful bop musicians got their start. Among them were Dizzy Gillespie, Charlie Parker, and Budd Johnson. In 1948 Hines rejoined Louis Armstrong, this time

in a small all-star jazz group with included Jack Teagarden and Barney Bigard. This group toured the United States and Europe with great success. But eventually the relationship between Hines and Armstrong deteriorated, and Hines left the group.

In 1951 he re-formed his own band, this time a small group with which he soon moved to the West Coast, establishing his home in San Francisco. For several years he was featured quite steadily at clubs in the Bay Area, taking occasional time out for tours to the New York area and even into Canada. In 1966 he made a European tour, a State Department tour into Russia, and there appeared to be no letup in the demand for his music in the United States. He was still active through the seventies and into the early eighties. But after a series of hospital stays he passed away in Oakland, California on April 22, 1983, at age 77.

The Earl Hines group of the early 1970s.

LES HITE

Started First Band 1930
Where Southern California
Sidemen With Band Included Charlie Jones, Sonny Graven, George Orendorff, Henry Prince, Harvey Brooks, Bill Perkins, Harold Scott, Lionel Hampton, Joe Bailey, Marvin Johnson, Lloyd Reese, Marshall Royal, Charlie Lawrence, Hubert Myers, Lawrence Brown, Britt Woodman, Allen Durham, Nat Walker, Al Morgan, T-Bone Walker, Joe Wilder, Alfred Cobbs, Dizzy Gillespie, "Snookie" Young, Ralph Bledsoe
Theme Song "It Must Have Been A Dream"

Hite's name is best identified with Frank Sebastian's Cotton Club in Culver City, California, where he was the featured attraction for nearly ten years, although he occasionally surrendered the fronting of the group to other people. Born in Du Quoin, Illinois in 1903, he moved to the West Coast in the mid-twenties. In 1930 he took over Paul Howard's band and became its leader. He was not pri-

marily a musician himself, although he did play alto sax, but during the Cotton Club stay he had some impressive talent in the band. Lionel Hampton spent four years in the outfit as the drummer, an attraction all by himself. For nearly two years in the early thirties, and not too long after Hite had taken over the band, it was fronted by Louis Armstrong, or perhaps it would be more accurate to say that Armstrong used it as a backing for his famous trumpet playing. It was during that period that Hampton took up the vibes, making his first record on the instrument with Armstrong. After his long Cotton Club stand, Hite toured the East Coast in the early forties. While there, Dizzy Gillespie played briefly with the band. Back on the West Coast, Hite gave up his bandleading career in the mid-forties to become a partner in the Hite-Fain Booking Agency. He died in 1962 in a Santa Monica hospital, the victim of a heart attack.

Les Hite and the Cotton Club Orchestra, 1936.

Claude Hopkins and his orchestra.

CLAUDE HOPKINS

Started First Band   1927 (A small group)
Where   Washington, D.C.
Previous Band Affiliations   Wilbur Sweatman
Sidemen With Band Included   Ovie Alston, Fred Norman, Sylvester Lewis, Fernando Arbello, Walter Jones, Pete Jacobs, Eugene Johnson, Bobby Sands, Henry Turner, Edmond Hall, Jabbo Smith, Shirley Clay, Lincoln Mills, Floyd Brady, Vic Dickenson, Chauncey Haughton, Ben Smith, Arville Harris
Vocalists With Band Included   Belle Powell
Theme Song   "I Would Do Anything For You"

Hopkins was born in Washington, D.C. in 1903 and went to school at Howard University, where he got a degree. In 1924 he joined the Wilbur Sweatman orchestra to play piano with the group for about a year. After a European trip as musical director for Josephine Baker, he started a group of his own in Washington, D.C. In 1930 he took over the band of Charlie Skeets and during the next six years played the Savoy Ballroom, the Roseland, and the Cotton Club, becoming for a brief period one of the most popular bands to play those locations. Good air time and the astute management of Harold Oxley both brought the band nationwide popularity, even though it was on a limited scale and of short duration. In the early forties he broke up the band and worked as an arranger for various bandleaders. Then about 1945 he formed and fronted a combo of his own. For the next several years he was active as a leader, usually with a small group and primarily in the New York area.

EDDY HOWARD

Started First Band   1942
Previous Band Affiliations   Dick Jurgens
Vocalists With Band Included   Howard did his own vocals
Theme Song   "Careless"
Songs Written   "Careless," "If I Knew Then," "My Last Goodbye," and "A Million Dreams Ago"
Recording Affiliations   Columbia and Majestic

Prior to becoming a bandleader himself, Howard made a strong contribution to the success of the Dick Jurgens band, not only as an instrumentalist and vocalist but also with his original compositions which the band recorded. Although he was known as a guitar player, he played enough trombone to audition successfully for the Jurgens band, because it was a trombonist they were looking for. Not able to read a note, he committed the audition tunes to memory. By the time Jurgens discovered he could not read music he had made such a good impression as a vocalist that he was kept on, and the guitar spot was created. Throughout the years he spent with Jurgens he was one of the band's most featured members.

Eddy Howard.

The Eddy Howard Orchestra during the peak of his band-leading career.

With a smaller band at Catalina Island, 1962.

The first few years with his own band were rather uneventful, but in 1946 he became the band of the year when his recording of "To Each His Own" became one of the year's biggest hits. With the stimulus of this wave of popularity, he kept his smoothly styled organization continually employed for several years on a coast-to-coast basis, and was particularly popular in the Chicago area. In addition to his recording activities he appeared, along with his orchestra, in one or more musical featur-

ettes made for Universal-International Pictures. The decline of the band business during the fifties affected his group along with the others. He eventually moved to California to make his home in Palm Springs, where he played winter engagements as well as occasional summer engagements at Catalina Island. He was preparing to open the 1963 Catalina season when he died one night in his Palm Springs home, apparently choking to death in his sleep on food particles.

201

WILL HUDSON

Started First Band 1938 (Had previously been co-leader of the Hudson-De Lange Orchestra with Eddie De Lange)
Where New York City
Previous Band Affiliations As an arranger with Fletcher Henderson, Cab Calloway, Don Redman, Andy Kirk, Earl Hines, Louis Armstrong, Jimmie Lunceford, and Ina Ray Hutton
Sidemen With Band Included Charles Mitchell, Rudy Novak, Joe Bauer, Jack Andrews, Edward Kolyer, George Bohn, Gus Bivona, Pete Brendel, Charlie Brosen, Mark Hyams, Doc Goldberg, Buss Etri, Billy Exner, Will Hutton, Mike Rosati, Max Herman, Frank Beraldi, George Siravo, Walter Burleson, George Berg, Bob Dukoff, Tommy Morgan, Ernie Mathias
Vocalists With Band Included Ruth Gaylor, Jane Dover, Elyse Cooper, Kay Kenny
Theme Song "Eight Bars In Search Of A Melody"
Songs . Written "Jazznocracy," "White Heat"

Recording Affiliations Brunswick, Decca

Hudson was born in Barstow, California in 1908 but went to school in Detroit. It was there he began the study of music and arranging. He became so skilled at arranging that he was occasionally called on to turn out an arrangement for McKinney's Cotton Pickers. This led to other arranging jobs on a full-time basis, with a number of popular bands as shown above. In 1936 the Hudson-De Lange Orchestra was formed, with both Hudson and De Lange carrying leadership billing. It was a twelve-piece band and for a time its vocalist was Nan Wynn. The band was active for some two-and-a-half years. Then it disbanded and Hudson formed a band of his own with many of the same personnel who had played in the first band. The musical styles of both bands were very similar: both were styled for the hotel and ballroom dancers. In the early forties Hudson gave up his bandleading career to concentrate on free-lance arranging.

The Hudson-DeLange Orchestra, 1937. The vocalist is Nan Wynn.

The Will Hudson Orchestra in the early 1940s.

INA RAY HUTTON

Started First Band   About 1934
Previous Band Affiliations   None—had worked in Broadway shows
Sidemen With Band Included   Ina Ray Hutton and Her Melodears, the all-girl orchestra, included: Kay Walsh, Estella Slavin, Ruth McMurray, Elvira Rohl, Althea Heuman, Ruth Bradley, Helen Ruth, Betty Sticht, Audrey Hall, Jerrine Hyde, Miriam Greenfield, Helen Baker, Marie Lebz, Lil Singer and others who came and went in later years. Her all-male orchestra included: Clarence Willard, Mac Adams, Guy Fusco, Johnny Mendell, Charles Maxon, Bill Westfall, Phil Olivella, Len Goldstein, Danny Cappi, George Paxton, Jack Purcell, Irv Orten, Pat Ruggles, Wally Gordon, Eddie Zandy, Joe Ortolano, Jack Andrews, Leonard Ray, Martin Berman, Sol Kane, Tony Alless, Ralph Collier, Hal Schaeffer, and others
Vocalists With Band Included   Ruth Bradley, Stuart Foster, June Hutton
Television With Band   A West Coast show in the early fifties which had a brief run on the networks about 1956
Theme Song   "Gotta Have Your Love"
Recording Affiliations   Victor, Vocalion, Okeh

Ina Ray Hutton did more than any other individual to prove that leading a dance band was not strictly a man's domain. The "Blonde Bombshell of Rhythm" got her professional start in show business tap dancing in a Gus Edwards revue, and later worked in the Ziegfeld Follies. The all-girl band which she put together in 1934 was billed as "Ina Ray Hutton and Her Melodears." Musically it was quite a swinging band, with Ina Ray in front, in a sexy gown, waving the baton and dancing. The band toured extensively, playing hotels, ballrooms and theaters, took a European tour, and worked in several short movie features. The personnel was quite consistent until a reorganization in the late thirties. In late 1939 she dropped the all-girl band to organize an all-male group, with arrangements done by George Paxton. This band was musically strong, with a style that was a combination of sweet and swing. A *Billboard* story in the fall of 1940 had such important fellow bandleaders as Tommy Dorsey predicting that the Hutton band would become one of the best in the business. By this time she was billing herself as "Queen of the Name Bands." Hutton's all-male band kept busy during the World War II years, but she disbanded them in the mid-forties, giving up the music entirely for awhile. She reorganized in 1946. In 1949 she married fellow bandleader Randy Brooks, a marriage which lasted until 1957. In the early fifties she was on the West Coast, once again with an all-girl band, which not only sounded good but was easy on the eyes. She was one of the first bandleaders to break into television successfully. She put together a show which was viewed for several years on the West Coast and had a brief fling on the networks. She dropped out of the music business permanently in the early sixties and passed away in Ventura, California in February 1984 at age 67.

Ína Ray Hutton and her orchestra.

HARRY JAMES

Started First Band 1939
Where New York City
Previous Band Affiliations Herman Waldman, Ben Pollack, Benny Goodman
Sidemen With Band Included Claude Bowen, Tommy Gonsulin, Jack Palmer, Russell Brown, Pruett Jones, Dave Mathews, Claude Lakey, Drew Page, Bill Luther, Jack Gardner, Brian Kent, Sherman Teague, Ralph Hawkins, Jack Schaeffer, Mickey Scrima, Al Stearns, Nick Buono, Dalton Rizzotto, Hoyt Bohannon, Harry Rogers, Vido Musso, Chuck Gentry, Al Lerner, Ben Heller, Sam Rosenbloom, Stan Stansfield, William Schumann, George Koch, Sam Marowitz, Glenn Herzer, Leo Zorn, Clint Davis, Lou Horvath, Henry Jaworski, Corky Corcoran, George Davis, Johnny McAfee, Ray Martinez, Willie Smith, Buddy Rich, Jack Percival, Bob Manners, Art Depew, Everett McDonald, Ziggy Elmer, Ray Conniff, Sam Donahue, Juan Tizol, Conrad Gozzo, Jackie Mills, Ray Sims, Louis Bellson, Sonny Payne, Gus Bivona, Bill Massingill, Bob Poland, Larry Kinnamon, Buddy Hayes, Allan Reuss, Lewis McGreery, Herb London, Bob Stone, Joe Comfort, Mickey Mangano, Dick Nash, George Roberts, Buddy

Harry James.

Combine, Ralph Ericson, Russ Phillips, Bob Robinson, Bob Turk, Larry McGuire, Vern Guertin, Vince Diaz, Ernie Pack, Jay Corre, Ernie Small, Terry Rosen, Tony De Nicola, Sam Frimature, Modesto Brisena, Cherry Kadowitz, Ernie Small, Dave Madden, Red

Kelly, Dave Wheeler, Joe Riggs, Larry Stof-
fel, Dick Carter, Bob Morgan, Phil Gilbert,
Tom Porrello, Al Yeager, Carl Saunders,
Dick Winters, Fred Haller, Dave Johnson,
Paul Humphrey, Bill King, Graham Ellis,
Jimmy Huntzinger, Everett Levey, Rod
Adam, Jack O'Keefe, Don Baldwin, Skip
Stein, Jack Poster, Al Patacca, Gino Baz-
zaco, Hal Espinosa, Rich Cooper, Rick Pat-
terson, Lon Norman, Steve Davis

Vocalists With Band Included Bernice
Byers, Connie Haines, Frank Sinatra, Dick
Haymes, Lynn Richards, Helen Forrest,
Kitty Kallen, The Skylarks, Buddy Moreno,
Buddy De Vito, Marian Morgan, Jilla Webb,
Ernie Andrews, Ruth Price, Joan O'Brien,
Rita Graham, Sundi Martino

Sponsored Radio Shows The "Danny Kaye
Show," "The Chesterfield Show," repeat appearances on Coca Cola's "Spotlight Bands
Show" and was one of three once-a-week
regulars during the last year of that show

Theme Song "Ciribiribin"

Recording Affiliations Columbia, MGM,
Capitol

Helen Forrest.

From the time he was born in Albany, Georgia in 1916 there was little doubt that Harry
James would be a musician. His father was
the leader of a circus band and James's musical training began at a very early age. By
the time he was eight he was sitting in with
the circus band and was soon doing trumpet
solos in the big top. His professional career
was launched in Beaumont, Texas when the
family moved there from Georgia. He played
for awhile with local bands, including Herman Waldman, who was very popular in the
Dallas area. While James was with Waldman, Ben Pollack heard him and offered him
a job, giving him his first move into the big
time where he played alongside other great
musicians of the day. It was with Pollack
that James made his first recordings, one
of which brought him to the attention of
another Pollack alumnus, Benny Goodman.
He joined the Goodman band in the late
summer of 1936.

James's trumpet choruses soon made him
a featured attraction with the Goodman

Kitty Kallen.

206

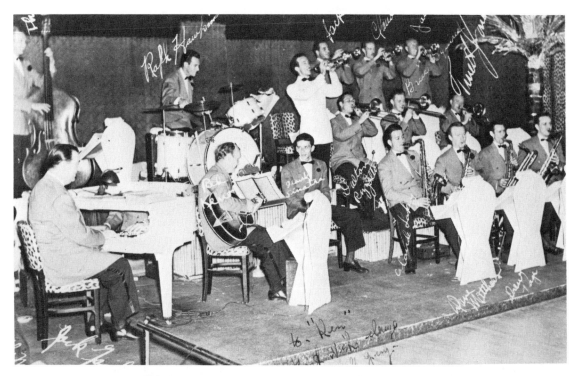

The 1939 Harry James Band, with young vocalist Frank Sinatra.

band, which was riding the crest of rising popularity at the time. He stayed with Benny nearly three years. By that time, his reputation was so well established that he felt ready to try it with a band of his own. Early in 1939 he made the move, with Goodman's blessing and at least a part of the financial support he needed for the venture.

Like other new bandleaders he found the best locations were not open to him in the beginning. They played the smaller spots, for equally small money, while the band worked itself into shape. In July of that year Frank Sinatra joined to do the singing chores, and stayed until Tommy Dorsey beckoned him about a year later. Recognizing that a job with Dorsey was a break for Frank, James released him from his contract. Sinatra was replaced by Dick Haymes, who also went to the Dorsey band when Sinatra left that organization to be a single. Another James vocalist to transfer to Dorsey was Connie Haines, who had been with James during Sinatra's stay. By that time James, an ardent baseball fan, must have

begun to believe he was an unpaid farm club for Dorsey.

When the James band was launched, MCA became its agency with Willard Alexander giving it his personal attention. Late in 1941 Frank (Pee Wee) Monte became Harry's personal manager, a job he still holds. Monte had also been Goodman's manager at one time. Rated one of the smartest and hardest working personal managers in the business, Monte made a major contribution to maneuvering the James band steadily towards the top of the heap and keeping it there once it had hit the top. At one time during the band's peak years there were three Montes associated with it — Frank, brother Fred who handled accounting, and brother Al who was the band boy.

In May 1941 James, who had been recording for Columbia with only moderate success, recorded "You Made Me Love You," which by the end of that year was one of the biggest records in the country. By the end of 1941, James's was rated the nation's Number One band. Other hit records followed,

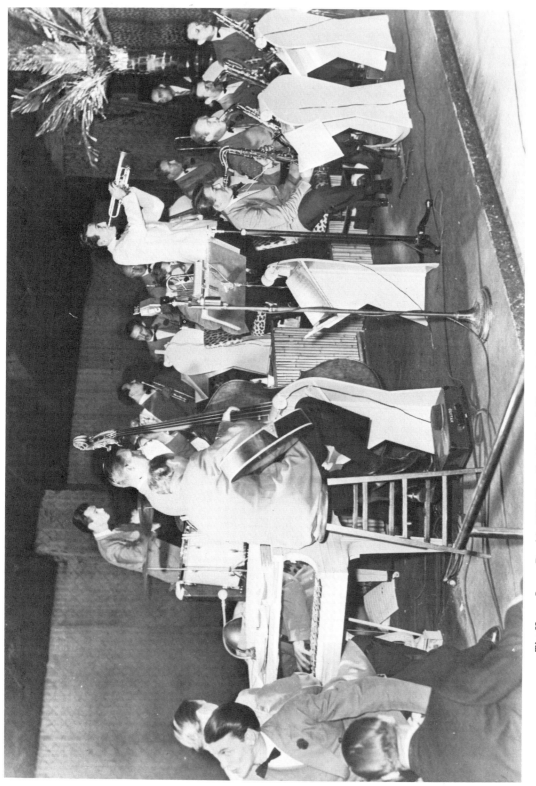

The Harry James Band in 1939. Yes, that is Frank Sinatra looking over his shoulder as the picture was shot.

establishing him firmly in the top bracket of the music business, a position from which he has not yet retreated. During the early and mid-forties James and the orchestra were featured in several motion pictures. In many of these films he did a creditable job as an actor as well as a musician. In addition to being heard almost nightly on remote broadcasts from the nation's best entertainment spots, he was quite successful on sponsored radio. He enjoyed the unique distinction of playing both the first and last of the "Coca Cola Company's Spotlight Band Shows," the first done from a marine camp in September of 1942 and the last from the Municipal Auditorium in Sacramento, California in November of 1946.

During the World War II period the James band had been augmented with a string section which eventually numbered nine violins. In late 1946 he disbanded briefly, and when he resumed activity in early 1947 the strings were gone. When the decline of the popularity of the name bands came during the fifties, James was one of the few able to weather the storm without reducing the size of his band or being content with local activity. Throughout the sixties he still kept "the big band sound" alive with coast-to-coast and international tours, and with steady bookings in the casino lounges of Las Vegas, Reno, and Lake Tahoe. In the early seventies he teamed up with Phil Harris for a series of successful appearances as headliners in the New Frontier Hotel in Las Vegas. By this time the Las Vegas scene was changing drastically as lounges dropped entertainment in favor of Keno. Those who made this change included the hotel where James had been a three-times-a-year attraction for many years.

But during the early seventies the big bands were enjoying a revival of interest. Even though it was slow in developing, this new interest furnished a replacement for the Las Vegas bookings, for these bands who were willing to travel. James went back on the road for one-nighters in the Midwest and East Coast and a six-weeks European tour which began in London on October 11, 1971. As the seventies moved along he continued to make an average of three or four

In 1943, the now oversize James band working in a motion picture.

tours of the Midwest, East Coast and the South, with annual stands at Disneyland and cruises with the Sitmar Lines.

Throughout his bandleading career James' musical style was always full and driving. Many of his arrangements reflected his admiration for Ellington. Numerically his bands ranged from fourteen plus vocalists to the twenty-six or twenty-seven it reached during the war. For thirty years the tenor saxophone of Corky Corcoran, so young when he joined the organization that Harry had to be appointed his guardian, sparked the sax section. Alongside him from 1945 until shortly before his death in 1967 sat Willie Smith, the only alto sax man who ever got a tone approaching that of Johnny Hodges. James always insisted on having the best people available in both the instrumental and vocal departments. During the late seventies and early eighties his was the most active band in the business playing to sellout houses on extended tours. In the early months of 1983 it was apparent to all his friends that Harry was a sick man. On July 5th cancer took his life in a Las Vegas hospital just forty years after he had married Betty Grable in the same city and on the same date.

The band in action, 1965.

ART JARRETT

Started First Band   January 1935
Where   Chicago at the Blackhawk Restaurant
Previous Band Affiliations   Ted Weems, Earl Burtnett, Phil Harris, Isham Jones, Red Nichols
Sidemen With Band Included   Jule Styne, Randy Brooks, James Fitzpatrick, Hal Sharff, Harold Dankers, Les Cooper, Jack Turner, Arthur Owen, Bruce Milligan, Rufus Smith, John Zellner, Floyd Sullivan, Babe Stuart, Ken La Bohn, Emery Kenyon, Sid Nierman, Ken Binford
Vocalists With Band Included   Jeri Sullivan, Gale Robbins, Eleanor Holm, Doris Singleton, Betty Barrett, Billy Blair; Jarrett usually handled the male vocals himself
Sponsored Radio Shows   "The Florsheim Shoe Show," "Dr. Pepper Show," guest shots on the "Fitch Bandwagon," and the "Coca Cola Spotlight Bands" program
Theme Song   "Everything's Been Done Before"
Songs Written   "Neath The Silvery Moon"
Recording Affiliations   Brunswick, Columbia, Victor

Art Jarrett.

In addition to being an accomplished vocalist, Jarrett played the guitar, the banjo, and the trombone. He successfully acted in the theater and in a number of motion pictures where he played with some of the top stars of the early thirties. Most of his bandleading career was spent in the Middle West and on the East Coast. He played several engagements at the Blackhawk Restaurant, the longest of which extended for seven months. His musical style was slanted towards the smoother side, and was aimed at encouraging patrons to get out on the floor and dance. Eleanor Holm, a swimming star as well as a vocalist, was married to Jarrett during the time she appeared with the band and until she left to participate in the 1936 Olympics. Shortly after Hal Kemp's untimely death in late 1940, Jarrett took over the Kemp band and its library, keeping the distinctive Kemp style alive for many years. He eventually gave up the music business to make his home in Yonkers, New York, where he went into the orange juice business.

JACK JENNEY

Started First Band   1939
Where   New York City
Previous Band Affiliations   Austin Wylie, Isham Jones, Freddie Rich, Richard Himber, Mal Hallett, Phil Harris, later with Artie Shaw, this between his first and second attempts at bandleading

Sidemen With Band Included   Nick Galetta, Oliver Suderman, Tommy Gonsoulin, Ray Noonan, Henry Singer, Hugo Winterhalter, Larry Gordon, Bunny Bardach, Marino Dallolio, Arnold Ross, Al Costi, Bob Shevak, Paul Richter, Rudy Novak, Joe De Paul, Don

The Art Jarrett Orchestra in the early 1940s.

Stevens, Bob Jenney, Jack Bigelow, Victor Garber, Morris Cohan
Vocalists With Band Included Louise Tobin, Meredith Blake, Bonnie Lake
Theme Song "City Night"
Recording Affiliations Vocalion, Columbia

Jenney's career as a bandleader was all too short, but he left his mark as one of the great musicians of the big band era. He was rated by his contemporaries as one of the finest trombonists of that period. He was born in Mason City, Iowa, in 1910 and began the study of the trumpet when he was eight years old. While he was in high school in Cedar Rapids he switched to trombone, taught to him by his father who was quite skilled on the instrument. His musical studies were continued at Culver Military Academy.

Austin Wylie gave him his first professional job. At the time he joined that organization Artie Shaw was also a sideman in the band. In the early thirties he went to New York where he became active in radio work, and where he remained throughout most of

Jack Jenney.

the decade. He became one of the most popular musicians in the studios, working regularly with such bands as those of Andre Kostelanetz, Freddie Rich, Richard Himber,

The Jack Jenney Band in action.

Lenny Hayton, and others. He was married briefly to Kay Thompson, who had a musical group of her own that later became quite famous.

His first bandleading venture in 1939, lasted less than a year. However, during that time his band did a substantial amount of recording. Probably the best remembered of these are his two versions of "Stardust," recorded for Columbia at one session. For many years it was a collector's item and was rereleased in a Columbia Golden Era Series in the mid-forties. In 1940 Jenney gave up his own band and joined Artie Shaw. Once again he recorded "Stardust" with Shaw's band, doing a small segment of the solo which he had done on his own recording.

In 1943 he took over the Bobby Byrne band when Byrne went into the service. The band was working in Florida at the time, but after concluding that engagement Jenney fronted them on engagements throughout the Middle West, including a stand at the Chase Hotel in St. Louis. His second venture as a bandleader was also short-lived, lasting only a few months. Then he was inducted into the service, going into the navy where he ended up in charge of a navy band. He was discharged from the service late in 1944 because of illness.

He then made his home on the West Coast where he once more became active as a studio musician, playing major radio shows. Among these was the Dick Haymes program, "Something for the Boys," beamed towards the men in uniform. Late in 1945 rumor had him contemplating the formation of a large orchestra, including strings, for recording sessions and possible personal appearances. But he suffered an attack of acute appendicitis and died on December 16, 1945 in a Hollywood hospital.

HENRY JEROME

Started First Band   1932
Where   Norwich, Connecticut
Vocalists With Band Included   Fran Warren, David Allen
Sponsored Radio Shows   "Dinner at the Green Room," a show originating from the Green Room of the Hotel Edison in New York City on the ABC network
Theme Song   "Night Is Gone" and "Nice People"
Songs Written   "Homing Pigeon," "I Love My Mama," "Night Is Gone," "Nice People," "Until Six," "Oh, How I Need You, Joe," "Theme from Brazen Brass"
Recording Affiliations   London, MGM, Roulette, Decca, Coral

Henry Jerome.

Radio listeners who picked up the Henry Jerome orchestra in the late forties and early fifties could well believe they were listening to the music of Hal Kemp. The Kemp style dominated his arrangements and, with a small band of eight to ten men, he did an excellent job of re-creating it. Most of Jerome's career was spent on the East Coast, with occasional swings through the Midwest to play the Chase Hotel in St. Louis, the Claridge or Peabody in Memphis, and the Roosevelt in New Orleans. Probably his longest stand was at the Hotel Edison in New York City, where he played for several years. He was consistently heard on radio remotes, and at one time had a sponsored show on the ABC network. His television work was limited to guest appearances. Although he did a great deal of recording during his career, including that done with the Kemp style band, probably the best known of Jerome's records was done during the sixties on a series of albums titled "Brazen Brass."

ARNOLD JOHNSON

Started First Band   Mid-twenties
Where   New York City
Sidemen With Band Included   Al Cassidy, Nat Natoli, Harold Sturr, Dudley Doe, Bernard Dailey, Ed Sheasby, Johnny Rose, Vic Graffrion, Charlie Dowski, Mickey Bloom, Pete Pumiglio, Chris Killinger, Roy Maxon, Bill Kranz, Roy Henderson, Ken Wittmar, Bobby Burns, Harold Arlen, Freddy Martin, Gary Gillis, and others

Songs Written   "Don't Hang Your Dreams on a Rainbow," "Goodbye Blues," "Sweetheart," "Teardrops," "All For You," "The Lovelight In Your Eyes"
Recording Affiliations   Brunswick, Vocalion

Prior to becoming a bandleader, Johnson had worked in vaudeville as an accompanist and soloist on the piano. He had also been

Jerome's arrangements gave the band a big sound, larger than the band's actual size.

215

Arnold Johnson and his "orchestra."

associated with Rudy Wiedoeft in a New York venture called the Frisco Jazz Band. With his own band he worked the New York and Chicago areas. Then he left the music business for awhile to try his hand at real estate. His best dance band was the one in the late twenties, which included several sidemen who later became important names in their own right. The Johnson band appeared in several Broadway musicals, including the *George White Scandals*. In the early thirties Johnson turned to radio to become a musical director and producer.

ISHAM JONES

Isham Jones.

Started First Band   1919
Where   Chicago
Previous Band Affiliations   None
Sidemen With Band Included   Louis Panico, Roy Bargy, Frank Quartell, Carrol Martin, Arthur Vanesek, Harold Moulding, Al Eldridge, Charles McNeil, John Kuhn, Joseph Frank, Leo Murphy, Joel Miller, Arthur Layfield, Wendell Detorly, Sonny Lee, Clarence Willard, Johnny Carlson, Red Ballard, Walter Yoder, Joe Bishop, Saxie Mansfield, Vic Halpric, Don Watt, Woody Herman, George Thow, George Wertenerr, Wally Lageson, Nick Hufner, Eddie Stone, Howard Smith, Jiggs Noble, Gordon Jenkins, Chelsea Quealey
Vocalists With Band Included   Carolina Lane, Frank Sylvano, Rita Smith, Joe Martin, Bob Carter, Woody Herman
Theme Song   "Spain," "You're Just A Dream Come True"
Songs Written   "I'll See You In My Dreams," "You've Got Me Crying Again," "It Had To Be You," "The One I Love Belongs To Somebody Else," "When My Dream Boat Comes Home," "Thanks For Everything," "Why Can't This Night Go On Forever?," "Swinging Down The Lane," "How Many Tears Must Fall?," and many more, in total well over 100
Recording Affiliations   Brunswick, Victor, Decca

There may be some who do not remember that Isham Jones was once one of America's most famous dance band leaders; but there is even less possibility of finding anyone in the English-speaking world who has not, at one time or another, hummed one of his compositions. During his lifetime he wrote well over 100 songs, many of which became standards. He was born in Ohio just before the turn of the century. But Chicago was where he began his bandleading career and where he made his headquarters during most of that career. In the early twenties he and his band were booked into the College Inn, where they stayed for nearly five years. Music Corporation of America was just getting its start, also in Chicago, and Jones was one of the first bandleaders to sign with them. They induced him to broaden his operations through tours of other major cities in the United States. Eventually he

The Isham Jones brass, 1934: George Thow, Clarence Willard, Johnny Carlson, Sonny Lee, and Red Ballard.

made a trip to England, where he found many fans waiting to hear the band which they had already heard on records. While many of the top bandleaders of the twenties were basically front men rather than accomplished musicians, such was not the case with Jones. His instrument was the saxophone. Not only did he play it well, but he consistently backed himself with an organization of well-qualified musicians. His radio broadcasts were considered the finest broadcasts of dance music during that period. Hundreds of records were turned out, the earliest of these on Brunswick, then on Victor; and his was one of the first bands to be signed by the new Decca label when it was launched in 1934. In 1936 Jones went into retirement due to poor health, playing his last engagement in Memphis, Tennessee. This retirement was short-lived. Within a few months he was back in New York once more fronting a band composed of all new members, for an engagement at the Lincoln Hotel. He was also competing with Woody Herman, who was playing another New York location with a band built around the key men from the former Jones orchestra. At least one more retirement followed before the early forties, at which time he returned to the music business, and remained active until the big band decline after World War II. He died in 1956.

The Isham Jones Band in Atlantic City, 1934.

About 1935, Woody Herman joined the sax section; in 1936 he would head the cooperative band formed from this group when Jones went into temporary retirement.

SPIKE JONES

Started First Band Early forties (small combo)
Where Southern California
Previous Band Affiliations Everett Hoaglund, Earl Burtnett, studio bands
Sidemen With Band Included Dick Morgan, Freddie Morgan, George Rock
Vocalists With Band Included George Rock, Red Ingall, Helen Grayco
Theme Song "Cocktails For Two," "The Shiek Of Araby," "Pass The Biscuits, Mirandy"
Tag Line "Spike Jones And His City Slickers"
Recording Affiliations Bluebird, Victor

Jones' identification with the dance band field is limited to his drumming with the bands of Hoaglund and Burtnett and the small combos with which he worked in the Los Angeles area in the early forties. With one of these groups he played the Rendezvous Room at the Biltmore Hotel for several years, a spot which did most of its business with late afternoon dancing.

Somewhere along the line Jones began to develop musical routines which were deliberately corny and which lampooned the popular songs of the day. The band's instrumentation gradualy began to include saws, bells, toy whistles, and the firing of guns. Shortly after the beginning of World War II they were signed by Bluebird to record some of this material and became an overnight sensation with a recording of a Jones' composition titled "Der Feuhrer's Face," the type number which could not help being successful at that particular moment. Other numbers in a similar vein followed including "Chloe," "Cocktails For Two," "The Glowworm," "You Always Hurt The One You Love," and "All I Want For Christmas Is My Two Front Teeth."

Shortly after the end of World War II Jones put together a big show unit which he called his "Musical Depreciation Revue" with which he toured the nation playing to packed theater houses wherever he went. Among his featured entertainers was Doodles Weaver whose own brand of zany comedy fit the Jones pattern perfectly. Another member of the unit was a pretty harpist who never played the harp but sat on a rocking chair knitting a scarf. Eventually she had a scarf ninety feet long but still had never played a note of music.

The show was very popular on radio throughout the latter forties and into the early fifties, at which time it converted to television where it was equally successful for several years. Eventually he reduced the size of his show unit and in the late fifties and early sixties was playing the casinos in Las Vegas and Lake Tahoe. Like the big dance bands of the day he too had been hurt by the advent of rock 'n roll, perhaps even more severely. He was quoted in a major music magazine as saying "My business is lousing up music but how can you slaughter a tune that is already a mess. The music of today is so bad that there's nothing I can do to make it sound ridiculous."

In March of 1965, while playing an engagement at Harrah's Club in Lake Tahoe, he was stricken with an asthma attack and forced to leave the show to enter St. John's Hospital in Santa Monica. After remaining there for several weeks he returned to his Trousdale Estates home, where he died in his sleep in the early hours of May 1, 1965, at the age of 53.

JIMMY JOY

Started First Band Mid-twenties
Where Texas
Sidemen With Band Included Gilbert O'Shaughnessy, Hollis Bradt, Jack Brown, Rex Preis, Lynn Harrell, Clyde Austin, Johnny Cole, Dick Hammell, Amos Ayalla, Norman Smith, Matty Matlock, Orville Andrews, Ernie Mathias, Al King, Oscar Reed, Elmer Nordgren, Oscar Miller
Theme Song "Shine On, Harvest Moon'
Recording Affiliations Okeh, Brunswick, Decca

When Joy was born in 1912, his name was James Monte Maloney. He took the name Jimmy Joy when he became identified with Joyland Park in Galveston, Texas, where he was playing with his band. He made his name change legal in a Kansas City court in 1929.

His band was originally formed on the campus at the University of Texas. For several years it was a big favorite in the Mid-west, playing regularly at the Muehlbach, the Peabody, and the Baker and Adolphus in Dallas. He also made occasional trips to the East Coast, and in the early forties was playing at the Casino Gardens in Santa Monica, California. His was a fine hotel and ballroom orchestra, playing music strictly styled for dancing. Joy was a competent sax man but he often surprised his audience by playing two clarinets simultaneously, a trick he borrowed from Wilbur Sweatman. He also enjoyed singing the blues, which he did in a style reminiscent of another Texan, Jack Teagarden. His native state of Texas was extremely proud of him, making him an honorary Texas Ranger. But his popularity was not restricted to Texas, for the state of Kentucky made him an honorary Kentucky Colonel, and for three consecutive seasons he was the official Kentucky Derby Orchestra. He died in Dallas in March 1962, where he had been semiactive as a bandleader during the fifties.

The Jimmy Joy Orchestra, Atlantic City.

DICK JURGENS

Started First Band Early 1930s
Where Sacramento, California
Sidemen With Band Included Louis Vacca, Art Aievoli, Stanley Noonan, Harold Winder, Eddy Howard, Carl Brandt, Floyd Adams, Bob Lee, Jimmy Shevenko, Eddie Kuehler, Ronnie Kemper, Lew Quadling, Clarence Lund, Frank Schrer, Charles Hands, Joe Contursi, Al Galente
Vocalists With Band Included Eddy Howard, Ronnie Kemper, Harry Cool, Buddy Moreno, Al Galente, Jimmy Castle
Theme Song "Daydreams Come True At Night"
Songs Written "Daydreams Come True At Night," collaborated on "Elmer's Tune"
Recording Affiliations Decca, Vocalion, Okeh, Columbia

Dick Jurgens.

During his school years in Sacramento, Jurgens' musical ability would not have qualified him as the most likely member of the class to succeed in the world of music. Nonetheless, for many years he fronted a first-rate, very popular dance orchestra. His bandleading career began by playing summer engagements in the resort locations at Lake Tahoe in the early thirties. While there his band attracted the attention of Music Corporation of America, and with the help of San Francisco radio announcer Mel Venter, they landed a 1933 engagement in the St. Francis Hotel. The next year they went back again for a much longer stay, which started them on the way to national success. From the St. Francis they went south to the Palomar Ballroom in Los Angeles, for a booking which lasted nearly a year. After that they felt ready to try the Midwestern and Eastern market. During the next several years the Jurgens' orchestra appeared in most of the nation's leading hotels and ballrooms. They were particularly identified with the Aragon in Chicago, Elitch's Gardens in Denver, and the Avalon Ballroom on Catalina Island.

World War II was not very far along before Jurgens entered the service, joining the Marine Corps. At the war's end he returned to Sacramento, reorganizing an orchestra which played its first engagement at the Hotel Claremont in Berkeley. That spot became one of the band's annual locations for the next nine years, usually during the football season. After that engagement, they would play one-nighters en route to Chicago, for an annual extended engagement at the Aragon.

When declining band business in the midfifties caught up with Jurgens and his contemporary leaders, he gave up the band to enter the electronics business in Colorado Springs, with his brother Will. For the next several years his bandleading activities were confined to occasional brief appearances at nearby Broadmoor Country Club. He returned to California in 1965 where he made infrequent appearances with a band, and talked of a comeback on a full-time basis. In the early seventies he launched that comeback, to play four or five annual tours of the Midwest, each including an extended engagement at Chicago's Willowbrook Ballroom. Eventually he gave it up once more to return to Sacramento where, when last contacted, he was in the real estate business.

The Jurgens Band in Denver, 1939.

The Jurgens Orchestra was a big favorite at Catalina, where this photo was taken in 1940. The pianists are Ronnie Kemper and Lou Quadling; the vocalist is Harry Cool.

ROGER WOLFE KAHN

Started First Band Early twenties
Where New York City
Sidemen With Band Included Manny Klein, Arthur Schutt, Joe Venuti, Nate Pisani, Perry Botkin, Vic Burton, Leo Arnaud, Larry Binyon, Joe Ross, John Williams, Tommy Gott, Earl Oliver, Chuck Campbell, Efrem Hanniford, Dick Johnson, Owen Bartlett, Joe Raymond, Licco Liggy, William Treesize, Raymond Romano, Arthur Campbell, Ken Whitmore, Arthur Lang, Leo McConville, Arnold Brilhart, Tommy Gott, Harold Sturr, Dominic Romeo, Miff Mole, Alfie Evans, Eddie Lang, Tony Colucci, Irving Brodsky, Herb Brodkin, Nat Shilkret, Stan King, Jack Teagarden (apparently recordings only), Charlie Butterfield, Dudley Fosdick, Jimmy Dorsey, Babe Russin, Henry Whiteman, Jack Russin, Joe Tarto, Chauncey Morehouse, Ruby Weinstein, Andy Russo, Artie Shaw, Elmer Feldkamp, Max Farley, Russ Carlson, Ward Lay, Gene Krupa
Vocalists With Band Included Elliott Shaw, Henry Berr, Johnny Marvin, Franklin Baur, Frank Munn, Scrappy Lambert, Libby Holman, Dick Robertson, The Foursome Quartet
Theme Song "Where The Wild, Wild Flowers Grow"

Recording Affiliations Victor, Brunswick, Columbia

Roger Wolfe Kahn was the scion of a wealthy family and a lover of popular music. With little or no need to make money with a band, he was able to recruit the best musicians available and put together an excellent band, often primarily for the satisfaction of having done so. In one instance he organized a band and paid them for several weeks of rehearsing, only to disband without ever having played a single job. A great deal of time was spent in the recording studios even though his recordings enjoyed only moderate success. Nonetheless Kahn was a potent factor in the New York band business scene through the twenties and into the thirties. His bands played various theaters and night clubs, and at one point he owned a night club of his own. He also had a booking office, and booked other musical units. In the mid-thirties his interest switched to aviation and he gave up the orchestra. During World War II he was a test pilot for an aircraft company. He died of a heart attack in July 1962 at age 54.

Reunion of Roger Wolfe Kahn musicians, Hollywood Athletic Club, 1948. *Left to right:* Manny Klein, Arthur Schutt, Joe Venuti, Nick Pisani *(standing)*, Perry Botkin, Vic Berton *(standing)*, Roger Wolfe Kahn, Leo Arnaud *(standing)*, Adolph Deutsch, Larry Binyon *(standing)*, Joe Ross, Dave Klein *(standing)*, Del Porter, John Williams, Ray Johnson.

ART KASSELL

Started First Band 1924
Where Chicago—Midway Gardens
Sidemen With Band Included Jack Davis, "Ponzi" Crunz, Ralph Morris, D. Johnson, Floyd Townes, Carl Bertram, Cliff Masteler, Bob Hill, John Jacobs, Ben Bensman, Thal Taylor, Paul Matlow, Emil Elias, Bob McReynolds, Don Gershman, Charlie Amsterdam, George Yadon, Mike Simpson, Lewis Math, Horace Robbins, Fred Benson, Bernie Woods, John Engro, John Gilliland, Larry Hall, Floyd Shaw, Mac Newton, Frank Folmar, Eddie Burbach, Art Wayne, Danny Bridge, James Hefti, Cub Higgins, Roy Henderson, Harvey Crawford, Don Baker, Charlie Kramer, Marty Rogers, Warren Smith, George Winslow, Pete Dudinger, Milt Samuels, Bob Dayton, Ken Switzer, John Byrne, Tom Taddonic, Jimmy McPartland, Benny Goodman, Bud Freeman, Dave Tough, and many others who came and went
Vocalists With Band Included Norman Ruvell, Thal Taylor, Billie Leach, Harvey

Art Kassell and vocalist Gloria Hart in the early 1960s.

225

Crawford, Grace Dunn, Marian Holmes, the Kassell Trio, Gloria Hart
Tag Line "Art Kassell and his Castles in the Air"
Sponsored Radio Shows "Shell Oil Company Show," "Elgin Watch Show," "Wildroot Hair Oil Show"
Television With Band A local show in the Los Angeles area in the early sixties, lasting a couple of seasons
Longest Engagement Fifteen years at the Bismarck Hotel in Chicago
Theme Song "Doodle-Doo-Doo"
Songs Written "Doodle-Doo-Doo," "Hell's Bells"
Recording Affiliations Victor, Columbia, Bluebird

A saxophone and clarinet man himself, Kassell's music was on the sweet side, except for his early Chicago years. His Midway Gardens stand led to engagements at both the Aragon and Trianon Ballrooms where, with heavy nightly air time, he became a big Midwestern favorite. Throughout most of his career he used Chicago as a base, finally migrating to the West Coast some time in the late fifties. For the next several years he kept busy playing a string of weekend engagements at the Hollywood Palladium in the early sixties, followed by an extended run at Myron's Ballroom, and finally into the Golden West Ballroom in Norwalk. That also became an extended engagement. His band was still playing there without him when he died in February 1965 after a lingering illness.

AL KATZ

Started First Band Early twenties
Where Chicago
Sidemen With Band Included The personnel was flexible and itinerant; included George Schechtman, Joe Magliatti, Fred Rollinson, Lewis Story, Jerry Bump, Eddie Kooden, Ray Kleemeyer, Joe Bishop, Greg Brown, Jess Stacy
Tag Line "Al Katz and his Kittens"
Recording Affiliations Gennett, Victor, Columbia

Katz was a very active bandleader in the Chicago area for many years, making appearances under many names in addition to his own, although the group with which he was best known was "Al Katz and his Kittens." During a luncheon conversation in the mid-sixties with Katz and veteran MCA executive Karl Kramer, Katz described some of his Chicago activities during the mid-twenties. It was interesting to note that even though MCA had handled his bookings, they had arranged several dates for Katz under other names without knowing he was the leader. Katz also toured the East Coast, including New York City, where he did some of his recording sessions.

AL KAVELIN

Started First Band 1933
Where New York City, Central Park Casino
Previous Band Affiliations Jean Goldkette
Sidemen With Band Included Personnel not available. Best known member of band was Carmen Cavallaro
Vocalists With Band Included Vivian Blaine, Bill Darnell, Don Cornell, Virginia Gilcrest

Longest Engagement Blackstone Hotel, Chicago—two years
Theme Song "Love has Gone," "I Give You My Word" (latter during ASCAP strike in early forties)
Songs Written "I Give You My Word," "Love Has Gone," "La Kiconga," "Blue Grass Region"
Recording Affiliations Columbia, Bluebird, Decca

Al Katz and His Kittens, 1924.

The Al Kavelin Orchestra, with Carmen Cavallero at the piano.

Kavelin was a graduate of the Royal Verdi Conservatory in Milano, Italy. His career as a bandleader began at the urging of Eddie Duchin, who wanted to leave the Central Park Casino to play a lucrative string of one-nighters, in order to cash in on his heavy air time from the Casino. To get the mangement's approval to do this, Duchin had to provide a satisfactory replacement, one which was not as brassy as many of the available name bands of that period. Kavelin organized a band sufficiently similar to the Duchin style to get the job. The band which he put together included Carmen Cavallaro on piano. They went in with an eight-week contract, which was extended on the second week to twenty-four weeks, when CBS picked them up on a national hookup and the fan mail began to come in. This broadcast also attracted the attention of MCA, who signed them to a contract making the band available on a national basis. During the next several years the Kavelin band played coast-to-coast in such spots as the Waldorf-Astoria, the Essex House, and the Biltmore in New York, the Blackstone in Chicago, the Mark Hopkins in San Francisco, the Peabody in Memphis, the Baker in Dallas, and the Roosevelt in New Orleans. In 1941, when the ASCAP ban on radio broadcasting was in effect, Kavelin penned a new theme song, "I Give You My Word," which became No. 1 on the Lucky Strike Hit Parade and sold a lot of records. Eventually Kavelin gave up bandleading and settled in the Los Angeles area, where he now operates Kavelin Tours, Incorporated, with an office on Wilshire Boulevard and another in Las Vegas.

HERBIE KAY

Started First Band   Late twenties
Where   Chicago
Previous Band Affiliations   College bands
Sidemen With Band Included   Information very limited. Charles "Bud" Dant, who later became an executive with Decca and Coral Records, played trumpet with the band in the mid-thirties
Vocalists With Band Included   Dorothy Lamour, Helen Conner, Ken Nealy
Theme Song   "Violets and Friends"
Recording Affiliations   Vocalion, Columbia

Herbie Kay's bandleading career really began on the campus at Northwestern. By the mid-thirties his had become one of the most popular dance bands in the Midwest, generally concentrating his activity in the Chicago area where he played repeated stands at the Blackhawk Restaurant. Dorothy Lamour joined the band in 1934, as its featured vocalist and remained until Hollywood beckoned her in 1936. She became Mrs. Herbie Kay in 1935, but the marriage ended in divorce in 1939. The August 24, 1940 issue of *Billboard* reviewed the Herbie Kay band on the stand at the Blackhawk Restaurant,

Herbie Kay.

pointing out that its charm with the dancers was because it concentrated on providing dance music, without any attempts to be cute. At that time the orchestra was a four-saxophone, four-brass, three-rhythm organization, basically the size which Kay maintained throughout his career. Some time in the early forties he gave up the band. He died in Dallas, Texas, on May 11, 1944 at the age of forty.

The Herbie Kay Orchestra, Chicago, 1936, with vocalist Dorothy Lamour at the mike.

SAMMY KAYE

Started First Band Early thirties
Where Cleveland, Ohio
Previous Band Affiliations Campus bands at Ohio University
Sidemen With Band Included Frank Blake, Lloyd Gillion, Oscar Reitz, Jimmy Brown, Charlie Wilson, Ralph Flanagan, Tommy Ryan, Paul Cunningham, Andy Russett, George Brandon, Ernie Rudisell, Glenn Long, Bob Niegron, Don Wallmark, Maury Cross, Gene Farraro, Frank Strasek, Henry Cole
Vocalists With Band Included The Three Barons, The Kaydettes, Tommy Ryan, Clyde Burke, Don Cornell, Arthur Wright, Marty McKenna, Allan Foster, Billie Williams
Tag Line "Swing and Sway with Sammy Kaye"
Sponsored Radio Shows "The Old Gold Cigarette Program," "Sammy Kaye's Sunday Serenade," "The Chesterfield Supper Club," "So You Want to Lead a Band"

Sammy Kaye.

The Sammy Kaye Orchestra at Cleveland's Statler Hotel, 1937. The pianist is Ralph Flanagan.

Sammy prepared to "Swing and Sway" at Elitch's Gardens in Denver, 1946.

Television With Band "So You Want to Lead a Band" (early fifties), the "Manhattan Shirt Program," (1958)
Theme Song "Kaye's Melody," "Until Tomorrow," and "Swing and Sway." "Kaye's Melody" was the one with which he was best known
Recording Affiliations Vocalion, Victor, Columbia

Although Kaye's "swing and sway" music generally had a great deal less swing than sway, it had a lot going for it when it came to reaping profits at the box office. Kaye was born in Cleveland and went to Ohio University where he majored in civil engineering. While there he put together a campus band and, delighted with the success it enjoyed, decided to make bandleading a full-time career. From the time his first band was launched, about 1933, he moved steadily towards the top ratings for the balance of the thirties. By the early forties he was in big demand from coast to coast in all the best places that featured name bands as attractions. A unique contribution to his success was made by an audience participation gimmick, which brought contestants up from the audience to try their hands at leading the Kaye band, with spectator applause deciding the winner. This feature of each evening's performance became so popular that he finally introduced it as a radio show, and later tried it briefly on television. Like most other bandleaders, he didn't enjoy the same success in television which he had with a number of sponsored radio shows. Another Kaye gimmick which paid off very well for him was the marketing on his radio show of a book of poems called *Sunday Serenade Book Of Poems.* This book was reported to have sold somewhere in the neighborhood of 100,000 copies annually for several years.

From the very beginning Kaye's musical style was predominantly on the sweet side, slightly reminiscent of Lombardo but still clearly identifiable as his own. For many years he featured singing song titles, in the same manner as Kay Kyser. The only change he made from his strictly "commercial" style was to record a swinging Dixieland album in the mid-sixties, which no one would have identified as Kaye's music unless they were told. Only intermittently did he have a female vocalist with the band, and supposedly fired the first one he had because she was slightly taller than he. Bandleaders who graduated from the Kaye organization included Ernie Rudy (Rudisill), Billy Williams, and Ralph Flanagan. Kaye passed away June 2, 1987, a victim of cancer.

JOE KAYSER

Started First Band 1921
Where Saint Louis, Missouri
Previous Band Affiliations Earl Fuller
Sidemen With Band Included Frankie Trumbauer, David Rose, Muggsy Spanier, Jess Stacy, Gene Krupa, and others less well known
Recording Affiliations Gennett, Brunswick

Kayser was one of the Midwest's pioneer bandleaders. Getting his musical training in St. Louis, he went to New York in 1917 to take a job as drummer in the Earl Fuller orchestra at New York's Rector's Restaurant. In this band one of his fellow musicians was Ted Lewis. He then did a World War I hitch in the navy. During that time he organized a small navy base band, which included a violinist named Benny Kubelsky, later better known as Jack Benny. Immediately after the war he fronted one of the Meyer Davis units, spending most of his time with it in the Carolinas. The Meyer Davis training contributed a great deal to his own success as a bandleader.

His own first band in St. Louis was a five-piece group, which grew larger with their success and the changing times. This band

Joe Kayser's Novelty Orchestra in the early 1920s.

Joe Kayser's band in the late 1920s.

was constantly on the road. Kayser maintains that he and Jan Garber were the pioneer travelling bands who originated the practice of one-night stands. Using an advance man to line up their dates, the band travelled impassable roads in Model T Fords but usually made it to their engagements. From St. Louis the band transferred its headquarters to Rockford, Illinois, and then moved into Chicago in 1924. During the next five years his was one of the featured bands at the Aragon and Trianon ballrooms. In 1929 Kayser switched to the stage band field and became director and master of ceremonies at the Diversey Theater in Chicago. That was followed by a similar position at Loew's Midland Theater in Kansas City.

In 1930 he was back in Chicago, where he played long engagements at the Arcadia and Mary Garden Ballrooms. During that period his band featured a lot of young Chicago musicians, many of whom later became prominent in the "Chicago style" school of jazz. During 1933 and 1934 his band was featured at the Chicago World's Fair, backing the Fair's top attraction, Sally Rand. In 1936 he gave up his band to join NBC Artists Service, booking some of the top radio artists of the day. In 1943 he joined Music Corporation of America, to take charge of their Chicago office name band department, handling bookings for the entire Midwest from Pittsburgh to Denver. He remained with MCA until 1955, when he retired. In the fall of 1977, while visiting Chicago, I had a lengthy telephone conversation with Kayser. At age eighty-two, he was as alert as most men thirty years younger, and a most interesting source of valuable information on the big band era.

HAL KEMP

Started First Band   Mid-twenties
Where   University of North Carolina
Previous Band Affiliations   Campus bands
Sidemen With Band Included   Saxie Dowell, Jack Purvis, "Bromo" Sulser, John Scott Trotter, Pinky Kurtzle, Jimmy Mullins, Ben Williams, Bob Mayhew, Jack Mayhew, Earl Beiger, Skinnay Ennis, Red Huneycutt, Buck Weaver, Joe Gillespie, Slatz Randall, Bill Simpson, Olly Humphreys, Reggie Merrill, Bill Brookins, Jimmy James, Paul Weston, Mickey Bloom, Bunny Berigan, Earl Geiger, Russ Case, Eddie Kusby, Harold Dankers, Phil Fent, Jack Shirra, Ralph Hollenbeck, Carl Loeffler, Bruce Milligan, Dave Barbour, Kenneth La Bohn, Jack Le Maire, Ralph Hall, Randy Brooks, Charlie Margulis, Lou Busch
Vocalists With Band Included   Skinnay Ennis, Scrappy Lambert, Bob Allen, Deane Janis, Maxine Gray, Judy Starr, Nan Wynn, Claire Martin, Janet Blair
Sponsored Radio Shows   "Chesterfield Program," "The Quaker Oats Program," the

Hal Kemp.

233

"Gulf Gas Program," "The Phil Baker Show," and the "Lady Esther Serenade."

Theme Song "How I'll Miss You When Summer Is Gone"

Recording Affiliations Columbia, Pathe, Brunswick, Harmony, Victor

James Harold Kemp was born in Marion, Alabama on March 27, 1904. He made his first attempt at bandleading while attending high school in Charlotte, North Carolina with a five-piece combination which he called "The Merrymakers." Later at the University of North Carolina, he played with various campus bands. During his senior year he put together the nucleus of the organization which he took with him when he left college and embarked upon a full-time career as a bandleader. It included pianist and arranger John Scott Trotter, saxophonist Saxie Dowell, and drummer Skinnay Ennis. Ennis later became the band's featured vocalist.

As their reputation in the North Carolina area grew, the Kemp band was given encouragement by the famous bandleader Paul Specht, and it was through him that they first met Fred Waring. Waring liked the band's unusual style and was instrumental in bringing them into New York, where he secured their first engagement, in a local ballroom. During the first evening's work a major hassle developed with the ballroom manager, resulting in their immediate termination. In the big city without reserve funds, they would have starved to death had it not been for Waring. Skinnay Ennis once told me that during a period of several weeks they were completely dependent upon Waring, who came to their hotel every morning and gave them each $1.00 to eat on for that day. Eventually with Waring's help they were able to get enough work to keep going.

Their first New York job of consequence was at the Strand Roof. They followed this with appearances at the Hotel Manger and the New Yorker. Although by now they were doing well in the New York area, their big break did not really come until Otto

Roth booked them into his Blackhawk Cafe in Chicago in 1932. During their long stay at the Blackhawk, regular air time over WGN and the Mutual Network established them firmly as one of the nation's top dance orchestras. At the end of this engagement, Kemp was able to help another University of North Carolina alumnus, Kay Kyser, by getting him booked into the Blackhawk. During the balance of the thirties the Kemp band was featured in such spots as the Astor Hotel, the Waldorf-Astoria, the Pennsylvania, the Drake, and the Palmer House in Chicago, and were doing very well on sponsored radio programs. They also were recording for RCA-Victor, with their records selling consistently well. In the fall of 1940 they came to the West Coast to play the Cocoanut Grove, after which they were booked into the Mark Hopkins Hotel in San Francisco. They closed at the Grove on December 19 and Kemp left immediately by car for an all-night drive to San Francisco. He was driving through the San Joaquin Valley in a heavy early morning fog when his car was struck head-on by another car and he was hospitalized in a Madera hospital. He died two days later. The band opened without him at the Mark Hopkins, and was fronted during its stay by several of his bandleading friends, including both John Scott Trotter and Skinnay Ennis. When the band left the Mark Hopkins, vocalist Bob Allen took over as the leader. But after a few months of unsuccessful attempts to keep it going, Allen turned it over to Art Jarrett.

The very distinctive stacatto style of Kemp was copied by several leaders following his death, perhaps most successfully by Henry Jerome. Fortunately most of Kemp's best numbers had been recorded, and at least one memorial album was released on the Victor label. In the early sixties, some twenty years after his death, Skinnay Ennis recorded on the Phillips label a Kemp salute, which included some of the best numbers with which Hal Kemp had been identified.

234

The Hal Kemp Orchestra in 1927, appearing at the Strand Roof, 47th and Broadway, New York.

Coral Gables Country Club, 1930. *Back row:* Paul Weston, Saxie Dowell, Bill Simpson, Pinkie Kintzle, Hull Humphreys, Reggie Merrill, Skinnay Ennis, Bill Brookins, Jimmy James, Gus Mayhew, John Scott Trotter. *Front row:* Mickey Bloom, Ben Williams, Hal Kemp.

By 1939 the Kemp orchestra was one of the nation's top bands.

RONNIE KEMPER

Started First Band 1942
Where Southern California
Previous Band Affiliations Dick Jurgens, Horace Heidt
Sidemen With Band Included The noteworthy sidemen who worked with his band included Claude Gordon, who became a bandleader in his own right.
Vocalists With Band Included Ruth Russell
Theme Song "Cecilia"
Songs Written "It's A Hundred To One I'm In Love," "Knit One—Purl Two," "The Doodlebug Song," "Downhearted Blues," "What You Gonna Do With Somebody Else"

Kemper gained his fame from the hit recording "Cecilia," made with the Dick Jurgens band. Later he played a prominent part in Horace Heidt's "Pot Of Gold" radio show and the motion picture of the same name. Eventually he decided that his personal reputation was strong enough to launch a band of his own. He was successful in obtaining the financial backing, but quickly learned

Ronnie Kemper with vocalist Ruth Russell.

that Heidt had no intention of letting him out of his contract to work with the Heidt band. That contract had been written just before the outbreak of World War II: and, because Heidt foresaw U.S. involvement in that war, he had insisted that the contract include a clause which cancelled it if the United States was attacked. Fate intervened on Kemper's behalf in the late summer of 1942, when a Japanese submarine fired a few nondestructive rounds into a mountainside near Brookings, Oregon. Kemper's attorney was successful in convincing Heidt that this constituted an attack, and Kemper became a bandleader. His bandleading career was cut short after little more than a year when he too was called into the service. He did not resume as a bandleader at war's end.

Ronnie Kemper and orchestra, 1942, at State Line Country Club, Lake Tahoe.

MART KENNEY

Started First Band   1931
Where   Vancouver, British Columbia
Previous Band Affiliations   Len Chamberlain, Sam Silverman
Vocalists With Band Included   Art Hallman, Roy Roberts, Wally Koster, Georgia Dey, Judy Richards, Norma Locke
Sponsored Radio Shows   "Home Oil Company," "Union Oil Company," "Purity Flour," "Borden's Canadian Cavalcade," and many CBC studio shows
Longest Engagement   Royal York Hotel
Theme Song   "The West, A Nest, And You, Dear"
Recording Affiliations   RCA Victor

Kenney got into the music business at an early age, and was a well-established dance orchestra leader in Vancouver even before he was old enough to vote. With the orchestra he toured British Columbia and Alberta in the early thirties, and played a season at Penley's Academy and Chestermere Lake in Calgary. He was first picked up on network radio while playing a repeat engagement at Waterton Park, Alberta, in 1934. C.P.R. management became interested in Kenney's broadcasts. This resulted in an engagement, in the fall of 1934, at their Hotel Saskatchewan in Regina; then to Lake Louise for the summer of 1935; and back home to the Spanish Grill of the old Hotel Vancouver in the fall of 1935. Kenney's band played many additional engagements there, as well as at Banff Springs Hotel, followed by the long run at the Royal York Hotel. During the war years Kenney toured extensively, and then returned to the Royal York for another long stay. He dropped out of band-leading, but returned in the mid-sixties to semiactivity and to record for RCA Victor again. RCA Camden also released a memorial album, produced by insurance man James Greer, of Kenney's best numbers from the heyday of his popularity in the late thirties and early forties.

Mart Kenney and his "Western Gentlemen," 1939.

STAN KENTON

Started First Band 1941
Where Los Angeles
Previous Band Affiliations Everett Hoagland, Gus Arnheim, Vido Musso, Johnny Davis
Sidemen With Band Included An impressive list of talent from the beginning; it included such people as Red Dorris, Bob Gioga, Howard Rumsey, Chico Alvarez, Shelly Manne, Johnny Anderson, Buddy Childers, Ray Wetzel, Ken Hanna, Bob Cooper, Gerry Mulligan, Bill Holman, Milt Bernhart, Jay Johnson, Art Peper, Bud Shank, Bart Calda-

rell, Ralph Blase, Dick Kenney, Harry Butts, Bob Fitzpatrick, George Roberts, Don Bagky, Johnny Howell, Shorty Rodgers, Maynard Ferguson, Max Bennett, Jack Nimitz and many others
Vocalists With Band Included Anita O'Day, June Christy, Gene Howard, Ann Richards, Jan Tober, Jay Johnson
Sponsored Radio Shows "The Bob Hope Pepsodent Show"
Theme Song "Artistry In Rhythm"
Recording Affiliations Decca, Capitol, and a label of his own called Creative World

The controversial music of Stan Kenton left no place for middle-of-the-roaders: it was either wholeheartedly endorsed or completely rejected. By his own description it was not intended for dancers, except for a brief period during his early career as a leader and an even briefer return to fronting a band styled for dancing in the early fifties.

Kenton's initial rise to the big name brackets was meteoric. He launched his band in 1941 with a summer engagement at the Rendezvous Ballroom in Balboa, California. The excitement he created there got him a booking into the Hollywood Palladium early in 1942, a location until then reserved for only the most firmly established names. From there he moved on to New York to play the Roseland Ballroom and Frank Dailey's Meadowbrook, the latter equally dedicated to playing name bands only. By mid-1942 the Kenton orchestra had carved a solid niche for itself in the American scene.

His initial recordings were on the Decca label, but he was one of the first bands to be signed by the newly formed Capitol label in 1942, and quickly became one of its leading attractions. Additional prestige was gained when Bob Hope selected the Kenton band to replace Skinnay Ennis and his orchestra on the Pepsodent radio show, while Ennis was in the service. This association continued until World War II ended. By that time Kenton was doing well on records and personal appearances, but his style had moved completely in what he identified as "progressive jazz." In 1947 he experienced a breakdown in health, probably resulting from both the strain of being constantly on the road and from the frustration of attempting to establish a musical style which the world was not totally ready for. He disbanded and there were rumors that he intended to give up music entirely to study medicine. He was back on the road by early 1948, however, but was attempting to limit his bookings to concert dates. Other layoffs followed, with each return to activity introducing a slightly different Kenton sound than the last one the public had heard.

Stan Kenton.

Palladium rehearsal time, about 1953.

Early in 1950 the ailing band business turned on Kenton, blasting him for creating the existing slump with his undanceable music. Kenton acknowledged this possibility, but insisted he had been helped by leaders who produced nothing new at all. Furthermore, he pointed out, he had long been asking bookers to promote him as a concert attraction, not a dance band, but they had ignored his request. Surprisingly, in the late summer of 1950, he was back at his old stand, the Balboa Rendezvous, with an organization styled for dancing. He even turned out some records, with a mammoth string section added.

This compromise with dance music was temporary, however. For the next fifteen years he continued to experiment, headquartering in Southern California and making periodic concert tours. A stretch of semi-retirement followed, but in the early seventies he was back in the business again with a new "creative jazz" band of eighteen men, playing innumerable one-nighters and making European tours. Except for occasional layoffs due to his health he remained active through the mid-seventies. In the spring of 1977, while on an Eastern tour, he was found unconscious in his hotel room, apparently the result of a fall in which he struck his head, resulting in a fractured skull. He underwent surgery in a Reading, Pennsylvania hospital for removal of a blood clot on the brain, and spent several weeks in recuperation and rest. When discharged from the hospital he returned to his California home for further rest. He died in a Hollywood hospital on August 25, 1979, at age 67.

The powerhouse Kenton trumpet section, 1947: Johnny Anderson, Buddy Childers, Ray Wetzel, Ken Hanna, and Chico Alvarez.

"Innovations of 1950" included strings.

On the Catalina bandstand, 1951: *back row:* Don Bagley, *unidentified*, Buddy Childers, Johnny Howell, Shorty Rogers, Maynard Ferguson. *Middle row:* Ralph Biose, Shelley Manne, Dick Kenney, Harry Betts, Bob Fitzpatrick, George Roberts, Milt Bernhart. *Front row:* vocalist Jay Johnson, Bob Cooper, Art Pepper, Bud Shank, Burt Caldarell, Bob Gioga.

AL KING

Started First Band 1926
Where New York City
Previous Band Affiliations The New Orleans Jazz Band, Original Dixieland Jazz Band, California Ramblers
Sidemen With Band Included Tony Spargo, Dick Wilson, John Turner, Elmer Ronka, Billy Wolfe, Herman Drewes, Eddie Yederman, Jack Teagarden, Charlie Spivak, Eddie Miller, Matty Matlock, Nappy La Mare, Doc Rando, Nat Farber, Sterling Bose, and others
Longest Engagement New Yorker Hotel
Theme Song "It's No Fun Dancing If The Band Don't Swing"
Songs Written "It's No Fun Dancing If The Band Don't Swing," "Kiss Me, My Darling," "Pasta Fazoola," "Alone In A Crowd," "Hop, Skip And Jump"

King's bandleading career occurred in a five-year period from 1926 to 1931, and was primarily concentrated in the New York-Atlantic City area. He played engagements at such locations as the Roseland Ballroom, Manhattan Towers Hotel, the New Yorker Hotel, and various clubs in Atlantic City. It was King who gave Jack Teagarden his first New York job in 1927. While playing with King's band Teagarden was offered a job with Ben Pollack. No recordings were cut by the King band. King terminated his own career as a bandleader to play trumpet in a long string of name bands, including the A & P Gypsies, Gus Arnheim, Skinnay Ennis, Alvino Rey, Freddy Martin, Red Nichols, Bob Crosby, Matty Malneck, and Jack Fina. He became a talent agent in Northern California, where he died at the age of 84 in March 1989.

Al King and His Rhythm Kings, Atlantic City, 1928.

HENRY KING

Started First Band   Early thirties
Where   Probably New York City
Sidemen With Band Included   Jack Diamond, George Tudor, Joe Sudy, Leo Arends, John Porpora, Neil De Luca, Jules Losch, Sidney Sudy, William Weems, Al Wallack, Phil Hart, Tubby Mertz, Vince Raff, Tom Enos, Eddie Bergman, Bobby Yacoubian, Johnny Paliso, Buss Michaels, Henry Jaworski, Charlie Enright, Harold Dohrman, Bill Jablonski
Vocalists With Band Included   Dick Robertson, Ray Hunkel, Don Reid, Sidney Sudy, Sonny Schuyler, Carmina Calhoun, Don Raymond, Bob Carroll, Phil Hanna, Eugenie Marvin
Sponsored Radio Shows   "The Burns and Allen Show"
Theme Song   "A Blues Serenade"
Recording Affiliations   Vocalion, Victor, Columbia, Decca

Henry King.

King was the son of a concert pianist and initially headed his career in the direction of classical music. Early in the thirties he switched to popular music, and became one of the nation's most active piano-playing bandleaders. His was definitely a hotel or society band, featuring smooth, danceable tempos with emphasis on violins rather than a heavy brass section. Those hotels in which he usually made at least one annual appearance included the Mark Hopkins in San Francisco, the Cosmopolitan in Denver, the Claridge and Peabody in Memphis, the Roosevelt in New Orleans, and the Shamrock in Houston. He also had an extended stand at the Biltmore in Los Angeles. During the heyday of radio remotes, he claimed to have racked up a score of more than 5,000 remote broadcasts. In the late fifties he moved to Houston, Texas, to live and eventually went into semiretirement. He died in that city in August 1974, after a long illness, at age 68.

WAYNE KING

Started First Band   1927
Where   Chicago's Aragon Ballroom
Previous Band Affiliations   Del Lampe
Sidemen With Band Included   Tony Hillis, Lee Keller, Louis Henderson, Burke Bibens, Andy Hansen, Ernie Birchill, Bill Heller, Paul Mack, Bill Egner, Johnny Kozel, Roger Wilson, Harry Waidley, Dick Harry, Sugar Harold, G. Belogh, Wayne Barclay, Oscar Kobelke, Herbert Miska, Wayne Alexander, Art Ellefsen, Ray Bluett, Lou Kastler, Emil Vanda, George Bay, Earl Schwaller, Kenneth La Bohn, Ray Johnson, Jerry Vaughan, Bill Kleeb
Vocalists With Band Included   The Aragon Trio, Elmo Tanner, Charles Farrell, Buddy Clark, The Barry Sisters, Linda Barrie
Tag Line   "The Waltz King"

Sponsored Radio Shows The "Lady Esther Serenade," "The Wayne King Show" for United Drug Company, "The Elgin-American Watch Company Show"
Theme Song "The Waltz You Saved For Me"
Songs Written "Josephine," "Goofus"
Recording Affiliations Victor

Although his critics did not always rate his saxophone playing as "incomparable," as his publicity indicated, King's box office popularity endured much longer than that of many of his contemporaries. Prior to launching his own bands he had been a featured saxophonist with the popular Del Lampe orchestra at the Trianon Ballroom. With the Lampe organization he had been rated as one of Chicago's best jazz saxophonists; but he quickly dropped this style in favor of smoother melodies when he took over his own band. Before long the Aragon's consistent air time had made him known as "The Waltz King" to the entire Midwest and a good share of the nation. His engagement at the Aragon ran for eight years.

In 1935 he announced he was going to retire from the music business, but if he was ever serious about doing so he apparently thought better of it. By that time he was

Wayne King.

active in commercial radio with two sponsored shows weekly, including the very popular "Lady Esther Serenade." His Victor recordings were selling well, and when his recording of "Josephine," a composition of his own, became a big hit about 1937 any thought of retirement doubtless receded into the background.

In mid-1942 he went into the army, returning to his bandleading at the war's end. His

1936, at Atlantic City's Steel Pier. Everyone who played the "Pier" had this "audience in background" shot made.

wartime absence apparently did nothing to diminish his popularity and he was soon once again doing very well on personal appearances in all categories. During the decline of the fifties he still picked and chose his engagements as he saw fit. Most of them were in the Midwest. Eventually he went into semiretirement in Scottsdale, Arizona.

But he still occasionally made tours through the South and Midwest. In February 1964, the Aragon invited him back to the bandstand where he had started thirty-seven years earlier, to play the final dance in the once-famous ballroom before its doors closed forever. On July 16, 1985, he passed away at age 84.

ANDY KIRK

Started First Band   1929
Where   Oklahoma City
Previous Band Affiliations   George Morrison, Terence Holder
Sidemen With Band Included   Jim Lawson, Allan Durham, Alvin Wall, John Harrington, Lawrence Freeman, Marion Jackson, William Dirvin, Ed McNeil, Mary Lou Williams, Bob Moseley, Gene Prince, John Williams, Claude Williams, Floyd Brady, Ben Webster, Irving Randolph, Buddy Cate, Dick Wilson, Henry Wells, Earl Miller, Cheney Kersey
Tag Line   "Andy Kirk and His Clouds of Joy"
Theme Song   "Clouds," "Until The Real Thing Comes Along"
Recording Affiliations   Brunswick, Decca

Kirk's bandleading career began when he took over the Terence Holder band after

Holder stepped out. At the time a long period of economic prosperity was just coming to an end and the depression was beginning. Before it was over the Kirk band of twelve and sometimes fifteen men would travel from its Kansas City headquarters as far as 150 miles to play jobs for a guarantee of $50. Their first Kansas City job was at the Pla-Mor Restaurant and Ballroom. During that stay they caught the attention of Jack Kapp, who recorded them on the Brunswick label. On the strength of the popularity of those records, the band obtained bookings in Chicago and Philadelphia, and eventually went into the Savoy and Roseland Ballrooms in New York. They returned to Kansas City to work in that area for the next several years. When Decca was formed Jack Kapp took the Kirk band with him and it was on that label that the majority of their records

The 1929 Kirk Orchestra.

were issued. Probably the biggest selling record they made was "Until The Real Thing Comes Along." Stylewise the Kirk band might have been described as a combination of "sweet" and "swing," but it had a sound that was all its own. In addition to some great section work and occasional instrumental solos, a major contribution was made to the band's efforts by vocalists Fha Terrell and June Richman. Kirk's greatest success came in the late thirties and early forties. He retired as a leader about 1948, but in the early sixties he returned to the music business to book a number of units under his own name for private engagements.

The "Clouds Of Joy" at the Rainbow Ballroom in Denver, 1935. Mary Lou Williams was the band's pianist and arranger.

On the stand in Kansas City, with Mary Lou Williams on piano.

ORVILLE KNAPP

Started First Band About 1934
Where Los Angeles
Sidemen With Band Included Michael Paige, George Mays, Jack Miller, Chick Floyd, Clarence Nelson, Jess Randall, Wally Rutan, Bill Echolstone, Guy Dick, Donald Swihart, Charlie Broad, Leighton Noble
Vocalists With Band Included Virginia Verrill, Edith Caldwell, Don Raymond, Ray Hendricks, Dave Marshall, Leighton Noble
Longest Engagement Beverly Wilshire Hotel, 1934 and 1935.
Theme Song "Indigo," "Accent On Youth"
Recording Affiliations Decca, Brunswick

Knapp's music was styled for dancing, with a distinctive sound that was imitated in part by some other bands, including Freddy Martin. With it Knapp played coast-to-coast, including such spots as the Aragon Ballroom in Chicago, and by 1936 was well on his way to becoming one of the nation's most popular dance bands. Late that year he died in the crash of a light plane which he was piloting himself. The Knapp band was taken over

Orville Knapp.

intact by George Olsen, who kept it going as "The Music of Tomorrow."

BENNIE KRUEGER

Started First Band Early twenties
Where Chicago
Sidemen With Band Included Hymie Farberman, Benny Bloom, Fred Schilling, Herman Kaplan, Perry Billitzer, Lester Morris, Bill Arenburg, Dick Cherwin, Happy Reis, Harry Reser, Benny Goodman
Vocalists With Band Included Al Bernard, Billie Jones, Ernest Hare, Scrappy Lambert, Dick Robertson, Fran Frey
Theme Song "It's Getting Dark On Old Broadway, Honey"
Recording Affiliations Gennett, Pathe, Brunswick, Embassy, Columbia. The majority of his recordings was on Brunswick

Most of Krueger's appearances were in theaters although his band occasionally booked dance dates. MCA was getting its start in the Chicago area in the early twenties, and his was one of the first bands they signed. The band was featured in what has been identified as MCA's first trade journal ad, appearing in *Billboard* on May 15, 1926. In addition to Krueger, the dozen bands which it listed included Coon-Sanders, Ted Weems, Charley Straight, and Isham Jones. The price quoted, compared to what bands would earn later, was infinitesimal and reflected the infancy of the band business at that time: one-nighters were quoted as low as $100, and a weekly rate of $600, both with percentage privileges. Krueger was best known outside the Chicago area for his recordings.

GENE KRUPA

Started First Band   1938
Where   New York City
Previous Band Affiliations   Joe Kayser, The Benson Orchestra, Red Nichols, Irving Aaronson, Russ Columbo, Mal Hallett, Buddy Rogers, Benny Goodman
Sidemen With Band Included   Murray Williams, George Siravo, Vido Musso, Carl Biesacker, Milt Raskin, Ray Piondi, Dave Schultze, Tom Gonsoulin, Tom Di Carlo, Bruce Squires, Charles McCamish, Chuck Evans, Nick Prospero, Charles Frankhauser, Toby Tyler, Dalton Rizzotto, Sam Donahue, Sam Musiker, Ray Cameron, Corky Cornelius, Nate Kazebier, Al Jordan, Floyd O'Brien, Rod Ogle, Clint Neagley, Bob Snyder, Sid Brantley, Tony D'Amore, Shorty Sherock, Howard Dulany, Rudy Novak, Babe Wagner, Walter Bates, Norman Murphy, Graham Young, Roy Eldridge, Tommy Pederson, Teddy Walters
Vocalists With Band Included   Helen Ward, Irene Daye, Howard Dulany, Anita O'Day, Johnny Desmond, Buddy Hughes, Dave Lambert, Buddy Stewart, Carolyn Gray, Ginnie Powell, Lillian Lane, The G-Noters, Dolores Hawkins
Theme Song   "Apurksody" was first used, later it became "Starburst"
Recording Affiliations   Brunswick, Columbia, Okeh

Gene Krupa.

Krupa was born in Chicago in 1909. Before music became the dominating force in his life, he spent at least a year in an Indiana seminary. After working with Chicago bands, he migrated to New York in 1929, where he quickly went to work with Red Nichols. Krupa's drums can be heard on many of the great Nichols' records of that period. He also recorded with Bix Beiderbecke and other jazz greats of the time. In 1935 he joined the Goodman band and was soon one of its featured attractions.

Early in 1938 he left Goodman to form the first band under his own name, built around his sensational performance as a drummer.

Roy Eldridge takes a solo with the Krupa band in the early 1940s.

The postwar Krupa band complete with nine strings and a vocal group called the "G-Noters."

His ability, his popularity, and his previous affiliations enabled him to quickly make a place for himself among the top names. Almost immediately the band began recording for Brunswick, adding another dimension to his popularity. During the first year their itinerary included a West Coast trip, for a very successful engagement at the Palomar and additional recording sessions in Hollywood studios.

Krupa was one of the pioneers in breaking the color line by bringing black musicians into his band. Not only did he employ them, he took a strong stand on their behalf to see that they were treated as well as his other musicians. In the early forties Roy Eldridge joined the Krupa trumpet section, and on at least one occasion Krupa challenged the management of a restaurant who declined to serve Eldridge along with the others.

In the early months of 1943, with the popularity of the Krupa band well established, misfortune overtook him while playing a theatre date in San Francisco. He was caught up in what those close to him felt was one of the San Francisco Police Department's periodic "clean city" drives which needed a prominent personality to insure headline publicity. Krupa was booked on a marijuana charge. The fact that the marijuana involved was actually in the possession of the bandboy (who, incidentally, had a long record of delinquency) did not prevent Krupa from drawing a jail sentence, which put him out of the business at the peak of his career. Twenty-five years later San Francisco would have been more likely to arrest him for drinking a Coca Cola in a cocktail lounge.

When this ordeal was over he joined the Tommy Dorsey band and was its featured drummer until he resumed his bandleading activities early in 1945. In keeping with the trends of that period, the new band was big in personnel, a powerhouse organization that had to be reduced in size to survive in the late forties. Some time during the mid-fifties he followed the course of many of his "swing era" colleagues and concentrated on appearances which could be handled with a small jazz combo, with his bookings confined to the New York area. A heart attack in 1960 sidelined him for awhile, but he returned again for occasional appearances until 1967 when he retired. In 1970 he appeared briefly at the Plaza Hotel in New York with a small combo. In 1972 he appeared in a television special with other jazz greats, and was featured in a segment with his old boss Benny Goodman. He died in his Yonkers, New York, home on October 17, 1973, a victim of leukemia at the age of 64. His life story was depicted (not very accurately) in a 1959 Columbia film titled *The Gene Krupa Story*, with Sal Mineo playing the title role.

The "G-Noters," with the Gene Krupa Band of the mid 1940s.

Lillian Lane.

Ginnie Powell.

Gene Krupa at the Aquarium, New York, in 1946: bass — Bob Strahl; piano — Buddy Neal; guitar — Bob Lesher; saxophones — Buddy Wise, Charley Kennedy, Harry Terrill, Mitch Melnick, Jack Schwartz; trumpets — Don Fagerquist, Armand Anelli, Ray Triscari, Al Porcino; trombones — Dick Taylor, Jack Zimmerman, Clay Harvey, Warren Covington; vocals — Bob Berry, Carolyn Grey.

KAY KYSER

Started First Band Mid-twenties
Where University of North Carolina
Sidemen With Band Included Marion Reed, George Weatherwax, Charles Kraft, Sully Mason, John White, Art Walters, Benny Cash, George Dunning, George Sturm, Bill Rhoads, Maddy Berry, Frank Fleming, Richard White, Ray Michael, Merwyn Bogue, Bill Stoker, Pokey Carrie, Bobby Guy, Max Williams, Harry (Breezy) Thomas, Morton Gregory, Armand Buissaret, Hymie Gunkler, Lyman Gandee, Lloyd Snow, Eddie Shea, Charlie Chester, Larry Duran, Roc Hillman, Bob Fleming, Noni Bernardi, Jack Martin, Willard Brady, Herbie Haymer
Vocalists With Band Included Ginny Simms, Merwyn Bogue, Sully Mason, Bill Stoker, Harry Babbitt, Julie Conway, Trudy Erwin, Jane Russell, Dotty Mitchell, Georgia Carroll Mike Douglas·
Sponsored Radio Shows "Kyser's Kollege of Musical Knowledge" for American Tobacco Company

The "Old Puh-Fessuh."

Television With Band "Kyser's Kollege of Musical Knowledge"
Theme Song "Thinking Of You"
Recording Affiliations Victor, Brunswick, Columbia

Kyser made little pretense of being a great musician himself, but concentrated heavily on showmanship. He consistently featured very capable vocalists and entertainers, backed by a band of adequate musicians, some of those who worked with him having either previously worked with some of the best swing bands of the period or ending up with them later.

Starting his bandleading career while attending the University of North Carolina, he apparently never seriously considered any other career except music. After completing his college education, he began his career as an orchestra leader on a full-time basis, enjoying moderate but not outstanding success until his friend Hal Kemp, another University of North Carolina alumnus, assisted him in moving into the Blackhawk Restaurant in Chicago. There, in the mid-thirties his "Kollege of Musical Knowledge" was started as a Monday night audience participation program, to stimulate business on a night when most clubs remained closed. It caught the attention of radio station WGN, who began broadcasting it, and soon the American Tobacco Company sponsored it as a network show. It very quickly made Kyser one of the most popular bandleaders in America. By the early forties he was probably the biggest attraction in the business, in demand everywhere for concert appearances, dance dates, and theater engagements. Attendance records were set wherever the band appeared.

During the war Kyser, along with other leading bandleaders, felt the urge to make his own personal contribution to the war effort and attempted to enlist. For several months rumor had it that Kyser was going into the army with the rank of major but he was eventually turned down on a physical disability. During the balance of the war he directed as much of his effort as possible

Harry Babbit and Ginny Simms share the mike on the Catalina Bandstand.

Jane Russell took her turn as a Kyser vocalist.

towards morale-building, playing for USO shows at military bases and defense plants, with each of his weekly radio programs originating from some such installation.

His popularity continued when the war was over, but his activity on radio diminished as television began to take over nighttime entertainment. In the early fifties he attempted to adapt the "Kollege of Musical Knowledge" to television, but it was unsuccessful. Shortly after this venture ended, he retired to Chapel Hill, North Carolina, to enjoy the fruits of his productive years as a top attraction. He divorced himself completely from his music business past in favor of Christian Science. A heart attack took his life on July 23, 1985, at age 79.

The Kyser Band in front of the Casino Ballroom, Catalina Island. The band made two appearances there, in 1939 and 1940.

The Kyser band during the war years.

ART LANDRY

Started First Band Early twenties
Sidemen With Band Included John Maitland, Dean Duel, George De Kay, Hal Sorensen, Joe Smith, Ted Mack, Sam Carr, Wilbur Edwards, Howard Emerson, Jimmie Greco, Boyce Cullen, Carl Gauper, Red Thomas, Dick Humphrey, Howard Emerson, Al Marineau, Henry Burr
Tag Line "Art Landry's Call of the North Orchestra"
Recording Affiliations Gennett, Victor

Landry was a clarinetist himself and usually fronted a band consisting of three saxophones, two trumpets, trombone, bass, piano, drums, banjo or guitar, and occasionally violins. Although not one of the better known bands of the twenties, their activities did take them from coast to coast. They did a great deal of recording, most of it in New York or Camden, New Jersey, but with at least one recording session done on the West Coast. Landry ended his bandleading career before the big band era really came into its own.

The Art Landry Band.

SAM LANIN

Started Band 1920
Where New York City
Sidemen With Band Included Sorting out those who simply recorded with him from those who appeared with him is difficult. Lanin's Roseland Dance Orchestra in the early twenties included the following: Hymie Farberman, Jules Levy, Miff Mole, Arnold Brilhart, Larry Abbott, Jack Lube, Morris Dixon, Harry Perrella, Tony Colucci, Bill Short, Irving Farberman, Red Nichols, Merele Johnston, Vic d'Ippolito, Herb Winfield, Clarence Heidke, Alfie Evans, George Slater, Eddie Schasby, Arthur Fields, Joe Tarto, Rube Bloom, Vic Burton, Arthur Hall, Leo McConville, Tommy Dorsey, Jimmy Dorsey, Andy Sanella, Arthur Schutt, Harry Reser, and many others. Among other famous musicians who recorded with Lanin were Manny Klein, Jack Teagarden, Jimmy McPartland, Joe Venuti, Eddie Lang, Benny Goodman, Phil Napoleon, Glenn Miller, and Bunny Berigan
Theme Song "A Smile Will Go A Long, Long Way"
Recording Affiliations Columbia, Okeh, Paramount, Embassy, Camden, Banner, Harmony

During the twenties and into the early thirties Sam Lanin was one of the most popular bands in the New York area. In addition to playing such famous locations as the Roseland Ballroom for several years, he was also musical director of the Ipana Troubadours. His activity was not concentrated so much on personal appearances as it was on records. With the possible exception of Ben Selvin, who was almost totally a recording bandleader, no one else spent so much time in the recording studios as Lanin. A long list of recording names was used: Lanin's Roseland Orchestra, Bailey's Lucky Seven, Lanin's Southern Serenaders, Lanin's Arcadians, the Ipana Troubadours, the Broadway Bellhops, the New York Syncopaters, the Broadway Broadcasters, Sam Lanin and His Famous Players, the Okeh Melodians, and the Melody Sheiks. The scope of his recording activity is indicated by the fact that Brian Rust, in his "American Dance Band Discography," uses sixty pages to list Lanin's recordings.

ELLIOT LAWRENCE

Started First Band Mid-forties
Where Pennsylvania
Previous Band Affiliations College bands
Theme Song "Heart To Heart"
Songs Written "Five O'Clock Shadow," "Heart To Heart," "Once Upon A Moon," "Sugar Town Row," "Brown Betty," "Sugar Beet"
Recording Affiliations Columbia, Decca, King

Elliot Lawrence's band was put together while he was attending the University of Pennsylvania. Once out of college, he took over the post of musical director for station WCAU in Philadelphia. His broadcasts over that station were quickly expanded to full-time broadcasts for the whole CBS network, giving his prestige a substantial boost. In 1946 he took his band into New York to play the Hotel Pennsylvania. The success of that engagement got him bookings into Frank Dailey's Meadowbrook in Cedar Grove, New Jersey, the Paramount Theater in New York, the Sherman Hotel in Chicago, and the Palladium in Hollywood. In between important location bookings he played every important college date, becoming one of the most popular bands for college proms of that period. His popularity continued through the forties and into the early fifties, at which time he gave up the band. He then concentrated his activities on arranging and conducting for television. He also did some Broadway shows, only occasionally returning to the dance band field with a pickup band for college dates.

The Elliot Laurence Orchestra.

HARLAN LEONARD

Started First Band 1934
Where Kansas City
Previous Band Affiliations George E. Lee, Benny Moten, Lon Basquette, Bob Adams, Thamon Hayes
Sidemen With Band Included Henry Bridges, Fred Beckett, Bill Hadnot, Jesse Price, Tad Dameron, Rozelle Claxton, Charlie Parker, Jimmy Ross, Richard Smith, Herman Walder, Woody Walder, Charles Goodwin, Leonard Johnson, Samuel Lovett, Carlos Smith, Bill Sanders, Ben Curtis, Edward Phillips, Darwin Jones, Bernie Cobb, Winston Williams, Edward Johnson, Richman Henderson, Jimmy Keith, Ernest Williams, Curtis Foster, Freddie Hopkins, Raymond Howell, Miles Jones, Norman Bowden, Russell Moore, James Wormick, Earl Jackson, Merill Anderson, Arvella Moore, Rodney Richardson, Johnny Otis, Jack McVea, Teddy Buckner, Preston Love
Vocalists With Band Included Myra Taylor, Helen Rothwell, Darwin Jones, James Ross, Ernest Williams
Theme Song "A Mellow Bit Of Rhythm," "Rockin' With The Rockets," "Southern Fried"
Recording Affiliations Victor, Bluebird

Harlan Leonard was part of the Kansas City scene which produced so many great black musicians during the twenties and thirties. During the twenties George E. Lee was one of the most important bands in that area, and perhaps the best known on records. Leonard worked with him during 1923. Then he joined Benny Moten, staying with him until the early thirties. He then went with Thamon Hayes' Kansas City Rockets, eventually taking over the leadership of the band in 1934. The band then became known as "Harlan Leonard and His Kansas City Rockets," a tag line which Leonard retained until he retired from the business. That first band broke up in 1936 and he took over the Jimmy Keith band in either 1937 or 1938. During the balance of the thirties Leonard kept busy in the Kansas City area, playing such spots as the Dreamland, Street's Blue Room, and the Century Room. In 1940 they were booked into Chicago to play the Aragon and Savoy Ballrooms. At that time they also did their first recording session on the Victor label. Returning to Kansas City, they spent 1941 playing the College Inn and other locations in Kansas City, plus tours through the Middle West. Late in 1941 the Leonard band went to New York City to compete in a battle of bands at the Municipal Auditorium. They were not too successful with their New York appearance, and returned to the Kansas City area. But in the early part of 1943 Leonard made a West Coast tour, playing one-nighters en route, and played the Club Alabam in Los Angeles for a year.

Harlan Leonard.

He remained in the Los Angeles area, playing other local club dates, the last of which was Shep's Playhouse in Los Angeles. At the end of that engagement Leonard gave up the music business entirely to work for the Internal Revenue Service, staying with them until he reached retirement age.

TED LEWIS

Started First Band 1916
Where New York City
Previous Band Affiliations Bessie Clayton
Sidemen With Band Included The list includes some jazz greats such as Muggsy Spanier, Benny Goodman, Frank Teschemacher, George Brunis, Manny Klein. Others included were Walter Kahn, Harry Raderman, Dick Reynolds, John Lucas, Vic Carpenter, Don Murray, Frank Ross, Tony Gerhardt, Sol Klein, Jack Aaronson, Hymie Wolfson, Sam Shapiro, Sammy Blank, Nat Lobovosky, Harold Diamond, Al Podova, Moe Dale, Rudy Van Gelder. Jack Teagarden also worked with the band on some recordings

Vocalists With Band Included Lewis did most of the vocals himself. Recordings were made with several great female vocalists during the twenties, including Ruth Etting
Sponsored Radio Shows The "Valspar Paint Program," the "Van Merritt Beer Program"
Theme Song "When My Baby Smiles At Me"
Songs Written "When My Baby Smiles At Me," "Show Me The Way," "While We Danced til Dawn," "Fair One," "Walking Around In A Dream"
Recording Affiliations Columbia, Victor, Decca, and RKO

The Lewis band working in a motion picture. Lewis and the orchestra made several trips to Hollywood to work before the cameras.

On the Coca Cola Spotlight Band Show, 1945.

Lewis was primarily a showman and fronted a show band. He did, however, devote enough time to the dance field to be considered an important part of it. Although many considered what he offered to be pure corn off the cob, the fact remains that some of the greats of the jazz and swing world worked with him at various time, as evidenced by the list above.

Getting his start in vaudeville, the band which he organized in 1916 in Coney Island was initially intended to be a vaudeville act. He called it "Ted Lewis and his Nut Band." In addition to himself, it had only four members. By the early twenties he was well established in the New York area in the dance band field, with an organization which grew in size with the trend of the times. By the end of the twenties he was rated among the nation's most popular leaders. But when the swing bands began to dominate the dance field in the mid-thirties, Lewis once more developed a unit which was basically a show band, concentrating his bookings on theaters and night clubs. For years he was a headliner on the Orpheum Circuit, playing the top vaudeville houses not only in the United States but in Europe. His battered old top hat and his not-too-well-played clarinet were familiar trademarks to several generations, and when he did his "I'm Stepping Out With A Memory Tonight" in the soft light of a crowded theater, he could have the entire audience in tears. He made a number of motion pictures, the first of which was for Warner Brothers in 1929,

Ted Lewis.

titled *Is Everybody Happy?* That was the question which Lewis periodically asked his audiences, usually finding out that they were if the applause could be accepted as an indication. He and the band made other pictures for Universal.

His career covered sixty-two years of activity on the bandstand and stage. He retired at age seventy-seven, after making his final appearance with his band and revue in the lounge of the Desert Inn in Las Vegas. He died in his New York home in August 1971, victim of a heart attack at age 81.

ENOCH LIGHT

Started First Band   Late twenties
Vocalists With Band Included   Jerry Baker, Peggy Mann, Bunny O'Dare
Tag Line   "Enoch Light and his Light Brigade"
Theme Song   "You Are My Lucky Star"
Songs Written   Mostly novelty numbers —
"Rio Junction," "The Daddy Of Them All," "Big Band Bossa," "Private Eye Suite," "Cinderella," "Daniel Boone," "Via Veneto," "Carribe"
Recording Affiliations   Bluebird, RCA, Vocalion

Light was born in Canton, Ohio in 1907. He attended Johns Hopkins University, and started his own band in the late twenties. Its musical style was aimed at the hotel trade, a style which he maintained throughout most of his bandleading career, except for a brief leaning towards the swing side in the early forties. He became popular not only in the United States, but enjoyed a long European tour in the early thirties. One of his longest stands was at the Taft Hotel in New York, where heavy air time contributed to his popularity. In the late forties or early fifties he gave up the band to concentrate on recordings, both as a conductor and a producer. In the late sixties and early seventies, he recorded a series of note-for-note re-creations of the work of other leaders from the big band era. He died in New York on July 31, 1978.

Enoch Light.

GUY LOMBARDO

Started First Band   Early twenties
Where   London, Ontario
Sidemen With Band Included   The band was built around members of the Lombardo family, including Lebert, Carmen, and Victor. Other sidemen included Jack Miles, Fred Higman, Francis Henry, George Gowans, Fred Kreitzer, Larry Owen, Dudley Fosdick, Frank Vigneau
Tage Line   "Guy Lombardo and his Royal Canadians"
Vocalists With Band Included   Rosemarie (Lombardo's sister), Kenny Gardner (Lombardo's brother-in-law)
Sponsored Radio Shows   "The Robert Burns Panatela Show," the "Lady Esther Serenade," "Spotlight Bands" (In its last years "Spotlight Bands" featured three bands on a permanent basis: Lombardo was one of these)
Television With Band   A show in the late fifties stayed on the network for only a single season. Other television activity was limited to specials, including an annual "New Year's Eve Show"
Theme Song   "Auld Lang Syne"

Recording Affiliations   Gennett, Columbia, Brunswick, Decca, Victor, Capitol. The biggest percentage of his recording was done on Decca

No one did so much as Guy Lombardo to establish the fact that the melody was important. His "sweetest music this side of heaven" may have been an irritant to jazz and swing fans, and if he placed at all in such trade journal ratings as the *Downbeat* poll, it was usually as "The King of Corn." This bothered Lombardo very little for he was consistently strong at the box office, the only poll which he considered of any real value. The style of his music was never altered from the time he first started his band in the early twenties to his death in 1977.

Lombardo brought his Royal Canadians down from Canada in the mid-twenties. They headquartered for a time in the Cleveland area, building their popularity through radio broadcasts, some of which Lombardo paid for himself. He was quick to recognize radio's value, through which the band's first

Lombardo and "The Royal Canadians" in the early 1930s.

At the Roosevelt Hotel, 1948.

big break developed. In Chicago, Jules Stein, heading up his newly formed Music Corporation of America, heard some of the Lombardo broadcasts and went to Cleveland to sign them up. He induced Al Quadbach, proprietor of a small cabaret on the south side of Chicago, to hire the band for their first Chicago appearance. For the Lombardo opening Quadbach changed the name of his place to the Granada Cafe. The first six weeks after their October opening was unimpressive. Convinced that radio was the answer, Lombardo and Jules Stein finally talked Quadbach into putting in a wire, the cost of which was split three ways. The band's first broadcast from the Cafe over WBBW occurred on New Year's Eve at nine o'clock, with little or no one in the place, but by closing time they had a packed house, clearly showing the power of radio remotes in the late twenties. Needless to say the wire and the broadcasts stayed, and through them Lombardo became one of the most popular bands in the land. The Granada became second only to the Blackhawk Restaurant in terms of popularity in Chicago.

Two years later Lombardo felt that he was ready to leave Chicago and invade New York. But Quadbach had other ideas, and his contacts and associates in the Chicago area were not the kind that anyone would be inclined to intentionally aggravate. The engagement dragged on, with its termination taking several months to work out. Some of the stories about how the engagement was ended were not told until several years later. Finally Lombardo was able to open in New York's Roosevelt Hotel in late 1929, starting the beginning of a very long engagement which was interrupted only as Lombardo saw fit, until the hotel finally closed the Roosevelt Grill in the late sixties.

In 1934 Lombardo was one of the first bandleaders to be signed by the newly created Decca label, and for the next twenty years turned out a consistent string of best sellers for them, including at least four which topped the million mark. Many of these were the original compositions of brother Carmen, including "Coquette," "Sweethearts On Parade," "Powder Your Face With Sunshine," "Boo Hoo," and "Seems Like Old Times." The Lombardo band was a closely knit organization with little change in personnel throughout the years. In the mid-sixties Victor left for a brief try at leading his own band, but returned very shortly. Practically all the band's arrangements were written by Larry Owen, who joined in the late twenties and remained until his retirement in the mid-seventies, except for a brief period which he spent with the similarly styled Jan Garber band in the early postwar years. Like many of the bandleaders who rose to popularity during the twenties, Guy was a violinist, although he seldom played the instrument, usually confining his efforts to wielding the baton in a manner which sometimes made one wonder whether he was leading the band or the band was leading him. Much of the Lombardo sound was built around Carmen's alto saxophone. In the fall of 1970, Carmen left the band because of illness, and died of cancer in his Florida home in April 1971 at the age of 67. His death was quite a blow to his family, which had worked so closely together for so many years.

A writer once headlined Lombardo as "the man who invented New Year's Eve." Perhaps this was because his theme song, "Auld Lang Syne," was the melody which every other band also played to welcome in the New Year. It could also be because beginning with the late twenties no New Year's Eve arrived without Lombardo's music being featured at midnight from some location on either radio or television. For many years it was from the Roosevelt Grill, but some also originated from the Waldorf-Astoria and even from Grand Central Station in New York.

When the decline of big band popularity was approaching the tobogganing stage in the early fifties, one of the better known music magazines polled several bandleaders for their opinions as to the cause. Lombardo's answer was that for his band there had been no decline; and that the answer lay in giving the patrons dance music, which was really the name of the game. The fact that he continued to roll steadily along while others fell by the wayside indicated that there were a lot of people who thought he was right. Twenty-five years later there was still no indication that Lombardo's popularity would ever end, for he was booked steadily, usually a couple of years in advance. In the summer of 1977 a heart ailment took him into Methodist Hospital in Houston, Texas for open heart surgery. Apparently recovered, he rejoined the band in the early fall, but by mid-October a relapse sent him back to the hospital. He died on November 5 at age 75.

The four brothers in 1958.

JOHNNY LONG

Started First Band 1932
Where Duke University, a campus band which remained intact to embark on a professional career upon graduation
Previous Band Affiliations None
Vocalists With Band Included Paul Harman, Helen Young, Bob Houston, Julie Wilson, The Beachcombers
Sponsored Radio Shows "The Teen-Timers Show," "Judy, Joe, and Johnny"
Television With Band Guest appearances and specials

Theme Song "The White Star of Sigma Nu," and "Shanty Town"
Songs Written "Just Like That"
Recording Affiliations Decca, Coral, Mercury, King, Signature, Forum, Roulette

Johnny Long, the nation's best known, if not its only, successful left-handed violinist, was born on a farm in North Carolina. The eleven-piece orchestra which he organized in 1932 on the Duke University campus was a group initially called "The Freshman." With it he competed with fellow student bandleader Les Brown for the jobs on the

Johnny Long and his orchestra at the Statler Hotel, Buffalo, New York, in the mid 1930s.

In the late 1950s Long still maintained a full-sized band.

campus. Most of the band graduated together in 1935 and began their professional careers. Some assistance was given them in those early years by another North Carolina bandleader who had already established himself, Hal Kemp. Long's orchestra became one of the most popular at college proms, particularly in the South and Midwest. They also played every major hotel, ballroom, and theater east of the Rockies, and came to the West Coast for at least one engagement at the Hollywood Palladium.

A great deal of momentum was given Long's career in 1940 when he recorded "In Old Shanty Town," which went on to sell well over a million copies. A long list of other successful records followed, although none did quite so well as "Shanty Town." The Long band was heard regularly on radio remotes, with a couple of sponsored shows doing much to boost its popularity. When television replaced sponsored radio he, like most other bandleaders, had difficulty finding a place in the new field, although several attempts were made. During the fifties Long reduced the size of his band substantially, but kept on the road with it, including several trips to Las Vegas for appearances in an upstairs dancing room at the Hotel Fremont. In the early seventies he returned

Johnny Long.

to school to get a bachelor's degree at Marshall University, with the express intention of teaching. In January 1972 he suffered a heart attack and died in a Parkersburg, West Virginia hospital at the age of 56.

VINCENT LOPEZ

Started First Band About 1917
Where New York City
Sidemen With Band Included Bob Biers, Bob Effros, Billy Hamilton, Harry Brown, Ernest Holt, Harold Geiser, Dave Barend, Henry Waak, Eddie Scheer, Larry Abbott, Jim Cassidy, George Napoleon, Joe Gold, Frank Reino, Willie Kessler, Norman Weiner, Xavier Cugat, Dan Yates, Charlie Butterfield, Joe Tarto, Einar Swan, Pete Gentile, Arthur Schutt, Jimmy Dorsey, Tommy Dorsey, Mickey Bloom, Vic d'Ippolito, Bud Wagner, Louis Heidelberg, Neil Golden, Ernie Charles, Leon Ziporlin, Ray Leone, Bob Lytell, Ernie Mathias, Red Dolan, Wesley Fogel, Jules Jacobs, Nick Pisani, Paul Rick-

enbach, Lew Green, Arthur Freidman, Bob Spangler, Dick Newman, Morty Bullman, Chick Dahlston, Milt Fried, Edgar Sweeney, Frank di Martino, Dick Morano, David Mordecai
Vocalists With Band Included Frank Munn, Dick Robertson, Jack Parker, Frances Hunt, Maxine Tappan, Johnny Morris, Betty Hutton, Sonny Schuyler, Penny Parker
Sponsored Radio Shows "The Realsilk Program," the "St. Joseph Aspirin Program," "The Nash Automobile Show"
Theme Song "Nola"
Recording Affiliations Paramount, Okeh, Brunswick, The Hit of the Week, Bluebird

Lopez was born in Brooklyn and during his growing years his parents were determined that he would enter the priesthood. He finally entered a monastery, but after a few uncomfortable years there Lopez and the monastery fathers agreed that he was cut out for some other career. He left, to concentrate on his love for playing the piano. The band which he organized in 1917 had, by the early twenties, become one of the most popular in the New York area. Following the practice of other bandleaders of that day, he soon had several bands he was booking and who were working under his name. Some of his groups were Vincent Lopez's Red Caps Vincent Lopez's Cadets, and Vincent Lopez's Debutantes. He even tried to sign up Guy Lombardo and his group as a Lopez band when Lombardo first came to the states from Canada.

Lopez was among the earliest bandleaders to see the potential of radio, and one of the first to be broadcasting regularly. From the bandstand of the Pennsylvania Hotel his brief introductory greeting, "Lopez speaking," became so famous and popular that he never dropped it. The success of his broadcasts in bringing business into the Pennsylvania Hotel influenced many other important leaders to send their music out over the air waves. He vied with Paul Whiteman and George Olsen for the services of the top musicians of the day, and rivalry between the three was strong. When Whiteman promoted and conducted his famous Gershwin Concert at the Aeolian Hall early in 1924, Lopez countered with a symphonic jazz concert at the New York Metropolitan Opera House in November of the same year.

In 1924 Lopez made a European tour, playing the Capitol Theatre, the Kit Kat Club, and the London Hippodrome. Late in 1925 he opened a supper club of his own called Casa Lopez, which he operated until March 1928. While he owned the club, it was destroyed by fire once, and in the long run cost Lopez a lot of money. Next he went into the St. Regis Hotel, where he stayed four years. Then he moved to Chicago, to play the

Vincent Lopez.

Congress Hotel and the Chez Paree during the World's Fair. He then returned to New York for another year at the St. Regis. During that time whistler Fred Lowery joined the band.

During the next several years the band spent more time away from New York, playing the Deauville Club in Miami, the Beverly Wilshire Hotel in Los Angeles, the Drake in Chicago, the Gibson in Cincinnati, Billy Rose's Aquacade in Cleveland, and the Palace Hotel in San Francisco. In 1940 friend Billy Rose brought the Lopez band in to play at the New York World's Fair Aquacade. Then early in 1941, he opened an engagement at the Taft Hotel, which continued for more than twenty years with only brief interruptions. By the mid-sixties his activity was curtailed by poor health, primarily problems with his eyes requiring repeated surgery. A limited market for big bands existed at that time so he was fronting a small group. In 1966 he and the group played for several months in a downtown Las Vegas location.

In a business where the mortality rate was extremely high, Lopez established a record for longevity which was equalled by only one or two others. He enjoyed the good life and when he began to make money was never reluctant to spend it. He was often heavily in debt. His name was linked with several wealthy society women, a reputation which he seemed to enjoy. His book, *Lopez Speaking—My Life And How I Changed It*, published in 1960, dwells on those romances as well as his falling in love with Betty Hutton when she sang with the band and his disappointment at her leaving. Never one to shy from controversial projects, he attempted in 1938 to rewrite the "Star-Spangled Banner" to make it more easily sung, which brought him both favorable and unfavorable publicity. In the early forties he took up numerology and from that point on it dominated his life. He died in a Miami, Florida nursing home at age eighty in September 1975.

Vincent Lopez and his orchestra, at the Claridge Hotel in Memphis, Tennessee, July 19, 1939.

BERT LOWN

Started First Band   Early twenties
Where   New York City
Sidemen With Band Included   Adrian Rollini, Chauncey Gray, Tommy Fulline, Irving Kaufman, Paul Mason, Johnny Costello, Rudy Adler, Miff Mole, Frank Cush, Eddie Farley, Ward Lay, Stan King, Elmer Feldkamp, Merrill Kline
Vocalists With Band Included   Smith Ballew, Scrappy Lambert, The Biltmore Rhythm Boys
Theme Song   "Bye Bye Blues"
Songs Written   "Bye Bye Blues," "You're The One I Care For," "Tired," "By My Side"
Recording Affiliations   Harmony, Columbia, Victor, Bluebird

Bert Lown, pride of the New York Biltmore in the 1920s.

Although Lown's was basically a hotel band he employed some good talent, as shown by the roster above. He was quick to recognize the value of radio and was heard regularly on remotes and in the New York area for a diamond sponsor. He also assisted Rudy Vallee both in getting his start as a bandleader and in obtaining a radio sponsor. He gave up the band in the mid-thirties for other interests. During World War II he was very active in relief work, and in the postwar years was Regional Field Manager for the Committee for Economic Development. He then became affiliated with the Columbia Broadcasting System. While on a trip to the Pacific Northwest in 1962, Lown was stricken with a heart attack and died in his Portland, Oregon hotel room. He was 59 years old.

CLYDE LUCAS

Started First Band   Early thirties
Where   West Coast
Sidemen With Band Included   Information not available
Vocalists With Band Included   Clyde Lucas, a musical group called "Four Men Only"
Tag Line   "Clyde Lucas and his California Dons"
Theme Song   "Dance Mood"
Recording Affiliations   Vocalion, Columbia

Lucas built his musical reputation on the West Coast in the early thirties, gradually expanding it through records and radio to the point that by the mid-thirties he was able to tour nationally with considerable success. He also gained quite a reputation for his work in motion pictures, including playing background music for some of the early talking pictures. The band's instrumentation was usually four saxophones, two trumpets, and a four-piece rhythm section, but often featured violins as well. The band's arrangements called for a great deal of doubling, making it essential that each musician be able to play more than one instrument. Lucas was most successful in hotel locations and theaters. He maintained his popularity through the war years and into the late forties, at which time he disbanded.

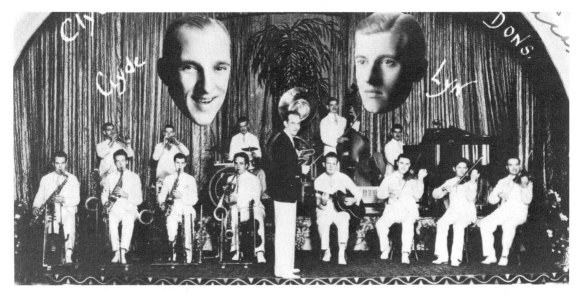

Clyde Lucas and His California Dons.

JIMMIE LUNCEFORD

Started First Band 1927
Where Memphis, Tennessee
Previous Band Affiliations Deacon Johnson, Elmer Snowden, Wilbur Sweatman. Studied music under Wilberforce J. Whiteman, father of Paul Whiteman
Sidemen With Band Included Sy Oliver, Willie Smith, Edmund Wilcox, Paul Webster, Eddie Tompkins, Russell Bowles, Elmer Crumbley, Eddie Durham, Earl Carruthers, Laforet Dent, Joe Thomas, Dan Grissom, Al Norris, Moses Allen, James Crawford, Trummy Young, Gerald Wilson
Vocalists With Band Included Dan Grissom, Sy Oliver, Joe Thomas, Henry Wells, Trummy Young
Theme Song "Jazznocracy," "Uptown Blues"
Recording Affiliations Victor, Decca, Vocalion, Columbia

Jimmie Lunceford.

Lunceford was born in Fulton, Missouri, on June 2, 1902. Somewhat later his parents moved to Denver, Colorado where he spent his boyhood and attended high school. During this period he also studied music under Wilberforce Whiteman. His formal education was completed at Fiske University and City College in New York. The band which he started in Memphis in 1927 was originally called the Chickasaw Syncopaters. They moved into the New York area and had become quite well established by the early thirties. His earliest recordings, made for Victor, produced only mediocre sales. After his switch to Decca in the fall of 1934, his discs began to catch on, adding a great deal to his reputation on a national basis.

Early in his bandleading career, Lunceford signed Harold Oxley to manage him. That association played a big part in the band's success. Oxley did a masterful job of promoting and publicizing the band, maintaining contact with all dance promoters coast-to-coast. Every important opening and tour was announced by postcard. At Christmas he sent greeting cards signed by both himself and Lunceford. I still have some of these in my file, received when I was promoting one-nighters in Southern Oregon in the late thirties and early forties. In the early months of 1940 Lunceford toured the West Coast, and I was offered the band for a February one-nighter at $500, a price which seems small now, but which was considered good money then, and on a level with most other top-rated bands who played the Pacific Northwest at that time. A prior commitment for an MCA band the same week prevented our using him.

Lunceford's greatest strength was in ballrooms, theaters, and colleges where he always drew big audiences. Aside from his theater engagements and his stands at such spots as the College Inn, the Fiesta Danceteria, and the Casa Manana in Culver City, he was usually on the one-nighter trail. Although he was master of all the reed instruments and even played trombone, he seldom played any of them when fronting the band. The Lunceford band was always made up of great instrumentalists, but they were not given the opportunity to perform often as soloists. It was a precision band, built around ensemble and section work rather than soloists.

The peak years of his popularity were from 1935 to about 1943. During World War II he faced the same personnel problems as other leaders, but managed to keep the band on the road. Perhaps he would have recaptured his old momentum in the post-war years had not fate intervened. On a tour of the Pacific Northwest he suffered a heart attack while playing a celebration in Astoria, Oregon, and died on July 12, 1947.

The great Jimmie Lunceford Band in the early 1940s.

ABE LYMAN

Started First Band   Early twenties
Where   Los Angeles
Previous Band Affiliations   Theater bands in the Chicago area
Sidemen With Band Included   Ray Lopez, Jim Welton, Howard Fenimore, Slim Martin, Al Baker, Horace Keyes, John Schonberger, Charles Kaley, Gus Arnheim, Charlie Pierce, Jake Garcia, Jimmie Grier, Al Newman, Fred Ferguson, Harry Podalsky, Teddy Powell, Dave Herman, Ted Dale, Ed Landry, Warren Smith, Arthur Most, Tommy Macey, Marty Gold, Carmen Cavallaro, Frank Parrish, Jack Pleis, Yank Lawson, Bill Clark, Frank Bruno, Ted Sandow, Gil Bowers, Murray Gaer, Al Pollack, Don Moore, Si Zentner
Vocalists With Band Included   Frank Sylvano, Phil Meely, Dick Robertson, Smith Ballew, Gracie Barrie, Sonny Schuyler, Barry Wood, Rose Blane, Billy Sherman
Tag Line   "Abe Lyman and his Californians"
Sponsored Radio Shows   NBC's "Waltz Time"
Theme Song   "California, Here I Come," "Moon Over America"
Songs Written   "Mary Lou," "Mandalay," "After I Say I'm Sorry," "I Cried For You"
Recording Affiliations   Brunswick, Decca, Bluebird

Lyman always headquartered on the West Coast but his territory was the forty-eight states and the continent of Europe. He was a drummer and learned his trade working in Chicago movie houses for as little as $5 per week, and sometimes for no pay at all. In later years he was able to laugh about being fired from one such nonpaying job because the management decided that even without salary they didn't want him in their band.

He was still quite young when he moved to Santa Monica, California, and it was there he formed his first band. He took it into the Ship Cafe in Venice, a spot patronized regularly by such movie stars as Norma Talmadge, Gloria Swanson, Bebe Daniels, and Thomas Meighan. They became his friends and decided he deserved better things. They prevailed upon Abe Frank of the Ambassador Hotel to audition the band, with the result that Lyman was invited to enlarge his orchestra and go into the Cocoanut Grove. They opened there in 1921 for an engagement which Lyman considered one of the highlights of his career. He remained there until 1926.

Abe Lyman.

When he left the Grove he made an Eastern tour, and then went to Europe to play the Kit Kat Klub and the London Palladium, as well as the Moulin Rouge and Perroquet in Paris. By the time he returned to the states he had both a national and international reputation, which was further enhanced by radio remotes and records which were selling well.

Lyman's philosophy of music was to give the public something it understood and he usually presented a balanced program pleasing to both the young and older people in his audience. That formula kept him busy in the nation's top locations throughout the thirties and well into the forties. *Billboard* magazine's special band issue of September 28, 1940, describes his activities for that year as having included an engagement at Chicago's Bon Air Country Club, the Royal Palm Club in Florida, the Beverly Hills Country Club in Cincinnati, the Casa Manana in Fort Worth and the Chez Paree in Chicago. It was about that time that the Lyman

Lyman at the microphone with vocalist Rose Blane, who was also Mrs. Lyman.

band began making weekly appearances on NBC's "Waltz Time." This show was still doing well in 1947, with Lyman still at the helm and drawing good ratings. In 1946 he also produced and appeared in a series of musical shorts called *Junior Prom*, turned out by Monogram.

In the late forties he retired from music to go into the insurance business and make his home in Beverly Hills with his wife Rose Blane, who had shared the bandstand with him for several years as featured vocalist. He died in 1957 at the age of 61.

The Lyman band in an appearance during World War II.

M

CLYDE McCOY

Started First Band 1920
Where Louisville, Kentucky
Previous Band Affiliations Walter Davidson
Sidemen With Band Included Bud Prentiss, John Cameron, Bobby Blair, Johnny Petrone, Freddy Taylor, Stanley McCoy, Mel Wilke, Tommy Miller, Eddie Lowth, Jack Fina, Mike Waller, Bud Smith, Frank Wagner, Lou Bush, Dale Butts, Eddie Kusby, Robbie Turk, Frank Carlson
Vocalists With Band Included Freddie Stewart, Rosalind Marquis, Wayne Gregg, The Bennett Sisters
Theme Song "Sugar Blues"
Recording Affiliations Columbia, Decca, Capitol

Clyde McCoy.

McCoy was born in Ashland, Kentucky and, according to press releases turned out after he became a popular bandleader, he was a descendant of the famous family which had the long feud with the Hatfields. With the band which he organized in 1928 he attained national prominence in the mid-thirties when his Decca recording of "Sugar Blues" became a big hit, eventually selling over a million copies. It was his band which in 1936 followed Benny Goodman's phenomenal engagement at New York's Paramount Theater, when the youthful fans were dancing in the aisles to the newly crowned "King of Swing." His trademarks were "Sugar Blues" and also his muted solos, on both his full-sized trumpets and a miniature model which he used for specialty numbers. An old Palomar program from the late thirties pictures the band as having twelve instrumentalists in addition to McCoy, with vocals done by the three Bennett Sisters and Wayne Gregg. Maxine Bennett eventually became Mrs. McCoy.

In 1942 McCoy surprised the music world by enlisting in the navy, taking his entire band with him. At the war's end he returned to the band business, this time with a somewhat larger organization of fifteen instrumentalists and two vocalists. He had little difficulty in picking up where he left off and remained active for several years, finally retiring in 1955 to take care of other business interests, including a Denver night club. He came out of retirement in 1960, organizing a Dixieland group which opened at the Round Table in New York. The reception was so encouraging that he once again took to the road to enjoy a whole new wave of popularity with this smaller group, which weathered the sixties and continued unabated into the seventies. In the mid-seventies he was still playing clubs from coast to coast, including the Nevada casinos. With a sharp little six-piece group sparked by his muted trumpet he booked solidly, playing to audiences ranging in age from their early twenties to some who were his fans in the 1930s. Eventually he retired to his home in Memphis where he died on June 11, 1990 at the age of 86, a victim of Alzheimer's disease.

The Bennett Sisters, who had joined the McCoy band in 1937, were the featured vocalists along with Wayne Gregg in 1938.

BILLY McDONALD

Started First Band 1936
Where Balboa, California
Previous Band Affiliations Carol Lofner, CBS staff
Sidemen With Band Included Ernie Barrell, Leon Gray, Harry Forbes, Hi Davidson, Ollie Mitchell, Bill Lamberton, Ian Bernard, Bob Handaway, and others

Tag Line Billy McDonald and the Royal Highlanders
Longest Engagement Florentine Gardens, Hollywood (two-and-a-half years)
Theme Song "Loch Lomond"
Songs Written "Friendly Arms and Western Skies," "I'm Going Home," "Everybody Dance," "It's A Rainy Day," "The Meaning

In the late 1950s, McCoy found a new career with a small band.

of Aloha," "Manoa," "Silver Isles," "Hula Drums"

Recording Affiliations Decca, D & S Records. Also Standard Transcriptions

Prior to starting his own band, McDonald had been a vocalist with the Carol Lofner orchestra and on the CBS staff in Hollywood. With Kay Thompson he formed a trio called the Three Midshipmen, which was featured by CBS on an eleven-western-state network, with McDonald as the soloist. By 1940 he had established himself as a bandleader, playing repeat engagements in the top West Coast ballrooms and in the Midwest, where he played the hotel and ball-room circuit. In the fall of 1941 he took his band to Honolulu, where they were playing when Pearl Harbor was attacked in December of that year. McDonald returned to the states and kept busy until he entered the service himself in 1942. After the war he reorganized a band with which he once again played most of the same locations he had covered in the prewar years. About 1948 he gave up his career as a bandleader to join the Fredericks Brothers Agency, later switching to William Morris, and in the early fifties joined the Associated Booking Corporation in its Hollywood office, where he is still working.

Billy McDonald and his orchestra in Honolulu, November 1941; Travis Pirtle; trumpets—Arnold Kay, Ollie Sudderman; drums—Glenn Redmond; bass—Ernie Barrell; piano—Art Roach; saxophones—Bert Dilly, Roy Noble, unidentified; violins—Hy Davidson and company; Billy McDonald; vocals—Dawn Meridith.

The McFarland twins—Art and George—and their orchestra.

THE McFARLAND TWINS

Started First Band Late thirties
Vocalists With Band Included Betty Engels, Dick Merrick, The Norton Sisters
Theme Song "Darkness"
Recording Affiliations Okeh

The McFarland Twins were saxophone-playing brothers who organized a dance band in the late thirties, styled in what was generally described as "Mickey Mouse," and which depended on a glee club for its presentation as much as on the musicianship of the band. In the early forties they switched their style to a more solid organization with a well-arranged library and featuring the piano work of Geoff Clarkson. It was a good hotel and ballroom band, and with it they kept busy for several years, winning a great deal of popularity because of the unusual twin-leadership arrangement. Shortly after World War II the band dropped from sight.

HAL McINTYRE

Started First Band 1941 (Had a previous brief attempt with own band in mid-thirties)
Where New York City
Previous Band Affiliations Glenn Miller, Smith Ballew, Dorsey brothers, Jimmy Dorsey
Sidemen With Band Included "Steady" Nelson, Clarence Willard, Bill Rubenstein, Paul McCoy, Don Ruppersberg, Howard Gibeling, Vic Hamann, Dave Mathews, John Dee, Larry Kinsey, Bob Poland, Jack Lathrop, Danny Hurd, Eddie Safranski, Ralph Tilken, Louis Mucci, Dick Rollins, Art Mendelsen. Arrangements were by Dave Mathews, Billy May, and Howard Gibeling
Vocalists With Band Included Penny Parker, Carl Denny, Jeanne McManus
Theme Song "Moon Mist," "Ecstasy"
Recording Affiliations Victor, Cosmo

Hal McIntyre.

McIntyre's band was launched with financial help from Glenn Miller. Like Miller, it was an engagement at the Glen Island Casino which gave him national prominence. In 1942 and again in 1943, he was voted in a college poll conducted by *Billboard* magazine, the most promising new orchestra. For the next several years his music was heard in the top hotels, theaters, and ballrooms in the country, including Frank Dailey's Meadowbrook and the Hollywood Palladium. He was the first leader to take his entire band on an overseas tour to entertain troops during World War II. During the mid-forties he appeared with his orchestra in at least two motion pictures for Paramount. In the postwar period he remained quite active, primarily in the Midwest and South and on the East Coast. In the late fifties he moved to the West Coast to live. In May 1959, at a time when he was preparing to organize for a Las Vegas lounge engagement, he was severely burned in a Los Angeles apartment house fire, and died a few days later in General Hospital at the age of 44.

The Hal McIntyre Orchestra on the stand at the Arcadia Ballroom.

MARION McKAY

Started First Band   Early twenties
Where   Indiana
Sidemen With Band Included   Ambrose Barringer, Le Roy Morris, Doc Marshall, Ernie McKay, Russell Mock, Henry Lang, George Agonost, Paul Weirick, Izzy George, Terry George, Skinny Budd, Harry Bason, Ed Johns, Jack Tillson, Roger Beals, Clem Johnson, Red Ginslar, Ernie Weaver, Marlin Skiles, Eddie Page
Vocalists With Band Included   Jack Tillson, Fred Stuart
Theme Song   "Dreamy Melody"
Recording Affiliations   Gennett

McKay was a banjo player who usually fronted an organization made up of three brass, three reeds, piano, bass and drums. His was one of the first bands to try what was then the new electrical recording system in Gennett's Richmond, Indiana studios. The attempt was not too successful and the initial sides were all scrapped, probably more the result of Gennett's inexperience with the new system than the efforts put forth by the band. McKay's was a territory band concentrating in the Richmond, Cincinnati, Cleveland, and Detroit areas but trumpeter-arranger Paul Weirick recalls at least one booking into New York for a night club engagement. McKay gave up his bandleading career in the mid-thirties.

RAY McKINLEY

Started First Band   1942, a short-lived venture broken up by the war, next band formed in 1946
Where   New York City
Previous Band Affiliations   The Duncan-Marin Orchestra, Beasley Smith, Tracy Brown, Smith Ballew, the Dorsey Brothers Orchestra, Will Bradley, (co-leader), Glen Miller
Sidemen With Band Included   Mahlon Clark, Brad Gowans, Dick Cathcart, Pete Condoli, Ray Beller, Deane Kincaide, Bill Ainsworth,

Marion McKay's orchestra, 1925, including: "Izzy" George, Elmer Hicks, Russ Mock, Ed John, Jack Gilson, Ralph Budd, Ernest McKay, Cliff Lang, Terry E. George, Paul Weirick.

"Peanuts" Hucko, Pete Terry, Mundell Lowe, Lou Stein, Paul Kashion, Vern Friley, Irv Dinkin, Jim Howard, Chuck Genduso, Joe Ferrante, Curly Broyles, Johnny Chance, Johnny Carisi, Ernie Terry, Nick Travis, Jim Harwood, Johnny Patoka, Johnny Gray. Arrangements were by Deane Kincaide and Eddie Sauter

Vocalists With Band Included McKinley did male vocals himself

Theme Song "Howdy, Friends"

Songs Written "My Guy's Come Back," "Howdy, Friends," "So Sweet," "Naughty But Nice"

Recording Affiliations Majestic, RCA Camden

McKinley's rightful image as a bandleader was probably diminished by the fact that for a ten-year period (1956 to 1966) he fronted the Glenn Miller orchestra and became too well identified in the public mind with the Miller music. In that capacity he was in a sense keeping the Miller sound alive, a first lieutenant or stand-in directing a band whose style was completely determined and from which there was no deviation. That image is incorrect, for McKinley very definitely had a musical identity which was all his own and the result of his own efforts.

His association with Miller began in the early thirties in the Smith Ballew orchestra, and continued when both played with the Dorsey Brothers band. When that band broke up in 1935 McKinley stayed with Jimmy for approximately four years. During that time he began to develop himself as a vocalist as well as a drummer. In 1940 he

279

joined up with trombonist Will Bradley to form a band, with the two billed as co-leaders. Primarily because his instrument better lent itself to fronting a band, Bradley became the front man. Managed by Willard Alexander the band was given heavy promotion and garnered a lot of space in music trade journals as well as in the conventional press. Within a year they were playing top locations, including New York's Famous Door and the Paramount Theater. Unfortunately the success they were enjoying was not enough to hold the band together. The built-in problems of having two leaders finally resulted in a breakup early in 1942.

McKinley immediately formed a band of his own which also included a rather impressive list of sidemen. Six months later, however, the draft caught up with most of its members including Ray. He was inducted into the service, where he immediately joined up with his old friend Glenn Miller and became a member of the Army Air Force Band. He remained with the unit throughout the war, and upon Glenn's tragic death in December 1944 McKinley was chosen to lead the band during its remaining eight months on the European continent.

Back home after the war, he once more formed an orchestra under his own name, launching it early in 1946. The arrange-

Drummer McKinley in action, 1946 or 1947.

ments for this band were written by Deane Kincaide and Eddie Sauter and musically it was rated as a top flight organization. A number of recordings were turned out, including six sides of Sauter originals done on the RCA Camden label. A few years earlier this band would probably have become very

Ray McKinley and his orchestra at the Commodore Hotel, New York City, 1946 or 1947: trumpets—Chuck Genduso, Joe Ferrante, Curley Broyles; trombones—Vern Friley, Irv Dinkin, Jim Howard; saxophones—Ray Beller, Dean Kincaide, Bill Ainsworth, Peanuts Hucko, Pete Terry; guitar—Mundell Lowe; piano—Lou Stein; drums—Paul Kashion; bass—Johnny Chance.

successful, but in the postwar years the downward trend of the nationwide band business overcame it. Triggered by some health problems, McKinley disbanded the group in late 1948. For a time he did a stint as a disc jockey and worked on the Morey Amsterdam television show.

Because of his previous association with the Miller band he was asked to take over its direction in 1956 when Tex Beneke gave it up. After ten years spent touring the United States, Europe, and Japan, McKinley tired of the constant travelling. He turned the band over to Buddy De Franco, and settled down to a quieter life working in television commercials and radio. He resides in Stamford, Connecticut.

McKINNEY'S COTTON PICKERS

Started First Band Mid-twenties
Where Detroit
Previous Band Affiliations Bill McKinney was a drummer who worked with small groups in the Springfield, Ohio and Detroit areas
Sidemen With Band Included Underwent constant change but included Benny Carter, Coleman Hawkins, Rex Stewart, Fats Waller, James P. Johnson, Todd Rhodes, Tench Robinson, Claude Jones, Quentin Jackson, Hilton Jefferson, Don Redman
Theme Song "If I Could Be With You One Hour"
Recording Affiliations Victor, Okeh

McKinney's Cotton Pickers.

This band was actually put together by Jean Goldkette and worked out of his Graystone Ballroom along with the other bands which Goldkette booked. They were constantly on tour throughout the Middle West, and even though McKinney gave the group its name he was seldom in front of it. Most of the time the band was under the direction of Don Redman, with McKinney as its business manager. The practice of the day was to fea- ture one or more bands on the same evening in "a battle of the bands" and McKinney's Cotton Pickers were constantly involved in that type of booking. The orchestra was considered one of the best black jazz orchestras of the late thirties. Recordings were made under various names including "The Chocolate Dandies." The band broke up in the mid-thirties and McKinney left the music business permanently.

JIMMY McPARTLAND

Started First Band   Mid-thirties
Where   Chicago area
Previous Band Affiliations   The Wolverines, Art Kassel, Ben Pollack, Benny Goodman, Russ Columbo, Horace Heidt, Smith Ballew, Harry Reser
Sidemen With Band Included   George Wettling, Joe Harris, Rosie McHargue, Royce Brown, Joe Rushton
Recording Affiliations   Decca

Although McPartland's activity as a leader was during the big band era, his unit was not a large band but usually a jazz-oriented group of no more than eight musicians, including himself on trumpet. His band was popular in the Middle West and New York City. After his first band was broken up in 1941, he joined the Jack Teagarden band, remaining there until he entered World War II service with the army. After the war he gained some experience as an actor and also occasionally led his own group.

Jimmy McPartland and his band, at the Three Deuces, Chicago, 1939.

The Jay McShann Orchestra.

JAY McSHANN

Started First Band   Early thirties
Where   Kansas City
Previous Band Affiliations   Played piano with local bands
Sidemen With Band Included   Little information available except for the fact that sax man Charlie Parker got his early start with this band
Recording Affiliations   Decca, Capitol

McShann was born in Oklahoma but migrated to Kansas City before he was twenty years old. Kansas City in the early thirties was one of the nation's musically great cities, with a wealth of fine black bands working around and out of there. McShann, who had become an accomplished pianist, fit readily into the scene and soon formed a band of his own. He lost little time in building it to a stature worthy of the Kansas City scene at that time. In the mid-thirties the newly formed Decca label signed up the band, thereby substantially increasing its popularity. In the early forties McShann made an East Coast tour, doing ballroom and theater dates, and at one time during that tour featured Al Hibbler on vocals. The band was broken up when McShann went into the army. He returned from service at the end of 1944. With a new band, he recorded for Capitol, including some sessions with Julia Lee. In the late forties he was working in the Hollywood area leading a small blues-oriented group. In the late fifties he returned to Kansas City to work as a single in night-clubs and was still active in that area during the early sixties.

ENRIC MADRIGUERA

Started First Band   Late twenties
Where   New York
Sidemen With Band Included   Joe Brittain,
John Fisher, Ray Hopfner, Bill Michails,
Jimmy Carroll, Rocky Jordan, Roger Haller,
Ernie Warren, Frank Carroll, Miguel Can-
dia, Tito Rodriguez, Alfredo Jamesworth,
James Cuarana, Miguel Duchene, Art Fos-
ter, Rocky "Rocco" Galgano, Fred Dombach,
Bernard Lazaroff, Harry Bloom, Jim Mig-
liore, Jimmy Dillon, Sol Amato, William
Mikulas, Tony de Simone, Pete Ippilito,
Leon Kellner, James Pasquerelli
Vocalists With Band Included   Tony Sacco,
Helen Dell, Patricia Gilmore (Mrs. Madri-
guera)
Theme Song   "Adios"
Songs Written   "Adios," "Forbidden Love,"
"Take It Away," "Flowers of Spain," "Min-
ute Samba," "The Language of Love"
Recording Affiliations   Columbia, Bruns-
wick, Victor, Decca

Enric Madriguera.

Madriguera was a pioneer in establishing
Latin-American music in the United States,
a style which was copied by others later.
Born in Barcelona, Spain, he studied music
at the Barcelona Conservatory and participated in concert tours as a youngster. His
instrument was violin. Before coming to
America, he was musical director for Columbia Records in South America for a brief
period of time. The American orchestra
which he formed in the late twenties played
its initial engagement at the Biltmore Roof
in New York. Radio time from that spot
earned him a recording contract which contributed substantially to his popularity.
Throughout the thirties and forties he
toured the nation, usually playing theaters
and hotels. In the early fifties he gave up his
bandleading career and dropped out of the
limelight.

MUZZY MARCELLINO

Started First Band   1938
Where   San Francisco
Previous Band Affiliations   The Lofner-
Harris Orchestra, Ted Fio Rito
Vocalists With Band Included   Gloria De
Haven, Marcellino handled male vocals him-
self
Theme Song   "I'll Take An Option On You"
Longest Engagement   Florentine Gardens
in Hollywood

Marcellino was born in San Francisco, where
he studied violin and guitar, breaking into
the music business at an early age with the
Lofner-Harris band at the Hotel St. Francis.
When Ted Fio Rito came into the St. Francis in 1932, Marcellino went to work for him
and during the next six years was featured
not only as the band's guitarist but also as
its male vocalist. During that time he also
worked with the Fio Rito band in such mo-

Muzzy Marcellino.

tion pictures as *The Sweetheart of Sigma Chi*, *Twenty Million Sweethearts*, and *Broadway Gondolier*. When he launched his own bandleading career in 1938, his first job was at Topsy's Restaurant in San Francisco. For the next several years he toured, primarily on the West Coast, playing hotels, amusement parks, and one-nighters. In the mid-forties he gave up a full-size band to work with smaller combinations playing Southern California locations, with occasional assignments in Las Vegas and Reno. In 1950 he joined the "Art Linkletter Show" as its musical director, a position which he maintained until the show went off the air in 1969. Since that time he has worked intermittently with small groups, keeping busy with the private party circuit. One of the few accomplished whistlers, he is the one called on when there is a whistling assignment on records, commercials, or in a motion picture.

RALPH MARTERIE

Started First Band   1946
Where   Chicago
Previous Band Affiliations   Paul Whiteman, Percy Faith, and studio work at NBC and ABC
Sidemen With Band Included   Joe Farrel, Jack Gaylo, George Roumanis, Charlie Callas
Vocalists With Band Included   Bill Walters, Janice Borla, Lou Prano
Sponsored Radio Shows   "Marlboro Cigarettes Show"
Television With Band   Guest shots but appeared on a program produced by station WGN, "The Cavalcade of Bands"
Theme Song   "Carla"
Songs Written   "Carla," "Truly"
Recording Affiliations   Mercury, United Artists, Musicor

Marterie's group started out as a recording orchestra and personal appearances followed later. One of his earliest engagements was at the Melody Mill Ballroom, where air time

Ralph Marterie.

began to make the band well known throughout the Midwest. Even though the band business began to decline during the late forties, Marterie built himself a strong position, one which retained its stability well into the fifties. During that time he appeared at Frank Dailey's Meadowbrook on the East Coast, the Hollywood Palladium on the West Coast, and most of the entertainment spots in between. Eventually he established an entertainment agency of his own in Chicago where, along with other units he kept his own band semiactive in the Midwestern area. He passed away on October 8, 1978.

FREDDY MARTIN

Started First Band 1931
Where Bossert Hotel, Brooklyn
Previous Band Affiliations The Mason-Dixon Orchestra, Arnold Johnson, Jack Albin
Sidemen With Band Included Bunny Berigan, Elmer Feldkamp, Elmer Rehmus, Joe Poretta, Jack Condon, Benny Eaton, Ross Dickson, Al Wagner, Terry Shand, Bobby Van Eps, George Van Eps, George Green, Manny Weinstock, Russ Morgan, Jack Fina, Al King, Harry McKeenan, Russ Klein, George Jean, Bill Stoker, Gene Walsh, Glenn Hughes, Ed Turley, Eddie Stone, Norman Bailey, Clyde Rogers, Eddie Bergman, Murray Arnold, Barclay Allan, Abe Siegel, Johnny Cochran, Dave Leonard, Jerry Kadovitz
Vocalists With Band Included Vivian Ruth, Lois Ellison, Russ Morgan, Gene Vaughan, Buddy Clark, Eddie Stone, Clyde Rogers, Bill Stoker, Stuart Wade, Merv Griffin, Johnny Cochran, Marty Barris
Sponsored Radio Shows "The Elizabeth Arden Show," "The American Oil Show," "The Maybelline Show," "The Campbell Soup Show," the "Lady Esther Serenade"
Television With Band A network all-band show which ran for two years in the early fifties. Later television attempts were on specials and a local West Coast show
Theme Songs "Bye-Lo-Bye Lullaby," "Early In The Morning," "Tonight We Love"
Recording Affiliations Columbia, Brunswick, Bluebird, Victor, Capitol

Martin began his musical career the hard way, demonstrating saxophones in a Cleveland music store. Prior to that, his interest in music developed in a Springfield, Ohio orphanage, where he lived from the time he

Freddy Martin and "Concerto," 1948.

was four years old until he was sixteen. Initially he had hoped to earn enough money from his musical work to finance a course in journalism at Ohio State. Instead he ended up as a full-fledged musician.

After a not too inspiring period spent working with a ship's orchestra, he played with the Mason-Dixon orchestra, then with Arnold Johnson and Jack Albin. When Albin retired from the music business, Martin was encouraged by Guy Lombardo, who had become his friend, to form an orchestra of his own. He did so, and with it he opened at the Marine Roof of the Bossert Hotel, in New York, on October 1, 1931. He remained there until 1934.

After the Bossert there followed appearances in other major New York hotels, in-

Freddy Martin and his orchestra at Chicago's Aragon Ballroom, 1936. Pianist Jack Fina had just joined the band that year.

cluding the Roosevelt, the Waldorf-Astoria the Ritz-Carlton, and the St. Regis. Then, after playing Chicago's best hotels, and the Aragon Ballroom, he went to the West Coast to play the St. Francis Hotel. In 1938 Martin played his first engagement at the Cocoanut Grove in Los Angeles. During the following years he played there so often that his fans gave him the title of "Mr. Cocoanut Grove."

Early in the forties, with the help of pianist Jack Fina, he began adapting the classics to popular tempos. His Victor recording of "Tonight We Love," based on Tschaikowsky's Piano Concerto No. 1 became one of the nation's biggest hits. This was followed by a long string of Martin hits, all adding to the stature of the band. In addition to his Cocoanut Grove assignments, he appeared on numerous sponsored radio shows, and made several motion picture appearances with the band. During the war years his absences from the Grove bandstand were very brief, until he took an extended tour in 1948. That "annual tour—back to the Grove" routine continued to be his pattern of operation well into the sixties, until the Grove finally went under new management and a total modification, including a change of policy.

In the early seventies he went into semi-retirement, moving to the Balboa Bay Club at Newport Beach, California, and confining his musical activities to playing special events, with occasional Midwestern tours and appearances in Las Vegas hotels. In the fall of 1972 he went on tour with the "Big Band Cavalcade," a musical production featuring three bandleaders alternating and fronting one band made up of some of Hollywood's ace sidemen along with the regular Martin crew. Most of the dates played were concerts, but the tour included some dance engagements. In addition to himself the headliners were Bob Crosby and Frankie Carle, with Margaret Whiting, never identified with big bands, presented as a vocal attraction. The success of the tour prompted repeats for the next two or three years. In 1977 Martin, a lifelong friend of Guy Lombardo, was asked to front the Lombardo band on tour while Lombardo was hospitalized with the heart condition that finally caused his death. He remained semi-active during the early '80s, primarily on the West Coast. He passed away in a Newport Beach hospital on October 1, 1983, after a lingering illness. He was 76 years old.

287

Freddy Martin on the Cocoanut Grove bandstand, 1952.

FRANKIE MASTERS

Started First Band   Late twenties
Where   Chicago
Previous Band Affiliations   Campus and theater house bands
Sidemen With Band Included   Woody Kessler, Jerry Borchard, Steve Brown, Jay Mathews, Stuart Charles, Bill Pritchard, Kahn Keene, Vincent Ferrine, Buddy Shiffman, Carl Bean, Howard Barkell, Don Elton, Buss Dillon, Orin Crippen, Ray Noonan, Johnny Barshark, Phil Gray, Joe Reisman, Eddie Baxter, Hy Lesnick, Morty Nathan, Fred Smith, Jimmy Nash, Bill Aimesworth, Jack Wald, Bobby Lewis, Max Anderson, Irving Trisco, Don Bell, Billy Johnson
Vocalists With Band Included   Harlan Rogers, Gordon Goodman, Lou Hurst, Phyllis Miles, The Swing Masters, the Masters Voices, Marion Francis
Theme Song   "Moonlight And You," "Scatterbrain"
Recording Affiliations   Victor, Vocalion, Okeh, Columbia, Mercury

Frankie Masters.

Like many other bandleaders Masters started his musical career while in college, where he enjoyed enough success to give him the incentive to make it a lifetime profession.

Eventually he dropped out of school to take a job in the house band of a leading Chicago theater, remaining there for several years, until he finally organized a band of his own. Initial engagements for his own crew were also in Chicago theaters. He died in October 1990 at age 86.

288

Frankie Masters and his orchestra at the Roosevelt Hotel, New York, in the early 1940s.

Eventually he was booked into the College Inn of the Sherman Hotel, for an engagement which lasted nearly four years. Nightly air time built up his reputation. But it was also during that period that he recorded "Scatterbrain," which quickly became a hit record, making Masters a national attraction. He invaded New York for successful engagements at the Pennsylvania, Taft, and Essex House Hotels, then went to the West Coast for two years, playing leading theaters and hotels in that area.

By the early forties his was one of the most steadily booked bands in the business, with a musical style combining both sweet and swing, and aimed at pleasing the dancing public. A 1942 *Billboard* review described it as "one of the few bands able to go into absolutely any kind of spot and be perfectly at home." When the Coca Cola Company launched its "Victory Parade of Spotlight Bands," Masters became one of its most frequent guest leaders. During the four years the program was on the air only one other bandleader appeared more often than he.

At the end of the war he spent several months on the West Coast at the St. Francis Hotel. Then he returned to Chicago where he was booked into the Stevens Hotel (now the Conrad Hilton) for an engagement which lasted several years. With the decline in the band business he went into semiretirement for a few years, making his home in Cary, Illinois, but returned to activity in the late sixties. In the mid-seventies he was still busy, concentrating on convention dates and special events in the Chicago area, with occasional out-of-town trips, usually private engagements. Masters was always a very capable front man but in addition handled many of the vocal numbers himself and occasionally played the guitar. His best-known female vocalist was Phyllis Miles, who soon became Mrs. Masters.

289

BILLY MAY

Started First Band   1952
Where   Los Angeles
Previous Band Affiliations   Barron Elliot, Charlie Barnet, Glenn Miller, Alvino Rey, plus arranging for many other bands
Vocalists With Band Included   Peggy Barrett, The Encores
Theme Song   "Lean Baby"
Recording Affiliations   Capitol

Peggy Barrett.

May's bandleading career was of short duration. It was launched after a lavish publicity buildup by Capitol Records, in the hope that they could accomplish what Victor had done with Ralph Flanagan. The band toured the country with only moderate success despite the fine musicianship of May, a well-qualified group of sidemen, and some fine arrangements. After two years on the road May tired of his bandleading duties, and the band, financed by Ray Anthony, was turned over to Sam Donahue. May settled down in Hollywood to concentrate on his arranging. In short order he was in big demand in both television and motion pictures. He also continued to arrange periodically for various bands, particularly for recording sessions. When the Time-Life series of big band records was produced in Capitol's studios in the early seventies, May did a great deal of the arranging, and also directed the entire series.

BENNY MEROFF

Started First Band   Mid-twenties
Previous Band Affiliations   None. Had been in vaudeville
Sidemen With Band Included   Norman Hendrickson, Harold White, Gene Gory, Pete Ross, Bill Hughes, Hymie Milrod, Al de Vito, M. Clauberg, Phil Grossi, Wild Bill Davison, Joe Rullo, Joe Quartell, Lenny Cohen, Tony Ciccone, Arnold Pritikin, Al Nillson, George Physter, Bennie Metz, Roy Cole, Al King, Larry Powell, Elmer Eberhardt, Meyer Druzinsky, Vernon Brown, Jack Marshall, Irving Barnett, Don Ellis, Bill Gollin, Marty Ross, Phil Stevens, Johnny Perrin, Danny Lynch, Al d'Artega, Fred Brown, "Mouse" Powell, "Pappy" Graham, Tommy Thomas, Santo Pecora, Carl Osborne, Rudy Bundy, "Red" Pepper
Theme Song   "Diane"
Songs Written   "What's the Use of Cryin' the Blues?," "Wherever You Go"
Recording Affiliations   Victor, Okeh, Columbia

Although Meroff concentrated on stage work, he was also quite active on the dance band circuit at various periods in his career. Playing both violin and saxophone-clarinet, he led a band which was usually made up of the top musicians of the day. In the late

The Billy May Orchestra at the Pennsylvania Hotel, New York.

twenties and early thirties the style of his band was predominantly jazz, with emphasis on showmanship. Meroff was a capable emcee, equally at home either conducting the band for dancing or directing a complicated stage show. Most of Meroff's time was spent in the Chicago area, particularly during the late twenties and early thirties. But throughout the thirties and into the forties he made periodic trips into New York to play hotel and theater locations. In the late forties he became semiactive, eventually giving up the band entirely for other interests. He died in 1973 at the age of seventy-two.

JOHNNY MESSNER

Started First Band 1936
Where New York City
Previous Band Affiliations Dick Messner
Sidemen With Band Included Shorty Skipper, Charles Cerborra, Shanty Diamant, Huff Allen, George Ward, Will Cottrell, Paul Kuhl, Augie Gonzales, Dick Cornell, Al Dell, Charles Gallant, Bobby King, Russell Moss
Vocalists With Band Included Gladys Tell, Jeanne D'Arcy, Mindy Carson

Sponsored Radio Shows Guest appearances on "Spotlight Bands" and "Fitch Bandwagon"
Longest Engagement Seven years at Hotel McAlpin
Theme Song "Can't We Be Friends?"
Songs Written "Catching the 802 Local," "Toy Piano Minuet," "Toy Piano Jump," "Piano Roll Rock," "Sing For Joy"
Recording Affiliations Brunswick, Vocalion, Bluebird, Varsity, Decca

Messner was one of five musical brothers who went on radio from New York in 1924. He was a graduate of New York's Institute of Musical Arts and an expert on all the reed instruments. He was also a skilled arranger. The band which he fronted was a hotel-style band, usually not more than twelve musicians with a vocalist. He and the band ap-peared in one or more motion pictures made by Paramount. He broke up his band to go into the army during World War II and did not resume as a leader at war's end. But he did remain in the music business, concentrating his activities on writing and producing advertising jingles for radio and television.

Johnny Messner and his orchestra.

GLENN MILLER

Started First Band 1937
Where New York City, first location job at the Roosevelt Hotel in New Orleans
Previous Band Affiliations Boyd Senter, Max Fisher, Georgie Stoll, Ben Pollack, Paul Ashe, Red Nichols, Smith Ballew, the Dorsey Brothers, Ray Noble
Sidemen With Band Included Leigh Knowles, John Best, Dale McMickle, Clyde Hurley, Paul Tanner, Jim Priddy, Frank D'Anolfo, Willie Schwartz, Al Klink, Hal McIntyre, Ernie Caceres, Tex Beneke, Maurice Purtill, Rollie Bundock, Chummy MacGregor, Billy May, Ray Anthony, Trigger Alpert, Jack Lathrop, Charlie Spivak, Claude Thornhill, Jerry Gray

Vocalists With Band Included Ray Eberle, Paula Kelly and the Modernaires, Gail Reese, Linda Keene, Dorothy Claire, Marian Hutton, Skip Nelson, Tex Beneke
Sponsored Radio Shows "The Chesterfield Supper Club"
Motion Pictures With Band *Sun Valley Serenade, Orchestra Wives*
Theme Song "Moonlight Serenade"
Recording Affiliations Decca, Bluebird, Victor

Glenn Miller's civilian bandleading career covered less than six years. But in that brief period he made a musical impression which has scarcely diminished more than thirty-

Glenn Miller.

five years after he played his last professional engagement.

Born in Iowa in 1904, he moved with his family first to Nebraska, and then to Fort Morgan, Colorado, where he studied music during high school and played on the football team. Soon after graduation from high school in 1921, he took his first professional job with the Boyd Senter orchestra, at that time quite popular in the Denver area. He stayed with the Senter band slightly more than a year. Then he enrolled at the University of Colorado, where he played with a college band. He left college in 1923 to devote full time to his career as a musician and arranger.

Early in 1924 he went to Los Angeles where, after brief periods with Max Fisher and Georgie Stoll, his first big break came. Ben Pollack asked him to join his band at the Venice Ballroom, where Miller worked alongside Benny Goodman, Gil Rodin, and other musical greats of the period. With the

Pollack band he went to Chicago, and eventually to New York in early 1928. It was in New York that Miller married his college sweetheart, Helen Burger, in October 1928. After leaving Pollack he played briefly with Paul Ashe in the pit band at the Paramount Theater. Then he became a free-lance trombonist and arranger, much in demand for recording sessions. For the next three years he was frequently in and out of the Red Nichols band and worked on most of the recordings Nichols and the Five Pennies made.

In 1932 he joined the Smith Ballew orchestra, which finally broke up in Denver in early 1934. Glenn then joined the newly-formed Dorsey Brothers band in New York and remained a year, leaving them just before they broke up, to assist Ray Noble in putting together his first American orchestra.

When he finally decided to launch his own band in January of 1937 he had firmly established his reputation both as a musician and an arranger. The band's first hotel job, at the Roosevelt in New Orleans, was set for two weeks, but Roosevelt owner Seymour Weiss liked the band so much that they stayed two months. But subsequent dates were less productive, and at the end of 1937 Miller disbanded, discouraged because of his inability to get the kind of men he wanted, and deeply in debt.

In the spring of 1938 he tried again, with financial help from his wife's family and from good friend Tommy Dorsey. This time he reassembled the men he wanted from the previous band and by carefully selecting, hiring, and replacing for the other chairs, he eventually had what he wanted. His search for a different style was ended when he developed in the reed section the clarinet-lead sound he had tried unsuccessfully to sell Ray Noble when he was arranging for him.

In the fall of 1938 he signed with Victor's Bluebird label, but initial sales were disappointing. Miller was almost ready to once again give up the venture when encouragement came in the form of financial help from Cy Shribman. Then the Miller records began to sell and although Glenn initially had a no-

At the Pennsylvania Hotel, New York, 1939: trumpets—Leigh Knowles, John Best, Dale McMickle, Clyde Hurley; trombones—Paul Tanner, Jim Priddy, Frank D'Anolfo; saxophones—Willie Schwartz, Al Klink, Hal McIntyre, Ernie Caceres, Tex Beneke; drums—Maurice Purtill; bass—Rolly Bundock; piano—Chummy MacGregor; vocals—Ray Eberle and Marion Hutton.

The Miller Orchestra working in the picture "Sun Valley Serenade," 1941. Trumpet section changes had brought in Billy May and Ray Anthony. Trigger Alpert was on bass, Jack Lathrop on guitar. The vocal group on the stand is the Modernaires, with Ray Eberle and minus Paula Kelly.

Glenn Miller and Marion Hutton. Miss Hutton joined the band in 1938, and except for a brief period in 1941 when she took time off to have a baby, she was with Miller until he disbanded at the end of September, 1942.

At the Pennsylvania again, 1941. Dorothy Claire had replaced Marion Hutton for a brief stay.

royalty contract (later rewritten), this boosted the band's prestige. In March 1939 they went into Frank Dailey's Meadowbrook, followed by a summer engagement at Glen Island Casino. Heavy coast-to-coast air time in both places, particularly the Glen Island Casino, gave the Miller style the exposure it needed. About that time his "In The Mood," arranged by Jerry Gray, became a top-selling hit, getting tremendous coverage both in juke boxes and by disc jockeys all over the country. By the time they left Glen Island in late August 1939, the band which had begun the year struggling for survival was the nation's hottest attraction. That fall they were signed by Chesterfield to do a three-a-week radio show.

From that time on the Miller band was magic on records and personal appearances. When World War II involved the United States, Miller added army camps to his busy schedule. Finally, at the peak of his professional career but feeling he should do more for his country, he entered the army in October 1942 to form what became the nation's most popular service band. The final engagement of the Glenn Miller orchestra was at the Central Theater in Passaic, New Jersey with both the audience and musicians in tears on the closing number. Miller entered the army a captain and was later promoted to major. Despite strong resistance and army red tape, he built a military band with a whole new musical concept.

In 1943, Captain Glenn Miller visits with Paula Kelly and the Modernaires.

That band went to England in the summer of 1944, with plans to move into the European war front zones to entertain troops. On December 15, Miller boarded a plane near Bedford, England to precede the band to Paris. The plane with its occupants disappeared into the low-hanging clouds and was never seen again.

What kind of man was Glenn Miller? Few people got to know him well. One of those who did was Don Haynes, for many years his personal manager, and with him up to the moment he boarded the plane for his final flight. It was Don who made the painful discovery that the plane had not made it across the Channel. Don and I became very good friends in the late fifties. He described Miller as a reserved person, but one who was extremely warm towards those near him.

Most of his associates were not so generous. All of them admired Miller, but described him as all business, generally cold, perhaps insecure, an individual who had a driving ambition to be successful. They all agreed that he was a perfectionist who knew what he wanted and would work until he got it. Millions of words have been written about Miller, his music, and his tragic death. There has been much speculation as to what musical course he would have pursued if he had returned from the war. Without detracting in any way from the Miller story, it seems reasonable to believe that his dramatic death contributed to the continued popularity of his music. In any event, the sound and musical style he created must be rated as one of those having the greatest effect on the music of the big band era.

HERB MILLER

Started First Band   Early forties
Where   West Coast
Previous Band Affiliations   Glenn Miller, Charlie Spivak
Recording Affiliations   Miller Tone Recording Company

Herb Miller was born in North Platte, Nebraska, the younger brother of Glenn Miller. Like his brother he too studied music during high school, and worked his way through college playing trumpet. After a brief period spent as business manager for Glenn's band,

The Herb Miller Orchestra, 1943: piano—Frankie Schenk; saxophones—Joe Reisman, Garth Andrews, Joe Lenza, Les Webel (playing clarinet solo), Dick Baker; trumpets—Bob Lewis, Danny Baxter, Herb Miller; drums—Bill Peri; bass—*unidentified;* trombone—*unidentified.*

and an occasional seat in the trumpet section, he left to play trumpet with Charlie Spivak. When the Glenn Miller orchestra became a sensational attraction in the early forties, Herb organized a band of his own, using publicity which made the most of the fact that he was the brother of the famous trombone player. Coast-to-coast tours were booked with mediocre success, with appearances at the Aragon Ballroom in Ocean Park, California, Jerry Jones' Rendezvous in Salt Lake City, and other ballrooms and hotels across the country. But only a small degree of the success his brother had enjoyed was to be Herb's. In the postwar years, he settled down in the Monterey, California area, concentrating his musical activities in that section of the country.

RAY MILLER

Started First Band Early twenties
Where New York City
Sidemen With Band Included Bernard Daly, Jim Welton, Phil Saxe, Mike Cirina, Tom Brown, Billie Fazioli, Louis Epstein, Gus Lazaro, Joe Brooco, Andy Sindelar, Harry Archer, Ralph Golati, Ward Archer, Earl Oliver, Ray Lodwig, Andy Sannella, Don Yates, Tom Satterfield, Frank Di Prima, Larry Abbot, Rube Bloom, Frankie Trumbauer, Miff Mole, Charlie Margulis, Bob Howard, Mike Durso, Fred Crissey, Andy Mansfield, Tony Briglia, Lloyd Wallen, Art Gronwal, Bill Paley, Muggsy Spanier
Vocalists With Band Included Irving Kaufman, Frank Wright, Harry Maxfield, the Downe Sisters
Recording Affiliations Okeh, Gennett, Columbia, Brunswick

Miller's first musical organization was a six-piece group which he called "Black and White Melody Boys," and which was featured in a number of New York musical productions. The larger dance band which he put together in the early twenties soon became rated in the New York area as a "musician's band," because he constantly employed some of the best white musicians of the day, as evidenced by the lineup above. Miller concentrated his activities primarily in the New York and East Coast area, appearing regularly at Atlantic City, the New York Hippodrome, and the Arcadia Ballroom. He dropped out of the business in the early thirties.

LUCKY MILLINDER

Started First Band Early thirties
Where Chicago area
Previous Band Affiliations None
Sidemen With Band Included J. C. Higginbotham, Charlie Shavers, Red Allen, Wilber De Paris, Tab Smith, Buster Bailey, Billy Kyle, Edgar Hayes, John Kirby, Bill Doggett, Freddy Webster, Sandy Williams, Dizzy Gillespie, Joe Guy, George Mathews, Lucky Thompson, Ellis Larkins, Bullmoose Jackson

Vocalists With Band Included Wynonie Harris, Rosetta Tharpe
Recording Affiliations Decca, Victor

Although Millinder was not technically a musician, he was an able front man and had a talent for attracting qualified musicians. A great deal of his success came from taking over other bands. After fronting a band of his own for the RKO circuit during the early thirties, he took over leadership of Doc

The Ray Miller Orchestra, Atlantic City, 1923. A large band compared to most of that time. *Left to right:* drums—Ward Archer; trumpet—Charlie Rocco; trombone—Miff Mole; violin—Danny Yates; trumpet—Roy Johnston; piano—Tommy Satterfield; tuba—Louie Chasone; leader—Ray Miller; saxophone—Frankie Trumbauer; saxophone—Andy Sandolar; piano—Ruby Bloom; saxophone—Billy Richards; banjo—Frank O. Prima; saxophone—Andy Sinnella.

The Lucky Millinder Orchestra, 1942, Savoy Ballroom. *Left to right:* piano—Bill Doggett; baritone sax—Ernest Purce; bass—George Duvivier; alto sax—Ted Barnett; alto sax—Tab Smith; drums—Panama Francis; tenor sax—Stafford "Pazuza" Simon; trumpet—Freddy Webster; trumpet—Nelson Bryant; guitar—Trevor Bacon; trumpet—Archie Johnson; trombone—George Stevenson; trombone—Ed Moran; trombone—Don Cole; leader—Lucky Millinder.

Crawford's band on a New York location in 1932. With that band he made a European tour, then returned to the New York area. In 1934 he took over Mill's Blue Rhythm Band, which already included a roster of heavy names. When this band broke up in late 1937 he took over Bill Doggett's band and toured with it for at least a year. This venture was not so successful and ended with Millinder going through bankruptcy. The next year he organized a band of his own, and remained intermittently active with it until the early fifties. He then went into the music publishing business. Throughout his bandleading career Millinder's orchestra was highly rated by fellow musicians. He died in New York City in September 1966.

VAUGHN MONROE

Started First Band 1940
Where Seilers Ten Acres, Wayland, Massachusetts
Previous Band Affiliations Austin Wylie, Larry Funk, Jack Marshard
Sidemen With Band Included Al King, Bobby Nichols, Dino Digiaro, Andy Bagni, Don Falco, Joe Connie, Frank Levine, Ziggy Talent, Paul Skersey, Guy Scafati, Jimmy Athens, Hy Levinson, Johnny Watson, Art Dedrick, Rudy Michaud, Arnold Ross, Charles Haggerty, Al Diehl, Irv Rosenthal, Joe Mack, Johnny Turnbull, Jack Hanson, Irving Goodman, Jack Bigelow, Joe Brantley, Jack Fay, Hal Burman, Harry Jaeger, George Esposito, George Matta, Carmen Mastren, Ray Heath, Roy Anderson, Ray Conniff, Murray Williams
Vocalists With Band Included Vaughn Monroe, Johnny Turnbull, Marilyn Duke, Mildred Law, the Four Lee Sisters, the Norton Sisters, the Moon Men, the Moon Maids. Novelty numbers were handled by Ziggy Talent
Sponsored Radio Shows "The Camel Caravan," guest appearances on "Spotlight Bands"
Television With Band "Camel Caravan," "The Vaughn Monroe Show"
Theme Song "Racing With The Moon"
Songs Written "Racing With The Moon," "Something Sentimental," "The Pleasure's All Mine"
Recording Affiliations Bluebird, Victor, and M and G Records, the latter his own company

Vaughn Monroe.

Monroe began his musical career with a battered old trumpet while he was still in grade school. Although never considered overly proficient on this instrument, he did very well as a bandleader, fronting a band which usually contained many talented musicians. Before forming his own organization he had fronted one of Jack Marshard's many society bands in the Boston area. With his own band he first began to attract national attention about 1941. During the World War II years

300

The Vaughn Monroe Orchestra in the early 1940s.

On stage at the Strand Theater in the mid 1940s. The vocalists are Rosemary Calvin, the Moonmaids, and the Moon Men.

he did better than average business on national tours, playing ballroom and theater locations and one-nighters.

He didn't achieve really big success, however, until 1945 when his RCA Victor record of "There, I've Said It Again" became a big hit. Its sales topped a million copies, and was followed in quick succession by other hits such as, "Let It Snow, Let It Snow," "Ballerina," "Cool Water," "Somebody Else Is Taking My Place," "Someday," and "Ghost Riders In The Sky." His popularity on records got him the "Camel Caravan Show" on radio, which would be tried on television somewhat later. From the late forties to the early fifties, Monroe was one of the strongest box office attractions in the band business, drawing guarantees equalling those of Tommy Dorsey, Benny Goodman, and Harry James.

In 1949 he made his first motion picture, a western entitled *Singing Guns*, produced by Republic. Others followed, and soon Monroe began to be identified more as a personality than a bandleader. His band was featured on several television shows, including the first sustaining color television show. Then in 1953 he disbanded his orchestra. Monroe remained active in show business as a single performer, playing the best clubs coast to coast and even making a number of international tours. When these tours and occasional television appearances did not keep him busy, he worked at managing his restaurant in Framingham, Massachusetts, known as The Meadows. In the mid-sixties he was still making occasional appearances, some of them in the Las Vegas area. He passed away in a Florida hospital on May 21, 1973 after a long illness. He was sixty-two years old.

ART MOONEY

Started First Band Late thirties
Where Detroit
Theme Song "Sunset to Sunrise"
Recording Affiliations MGM

The band which Mooney put together in the thirties spent most of its time in Detroit and the nearby Midwest area. In the early forties he gave it up to enter military service, returning to put together a new band in 1945. Neal Hefti was one of that band's arrangers. Like several other bands of that period, Mooney's style was similar to Glenn Miller's. In 1948 his MGM recording of "I'm Looking Over A Four Leaf Clover" became a big hit, putting the Mooney orchestra into the heavy money brackets for personal appearances. The recording had been done almost as a novelty number, not in the style which had previously identified the band. Because of the popularity this new style gave him, Mooney continued to feature group singing and the sound of a banjo. But the big band decline of the fifties substantially diminished the demand for his ser-

Art Mooney.

vices, and he eventually dropped the band entirely.

BUDDY MORENO

Started First Band 1947
Where Chicago
Previous Band Affiliations Guitarist and vocalist with Griff Williams and Dick Jurgens, vocalist with Harry James

Vocalists With Band Included Perri Mitchell (Mrs. Moreno), Frank Hudec, Buddy Moreno
Theme Song "It's That Time Again"
Recording Affiliations Victor

The Buddy Moreno Orchestra at the Commodore Hotel, New York, 1948.

Buddy Moreno.

Moreno, who was born in Los Angeles, was still quite young when he launched his musical career, singing with the newly organized Griff Williams band in San Francisco in 1933. Although also a guitarist, he was best known as a vocalist. In the late thirties he joined the Dick Jurgens band, and can be heard on many of the Okeh records the Jurgens band made in the early forties. In 1943 he joined Harry James as a featured male vocalist, and worked with the James orchestra in a couple of MGM pictures and on the Chesterfield Show on radio. By 1947 he felt ready to launch a band of his own. The organization he put together featured a conventional instrumentation, usually consisting of not more than twelve men, five reeds, four brass, and three rhythm. He and the band worked mostly in the Middle West, where he became a territory favorite. In 1948 the band was in New York, where it played the Paramount Theater, on a bill including the Weire Brothers, Lina Romay, and Henny Youngman. Regular appearances were made in the Midwestern and Southern hotel circuits, including the Muehlebach, the Peabody, the Roosevelt in New Orleans, and the Chase in St. Louis. In 1950 he settled down in St. Louis to become the house band at the Chase, and to do a local television show on KMOX called "The Buddy Moreno Show." In 1957 he cut back his band activities, playing only local conventions and other private jobs in the St. Louis area; and became active as a radio personality on station WIL. Later he switched to station WEW and is still there a program director.

RUSS MORGAN

Started First Band 1935
Where New York City
Previous Band Affiliations The Scranton Sirens, Paul Specht, Jean Goldkette, Phil Spitalny, Ted Fio Rito, Freddy Martin
Sidemen With Band Included Russ Case, Will Bradley, Charlie Butterfield, Toots Mondello, Arthur Rollini, Paul Ricci, Joe Venuti, Claude Thornhill, Jimmy Lewis, Charley Barbour, Chauncey Morehouse, Mert Curtis, Paul Roberts, Al Jennings, Eddie Bush, Cappy Lewis, Walter Ling, Jack Morgan, David Morgan
Vocalists With Band Included Jack Fulton, Judy Richards, Bernice Parks, Amy Terris, Carolyn Clark, Gloria Whitney, Jack Russell, Carol Kay, Jacquelyn Moore, Phyllis Lynn, Pat Laird, Manon Smith, Juanita Crowley. Russ did most of the male vocals himself, particuarly on records. He also occasionally featured a group called the Morganiaires
Tag Line "Music In The Morgan Manner"
Sponsored Radio Shows "The Rinso Show," "The Lifebuoy Show," "The Phillip Morris Program"
Television With Band A summer show for Admiral TV and Proctor and Gamble, plus local West Coast television shows
Theme Song "Does Your Heart Beat For Me?," closing theme was "So Long"
Songs Written "Does Your Heart Beat For Me?," "So Tired," "You're Nobody Til Somebody Loves You," "Sweet Eloise," "So Long," "Homespun," "Somebody Else Is Taking My Place," "Don't Cry, Sweetheart," "Tell Me You Love Me," "Lover's Rhapsody," "My Star of Love," "Goodnight Little Angel," "Whisper," "It's Time To Say Goddbye," "It's All Over But The Crying," "Flower of Dawn," "Snow Country," "Please Think of Me"

Russ Morgan.

Recording Affiliations Brunswick, Decca, Vocalion, Everest

Born in the coal section of Pennsylvania, Morgan earned the money for music lessons by working in the coal mines. Although he studied a variety of instruments, it was with the trombone and piano that he would be best identified throughout his career. He was also an accomplished arranger and prolific composer. While still a very young man, he started playing professionally, taking his first important assignment with Billy Lustig's Scranton Sirens. He then went on to work with a string of name bands, with

At the Claremont Hotel, Berkeley, California, 1945.

At the Casino Ballroom, Catalina Island, 1961. The trombonist at right is Russ' son, Jack Morgan, who took over the band after his father's death. The guitarist is son David Morgan.

most of whom he not only played trombone but also arranged. Following his time with Jean Goldkette (part of which was spent directing one of the Goldkette units), he served briefly as musical director for radio station WXYZ in Detroit. During that time he was seriously injured in an automobile accident, and spent several months in the hospital recuperating.

In 1935 in New York he left Freddy Martin to launch his first orchestra, encouraged by Rudy Vallee who assisted him in getting his first New York booking. For the next several years he maintained his headquarters in New York. From there he played the nation's best dance spots, with his popularity continuing on the upward swing, but with big success just beyond the reach of his fingertips. During the early years of World War II he came to the West Coast for a long engagement at the Claremont Hotel in Berkeley, California. After that he made his home in Beverly Hills. In 1946 he went into the Biltmore Bowl for a two-year run. Following that engagement he returned to the Claremont, and then made several Eastern tours. In 1949 his records, which up to this point had enjoyed only moderate success, became the hottest discs in the market, with every jukebox in the country playing such hits as "Cruising Down The River," "Forever and Ever," "So Tired," "Sunflower," and others. He was the year's Number One recording artist, thereby creating a demand for his orchestra which would not diminish for several years.

The musical style for which Morgan was famous was made to order for easy dancing, but it also had the big band sound that resulted from having seventeen musicians. He maintained an organization of this size even through the declining years of the dance orchestras, the mid and late fifties, when other leaders were substantially reducing their personnel or dropping out entirely. Finally in 1960, tired of making annual tours through the Midwest and Eastern areas, he reorganized and with a band of only twelve men concentrated on the available jobs in Los Angeles and the immediate area. For the next several years he played local spots as well as the Avalon Ballroom in Catalina and the clubs and casinos in Reno, Lake Tahoe, and Las Vegas. In 1965 he made his home in Las Vegas, where he became a fixture at "The Top Of The Strip" in the Dunes Hotel, playing an average of nine months annually in that location. He was still working there when he died on August 7, 1969 at the age of 65 after a month-long hospitalization resulting from a stroke.

His son Jack, also a trombonist, who had been working with the band for approximately ten years, took over the band's leadership to continue on at the Dunes and to make annual tours of the midwest. He is still active with the band.

BUDDY MORROW

Started First Band 1950
Where New York City
Previous Band Affiliations Paul Whiteman, Artie Shaw, Tommy Dorsey, Vincent Lopez, Bob Crosby
Vocalists With Band Included Pat Collins
Theme Song "Solo," "Night Train"
Recording Affiliations Victor

Before launching his own band in 1950, Morrow (born Moe Zudekoff) had established himself as a top flight trombonist who had played with a long string of the best bands in the business. His bandleading career began under rather unusual circumstances: he was sponsored by the biggest label in the recording industry, RCA Victor. According to trade paper stories at the time, Morrow's band was organized to be Victor's replacement for Tommy Dorsey, who had left the label in the late forties. With Ralph Flanagan they had proven that heavy promotion

The Buddy Morrow Orchestra at the Peabody Hotel, Memphis, Tennessee, in 1955.

Buddy Morrow.

Pat Collins, featured with Buddy Morrow.

on records could build a band to name status prior to any personal appearances. A similar buildup was given Morrow. Although the results did not quite equal Flanagan's, when the band went on the road in early 1951 it did have a ready-made market waiting. In addition to Victor's heavy promotion, Morrow's was one of several bands included in a 1952 attempt by Frank Dailey's Meadowbrook to revive the then-faltering band business via television remotes. These were intended to build the bandleader's appeal on road tours, as radio had done in the thirties. Unfortunately for Morrow and for the rest of the band business, Dailey's efforts were not sufficiently productive to either

307

build the bands who worked for him or to keep his Meadowbrook in operation. Morrow became a heavy favorite in the Midwest and South, with regular appearances at the Memphis Peabody and the Roosevelt in New Orleans. West Coast trips were also made, where the band did good business at the Hollywood Palladium. Morrow's base of operations continued to be New York City, however, and among the New York spots where he appeared regularly was the Roseland Ballroom. Morrow was rated by fellow musicians as a very accomplished trombonist. At an earlier time he might have equalled Dorsey's success. But time was running out for the big bands, and in the early sixties his appearances were reduced to weekends, with an occasional tour thrown in. Eventually he was limiting his activities to studio work in the New York area. But in the mid-seventies Morrow went back on the road as the front man for the still-active Tommy Dorsey orchestra.

N

FREDDY NAGEL

Started First Band Mid-thirties
Where West Coast
Vocalists With Band Included Lorraine Benson, Bob Locken, Ken Jackson, Allen Overend
Theme Song "Sophisticated Swing"

Much of Nagel's bandleading career was spent on the West Coast, where he played hotel locations and such amusement spots as Jantzen Beach in Portland, Oregon, and Natatorium Park in Spokane, Washington.

His first orchestra was best identified as a "society" band. He changed style in the early forties to front a more solid dance band, with which he toured the Middle West, playing both the Aragon and Trianon ballrooms in Chicago. As a front man he was sometimes described as a "Kay Kyser type," using showmanship as much as musicianship to sell the band. Eventually he dropped out of the music business to make his home on a ranch near Susanville, California.

Freddy Nagel and his orchestra.

PAUL NEIGHBORS

Started First Band   1948
Where   Los Angeles, first job was Mapes Hotel in Reno, Nevada
Vocalists With Band Included   Ralph Anthony. Neighbors did most of the vocals himself
Sponsored Radio Shows   A regional show for Ford over CBS from New Orleans in early fifties
Theme Song   "Love Thy Neighbor"
Recording Affiliations   Capitol

Paul Neighbors.

Although the Neighbor's band was organized on the West Coast, most of its time was spent elsewhere. Following his first job at the Mapes in Reno, he played other West Coast locations, including several stands at the Claremont in Berkeley. In the early fifties he moved to Houston, Texas to live, and established a base for coverage of the Midwest. During the next several years his became a favorite Midwest territory band, playing the hotel circuit, including the Peabody, the Chase, the Schroeder in Milwaukee, and the Dallas Shamrock Hilton. He also played the Pennsylvania in New York, and made several appearances at the Roseland Ballroom. From each of these tours he returned to Houston to play an average six-months engagement at the Shamrock, the first of which was played in 1956. He remained active in the southwest until his death in Houston, Texas, on August 26, 1983, at age 65.

Paul Neighbors and his orchestra in the mid 1950s.

OZZIE NELSON

Started First Band   June 1930
Where   New York City; had previously had campus band while at Rutgers College
Previous Band Affiliations   Various college bands
Sidemen With Band Included   Charlie Spivak, Donald Wright, Bill Nelson, Charlie Bubeck, Sid Brokaw, Sandy Wolfe, Fred Whiteside, Harry Murphy, Joe Bohan, Abe Lincoln, Harry Johnson, Bo Ashford, Hollie Humphreys, Bill Stone, Chauncey Gray, Irving Gellers, Bob Damos, Howard Bruno, Clayton Moore, Ray Crider, Oscar Haines, Norman Sipple, Robert Bann, Russ Mayhew, Bunny Jones, Billy Marcus, Jerry Colonna
Vocalists With Band Included   Harriet Hilliard (Mrs. Ozzie Nelson), Joy Hodges, Cass Daley, Rose Ann Stevens, Shirley Lloyd
Sponsored Radio Shows   "Joe Penner Show," "Bob Ripley Show," "Feg Murray Show," "Red Skelton Show"
Longest Engagement   Three consecutive summer seasons at Glen Island Casino, three consecutive winter seasons at Lexington Hotel, New York City
Theme Song   "Loyal Sons Of Rutgers"
Songs Written   "And Then Your Lips Met Mine," "Baby Boy," "Swingin' On The Golden

Ozzie and Harriet during their "big band" days.

Gate," "Mary," "I'm Looking For A Guy Who Plays Alto and Baritone, Doubles On Clarinet, And Wears a Size 37 Suit"
Recording Affiliations   Brunswick, Vocalion, Bluebird, Victor

The long run of television's "The Adventures of Ozzie and Harriet" may have caused even its older viewers to forget that Ozzie

January 1936: the Nelson orchestra on the stand at the Lexington Hotel, New York.

Ozzie and Harriet with the band in "Sweetheart of the Campus," 1942.

Nelson was once one of America's famous dance bandleaders and that Harriet Hilliard was his talented vocalist.

He was still in college when he organized a band to play the summer season at Glen Island Casino. Because of the public's enthusiastic response, he decided to forget a career in law and follow music on a full-time basis. Soon his band was playing the best spots in New York City and on the East Coast, and eventually on a nationwide basis. Harriet Hilliard joined the band as vocalist in 1932 and married Nelson in 1935. She remained with the band until the arrival of the first of their two sons, but even though he might be on tour with the band Ozzie was never further away from her than the nearest telephone. It was doubtless the Nelson-Hilliard duets won them places on the top radio shows.

The Nelson orchestra turned out a long list of recordings, the earliest ones on Bruns-wick but most of them on Victor and Blue-bird. They were also featured in motion pictures for several of the major studios in the early forties, when dance bands were the number one form of live entertainment. As his radio activity began to take more and more of his time, Nelson reduced his travels with the band, eventually giving it up altogether when "The Adventures of Ozzie and Harriet" became a popular weekly television series. Along with their two sons, David and Ricky, they developed one of the most popular family comedy shows on television, with a combined run on radio and television of twenty-two years. The show finally came to an end in 1966, but Nelson took another brief fling at television in the mid-seventies with a show called "Ozzie's Girls." That show was dropped because of Nelson's health. Late in the fall of 1974 he underwent surgery for cancer. He died in his home on June 3, 1975 at the age of 69.

RED NICHOLS

Started First Band About 1922
Where New York City
Previous Band Affiliations Syncopating Five, The Royal Palms Orchestra, Johnny Johnson, and brief periods with various other New York bands
Sidemen With Band Included Because Nichols was so active on records in the early years of his career, and with such a changing list of musicians on those dates, nothing resembling a complete listing could be made. Among those who worked with him in the early and mid-twenties were Joe Venuti, Joe Zigler, Chuck Campbell, Gerald Finney, Freddy Morrow, Dudley Fosdick, Arthur Schutt, Irving Brodsky, Vic Burton, Jack Mayhew, Dick McDonough, Perry Botkin, and Jimmy Dorsey. During the late twenties, his band included both Jimmy and Tommy Dorsey, Benny Goodman, Gene Krupa, Glenn Miller, Miff Mole, Eddie Lang, and Jack Teagarden. Throughout the thirties and into the early forties, he fronted a big dance band which included Ernie Mathias, Frank Sacco, Charlie Rodnick, Bill Lower, Tony Sacco, Frank Myers, Ted Kline, Fred Morrow, Snub Pollard, Alex Polascay, Joe Catalyne, Ray McCosh, George Schmidt, Buck Weaver, Howard Jenkins, Manny Strand, King Harvey, George Kennedy, Barney Zudecoff, Leo Moran, Frank Perry, Murray Williams, Don Stevens, Ray Schultz, Billy Maxted, Tony Colucci, Jack Fay, Vic Engle, Douglas Wood, Hal Mastran, Jack Knaus, Conn Humphries, Heinie Beau, and others. Among those who worked in his postwar Five Pennies band were Rollie Culver, Herbie Haymer, Joe Rushton, Matty Malneck, Bill Wood, Pete Beilmann, Al Sutton, Bill Campbell, Eddie Miller, Walter Yoder, Richard Nelson
Vocalists With Band Included Tony Sacco, June Rae, Bill Darnell, Marian Redding, Dottie O'Brien
Sponsored Radio Shows "The Bob Hope Show," "The Kellogg Show"

Red Nichols.

Theme Song "Parade of the Five Pennies," "Wail of the Winds"
Recording Affiliations Brunswick, Okeh, Vocalion, Victor, Bluebird, Capitol plus many obscure labels during the twenties

Technically Nichols qualifies for the big band era only during the thirties and into the early forties, for his first full-size dance band was formed about 1932 and given up approximately ten years later. But he was always part of the dance band scene. Although only a scattered few have ever denied that Nichols was one of the all-time great jazz musicians, he always insisted that jazz was not just for listening but should be danceable. "Jazz actually stems from dance music," he repeatedly said, "It is based on dance music — the best jazz can still be dance music." Even with his small bands of five to seven musicians, he insisted on having written arrangements for everything they played and if you couldn't read music you couldn't play in the Nichols band.

The Nichols Band in Cleveland, 1933. *Back row:* trumpets—Ernie Mathias, Frank Sacco; piano—Charlie Rodwick; trombone—"Little Miff"; tuba—Bill Lower; drums—Vic Angle. *Front row:* violin and vocals—Tony Sacco; saxophones—Frank Meyers, Ted Kline, Fred Morrow.

In Roseburg, Oregon, 1947. Nichols' postwar "Pennies" included: piano—Pete DeSantos; bass sax—Joe Rushton; vocals—Dottie O'Brien; drums—Rollie Culver; trombone—Brad Gowans; clarinet—Al Kavich; tenor sax—Don Lodice.

The Pennies in San Diego, 1951.

His musical training began under the tutelage of his father, who was a professor of music at Webber College in Ogden, Utah. By the time he had reached the age of twelve, Nichols was playing in the family's own little dance orchestra, which worked in the Ogden area and occasionally took trips into the hinterlands.

After a short period at Culver Military Academy (where he went on a scholarship in 1920), he played with a dance orchestra in Piqua, Ohio, on what at that time seemed an impressive salary of $50 weekly. He then joined the Syncopating Five, a cooperative group which travelled to Atlantic City for an extended run and then moved into New York. Red's fame on the cornet was growing steadily. His bandleading career began when Johnny Johnson gave him an opportunity to head up his own band at the Pelham Heath Inn, making him a full-fledged bandleader while still a very young man. It was this group which became known as the Five Pennies, a name given them by drummer Vic Burton.

During the next several years the band, billed as "Red Nichols and His Five Pennies," varied in size from six to nine men. Red alternated between leading his own band and playing as a sideman with such organizations as the California Ramblers, Sam Lanin, Vincent Lopez, Ross Gorman, George Olsen, and briefly with Paul Whiteman. With his own band he kept busy on recordings and was so much in demand that he recorded for various labels, using a variety of names for his recording groups. Because of his reputation as a musician, the best talent in the business was anxious to record with him and the personnel listing on his sessions reads like a Who's Who of the music business. Most of the great jazz bands of the 1920-30 period were the black groups, with Nichols standing out almost alone in the white field, producing music which was years ahead of its time.

By 1931 the jazz age seemed to have gone with the twenties, society bands of ten to twelve men were coming into style and by the mid-thirties swing was the thing. Red

315

changed with the times and for the next ten years fronted a band of ten and sometimes fourteen musicians, with featured vocalists and at times even including a vocal trio of girls. He continued to make records, but the sound of the finished product reflected a degree of compromise with commercialism necessitated by the trends of the period. Even though he continued to surround himself with the best musicians available, this was probably a stage of his career when he was not too pleased with what he was accomplishing. During the early years of World War II he gave up his bandleading career when his daughter Dorothy was stricken with polio. For the next several years he worked in the shipyards in Alameda, California, with only occasional brief activity in music in the Bay area. In 1944 he worked for six months for the Glen Gray Casa Loma band.

Then he returned to the West Coast to buy a home in Hollywood, and opened in the spring of 1945 at El Morocco Club on Vine Street with a small band of his own. This was the beginning of a whole new career for Red and the Five Pennies. They soon had regained their popularity and were in big demand for personal appearances on a nationwide basis. That popularity continued unabated for the next twenty years, during which time he was once more active in the recording studios. In 1959 his life was immortalized in a motion picture titled *The Five Pennies*, with the lead role played by Danny Kaye. In 1960 he made an extensive Far Eastern tour for the State Department, and three years later a trip to the Orient for a Jazz Festival.

Towards the mid-sixties he reduced his travel engagements to concentrate in the Southern California area, usually playing the winter months in the Zebra Room of the Sheraton-West Hotel. His last engagement was played there in the spring of 1965. Then he went to Las Vegas to play at The Mint. With two weeks of that engagement still to be played, he was stricken with a heart attack in his hotel room on June 28, and died at the age of sixty.

In 1960 the Pennies were trombone—Pete Beilmann; bass sax—Joe Rushton; clarinet—Bill Wood; drums—Rollie Culver; piano—Al Sutton; cornet—Red.

LEIGHTON NOBLE

Started First Band   1937
Where   New York City
Previous Band Affiliations   Hal Grayson,
Orville Knapp, George Olsen
Vocalists With Band Included   Johnny
McAfee, Edith Caldwell, Margie Lee. Noble
usually handled male vocals himself
Recording Affiliations   Vocalion, Bluebird

When Noble organized his first band, he did
what was generally considered impossible:
that is, he moved directly into Frank Dailey's
Meadowbrook for his opening job. He followed this with a stand at Philadelphia's
Arcadia Ballroom, and went on from there to
play the top hotels in the country for many
years. The movies gave him an opportunity
to play major picture roles in the early forties, and he continued to be active in the
Hollywood scene throughout the decade. He
tried to confine his musical engagements to
the West Coast during this period, with
occasional extended tours taking him across
the country. A handsome and capable front
man, he was still a favorite in the Las Vegas-
Reno entertainment centers as the sixties

Leighton Noble.

got under way. In 1961 he became leader of
the house band at Harrah's Club, Lake
Tahoe, where he remained until 1969. After
leaving Harrah's, he moved to Vancouver,
Canada to live, returning to the states only
occasionally for appearances, including some
at the Roosevelt Hotel in New Orleans.

Leighton Noble and his orchestra, Catalina Island, 1949.

RAY NOBLE

Started First Band   Late twenties
Where   London, England
Sidemen With Band Included   Glenn Miller, Charlie Spivak, Pee Wee Irwin, Will Bradley, Johnny Mince, Bud Freeman, Milt Yaner, Jim Cannon, Danny D'Andrea, George Van Epps, Claude Thornhill, Delmar Kaplan, Sterling Bose, Alex Polascay, Mike Doty, Frank Barnard, Gordon Connell, Jim Davidson, Herb Mason, Jack Madden, Ted Davidson, Cliff Timms, Jack Nielsen, Cliff Cadman, Johnny Burt, Red McGarvey, Joe Niosi, Earl Hagen, Carl Loffler, Bob Goodrich, Don Bonnee, Jack Dumont, Bud Smith, Manny Stein, Frank Leithner, Don Anderson, Milt Bernhart, and others
Vocalists With Band Included   Al Bowlly, Sally Singer, Howard Phillips, Ray Hendricks, Liz Tilton, Mary Ann Warren, Larry Stewart, Dorothy Cordray, Snooky Lanson
Sponsored Radio Shows   "Burns and Allen Show," "Charlie McCarthy Show"
Theme Song   Used several—"I'll See You In My Dreams," "Midnight Moon," "The Very Thought of You," and "Goodnight Sweetheart"
Songs Written   "The Very Thought of You," "The Touch Of Your Lips," "Cherokee," "Goodnight Sweetheart" and many others
Recording Affiliations   HMV, Victor, Brunswick, Columbia

Ray Noble.

Although he was perhaps one of the most gifted pianists to come out of England, Ray Noble seldom played piano in any of the fine orchestras which he fronted during his active career as an American bandleader. Born in 1908, the son of a British doctor, by the early thirties he had become one of England's most famous musicians. With his Mayfair orchestra, he was broadcasting regularly over BBC and was one of the most popular recording artists in his native land. Deciding that a greater market for his talent existed in the United States, he came to this country in the spring of 1935.

If he had any thought of bringing his own band with him, union problems which existed at that time prevented his doing so. Because of the strong position British unions had taken against American musicians working in that country, the unions in the United States had established an equally strong reciprocal position. Consequently Noble brought with him nothing but his talent, some of his original compositions, and a few arrangements. To assist him in organizing a band in the States, he hired Glenn Miller, who had just left the Dorsey band. Miller was not only instrumental in rounding up a group of fine musicians for Noble but did a great deal of the arranging. Fellow musicians for Noble who were in that band with him recall that he attempted to arrange for Noble the sounds which he later made famous with his own orchestra. But Noble was unimpressed and declined to use these sounds. Miller stayed with Noble for approximately eighteen months before leaving to begin the forming of his own orchestra.

Noble continued to hire the best musicians available, and his music quickly caught

This is the Ray Noble band that played the Rainbow Room in New York for over a year. At the extreme rear of the group is Glenn Miller, as well as future leaders Charlie Spivak and Claude Thornhill.

on in the United States. He enjoyed a long run at the Rainbow Room in New York City, with regular air time making him well known from coast to coast. When he left the Rainbow Room, he was in demand in all the nation's top hotels where good dance music was featured. The Victor people had quickly signed him to a recording contract and on that label he turned out a string of best sellers, ranging from sweet ballads featuring the vocal talent of Al Bowlly to some which compete with the best swing records of the period.

Noble's popularity quickly won him a place in commercial radio, and he joined the "Burns and Allen Show" early in 1940. This was followed by many years on the "Edgar Bergen-Charlie McCarthy Show," on which he was not only the featured bandleader but consistently played a leading part in the dialogue, with weekly exchanges of sarcasm with Charlie McCarthy. When television finally drove the big radio shows permanently off the airways, Noble retired from activity as a bandleader to make his home on an island in the Mediterranean, from which point he usually managed at least one trip annually to the United States, including a visit to the West Coast. In the seventies he returned to California to make his home in Santa Barbara. He died on April 3, 1978 in a London Hospital, a victim of cancer at age seventy-one.

In Denver, 1938. The vocalist is Larry Stewart. Liz Tilton was with the band but not present for the picture. Among the key sidemen were trombonist Earle Hagen, guitarist George Van Epps, and bassist Manny Stein.

The Noble band at Catalina Island, 1941, with singer Snooky Lanson at the mike.

RED NORVO

Started First Band 1936 (Had previously fronted small combos)
Where New York City
Previous Band Affiliations Paul Ashe, Victor Young, Paul Whiteman
Sidemen With Band Included Eddie Sauter, Ralph Burns, Aaron Sachs, Remo Palmier, Clyde Lombardi, Bill Hyland, Stew Pletcher, Leo Moran, Eddie Myers, Slats Long, Herbie Haymer, Frank Simeone, Joe Liss, Dave Barbour, Maurice Purtill, Al Mastren, Charles Lampheare, George Wendt, Louis Mucci, Hank d'Amico, Len Goldstein, Bill Miller, Red McGarvey, Pete Peterson, Jimmy Blake, Zeke Zarky, Barney Zudecoff, Wes Hein, Jerry Jerome, Al Hanlon, George Wettling, Andy Russo, Maurie Kogan, Bob Kennedy, Jimmy Salko, Leo Connors, Fred Artzburger, Mickey Folus, Sam Spumberg, Bob Kitsis, Freddy Sharp, Frank Vesely. Records were cut with a small combo including Buster Bailey, Charlie Shavers, Billy Kyle, Russell Procope, John Kirby, and O'Neil Spencer
Vocalists With Band Included Mildred Bailey (Mrs. Norvo), Terry Allen
Musical Style His big band was good, solid swing. His smaller combos, with which he has been better identified, played some of the best jazz of their period
Theme Song "I Surrender, Dear"
Recording Affiliations Brunswick, Vocalion

Red Norvo.

Norvo was the first jazz man to make his reputation on the xylophone. He was already quite well known when he joined the Paul Whiteman orchestra in the early thirties, but the Whiteman job substantially enhanced his career. Also working with the Whiteman band was vocalist Mildred Bailey, "The Rocking Chair Lady," who soon became Mrs. Red Norvo. With Mildred doing the vocals, Norvo launched his twelve-piece band in 1936. One of his first engagements was at Jack Dempsey's in New York City, followed by stands at the Commodore Hotel, the Sycamore Hotel, and the Blackhawk Restaurant in Chicago. In the fall of 1937 they travelled to the West Coast for an engagement at the Palomar, which was billed as the premier West Coast appearance of "Mr. and Mrs. Swing." Another West Coast engagement at the St. Francis Hotel in San Francisco followed. Then the band returned to the East Coast. Norvo's career as leader of a big band encompassed a period from 1936 through 1944, with intermittent breakups. He gave up the band entirely to work with Benny Goodman in 1945, then spent a couple of years with Woody Herman. During the next several years he alternated between working with Benny Goodman and other swing-oriented leaders and leading a small combo of his own, working the Nevada lounges.

Red Norvo and his orchestra.

HUSK O'HARE

Started First Band Mid-twenties
Where Chicago
Sidemen With Band Included Jimmy McPartland, Bud Freeman, Jimmy Lannigan, Frank Teschemacher, Bix Beiderbecke, Floyd O'Brien, Dave North, Arnold Sweatman, Harry O'Connor, Franklyn Marsh, and others
Theme Song "The One I Love"
Recording Affiliations Gennett, Decca

Husk O'Hare was one of the pioneer radio bands and better known for his studio work than for personal appearances. He was active, however, in the Chicago and Midwest area for several years on personal appearances, chosen as he saw fit, and a heavy drawing card because of his radio prestige.

The first organization under his own name was a small group called the "Blue Friars," the leadership of which he took over, changing its name first to "O'Hare's Red Dragons" and then to "Husk O'Hare's Wolverines," the latter a name which he used for several years. Its personnel included some of the famous Chicago Austin High musicians as indicated by the list above. With his group and other bands O'Hare took Midwestern tours which included locations played in Cleveland, Pittsburgh, Philadelphia, Atlantic City, and Baltimore. O'Hare remained active as a bandleader throughout the thirties. He retired completely from music in the early forties to engage in the novelty manufacturing business in Chicago.

PHIL OHMAN

Started First Band Mid-twenties
Where New York City
Previous Band Affiliations Paul Whiteman
Theme Song "Canadian Capers"
Songs Written "Lazy Rolls the Rio Grande," "The Cowboy and the Senorita," "Dream Awhile," "Strawberry Samba," "Zilda,"
"Each Time You Say Goodbye," "Only One," "I Close My Eyes," "Don't Believe All You Hear About Love," "If You Are There," "Dreaming To Music," "The Girl With The High Button Shoes"
Recording Affiliations Edison, Columbia, Victor, Brunswick

Initially Ohman was co-leader of the band with Victor Arden, billed as the Arden-Ohman Orchestra. Both were piano players and made many piano duo records, also appearing together in Broadway shows as featured pianists, and on the radio shows of the late twenties and early thirties. In the mid-thirties the two split up. With a band of his own, Ohman moved to the West Coast, where he not only kept busy with personal appearances made with the band, but did a great deal of movie writing and radio work. He was a big favorite at Hollywood's Mocambo, the "in" spot for the motion picture crowd during the late thirties, and enjoyed a long run at that location. He remained active as a bandleader into the early fifties. He finally retired shortly before his death in Santa Monica in 1954, at the age of fifty-eight.

The Phil Ohman Orchestra, 1936.

KING OLIVER

Started First Band   About 1919, may have had a small band briefly about 1915
Where   Chicago
Previous Band Affiliations   Several New Orleans bands, most notably Kid Ory, then with Lawrence Duhe, then Bill Johnson in the Chicago area
Sidemen With Band Included   Louis Armstrong, Lil Hardin, Kid Ory, Barney Bigard, Honore Dutray, Johnny Dodds, Baby Dodds, Albert Nicholas, Louis Russell

Songs Written   "Doctor Jazz," "West End Blues," "Canal Street Blues," "Sugarfoot Stomp"
Recording Affiliations   Paramount, Gennett, Okeh, Columbia, Victor, Brunswick, Vocalion

Oliver's work with the cornet in various marching bands in the New Orleans area earned him the title of "King," given to him by Kid Ory when he played with Ory's

The King Oliver Band, 1923. *Left to right:* Baby Dodds, Honore Dutry, King Oliver, Louis Armstrong, Johnny St. Cyr, Johnny Dodds, Lil Hardin Armstrong.

group. He was the idol of young Louie Armstrong, and played a big part in shaping and launching Armstrong's career. Shortly after he started his own band in Chicago, he sent for Armstrong and brought him in as second cornetist. The Oliver band, which he called The Creole Jazz Band, was one of the first, if not actually *the* first, black band to get on records, in about 1923. Oliver concentrated his activities in the Chicago area until the late twenties, when he moved to New York. While the band was in New York, Louis Russell left to start a band of his own, and took many of Oliver's sidemen with him. For the next couple of years Oliver worked in New York and was still making records, but quite often with a pickup group. By that time Oliver's career had long since peaked and was on the decline. He continued to put bands together for tours, but gave up the business entirely in the early thirties, settling down to live in Savannah, Georgia. He died in that city in 1938.

GEORGE OLSEN

Started First Band About 1917
Where Portland, Oregon
Sidemen With Band Included Rudy Wiedoeft, Don Lindley, Chuck Campbell, Floyd Rice, George Henkel, Eddie Kilfeather, Jack Hansen, Bob Borger, Jack Fulton, Milton Neul, Ed Joyce, Larry Mercy, Jack Gifford, Dick Gardner, Fred MacMurray, Lou

The George Olsen Orchestra, 1924. Olsen seated on floor.

Busch, Eddie McKinney, Ernie Mathias, Orville Knapp, Leighton Noble, Red Nichols, Fran Frey worked briefly with the band in the late twenties.

Vocalists With Band Included Billy Murray, Louis James, Jack Gifford, Jerry Baker, Dave Marshall, Ethel Shutta, Fran Frey, Bob Borger, Bob Rice

Sponsored Radio Shows The "Jack Benny Show" (briefly)

Theme Song "Beyond the Blue Horizon," in later years used "Music of Tomorrow"

Recording Affiliations Victor, Columbia, Decca

Olsen's career as an active bandleader spanned approximately thirty-five years. During most of those years he was a top name, working the best night clubs, hotels, and theaters as well as working in several New York musical comedies. It all began when he started his first band in Portland, Oregon about 1917, thereby disappointing his father, who had wanted him to take over the family moving van business. That first

George Olsen.

326

The George Olsen Orchestra in the late 1930s or early 1940s.

band was a six-piece group including himself, and one of its featured performers was Wilbur Johnson, billed as the "World's Only Mellophone Soloist." It also included a violinist named Herman Kanin, who many years later would become the president of the American Federation of Musicians. Olsen himself was a drummer.

After building his popularity in the Pacific Northwest, Olsen first moved southward to play ballroom and theater dates in Los Angeles and San Francisco. It was in the latter city that Florenz Ziegfeld contacted him, inviting him to come to New York with his band to play in the musical comedy *Kid Boots*, a show which starred Eddie Cantor. This was followed by a series of other Broadway shows including "Whoopee," "The Girl Friend" and "Good News." During the same period he was active with his band in New York night clubs, including Jack White's

54th Street Club, the Rendezvous, and the Club Richman.

In 1925 his Victor recording of "Who" became a nationwide hit, making him known from coast to coast. This launched him on a recording career which continued for many years. Many of the best musicians of the day recorded with him. These included Red Nichols, who also played for awhile in one of Olsen's pit bands, and Rudy Wiedoeft, who at that time was one of the nation's most famous and copied saxophonists. The Olsen band was also one of those in which Fred MacMurray played saxophone, on his way to becoming one of the best known and wealthiest motion picture stars in America.

By the end of the twenties the size of the Olsen band had grown to about sixteen men. The band's best known vocalist by then was Ethel Shutta, who also became Mrs. Olsen. About 1930 Olsen returned to the West

Coast to play in the Los Angeles area, where he was featured at the Plantation Ballroom, and also made a number of musical movie shorts. In 1936 Orville Knapp, who after working briefly for Olsen had started a band of his own, was killed in the crash of a plane which he was flying himself. Olsen, who had liked the Knapp band's musical style, took it over completely. Calling it "Music of Tomorrow," he toured coast to coast although he continued to make his headquarters in New York. During that period Leighton Noble was the featured male vocalist with the band. Noble once described Olsen to me as a nice guy to work for, but basically a front man rather than a musician. (This was true of most of the bandleaders who became famous during the twenties.) He seemed always to have a problem in giving the band a recognizable downbeat and this led at times to some embarrassing moments when they were playing stage shows and the background music for headliners. It was an even more serious problem when they were on a sponsored radio show.

Olsen gave up his bandleading career in 1951, playing his last engagement at the Edgewater Beach Hotel in Chicago. He then opened a restaurant in Paramus, New Jersey, which became quite successful. He died in Paramus on March 18, 1971, at the age of seventy-eight.

WILL OSBORNE

Started First Band 1924
Where New York City
Vocalists With Band Included Dick Robertson, Dorothy Rogers, Joan Whitney, Janice Todd, Lynn Davis, Eileen Wilson. Osborne usually did male vocals himself, particularly on records
Sponsored Radio Shows "The Blue White Diamond Show" in New York City, "The Corn Products Show," "The Camel Cigarette Show," and the "Abbott and Costello Show"
Theme Song "Beside An Open Fireplace," "The Gentleman Awaits"
Songs Written "Pompton Turnpike"
Recording Affiliations Columbia, Banner, Mellotone, Perfect, Decca, Black & White

The patented slide trombone effects which identified the Will Osborne style for many years resulted in a popular misconception that he was a trombonist himself. Actually the handsome leader was a drummer and even better known as a vocalist, with a style which became known as "crooning." His ardent fans claim that it was he who originated it. Rudy Vallee disagreed, touching off a much-publicized feud of considerable

Will Osborne.

duration, with Osborne apparently laughing quietly to himself and riding the crest of the publicity while Vallee fumed. He started his first band in 1924 in New York City, to play what he later laughingly described as

The Will Osborne Orchestra at a theater engagement in 1944.

the "Speakeasy Circuit." After several months of that routine, he had an opportunity to follow the fast-rising Duke Ellington into the Kentucky Club for a year's engagement. Here he established himself firmly as a bandleader headed for a national reputation.

The Vallee incident occurred when Vallee left the club where he had been appearing for a long run to go to the West Coast to make a motion picture, and Osborne moved in. The place had a remote pickup with regular airtime which Osborne made the most of. It was during that engagement that his broadcasts in the New York area were sponsored by Herbert's Blue-White Diamonds. Later a combination of steadily selling records and a couple of network shows made him a national attraction. The Osborne band took tours which included West Coast appearances at the Palomar in the late thirties.

In the mid-forties Osborne moved to the West Coast to make his home and headquarters, working out of the Los Angeles area. Like other bandleaders he made several appearances in motion pictures, both for Warner Brothers and Paramount. During that time the band he fronted was swing-oriented in keeping with the demands of war-time audiences. Shortly after the war, he softened his musical style to something which reviewers described as "smooth and rhythmic." In 1947 and 1948 he still had an organization totalling seventeen musicians and a vocalist. He remained active as a leader until the late fifties, when he gave up batoneering to become entertainment director of Harvey's, one of northern Nevada's most popular clubs, located at Lake Tahoe. He later retired to Newport Beach, California, where he died on October 22, 1981.

The Owens band and entertainers on a TV show in the early 1950s.

HARRY OWENS

Started First Band 1926
Where Los Angeles, California—The Lafayette Cafe
Previous Band Affiliations The Cocoanut Grove Orchestra, Vincent Rose
Sidemen With Band Included The early Los Angeles band included Ted Mack. His most popular band was formed in Hawaii with local men. On return to the West Coast he brought in Local No. 47 men, including Henry Jaworski and Al Galenti
Vocalists With Band Included Hilo Hattie, The Royal Hawaiian Sweethearts, Kenny Allen, Gil Mershon
Television With Band A show telecast on a special West Coast/Hawaii CBS network for Regal Pale and other sponsors, starting in 1949 and running nine years
Longest Engagement Royal Hawaiian Hotel

Theme Song "Sweet Leilani"
Tag Line "The Royal Hawaiians"
Songs Written "Linger Awhile," "Sweet Leilani," "Hawaiian Pradise," "To You Sweetheart Aloha," "Princess Poo Pooly," "Hawaii Calls," "Voice of the Trade Winds," "Polynesian Holiday," and many others
Recording Affiliations Decca, Capitol, Columbia, Hamilton

Owens, whose fame would come from writing and playing Hawaiian music, was born in Nebraska, a long way from the trade winds and banyan trees about which he would write so successfully in later years. His early musical career gave no indication it would turn in that direction. He played trumpet in several Los Angeles bands and enjoyed a fair amount of success with a conventional band of his own. In 1934 he went to

Harry Owens with daughter Leilani, who inspired the song "Sweet Leilani."

Honolulu to become musical director of the Royal Hawaiian Hotel with a four-months contract, during which time he was to build a dance orchestra which could combine the island music with that of the mainland. He quickly learned that the work habits of the native musicians he was to direct were not geared to his own and that his orchestrations must be kept simple if they were to play them. After much scoring and rescoring, the format which became his identification was developed, just in time to get a contract renewal. That contract continued on for seven years, interrupted only by trips to the mainland to appear with the band in motion pictures and to play West Coast location engagements, including the St. Francis and Beverly Wilshire Hotels. In 1941 he was once again touring the states, with a contract calling for a reopening at the Royal Hawaiian in late December when the bombing of Pearl Harbor eliminated any possibility of returning to the Islands for several years. For the next several years he concentrated on West Coast locations with occasional tours through the Midwest and South and one or more location jobs in New York City. When television's strength became apparent, he got into it. He started a West Coast show in 1949 for which CBS put together a special network covering the western states, Alaska, and Hawaii, and the show enjoyed a very successful run. Eventually Owens retired as a performing musician, to operate an Hawaiian tour agency for several years. In 1976 he sold his Santa Monica home and moved to Eugene, Oregon retaining no contact with his former musical career except the operation of his music publishing business. He died in a hospital in that city on December 11, 1986, victim of a heart attack at age 84.

WALTER PAGE

Started First Band Mid-twenties
Where Oklahoma City
Previous Band Affiliations Benny Moten
Sidemen With Band Included Le Roy White, Doc Ross, Lester Young, Buster Smith, Reuben Lynch, Abe Bolar, Jap Jones, Leonard Chadwick, George Hudson, Charlie Washington, Druie Bess, Raymond Howell, Hot Lips Page, Count Basie, Ted Manning, Eddie Durham, Jimmy Simpson, Reuben Roddy, Turk Thomas, Alvin Burroughs, and others. (Listing is not necessarily in the order of their working with the band)
Tag Line Walter Page's Original Blue Devils

Page is probably better remembered for his work with the Count Basie band, but for a few years during the late twenties and early thirties he led one of the best black bands in the Midwest area and for a part of that time Count Basie was a member of the Page orchestra. Page got his musical schooling in Kansas City, where he studied violin, piano, and the reed instruments as well as arranging and composition. He spent nearly five years in the Benny Moten band before joining a road show to tour the Southwest, which eventually broke up in Oklahoma City. It was in that city that the "Original Blue Devils" were formed, and out of which they worked, playing primarily one-nighters. In the early thirties the band transferred its base to Kansas City and was planning to attempt bookings in New York City. About that time Page encountered some difficulties with the Kansas City Musician's Union, so he turned the band over to James Simpson to complete the bookings which had already been signed. Page rejoined Benny Moten until Basie formed his own group in 1935. Then Page joined the Basie band, remaining with them until 1942, and rejoining them for awhile in the late forties. During the early fifties he freelanced around New York with various jazz groups, remaining active until shortly before his death in December 1957, a victim of pneumonia.

JIMMY PALMER

Jimmy Palmer.

Started First Band 1945
Where New York City
Previous Band Affiliations Bobby Byrne, Les Brown, Blue Barron, Lou Breese, Dick Stabile
Vocalists With Band Included Thelma Gracen, Julio Maro, Larry Dean
Longest Engagement Hilton Hotel, Chicago, five-and-a-half years
Theme Song "It's A Lonesome Old Town"
Songs Written "Dancin' Shoes"
Recording Affiliations Mercury, United Artists

Jimmy "Dancin' Shoes" Palmer was both a trumpet player and a vocalist, although it was the latter which launched his career. Just out of high school, he entered a Paul Whiteman contest as a singer and won. As a result he was offered a sustaining show on radio station KDKA in Pittsburgh, which gave him sufficient recognition to break into the band business as a vocalist. One of his singing jobs was with the Dick Stabile band, where he went in on a temporary "fill-in" basis and remained on as a permanent replacement. Jobs with Blue Barron,

The Jimmy Palmer Orchestra at the Hollywood Palladium, late 1950s.

Bobby Byrne, Les Brown, and Lou Breese were followed by an eventual return to Stabile. When Stabile went into the service Palmer fronted the band for a brief period of time. Immediately after the war he formed his own band and eventually became a strong favorite in the Midwest, appearing repeatedly at the Chase Hotel, the Muehlbach, the Claridge, the Peabody, the New Orleans Roosevelt, the Rice in Houston, the Casa Loma Ballroom in St. Louis, the Melody Mill in Chicago, and in a long run at the Chicago Conrad Hilton. Although the Midwest was his main base of operations, he also made at least one trip to the Hollywood Palladium, and played such major East Coast locations as the Shoreham Hotel in Washington, D.C., the Steel Pier in Atlantic City, Frank Dailey's Meadowbrook, the Glen Island Casino, the Roosevelt Grill in New York, and the Roseland Ballroom. His musical style is indicated by the fact that he was chosen by the National Ballroom Operators of America as the most promising sweet band in the country. In the mid-seventies Palmer was still active in the Chicago area.

BILL PANNELL

Started First Band 1945
Where Fresno, California
Previous Band Affiliations Army Air Force Band
Vocalists With Band Included Allan King, Kenny Kenniston
Television With Band A West Coast show with Jack Owens
Longest Engagement Ten years at the Hollywood Roosevelt Hotel
Theme Song "Twilight Time"
Recording Affiliations London, Fanfare, Amco, and Val

Pannell's was a hotel-style dance band, which spent most of its time on the West Coast. After a couple of years at the California Hotel in Fresno, with good air time, they came into Los Angeles to play the Hollywood Roosevelt, and soon became a very popular favorite in the Southern California area. During a twenty-six year span Pannell came and went at the Roosevelt, with one continuous engagement of ten years. The band toured throughout the West Coast and Southwest, playing Catalina Island, the Las Vegas lounges, and the Westward Ho in Phoenix. In the early years of his bandleading career Pannell fronted a band of twelve men, but reduced it in size as the decline in big band popularity developed. He remained active until the early seventies, at which time he gave up the band because of a bad arthritic condition.

TONY PASTOR

Started First Band 1939 (Had briefly fronted own band in a Hartford night club in the early thirties)
Where New York City
Previous Band Affiliations Irving Aaronson, Smith Ballew, Joe Venuti, Vincent Lopez, and Artie Shaw
Sidemen With Band Included Buddy Morrow, Cappy Crouse, Lou McGarity, Charley Trotta, Bill Robbins, Irving Berger, Andy Ferretti, Leonard Ross, John Wade, Bill Schine, Gary Rains, Fred Isnardi, John Niccolini, Bill Shultz, Marvin Wittstein, Chuck Peterson, Les Burness, Sam Shapiro, Russ Brown, Hank Freeman, Johnny Morris, Max Kaminsky, Ray Noonan, Al Avola, Bill Pritchard, Bobby Gyer, Tommy Farr, Stan Worth, Ed McKinney, Stubby Pastor, George

Bill Pannell and his orchestra at the Hollywood Roosevelt.

Horvath, Bill Abel, Nick Henderson, Joe
Camilleri, Ed Dougherty, Dave Maser, Bob
Ascher, Russell Grant, and others
Vocalists With Band Included Elisse
Cooper, Kay Little, Eugenie Baird,
Rosemary Clooney, Dolores Marvin
Theme Song "Pastoral," "Blossoms"
Recording Affiliations Bluebird, Victor,
Cosmo, Columbia

Born in Middletown, Connecticut in 1907,
Tony Pastor was playing tenor saxophone
with local bands before he was out of high
school. He made his first step into the big
time in 1928, when he joined Irving Aaronson's Commanders, staying with them for a
couple of years. A few years later, while
working with Vincent Lopez, he began to
sing as well as play in the sax section, a
gravel-throated style resembling that of
Louis Armstrong, so that he was sometimes
mistaken for Armstrong when heard on a
jukebox record.

When he joined Artie Shaw he was given
wide latitude in the vocal department. His
biggest break probably came when Shaw
featured him on his Bluebird recording of
"Indian Love Call," which became a big hit.
The recognition which he gained from that
record made it possible for Pastor to start
his own band in 1939 when Shaw disbanded

Tony Pastor.

briefly. One of his first bookings was into
the Lincoln Hotel in New York, where he remained for seven months. Before long Pastor's band, styled similarly to the Shaw

336

Tony Pastor and his orchestra, Catalina Island, 1951.

Tony Pastor and Phil Harris at the Hollywood Palladium in the early 1950s.

organization, was well known coast to coast, with bookings in the top hotels and ballrooms available to them. Pastor's own recordings on Bluebird and Victor did well in the marketplace. During the early and midforties the band made several musical short subjects for Columbia and Universal Pictures and at least one full-length film, *Two Blondes And A Redhead*, the latter for Columbia.

Pastor's success with a big band continued unabated throughout the fifties, although by that time he was concentrating his activities in the area east of the Mississippi.

He played regular annual engagements at such hotels as the Peabody in Memphis and the Roosevelt in New Orleans, with an occasional trip to the West Coast to play the Palladium. In 1959 he gave up the big band to form a smaller group, primarily a vocal act, which included his two sons Tony Jr. and Guy. Most of his time with this group was spent playing the lounges in Las Vegas, where they were extremely popular. Pastor passed away at the age of sixty-two in New London, Connecticut, in October 1969 after a long illness.

RAY PEARL

Started First Band 1937
Where Pennsylvania
Previous Band Affiliations Barney Rapp
Sidemen With Band Included Walter Link, Buddy Madison, Nicky Barile, Sully Walker, Bob Berkey, Memo Bernabei, Walter Bloom, and others
Vocalists With Band Included Best known was Jean Gordon
Theme Song "A Kiss From Me To You"
Recording Affiliations Transcriptions only

Throughout his bandleading career Pearl's musical style was definitely on the sweet side. The instrumentation was usually three saxophones, four brass, guitar, drums and piano, with both a string bass and a tuba. Trade journal reviewers sometimes described Pearl's music as a combination of the styles of Wayne King, Sammy Kaye, Jan Garber, and Russ Morgan. The band quickly became a strong dance attraction in the Pennsylvania/Ohio area. It was considered strong enough for MCA to book a summerlong West Coast tour in 1940, which included playing such locations as Jantzen Beach in Portland and the Casino Gardens in Santa Monica. Perhaps if World War II had not intervened Pearl might have found success similar to that of the leaders whose styles he borrowed: for despite the popularity of swing bands, the demand for sweet music

Ray Pearl.

in the early forties was also very strong. Pearl was a likeable individual, but per-perhaps he should have been a fighter rather than a bandleader. When he took a stand on something, he considered no adversary too tough to tangle with. I recall spending a weekend with him in Portland, Oregon in 1940, when most of our time was spent going to the

At the Casino Gardens, Santa Monica, California, in the summer of 1940.

police station to recover his car, where it was repeatedly towed after he insisted on parking it in yellow zones. He was drafted into the army early in the course of the war and stationed at an army post in Kansas. He quickly discovered that the manner in which the army was conducting military affairs did not meet with his approval, a fact which he made clear to everyone, including the company commander. The consistency with which he expressed his opinions in the matter resulted in his contribution to the war effort being fairly well limited to latrine duty. There was a great deal of conjecture as to whether he or the army was happier to terminate their association at the war's end. In the postwar years his was one of the Midwest's busiest territory bands, with headquarters in Chicago where he was brought back time and again to play the Melody Mill. He was also a regular at the Roosevelt Hotel in New Orleans and the Peabody in Memphis. His popularity in that area continued through the early fifties until about 1955, when the band business was in a decline. Pearl placed the blame for the slumping business squarely on the shoulders of the Union's president, Jimmy Petrillo. In 1956 at the close of an engagement at the

Jean Gordon, vocalist with Ray Pearl in the early 1940s.

Peabody Hotel, he purchased a large ad in the Memphis newspapers blasting Petrillo, and announcing his retirement from the music business. It hardly needs noting that his retirement was permanent.

PAUL PENDARVIS

Started First Band   Early thirties
Where   Kansas City
Theme Song   "My Sweetheart"
Recording Affiliations   Columbia

Pendarvis was born in Oklahoma, but moved to California for his college education where he attended UCLA. After a short business career and some minor motion picture parts, he put together a band in Kansas City, where it was immediately successful. Pendarvis was a violinist, who was brought on the air with this announcement: "When you hear the violin it's Paul Pendarvis," followed immediately by the band's theme. Following his Kansas City success, he moved into the Congress Hotel in Chicago, and for the next several years played the Midwestern circuit with occasional trips into the New York area. In the late thirties he moved to the West Coast, to settle in Los Angeles and play West Coast locations. He gave up his bandleading career in the early forties to become musical director of a radio station.

RED PERKINS

Started First Band   Mid-twenties
Where   Omaha, Nebraska
Sidemen With Band Included   Jesse Simmons, A.C. Oglesby, Charlie Watkins, Eugene Freels, Harry Rooks, Louie Van, Sylvester Freels, Clarence Gray, Bernard Wright, Jabbo Smith, Ernie Redd, Bill Osborn, Bob Hall, Louis Evans, Sam Grievous, Bob Canslar, Leslie Canslar, Jim Alexander, Johnny Redd, Richard Hart, Herb Wiggins, Jay Green, Francis Whitby, Willie Parr. Perkins played trumpet and did vocals
Tag Line   Red Perkins and His Dixie Ramblers
Recording Affiliations   Gennett

Perkins' first group was a sextet, but as his reputation grew so did the size of his band. For a period of approximately twenty years his was one of the most popular dance bands to play out of Omaha. Booked by National Orchestra Service, he covered Nebraska, Kansas, Iowa, and the Dakotas, and was constantly on the road playing one-nighters. The band was always good instrumentally, but also a very entertaining band. Perkins usually maintained a group of versatile musicians, all able to double on several instruments. When Perkins finally gave up the band, he settled down in Minneapolis to become a photographer.

TEDDY PHILLIPS

Started First Band   1946
Where   Chicago, Illinois
Previous Band Affiliations   Ben Bernie, Ted Weems, Lawrence Welk, and studio work with both CBS and ABC networks
Sidemen With Band Included   Bill Paige, Ethmer Roten, Tommy Shephard, Elmer Bloomquist, Bobby Burgess, Arnold Oberstein, and others. During most of his career he worked with a twelve- to fourteen-piece band
Vocalists With Band Included   Lynn Hoyt
Television With Band   Original show called "The Teddy Phillips Show for Pontiac," originating in Chicago. Duration one year
Longest Engagements   Annual repeat appearances at the Aragon and Trianon Ballrooms in Chicago for a seven-year period
Theme Song   "Thankful"
Songs Written   "Wishin'," "Don't Call Me Sweetheart Anymore," "Little Canole," "Camel Hump," "Open House"
Recording Affiliations   London, Decca, Brunswick, Mercury, Dot, Liberty, MGM, Coral, and Tower

"Red" Perkins and his Original Dixie Ramblers.

When Phillips came out of the army in 1945 he went to work as a staff musician at CBS in Chicago for a year. Prior to the war he had been with ABC. In 1946 he organized his first band, a jazz-oriented pit band for Chicago's Downtown theater, where they remained for a year. The following year MCA signed the band and took Phillips on a tour through the South and Southwest, keeping him on the road until early 1948. At that time he changed his musical style to that of a commercial dance band, a style which he still maintains. For the next several years Phillips kept busy in the Chicago area, playing both the Aragon and Trianon, with time out for tours through the South to play the Peabody, Roosevelt, and Baker and Muehlbach Hotels. Eventually he moved to the West Coast to live in Los Angeles, where he played such locations as Myron's Ballroom and the Golden West Ballroom. During the early seventies he was still making annual Midwestern tours. Early in 1975 a serious injury in an auto accident hospitalized him for several months and from that point on reduced his ability to travel. Now he is concentrating on writing and arranging, and also playing private and public one-nighters in the Los Angeles area, including an occasional appearance at the new Palace Ballroom in North Hollywood.

341

Teddy Phillips.   Teddy Phillips and his orchestra, Chicago, 1956.

The Teddy Phillips Orchestra backing the Ritz Brothers at the Flamingo, Las Vegas, 1956.

BEN POLLACK

Started First Band 1925
Where Los Angeles area
Previous Band Affiliations New Orleans Rhythm Kings
Sidemen With Band Included Glenn Miller, Benny Goodman, Gil Rodin, Fud Livingston, Harry Greenberg, Harry Goodman, Victor Young, Al Harris, Wayne Allen, Al Beller, Nick Breidis, Lou Kessler, Jimmy McPartland, Frankie Quartell, Larry Binyon, Dick Morgan, Eddie Bergman, Jack Teagarden, Ray Bauduc, Smith Ballew, Ruby Weinstein, Snub Pollard, Joe Catalyne, Charlie Teagarden, Charlie Spivak, Sterling Bose, Joe Bowers, Nappy Lamare, Matty Matlock, Eddie Miller, Ray Cohen, Jerry Johnson, Yank Lawson, Harry James, Shorty Sherock, Irving Fazola, Opie Cates, Dave Mathews, Freddie Slack, Thurman Teague, Muggsy Spanier, Mort Friedman, Gene Krupa, George Thow, Clyde Hurley, Earle Hagen, George Hill, Bob Laine
Vocalists With Band Included Frank Sylvano, Frank Bauer, Belle Mann, Dick Robertson, Scrappy Lambert, Doris Robbins, Lois Still, Jim Hardy, Peggy Mann, Paula Gayle, Armide Whipple, Mel Torme
Theme Song "Song of the Islands"
Recording Affiliations Victor, Variety, Columbia, Decca

Ben Pollack deserves a much higher place in the musical history of the big band era than the financial success he attained during his nearly thirty years of activity. His skill as a developer of musical talent was equalled by

The late 1920s Pollack band included Benny Goodman, Fud Livingstn, Harry Goodman, Jack Teagarden, and Gil Rodin.

343

The Pollack band in the early 1940s at the Sherman Hotel.

very few. Many of those who later became successful bandleaders of the twenties and thirties got their start working with Pollack, before moving on to work with other name bands.

Born in Chicago, he became active in music by playing drums in high school bands. His first professional job was with the New Orleans Rhythm Kings, with whom he spent approximately three years and did his first recording. In 1924 he went to the West Coast, where in early 1925 he formed his own first band and booked it into the Venice Ballroom. That organization included Glenn Miller on trombone and Benny Goodman on clarinet. After a successful California run, he returned to Chicago to play the Southmore Hotel, then moved on to the

Park Central in New York, where he stayed for more than a year. He then went into a prominent Gotham supper club called the Silver Slipper.

Pollack had a talent for discovering and assembling good musicians, and a long list of future great names worked for him. But he seemed to have trouble keeping them together. It was not for any lack of money, for he paid better than average salaries and his weekly payroll often exceeded the band's income. In 1935, with an all-star organization, he once again made a tour to the West Coast. Dissension within the band developed, and it returned to the East without Pollack. That group remained virtually intact and shortly later became the Bob Crosby band.

Pollack and his "Pick-A-Rib Boys" on the Sunset Strip in the late 1950s.

Pollack reorganized and remained active, but in the early forties he made a deal for Chico Marx to front the Pollack organization, relegating himself to the capacity of a manager. Male vocals in the band at that time were handled by Mel Tormé, who was only sixteen years old. In addition to singing Tormé did some arranging, and occasionally played the drums. This band also broke up on the West Coast at the end of 1942.

Next, Pollack started a talent agency and a recording company of his own, confining his activities to these operations for the next several years with only moderate success.

Eventually he liquidated both the talent agency and the recording company to engage in the restaurant business in Hollywood and later in Palm Springs. But he made

periodic returns to bandleading activities, with a Dixieland group sometimes billed as "Pollack's Pick-A-Rib Boys." During those years he often expressed, to friends who dropped in to see him, a feeling of bitterness towards the music business and what he felt was ingratitude on the part of those he had helped along the road to success.

In June 1971, despondent over financial problems, he hanged himself in his Palm Springs home. He was laid to rest in Hollywood, with services in a chapel jammed to overflowing with his old friends and coverage by the television networks. Such is the irony of life. If just a few of those friends had thought to call him on the phone two weeks earlier, they would probably not have been assembled to pay their last respects on that June day.

345

PETE PONTRELLI

Started First Band 1919
Where Los Angeles
Sidemen With Band Included Everett Hoagland, Bernie Snyder, Joe Pally, Ernie Lohrman, Bill Cooper, Hal Barnett, Joe Norden, Cliff Barber, Claude Bowen, Dalton Rizutto, Steve Allen, Les Pinlar, George Pope, Leo Wàrez, "Breezy" Thomas, Harry Green, John De Soto, Bobby Small, Ted Romero, Pat McCartney, and many others
Longest Engagement Figueroa Ballroom, Los Angeles
Recording Affiliations Senate (Pontrelli's own label)

Pontrelli started out to be a barber and ended up a musician and bandleader. The bands he fronted varied in size, starting with a five-piece unit in 1919 and growing to as many as fifteen men, with the average about twelve. Pontrelli played a saxophone. During most of what turned out to be a long musical career, Pontrelli had a very popular Southern California band, with no ambition

to travel. Coast-to-coast air time from some of the locations where he played gave him seminame status over a wide area. Those locations included four years at the Palace Ballroom in Ocean Park, beginning in 1928; a long stand at the Rainbow Gardens (later the Palomar) with coast-to-coast air time over KTM; five years at the Paris Inn in downtown Los Angeles, with a daytime and a nighttime pickup on CBS. In 1937 the Fox Theater chain gave him an award as having the best dance band on the air, with Edward Arnold making the presentation. In 1944 he took over operation of the Figueroa Ballroom, and for the next fourteen years ran it himself, with his own band featured. Throughout that period the band was heard steadily on radio and made occasional appearances on KHJ-TV. During the sixties Pontrelli worked at Myron's Ballroom in downtown Los Angeles, but by that time had decreased the size of his band to seven men. When I interviewed him, he was still occasionally active with a small group at the age of eighty.

Pete Pontrelli and his orchestra, Figueroa Ballroom, Los Angeles, 1952.

TEDDY POWELL

Teddy Powell.

Started First Band 1940

Where New York City

Previous Band Affiliations Abe Lyman

Sidemen With Band Included George Esposito, Irving Goodman, Pete Skinner, George Koenig, Gus Bivona, Don Lodice, Pete Mondello, Milt Raskin, Ben Heller, Tom D'Agostino, Howard Gaffney, Tom Reo, John Grassi, Harry Davis, Lenny Hartman, Buddy Weed, Dick Fisher, Bill Westfall, Mickey Folus, Tony Aless, Bobby Domanick, Mickey Clocielo, Tino Isgrow, Barry Galbraith, Wilbur Hoffman, Dave Bastien, Louis Fromm, Chuck Gentry, Irving Fazola, Carmen Mastren, Charlie Ventura, Pete Candoli, Milt Bernhart. Arrangements were done by Fred Norman, Ray Conniff, Dave Mathews

Vocalists With Band Included Ruth Gaylor, Jimmy Blair, Peggy Mann, Skip Nelson, and Gene Barry, who later became famous as a television star

Musical Style A good solid swinging dance band

Sponsored Radio Shows Several appearances on the "Coca Cola Spotlight Band Show"

Longest Engagement One year at the Rustic Tavern

Theme Song "Blue Sentimental Mood"

Songs Written "You Won't Be Satisfied Until You Break My Heart," "Heaven Help This Heart Of Mine," "Unsuspecting Heart," "Boots And Saddles," and "Ooh, My Aching Heart"

Recording Affiliations Decca, Bluebird, and Victor

The Teddy Powell Orchestra on stage in New York in the mid 1940s.

Powell was born in Oakland, California, and joined the Abe Lyman orchestra when he was only sixteen years old. With the Lyman band, he was not only a sideman but did a great deal of the band's arranging. His own band included, at various times, some very talented musicians as the roster above will indicate. With it he toured coast to coast playing ballrooms, theaters and night clubs and enjoying several years of strong popularity. His recordings sold well, but few of them reached the hit category. Many were novelties. With the entire band he was featured in two movies, *Jam Session* at Columbia and *Melody Gardens* at Universal. Powell was an accomplished songwriter with a long list of credits, one of which ("Boots And Saddles") won the ASCAP award in 1935 for being the greatest western song of the year. During the war years Powell disbanded briefly because of problems created by the draft, and resumed bandleading at war's end. He retired from bandleading in 1954 to enter the music publishing business.

LOUIS PRIMA

Started First Band   Early thirties
Where   New Orleans
Theme Song   "Sing, Sing, Sing," "Way Down Yonder In New Orleans"
Songs Written   "Sing, Sing, Sing," "Robin Hood," "Little Boy Blew His Top," "Boogie In Chicago," "It's The Rhythm In Me," co-composer of "A Sunday Kind Of Love"
Recording Affiliations   Brunswick, Majestic, Victor, Mercury, Columbia

Prima is best known for his work with small jazz-oriented groups with a New Orleans flavor, but throughout the late thirties and forties he fronted a full-sized dance band which recorded regularly, with many of the recordings featuring Prima himself on the vocals. He worked with the band in several motion pictures, including *Rhythm On The Range, Manhattan Merry-Go-Round, Start Cheering,* and *You Can't Have Everything.* Many prominent sidemen worked with him from time to time, including Pee Wee Russell, George Brunis, Eddie Miller, Nappy Lamare, Ray Bauduc, George Van Eps, and Claude Thornhill. In the mid-fifties Prima became a consistent headline attraction in the Las Vegas casinos, with a small group which featured the saxophone work of Sam Butera, and Prima's wife Keely Smith along with Louis on vocals. About 1958 their re-

Louis Prima.

cording of "Old Black Magic" became a sensational hit, boosting their drawing power for many years to come. When Keely Smith left the band, other vocalists were brought in to work with Prima, but without the same success. He remained active into the early seventies. In 1976 he entered a Los Angeles hospital for surgery because of brain tumor, and was later transferred to a New Orleans hospital where he died in August of 1978.

HAL PRUDEN

Started First Band 1946
Where Los Angeles
Previous Band Affiliations Chuck Foster,
Bob Crosby
Longest Engagement Flamingo Hotel, Las
Vegas
Theme Song "Busybody"
Songs Written "Busybody," "Powder Blue,"
"Ivory Mischief"

Pruden describes his band as a "piano showcase band" that played danceable music. He
was often billed as the world's fastest pianist, claiming the ability to play more notes
per second on the piano than anyone else.
His ability in that area was somewhat remarkable, considering that as a child he at
one time had completely lost the use of his
hands, because of the residual effect of scar-
let fever and inflammatory rheumatism.
Booked by MCA, the Pruden band played
coast-to-coast in such locations as the Mapes
Hotel in Reno, the Baker Hotel in Dallas, the
Shamrock in Houston, the New Orleans
Roosevelt, the Peabody in Memphis, and the
Statler in Boston. Pruden gave up his bandleading career in 1953.

Hal Pruden.

BOYD RAEBURN

Started First Band   About 1933
Where   Chicago
Previous Band Affiliations   College bands
Sidemen With Band Included   Johnny Bothwell, Al Cohn, Ike Carpenter, Don Lamond, Benny Harris, Oscar Pettiford, Hal McKusick, Trummy Young, Dizzy Gillespie, Buddy de Franco, Johnny Mandell, Dodo Marmarosa, Harry Babisin, Milt Bernhart, and many others who came and went
Vocalists With Band Included   David Allen, Don Darcy, Ginnie Powell (later became Mrs. Raeburn)
Theme Song   At various times used three: "Man With A Horn," "Over The Rainbow," "Raeburn's Theme"
Recording Affiliations   Grand, Guild, Jewel

Boyd Raeburn.

After winning a college band contest sponsored by the Sherman Hotel, Raeburn launched his professional bandleading career at a restaurant at the Chicago World's Fair in 1933. During the next several years he worked the Middle West with a "sweet" hotel style band, but towards the end of the thirties he switched to swing. In 1940 he took his band into the Chez Paree in Chicago, where good nightly air time built his prestige. In 1942 he made his first trip to New York City to play briefly, and then returned to Chicago to play at the Bandbox for at least a year. In 1944 he changed his style completely, putting together a progressive jazz organization to compete with Woody Herman and Stan Kenton in that selective category. With the new band he went into

350

The Boyd Raeburn Orchestra in 1945.

the Lincoln Hotel in New York City to play an extended engagement. Late that year he was given a setback when the band lost most of its instruments and library in a fire. During the balance of the forties he reorganized and disbanded several times, with some periods of complete layoff. In the early fifties he concentrated his activities in the New York City area, usually with a pickup band. In 1952 he dropped out entirely to engage in a business venture in New York, which he gave up in the mid-fifties to move to the Bahamas. In the late fifties he once again organized a band, this time somewhat more styled for dancing, this venture also of short duration. He died in Lafayette, Louisiana in August 1966 at the age of 52. Family and friends attributed his death to injuries suffered in an auto accident three years ealier.

BARNEY RAPP

Started First Band   Early twenties
Where   East Coast, apparently in Connecticut
Vocalists With Band Included   Eddie Ryan, Bunny Welcome, Ruby Wright, Doris Day
Tag Line   "Barney Rapp and his New Englanders"
Recording Affiliations   Victor, Bluebird

Rapp was primarily a Midwest attraction who built his reputation with the help of good air time from a night-club of his own in Cincinnati. His smoothly styled orchestra was ideal for dancing and came off well on records, which sold moderately well. Perhaps his biggest claim to fame was that future motion picture and television star Doris Day got her start singing in his band. He seldom wandered far from Cincinnati, although he did get to the West Coast to appear in at least one motion picture. He died in Cincinnati in the early seventies.

Barney Rapp and his New Englanders.

CARL RAVAZZA

Started First Band   Mid-thirties
Where   San Francisco
Previous Band Affiliations   Violinist and vocalist with Tom Coakley. Took over Coakley's band when Coakley gave it up for the practice of law
Sidemen With Band Included   Paul Durand, Bobby Blair, Bud Crossman, Bill Hammett, George Porter, Paul Faria, Lester Randolph, Joe Coates, Russell Doxaras, Neil Bondshu, Ted Bering, George Hewett, Marshall Cram
Vocalists With Band Included   Ravazza did male vocals himself. Among the early female vocalists was Dawn Meredith
Theme Song   "Vieni Su"
Recording Affiliations   Decca, Bluebird

During his early years as a bandleader, Ravazza enjoyed a long engagement at the Sir Francis Drake in San Francisco. Next he took the band on the road for tours that booked him through the South and Midwest, and occasionally into New York City. His

Carl Ravazza.

was primarily a hotel band, and its list of regular stops included the Adolphus in Dallas, the Peabody in Memphis, the Muehlbach in Kansas City, the Nicollet in Minneapolis, and the Lexington in New York. Return engagements to his home town of San Francisco were usually played at the St. Francis. His singing style was his biggest asset and

eventually he gave up the band to become a single, playing leading night-clubs throughout the country for several years. Eventually he settled down in Reno, Nevada, where he owned a ranch, and put together a very successful talent agency. He died in a Reno hospital in the summer of 1968.

DON REDMAN

Started First Band Early thirties
Where New York City
Previous Band Affiliations Fletcher Henderson, McKinney's Cotton Pickers, arranged for several bands including Paul Specht
Theme Song "Chant of the Weed"
Songs Written "Cherry," "Chant of the Weed," "How'm I Doin'?"

Although he was best identified with the saxophone, Redman was able to play any

instrument in the band and started out with the trumpet even before he entered grade school. He was born in West Virginia, the son of parents who were both involved in music, and who supervised his early musical study of the instruments and encouraged his study in arranging and composition. He later pursued those studies at musical conservatories in Boston and Detroit. In 1923 he joined Fletcher Henderson's band for a recording session at Columbia's Columbus

Don Redman and his orchestra.

353

Circle Studio, and was invited to become a permanent member when the band opened at the Club Alabam. He quickly became a strong influence on the Henderson style and remained with Henderson for four years, finally leaving in 1927. At that time he went to Detroit where he joined McKinney's Cotton Pickers, quickly becoming musical director of the unit, which was booked by Jean Goldkette. With them he toured the Midwest until 1931. He then returned to New York, where he formed a band of his own.

During the early thirties the Redman orchestra was rated as one of the top black bands in the New York area. With it he became the first black leader to have a sponsored radio program (for a soap sponsor). He gave up the band in the early forties to devote his time to arranging, but periodically reassembled a group for night-club appearances and for at least one European tour. In the early fifties he put together a band to back Pearl Bailey on theater engagements. He died on November 30, 1964.

TOMMY REED

Started First Band 1946
Where San Francisco
Previous Band Affiliations Joe Venuti, Henry King, Russ Morgan, Jimmy Dorsey, Richard Himber, Dick Jurgens, Ernie Hecksher, Del Courtney, Ran Wilde
Vocalists With Band Included Sue Mouro
Theme Song "Two Clouds In The Sky"
Songs Written "Fishin' For Love," "Two Heavens," "After All"
Recording Affiliations MGM, Camelback Records

Although Reed started his band on the West Coast, he spent little time working there once the band was organized. With a full-size band of thirteen men playing some good arrangements he toured the Middle West and then played at least one engagement at the Lexington Hotel in New York City. Finally he settled in the Midwest, where he became a heavy favorite playing regularly at the Oh Henry Ballroom (now Willowbrook), the Chase Hotel in St. Louis, the Peabody in Memphis, the Roosevelt in New Orleans, the Pier in Galveston, Texas, and a five-year run (1954-1959) at the Muehlbach in Kansas City. Somewhere along the way he reduced the band in size, but with the use of some fine arrangements retained a sound which would have done justice to a larger unit. When the big band in the Midwest declined in the early sixties, Reed

Tommy Reed.

moved to Phoenix, Arizona where he opened a talent agency (Southwest Booking Agency, Inc.), and quickly established himself as the most active talent booker in the Arizona market. Meanwhile he still found time to play most of the city's conventions and special events, with a band of eight men, including himself on saxophone and clarinet. He is still prosperously active in both categories.

Tommy Reed and his orchestra at the Lexington Hotel, New York, 1948.

JOE REICHMAN

Started First Band Late twenties
Where St. Louis area
Sidemen With Band Included Art Lewis, Burt LaMarr, Charles Grifford, Joseph Sudy, Joe Martin, Clem Zuzensk, James Williamson, Fred Fellensby, Eddie Mihas, Jim Bishop, Leon Schwartz, David Kellner, Ernie Mathias, Ed Turley, Larry Neill, George Werth, Bernie Gold, Joe Perrin, Chester Le Roy, Milt Bernhart, Les Penner, Mort Corb, Irving Edelman, Cecil Horowitz, Ben Ribble, Frankie Ortega
Vocalists With Band Included Marion Shaw, Margie Stuart, Jane Fulton, Margie Lee
Theme Song "Variation in G," and "Pagliacci"
Recording Affiliations Perfect, ARC, Victor

During a bandleading career that spanned several decades, Joe Reichman, "The Pagliacci of the Piano," probably played every major hotel in America. He was a regular attraction at New York's Waldorf-Astoria, the Chase Hotel in St. Louis, the Adolphus in Dallas, the Biltmore and Cocoanut Grove in Los Angeles, the St. Francis and Mark Hopkins in San Francisco. His music was styled for the sophisticated set who dined and danced regularly in the top hotels and

supper clubs. The size of the band scarcely varied throughout its existence. It was usually four saxes, three brass, drums, bass, and two pianos. One piano was played by Reichman himself when he was not standing on the edge of the bandstand taking requests. Sometimes he played from a standing position. He was a showman, but also a man with a volatile temper. It was not uncommon to see him pitch a piano stool onto the dance floor. Observers were never sure whether they were witnessing his idea of showmanship or a manifestation of his temper. He insisted that radio announcers bring him on the air by drawing out "Joe" to "Jo-o-o-e," in a manner supposedly achieved by an announcer one night when he was fighting an urge to sneeze. Reichman was also an accomplished mimic, an art which he occasionally practiced on radio broadcasts. In 1948 he moved to Dallas to make his permanent home, where he eventually gave up the band to become a disc jockey. In the mid-fifties he again became periodically active, playing the Muehlbach Hotel in Kansas City and the Peabody in Memphis. He died in a Dallas hospital in April 1970, at the age of seventy-two.

On the Strand stage in the early 1940s.

A slightly smaller Reichman band in the early 1950s.

LEO REISMAN

Started First Band   Early twenties
Where   Boston
Previous Band Affiliations   College orchestras
Sidemen With Band Included   Ernie Gibbs, Louis Shaffrin, Bert Williams, Bill Tronstein, Lew Conrad, Raymond Pugh, Andrew Quenge, Harry Atlas, Harry Sigman, Chuck Campbell, Eddy Duchin, Ned Cola, Pete Eisenberg, Adrian Rollini, Don Howard, Philip Steele, Jack Shilkret, Jeff Smith, Fran Frey, Lew Sherwood, Arthur Schwartz, Joe Poretta, Carl Prager, Ernie Mathias, Frank Hasselberg, Cliff Heather, John Helfer, Bernie Ladd, Harry Katzman, Leo Kahn, Frank Petrilli, Bob Richardson, Harry Walter, Ben Kanter, Art Quenger, Jess Smith, Dave Goldfarb, Martin Black, Felix Slatkin, Hillard Lubre, George Borres, Joe Yukl
Vocalists With Band Included   Smith Ballew, Frank Luther, Philip Steele, Frank Munn, Dick Robertson, Frances Maddux, Sally Singer, Bernice Claire, Lee Sullivan, Lee Wiley, Larry Stewart, Dinah Shore, Anita Boyer
Sponsored Radio Shows   "The Phillip Morris Show," "The Lucky Strike Hit Parade," "The Pond's Cream Show," "The Fleishman's Yeast Show," "RKO Theater of the Air"
Theme Song   "What Is This Thing Called Love?"
Recording Affiliations   Columbia, Vocalion, Brunswick, Victor, Decca

Throughout his career the Reisman orchestra was classed as a "society band," even though during the late twenties he called himself a jazz bandleader, a term which was not at that time as restrictive as it became later. He even authored a series of articles on jazz for a music magazine; and in one article took issue with Henry Ford, who had been quoted as having a very low opinion of jazz and anyone who played it.

Except for some school bands (most of which he put together himself) and appearances with the Boston Symphony Orchestra,

Leo Reisman, famed Victor-NBC music king.

he never worked with any other musical organization except his own. Like many other leaders of that period his instrument was the violin. During his early years as a leader, except for coastwise tours, he worked steadily at the Egyptian Room of the Hotel Brunswick in Boston. At that time it was common practice for name leaders to have several musical organizations which they booked under their own name, and Reisman also followed this practice. In 1929 he went into New York's Central Park Casino, for an engagement supposedly arranged by New York's Mayor Walker and an opening that was highly publicized. He eventually became one of the most popular dance orchestras on the East Coast, with regular appearances at the Waldorf-Astoria and occasional European tours.

Reisman was once described by a columnist as, "looking like a continually irritated rooster" when he was on the bandstand. If this were true, it was probably because he permitted no nonsense from the members of the band, and not a great deal from the audience out front. He resented adverse criticism and reacted strongly to it. In an exchange of correspondence with him in early 1961, he told me emphatically that he made and sold more records than any orchestra leader in the world. By that time he was retired from the music business and making his home in Miami, Florida. He died there on December 18, 1961.

Leo Reisman and his orchestra at the Central Park Casino, New York, 1934.

ALVINO REY

Started First Band 1939
Where California
Previous Band Affiliations Horace Heidt
Sidemen With Band Included Rafael Mendez, Jack Cathcart, Skeets Herfurt, Levon Urbanski, Willy Morinez, Buddy Cole, Don Whittaker, Dick Morgan, Charlie Price, Frank Strasek, Danny Vanelli, Paul Fredricks, Jerry Rosa, Wally Barron, Bill Shine, Kermit Levinsky, Jerry Sanfino, Milt Raskin, Gene Traxler, Bunny Shawker, Bill Schallen, Ted Julian, George Sedola, John Fallstitch, Charlie Lee, Charles Brosen, Sanford Block, Jack Palmer, Sam Levine, Ralph Muzillo, Nick Fatool, Justin Gordon, Irving Goodman, Ron Perry, Kai Winding, Stan Fishelson, Jack Gerheim, Russ Grainger, John Martell, Frank Nelson, Chuck Peterson, Bill Young, Kelly Bowman, Bill Haller, Bob Swift, Earl Swope, Bob McReynolds, Roger Thorndyke, Moe Schneider, Ed Kiefer, Hal McKusick, Jack McGowan, Bob Walch, Bud Estes, John Gruey, Herbie Steward, Zoot Sims, Bob Greattinger, Lee Yardum, Rocky Coluccio, Moe Defenbach, Eddie Robertson, Jim Bates, Chick Parnell, Jimmy Pratt, Don Lamond, Al King, and others
Vocalists With Band Included The Four King Sisters (solo numbers were taken by Alyce and Yvonne), Bill Schallen, Andy Russell
Theme Song "Blue Rain," "Nighty-Night"
Recording Affiliations Bluebird, Victor, and Capitol
Before starting his own organization, Alvino Rey and his electric guitar were featured for several years with Horace Heidt and His

The Alvino Rey Orchestra and the King Sisters at the Pasadena Civic Auditorium in 1939. The band included some great talent: piano—Buddy Cole; trumpet—Rafael Mendez, Jack Cathcart; saxophone—Skeets Herfurt; guitar—Dick Morgan.

Musical Knights. Also featured with the Heidt orchestra during those years was a quartette of lovely vocalists from Salt Lake City, Utah: the King Sisters. Since Alvino was married to one of the group (Luise), they too left Heidt to participate in the new musical venture. The combination of a top vocal group and the Rey orchestra eventually became a smooth working package which was pleasing to both listeners and dancers in the best hotels, ballrooms, and theaters in the nation.

But success did not come as easily as that makes it sound. At a Hollywood Press Club "Salute To The Great Dance Bands," which I produced in April 1977, Alvino told of the early day struggles, including auditioning for a major agency who did not even give the group the courtesy of telling them they were not interested. Deciding then to handle their own bookings, the band worked its way to the East Coast, playing one-nighters and a three-weeks location job for which they did not get paid. Eventually they booked themselves into a leading New York hotel, where they were cautioned by the management to "make as little noise as possible." This was somewhat difficult for the Rey band, which had a very heavy brass section with arrangements to match. All

The King Sisters, after they were performing as an attraction without the band.

went well for a few weeks until a friend who had heard the band on the road came in and asked for a special request. Rey decided they would play it as written and the sound that resulted practically brought down the room's draperies. It also brought the hotel manager in from his suite in his dressing robe, to fire them on the spot.

Eventually the band caught on, with the aid of their Bluebird and Victor records, which began to sell well. Most of these featured the King Sisters, with the band well identified in the background, but there were also many good instrumentals. During the early forties the band was sufficiently popular to be featured in several motion pictures.

At the peak of the band's popularity, Rey was forced to disband to enter the navy, where he remained for the duration of World War II, a great deal of his time being spent at the Great Lakes Naval Training Station. Returning at war's end, he once again re-sumed with a big band, but without the King Sisters who had retired to do only occasional personal appearances and record dates. With this new band he enjoyed moderate success for several years, reducing it in size to a smaller combination during the early fifties. The smaller group remained active until the early sixties with occasional tours to Europe and Hawaii. In the fall of 1964 he and the King Sisters found a whole new career in television with the "King Family" show which featured the original King Sisters, their children, and occasionally the full Rey orchestra. The television show lasted only a few seasons, but it created a steady demand for personal appearances which continued unabated into the seventies. Rey is still periodically active with a band of varying size.

In the early 1940s at the Log Cabin in New Jersey.

TOMMY REYNOLDS

Started First Band 1939
Where Cleveland, Ohio
Previous Band Affiliations Isham Jones
Sidemen With Band Included Louis Colombo, Joe Fandel, Tino Iscro, Harold Raymond, Dick Hathaway, Don Cavanaugh, Chuck Hill, Marshall Hutchins, Pete Abramo, George Kohler, Parker Lee, Wilfred Dufresne, Julio Cancredi, Hank Maddalena, Cy Siok, Tom Bell, Dick Di Maio, Lenny Ross, Al Anthony, Floyd Smith, Nick Peters, George Robinson, Joe Cribari, Joe Kurtz, Eddie Spear, Rollie Michaels, Art Smith, and others
Vocalists With Band Included Marion Page, Penny Porter, Sally Richards, Mary Ann McCall, Ralph Young
Theme Song "Pipe Dreams"
Songs Written "Pipe Dreams," "Once Over Lightly," "I'll Tell It To The Breeze"
Recording Affiliations Vocalion, Okeh, Columbia

Reynolds, who played clarinet in a style patterned after Artie Shaw, attended Akron University before becoming a sideman with Isham Jones. He spent two years in the Jones band, then in late 1939 put together his own organization. Access to good air time built his popularity in the Cleveland area and throughout the Midwest. He gradually expanded that popularity and retained it through the forties, playing such spots as the Roseland Ballroom in New York, Frank Dailey's Meadowbrook, the Paramount Theater, the New Yorker Hotel, the Bandbox in Chicago, and the Palladium in Hollywood. He kept the big band alive until the mid-fifties, when he gave it up to become musical director for radio-television station WOR in New York City. During his stay there, he produced the popular show, "Bandstand U.S.A."

BUDDY RICH

Started First Band 1946
Where New York City
Previous Band Affiliations Joe Marsala, Bunny Berigan, Artie Shaw, Tommy Dorsey, Benny Carter
Sidemen With Band Included Pinky Savitt, Louis Oles, Bitsy Mullens, Carl Warwick, Sid Illardi, Earl Swope, Johnny Mandel, Sam Hyster, Dave Sickles, Les Clark, Aaron Sachs, George Berg, Mike Blanos, Sid Brown, Tony Nichols, Lenny Mirabella, Joe Shulman, Stan Kay, Tommy Allison, Al Loraine, Mickey Rich, Jimmy Johnson, Red Rodney, Irv Markowitz, Harry Bist, Phil Gilbert, Bill Howell, Mario Daone, Bob Ascher, Eddie Caine, Allen Eager, Harry Levine, Harvey Leonard, Tubby Phillips, Dale Pierce, Jack Carmen, George Handy, Terry Gibbs, Chauncey Welsch, Sam Marowitz, Stan Weiss, Buddy Guyer, Frank Defabio, George Shaw, Bill Rubinstein, Sonny Russo, Emmett Berry, Harry Edison, Joe Ferrante, Jimmy Nottingham, Earl Warren, Phil Woods, Benny Golson, Steve Perlow, John Bunch, Sam Herman, Phil Leshin, Tony Scodwell, Bob Faust, John Sottile, Jim Tremble, John Boice, Bob Brawn, Tom Hall, Sam Most, Jay Corre, Marty Falx, Barry Zwig, Gary Walters, Ray Stalling, Chuck Findley, Oliver Mitchell, Ernie Watts, Jimmy Moser, Bob Keller, Jimmy Gannon, Meyer Hirsch, Herb Ellis, Charley Davis, John Hoffman, Larry Hall, Allen Kaplan, Keith O'Quinn, John Lays, Joe Robano, Bob Martin, Pat La Barbera, Bob Crea, Buddy Hudson, Joe Beck, Tony Levin, and many others. Turnover was heavy, due to many starts and restarts
Vocalists With Band Included Dorothy Reid, Lynn Warren, Linda Larkin, Marjorie Dean, Muriel James, Jean Weeks
Recording Affiliations Mercury, Verve, Liberty, Pacific, Victor

361

The Buddy Rich Orchestra in the late 1940s.

Rich has been rated by many as one of the greatest—perhaps *the* greatest—of all the white big band drummers. Those who rated him so highly could hardly have been influenced by personal reasons, for he was never one to be concerned with winning personality awards. Born in Brooklyn in 1917, he broke into show business with his parents' vaudeville act, and worked with a band before he was a teenager. By 1938 he was drumming with Joe Marsala's sextet at the Hickory House in New York. Later that year he joined Bunny Berigan; then moved on to play with Artie Shaw; then left him to join Tommy Dorsey, with whom he played from late 1939 through most of 1942. At that time he went into the service, to spend two years in the marines.

Out of uniform in late 1944, he rejoined the Dorsey band. In 1946 he formed his own band, the first of several such ventures, this one of short duration. Despite financing by Frank Sinatra and some excellent bookings, the band didn't catch on and he broke it up after a couple of years, to tour with Norman Granz and his Jazz at the Philharmonic.

The fifties saw him alternately fronting a band of his own and working for Tommy Dorsey and Harry James. He finally settled down with James in the late fifties for a long stay at what trade stories indicated to be a $35,000 annual salary. A heart attack in 1959 caused him to drop out for awhile, returning to the James band in early 1961 after a short try at a singing career. Except for brief interludes related to his health, he remained with James into early 1966, during which time he was the band's most publicized sideman.

In the spring of 1966, he once again formed a big band of his own, a driving, swinging jazz band with arrangements designed to give it what Rich described as "the sound of today." Skeptics who predicted he wouldn't make it were changing their minds by the end of the year, when he was booked solidly for months ahead. In January 1967 the somewhat conservative "National Observer" devoted nearly a full page to predicting that Rich might be sparking a big band revival. Late the same month Earl Wilson made him the subject of an entire column, apparently intended to remind those who knew Rich that the prospect of big success had not diminished the sharpness of his tongue. In this column Rich was quoted as putting down the rest of the band business, with Vaughn Monroe, Russ Morgan, and his old boss Artie Shaw as special targets. That summer "Mr. Warmth," as his fan Johnny Carson had named him, surprised everyone by being selected as the summer replacement for Jackie Gleason. He was still on the road with his band when a brain tumor and resulting heart attack took his life on April 2, 1987.

FREDDIE RICH

Started First Band Early twenties
Where New York City
Sidemen With Band Included Jimmy Dorsey, Tommy Dorsey, Joe Venuti, Eddie Lange, Manny Klein, Tony Parenti, Bunny Berigan, Leo McConville, Hymie Farberman, Earl Kelly, Ted Klein, Rudy Adler, Jimmy Johnston, Jack Hansen, Ray Bauduc, Chelsea Quealey, Bobby Davis, Sam Ruby, Adrian Rollini, Irving Brodsky, Tommy Felline, Stan King, Ray Stilwell, Benny Bloom, Benny Fairbanks, Phil Walzer, Al Duffy, Bob Mayhew, Jack Mayhew, Joe Tarto, Karl Kress, Fred Cusick, Arthur Schutt, Frank Signorelli, and many others. Also used on record dates were Red Nichols, Roy Eldridge, Benny Carter, Babe Russin, and other all-stars of the day
Vocalists With Band Included Ray Stilwell, Lewis James, Franklyn Baur, Frank Luther, Elliott Shaw, Smith Ballew, James Melton, The Rollickers, Scrappy Lambert, Dick Robertson, Rosemary Calvin
Sponsored Radio Shows "The Family Hotel," "Penthouse Party," "The Abbott and Costello Show"
Theme Song "I'm Always Chasing Rainbows," "So Beats My Heart For You"
Songs Written "I'm Just Wild About Animal Crackers," "Cap And Gown," "Blue Tahitian Moonlight," "Time Will Tell," "Penthouse," "On The Riviera" plus the scores for many motion pictures

Recording Affiliations Harmony, Banner, Gennett, Okeh, Columbia, Paramount, Camden, Vocalion

Rich is best known for his work on radio and in the recording studios, although he was the leader of a very successful dance band for several years. Most of that time was spent in the New York City area. The band which he put together in the early twenties went into the Astor Hotel in 1922 and stayed there until 1929. In 1928 he became the musical conductor for the CBS Radio network, a post which he held for over ten years. During that time he appeared with his band on a string of successful radio shows. His recording activity was on a variety of labels, including most of those in the business during the twenties and thirties. He also used a variety of recording names, sometimes Freddie Rich and His Orchestra, sometimes Fred Richard's Dance Orchestra, the Astorites, the Hotel Astor Orchestra, and many others. Because he was so busy on records he attracted most of the prominent sidemen of the day, who became the name bandleaders a few years later. This pace continued into the early forties, when he moved to the West Coast to concentrate on composing and directing background music for motion pictures. He died in Beverly Hills in September 1956 at the age of fifty-eight.

JOHNNY RICHARDS

Started First Band Early forties
Where Los Angeles
Previous Band Affiliations Victor Young
Recording Affiliations Musicraft

Richards was best known as an arranger, a skill which he learned while attending Syracuse University. During the early thirties he scored motion pictures in England, and then moved to Hollywood where he performed the same chores. Capable of playing various instruments himself, he put together a band which created quite a sensation for its style. But after playing many good locations, he disbanded in Chicago in mid-1945. During the next several years he concentrated on arranging for such bands as Boyd Raeburn's, Dizzy Gillespie's, Charlie Barnet's, and Stan Kenton's. Equally brief bandleading ventures were attempted in the late fifties and early sixties.

MIKE RILEY

Started First Band 1934 (The Riley-Farley Band)
Where New York City
Previous Band Affiliations Irving Aaronson, Ben Bernie, Rudy Vallee, Vincent Lopez, Will Osborne
Sidemen With Band Included Frank Langone, Arthur Enz, Frank Froeba, George York, Conrad Lanoue, Harry Prebal, George Tookey, John Montelione, Llana Webster, Sam de Bonis, Joe Butaski, Bill Flanagan, Pops Darrow
Vocalists With Band Included Eddie Farley, Mike Riley, Vic Engle, Wayne Gregg, Hal Burke
Theme Song "The Music Goes 'Round And 'Round"
Songs Written "The Music Goes 'Round And 'Round," "Laughing Through Tears," "I'm Gonna Clap My Hands," "Rip Van Winkle," "Lookin' For Love"
Recording Affiliations Champion, Decca

Most of Riley's fame was shared with Eddie Farley and was based on their novelty hit record, "The Music Goes 'Round And 'Round." The two met in the early thirties while working with Will Osborne's band and left to form a combo of their own in 1934. With it they played New York night clubs. Their first important job was at the Onyx Club in 1935. Meanwhile the newly-formed Decca Records had signed them to a contract. In the fall of 1935 they introduced their novelty number (composed by the two of them along with Red Hodgson) at the Onyx Club, and it quickly caught on. In the early months of 1936 the record was being played on every jukebox in the country. Its sales were reported to have been the biggest single contributor to Decca's becoming a profitable and successful enterprise. In addition to record sales, every band in the country was playing the hit and Paul Weirick's stock arrangement (for Santly-Joy) sold 25,000 copies—which was also probably a record. Their popularity permitted them to augment the size of the band. Late in 1936 the two separated, with each fronting a band of his own. Riley remained active into the early fifties, sometimes fronting a Dixieland group. He passed away in September, 1985, at age 80.

BUDDY ROGERS

Started First Band Late twenties
Where New York City
Sidemen With Band Included Corky Cornelius, Andrew McKinney, George Macy, Tommy Reo, Mark Bennett, Jack Henderson, Ben Freeman, Herman Stanchfield, Steve Benorick, John Nicolini, Joe Mooney, Bob Domenick, Tony Federici, Russ Isaacs, Ernie Mathias, Murray Williams, Gene Krupa
Vocalists With Band Included Bob Hannon, Jack Douglas, Marvel Maxwell (later Marilyn Maxwell), Liz Tilton; Rogers handled many of the male vocals himself
Theme Song "My Buddy"
Recording Affiliations Victor, Vocalion

Rogers was born in 1904 in Olathe, Kansas, a suburb of Kansas City, Kansas. By the late twenties he was well established as a bandleader and was also working in motion pic-

Mike Riley and his orchestra.

tures. Eventually his motion picture work
began to take precedence over his interest
in leading a band although he did continue
active through the thirties and into the forties. A 1938 Palomar bulletin announces his
opening at that location on May 18, 1938 and
bills it as his first Southern California appearance. At the time he had just returned
from a tour of the Eastern states and England. In keeping with the musical style of
that period, the Rogers orchestra was billed
as "The Newest Thing In Swing." The bulletin also announced that Rogers was the only
bandleader in America who could play every
instrument in his orchestra, and would do so
each evening. The May 18 opening brought
out a houseful of motion picture people, with
a special party hosted by Mary Pickford,
whom Rogers had recently married. During
that same West Coast trip the Rogers orchestra made its first appearance at the
Avalon Ballroom in Catalina. Eventually
Rogers gave up his activity as a bandleader
to concentrate on motion pictures and also
to assist Miss Pickford in handling business
interests in which they had both invested.

Buddy Rogers.

On the Catalina bandstand in 1938.

VINCENT ROSE

Started First Band Early twenties
Where Southern California
Sidemen With Band Included Harry Owens, Buster Johnson, Bobby Burns, Jackie Taylor, Bob Stowell, Albert Jaeger, Jack Van Cott, and others

Vocalists With Band Included Joe Prince, Irving Kaufman, Scrappy Lambert, Chick Bullock, Smith Ballew, Dorothy Brent, Dick Robertson
Recording Affiliations Victor, Columbia, Gennett, Perfect, Banner

Vincent Rose and his Montemarte Cafe Orchestra.

Rose was a very popular bandleader in Southern California for many years, several of which were spent at the Montmarte Cafe in Hollywood. During that time Harry Owens was the featured trumpet player, before starting a band of his own. The Montmarte was a favorite dining and dancing place for the motion picture people, who would often take the entire band to their own mansions to play and entertain until daylight. They also sat in with the band at the Montmarte and it was not uncommon to see Fatty Arbuckle playing drums or Tom Mix playing Harry Owens' trumpet. When Owens and Rose collaborated to write "Linger Awhile," which quickly became a big hit, the band's reputation was sufficiently broadened to earn them engagements at the College Inn in Chicago and the Ritz-Carlton in New York City. Eventually the fickle film colony deserted the Montmarte for other newer spots. The Rose band was forced to seek other California locations and spent a great deal of its time on tour. Sometime during the mid-thirties Rose gave up the band for other music business interests.

JACK RUSSELL

Started First Band 1929
Where Waukegan, Illinois
Previous Band Affiliations The Kentuckians
Sponsored Radio Shows "The Dodge Program," CBS, 1940
Longest Engagement The Melody Mill, three years
Theme Song "Into My Heart"

Russell's was strictly a local Chicago band but was very popular in that area for the approximately ten-year period of its existence. The band was launched in the Valencia Ballroom in September 1929, and then went on to play such locations as the Drake Hotel, the Granada Cafe, and the Vanity Fair; and was featured at the World's Fair in 1933 with Texas Guinan. Russell then played the Congress Hotel, the Canton Tea Gardens, the Merry Garden Ballroom, and then the Morrison Hotel Terrace Gardens. The summer of 1934 was spent at the Grand Beach Hotel, Grand Beach, Michigan. After that they went into the Melody Mill Ballroom in 1935, and remained there through 1937. The band was also featured at both the Aragon and Trianon Ballrooms, the Boulevard Room of the Stevens Hotel, the Panther

Jack Russell.

Room of the Sherman, the Marine Dining Room of the Edgewater Beach, and the Radison Hotel in St. Paul. Russell terminated his bandleading career in 1938 to become a talent agent.

DANNY RUSSO

Started First Band Early twenties, the Russo-Fio Rito orchestra
Where Chicago area
Sidemen With Band Included Max Williams, Ralph Pierce, George Weisheipl, Roy Johnson, Fritz Holtz, Hector Herbert, Ralph Barnhart, Paul Wittenmeyer, Don Hughes, Jim Jackson, and others
Recording Affiliations Brunswick, Columbia

Danny Russo, a violinist himself, teamed up in the early twenties with Ted Fio Rito to put together an orchestra which they soon booked in to the Oriole Terrace in Detroit. After some hassling with the local unions over the right for travelling musicians to play in Detroit, the band became very popular there. Eventually they returned to the Chicago area, where Fio Rito and Russo parted company about 1927. Two bands were then formed, with Russo continuing to call his the Oriole Orchestra. The instrumental combination was usually three saxophones, two trumpets, one trombone, piano, banjo, tuba, and drums with Russo fronting on the violin. That was an average size and average instrumentation for most of the white bands of that period. Russo's popularity continued for several years, with his activities concentrated on Chicago and the Middle Western area. He eventually gave up the band, and died on December 15, 1944.

The Danny Russo Band.

SAUTER-FINEGAN

Started Band 1952
Where Los Angeles
Previous Band Affiliations Both Eddie Sauter and Bill Finegan had worked with a long list of name bands including Charlie Barnet, Red Norvo, Benny Goodman, Artie Shaw, Tommy Dorsey, Woody Herman, Ray McKinley, Glenn Miller, Horace Heidt, Les Elgart
Theme Song "Doodle Town Fifers"
Songs Written By Finegan: "Pussywillow" By Sauter: "Benny Rides Again," "Clarinet A La King," "Superman," "All The Cats Join In," "Night Rider," "The Maid With The Flaccid Air," "Concerto for Jazz Band and Symphony Orchestra," and others
Recording Affiliations Victor

The unconventionally styled Sauter-Finegan orchestra was born in 1952, at a time when the state of band business was so poor that observers were unanimously predicting that the band would not make it. Despite those predictions of doom, the band did successfully survive for a period of approximately five years, playing mostly the arrangements of the two leaders and featuring such normally unnoticed instruments as the flute, the piccolo, the oboe, the English horn, bass clarinet, and harp. Unusual percussion effects were also utilized, including the tympany. The band broke up in 1957, with the two leaders going their separate ways to concentrate on arranging. They teamed up again in the early sixties, to produce jingles for both television and radio.

JAN SAVITT

Started First Band About 1935
Where Philadelphia
Previous Band Affiliations No dance bands, had been violinist with Leopold Stokowski and the Philadelphia Symphony, then conducted the studio orchestra at Philadelphia's station KYW

Sidemen With Band Included Jack Hansen, Harold Kearns, Chuck Evans, Al Leopold, Johnny Warrington, James Schultz, Gabe Galinas, Harry Roberts, Irv Leshner, Frank Rasmus, Howard Cook, George White, Charles Jensen, Johnny Augustino, Bob Spangler, Jimmy Campbell, Cutty Cutshall,

The Sauter-Finegan Band was more for listening than for dancing.

Fred Ohms, Norman Sipple, Ed Clausen, Frank Langone, Jack Pleis, Guy Smith, Morris Rayman, Don Simes, Buddy Schutz, Georgie Auld, George Bohn, Frank Cudwig, Jack Ferrier, Gene De Paul, Russ Isaacs, Chubby Jackson, George Siravo, Jack Palmer, Al George, Ted Duane, Ben Pickering, Joe Aglora, Ray Tucci, Danny Perri, Andy Egan, Ralph Harden, Joe Weidman, Gus Bivona, Albert Davis, Ed Stress, Bob White, Jack Daugherty, Harry Gozzard, Pete Lofthouse, Bill Hamilton, Allen Harding, Hollis Bridwell, Hugh Huggings, Vic Valente, Jess Bourgeois, Ray Hagen, Joe Martin, Urbie Green, Earle Hagen, Nick Fatool, and others

Arrangers For Band Included Eddie Durham, Billy Moore, Abe Osser, Johnny Watson, and Jan Savitt

Vocalists With Band Included Bon Bon, Phil Brito, Bob D'Andrea, Carlotta Dale, Gloria De Haven, Allen De Witt, Joe Martin, Ruth Robin, Jane Ward, Helen Warren, and the Three Top Hatters

Tag Line "Jan Savitt and His Top Hatters"

Sponsored Radio Shows "Rhapsody In Rhythm," a CBS network show for P. Lorillard Company

Motion Pictures With Band *Betty Coed, High School Hero, That's My Gal*

Theme Song "Quaker City Jazz," and "It's A Wonderful World"

Songs Written "720 In The Books," "Now And Forever"

Recording Affiliations Variety, Bluebird, Thesaurus, Decca, Victor

Savitt was born in Petrograd, Russia, on September 4, 1912. His father was leader of the Imperial Regiment Band under Czar Nicholas II. The family came to America when Jan was eighteen months old, to settle in Philadelphia, where Jan began the study of violin at the age of six. Later he won a number of scholarships, and at the age of fifteen was invited by Leopold Stokowski to join the Philadelphia Symphony. From the classics he switched to popular music and eventually joined the NBC station in Philadelphia, KYW, where he led a studio band broadcasting popular music programs. The popularity of those programs led him to take the band on the road early in 1936. Not only was he directing the band but also doing the arrangements and turning out a musical style identified as "shuffle rhythm." Their respective fans are still arguing as to whether that style was originated by Savitt or by Henry Busse. During the next several

Savitt fronts his "Top Hatters."

Jan Savitt and vocalist Bon Bon.

The full Savitt band at the peak of his career.

years Savitt, with an orchestra ranging from fifteen to eighteen instrumentalists plus vocalists, played the top hotels, theaters, ballrooms, and college proms, as well as working in a number of motion pictures for Columbia and Warner Brothers. Records usually sold well, one of his most popular being "Tuxedo Junction," recorded in the early forties. In the postwar period the Savitt band was reduced in size to eight men in addition to himself. By that time he had moved to the West Coast and was making his home in North Hollywood. On October 3, 1948, en route to a one-nighter in Sacramento, he was stricken with a cerebral hemorrhage while riding in a car with one of his band members, and passed away in a Sacramento hospital at the age of thirty-six. Barry Ulanov, who had been the Savitt band's publicity man in 1939, eulogized Savitt in a magazine article as a great jazz musician, a hard-luck guy who never totally found his niche, and whose death at such a young age deprived him of many years of productivity and the opportunity to realize his lofty musical ambitions.

RAYMOND SCOTT

Started First Band About 1939 (had previously had a popular quintette)
Where New York City
Sidemen With Band Included Willie Kelly, Gordon Griffin, Mike Meola, Reggie Merrill, Dave Harris, Art Drellinger, Pete Pumiglio, Joe Vargas, Irving Sontag, Walter Gross, Vince Massi, Lou Shoobe, Johnny Williams, Bert Lamarr, Steve Market, Lloyd Stearns, Charles McCamish, Wendell De Lory, Ben Lagasse, Stanley Webb, Hugo Winterhalter, Bernie Lazaroff, Art Ryerson, Chubby Jackson, Andy Picard, Jimmy Maxwell, Ray Schultz, Jack Walker, Graham Young, Jack Hall, Charlie Spero, Frank Calludaro, Don Tiff, Mike Ruben, Carl Maus, Vincent Bardale, Joe Ortolano, Sam Levine, Joe Olivella, Zeb Julian, Milton Holland, Buzz King, Bob Aston, Bill Siegel, Ed Aversano, Mack Marlow, Pete Tumiglio, Charlie Kiner, Lester Merkin, Bill Halfacre, Sid Kaye, Charlie Shavers, Ben Webster, Cliff Lehman, Johnny Guarnieri
Vocalists With Band Included Nan Wynn, Clyde Burt, Gloria Hart, Dorothy Collins
Sponsored Radio Shows "The Hit Parade"
Television With Band "The Hit Parade"
Theme Song "Toy Trumpet," "Pretty Little Petticoat"
Songs Written "Toy Trumpet," "In An

Raymond Scott.

Eighteenth Century Drawing Room," "Huckleberry Duck," "Twilight In Turkey," and others
Recording Affiliations Columbia, Decca, Coral, Victor

Scott had a reputation as a musical perfectionist who placed heavy demands on those who worked for him. It was not uncommon for him to express his opinion of an arranger's work by tearing up the manuscript and throwing the pieces on the floor. He studied music in New York and in the early thirties went to work on the CBS staff in that city. By 1936 he had organized his Quintette, which played primarily novelty instrumentals and with which he was active on radio, records, and even in some motion pictures. His first full-size band was put together in 1939 and although it was swing-oriented, he featured many of his own compositions, which had a style all their own. This band remained active for about three years. Then Scott once more returned to CBS, where he conducted a studio band during most of World War II. In the mid-forties he was once again on the road with a full-size band, this time playing a style which had a touch of Glenn Miller in it. He kept it active with coast-to-coast tours until the fall of 1949. At that time the sudden death of his brother, Mark Warnow, (Scott's real name was Harry Warnow) who had been conducting the "Hit Parade" for several years left that very popular program without a leader. Scott was offered the assignment and remained with it throughout its run on radio and later on television. When the show left the air in 1957 Scott retired from television to other musical interests, including a recording studio of his own.

BOYD SENTER

Started Band Early twenties
Where Atlantic City
Previous Band Affiliations Theater bands
Theme Song "Bad Habits"
Recording Affiliations Paramount, Okeh, Victor

Senter's professional musical career began while he was a teenager and probably because of his ability to double on a variety of instruments. During 1921, after forming a band of his own, he concentrated his activities on the East Coast, fronting groups of varying sizes. About 1922 he was headquartering in Denver, during which time Glenn Miller worked with the band as trombonist and arranger. That band toured the Midwestern area, eventually leaving the Rocky Mountain section to settle in Chicago. During the next several years Senter's activities were concentrated in the Chicago-Detroit area; at times he led a theater band. He gave it up during World War II to work in a defense plant. Following the war, he again put together a band, but only for occasional

Boyd Senter.

appearances. Eventually he quit the band business for a business venture.

ARTIE SHAW

Started First Band   1936
Where   New York City
Previous Band Affiliations   Johnny Cavallaro, Paul Specht, Austin Wylie, Irving Aaronson, Johnny Green
Sidemen With Band Included   Lee Castle, Zeke Zarchy, Tony Pastor, Mike Michaels, Jerry Gray, Ben Plotkin, Sam Persoff, Jimmie Oderich, Joe Lippman, Gene Stultz, Ben Ginsberg, Sammy Weiss, Tony Gottuso, George Wettling, Buddy Morrow, Johnny Best, Tom Di Carlo, Malcolm Crain, Harry Rogers, Les Robinson, Art Masters, Fred Petry, Les Burnuss, Al Avola, Cliff Leeman, Harry Freeman, Chuck Peterson, Claude Bowen, Ted Vesley, Ronnie Perry, Bernie Privin, Les Jenkins, Hank Freeman, Georgie Auld, Bob Kitsis, Buddy Rich, Dave Barbour, Charlie Margulis, Mannie Klein, George Thow, Randy Miller, Bill Rank, Babe Bowman, Blake Reynolds, Bud Carleton, Jack Stacey, Joe Krechter, Mark Levant, Mort Cruderman, Harry Bluestone, Peter Eisenberg, Sid Brokaw, David Cracov, Alex Law, Jerry Joyce, Stan Spiegelman, Jack Gray, Irving Lipschultz, Jules Townbaum, Stan Wrightsman, Bobby Sherwood, Harry Geller, Happy Lawson, Skitch Henderson, Jack Cathcart, Billy Butterfield, Jack Jenney, Vernon Brown, Jerry Jerome, Johnny Guarnieri, Al Hendrickson, Nick Fatool, George Wendt, Ray Conniff, Neely Plumb, Buss Bassey, Dave Tough, Conrad Gozzo, Claude Thornhill
Vocalists With Band included   Peg La Centra, Dorothy Howe, Bea Wain, Dolores O'Neil, Anita Bradley, Billie Holliday, Helen Forrest, Pauline Byrne, Anita Boyer, Lena Horne, Bonnie Lake, Georgia Gibbs
Sponsored Radio Shows   "The Old Gold Show"
Theme Song   "Nightmare"
Recording Affiliations   Brunswick, Thesaurus, Bluebird, Victor, Musicraft

In his book, "The Trouble With Cinderella," published in 1952, Shaw pictured himself as having mediocre basic talent which he overcame by driving himself to long hours of

Artie Shaw.

rehearsal. Chances are he didn't really believe that—other musicians who were his contemporaries rated him as one of the best. Born in New York City, he began to study saxophone and clarinet in grade school and while still in high school was playing with local dance bands. There followed a string of jobs with name bands and a great deal of free-lancing in New York City, including numerous record dates.

His first band attempt in 1936 was not successful and was junked after a very brief existence. In 1937 he put together a full-size swing band and the next year hit the big time as a bandleader on the strength of his record of "Begin The Beguine," arranged by Jerry Gray, which was one of the year's biggest hits.

This was the start of many years of success, during which Shaw alternately fought and reembraced the band business. After

The Shaw orchestra in the late 1930s.

little more than a year at the top he disbanded again and published an article in a magazine in which he described the whole music business as a "racket." He moved to Mexico for awhile. But in less than a year Shaw was back in the band business and busier than ever. If his absence had had any effect on his popularity, it apparently served to increase it. Meanwhile his attitude towards the business and his fans was not in keeping with the determination which had made him a top name. When the long-sought breaks started to come he was reported to have purchased a new wrist watch every week, just to convince himself that it was all true. Yet there usually appeared to be little love lost between the leader and any audience for which he performed. Sideline observers often had the impression that the crowd out front loved what they heard, but wished someone else was producing it. Meanwhile Shaw's expression implied that while he loved having them pay their way past the box office, he was unable to forgive them for staying around to listen. Shaw did a good job of explaining that impression with his candid answers on a television interview in 1977. He made it clear that he

enjoyed success as much as any other bandleader, but the monotony of playing his hit record tunes night after night for the fans who requested them became totally boring, to the point that he finally had to get away from it all for awhile with repeated band layoffs. Shaw was an intellectual who proved time and again that his interest lay only in moving forward and not looking back.

Shaw was a pioneer in the use of large string sections, an innovation which he introduced in the early forties. He was also an early volunteer for service in World War II. When he disbanded to put on a navy uniform, he was fronting a mammoth organization of thirty-two musicians, with a smaller combo within the band called the Gramercy Five. During his navy service he fronted a navy band which toured the South Pacific theater of action and was highly rated by those who heard it. Once out of the service, he reorganized the big band, which he kept active until the early fifties. Then he put together a smaller group, with which he played selected engagements, including the Las Vegas casinos, until the mid-fifties when he retired permanently. When interviewed on the Johnny Carson Show in the mid-seventies he stated that he had not played his clarinet for at least twenty years.

Shaw has to be rated as one of the giants of the big band era. Among the white leaders he was one of the big four, along with Goodman, Tommy Dorsey, and Miller. In retrospect he may well deserve rating as number one. It's been a long time since America's disc jockeys have been playing the music of Artie Shaw or any one else from the big band era. But in a mid-fifties *Billboard* magazine Annual Disc Jockey Poll they were asked to name their all-time pop record favorites. The disc jockeys' respect for Shaw was apparent when twenty out of the top twenty-five favorites were big band records and five of those twenty selections were Shaw's.

Artie Shaw's first appearance at the newly opened Hollywood Palladium early in 1941.

BOBBY SHERWOOD

Started First Band   1941
Where   West Coast
Previous Band Affiliations   Georgie Stoll, Benny Goodman, as a sideman and had done arranging for Tommy Dorsey, Larry Clinton, Artie Shaw, Charlie Barnet, and Goodman
Theme Song   "Elk's Parade" (also used "Cotton Tail" and "Sherwood's Forest")
Songs Written   "Elk's Parade," "Sherwood's Forest"
Recording Affiliations   Capitol, Victor

Sherwood was a very accomplished musician, playing banjo, guitar, and trumpet, and was self-taught on all instruments. He was also a highly competent arranger, with many compositions to his credit. He was appearing in vaudeville by the time he was ten years old. He moved to the West Coast in the mid-thirties to work with Bing Crosby on recording sessions as a replacement for the deceased Eddie Lang, a close friend of Bing's. After the Crosby association ended, he joined the Hollywood MGM staff and worked for several years as a studio musician. Sherwood's big band instrumentation was usually four (occasionally five) reeds, three trumpets, two trombones, and three rhythm. I first heard the band at the newly opened Avadon Ballroom in the early summer of 1946. It was a swinging organization with the versatile Sherwood working in front and alternating between trumpet and guitar, and occasionally trombone. When a vocal was in order he handled that also and acquitted himself equally well. He remained

The Bobby Sherwood Orchestra.

active with that band until 1949, when he gave it up to go into a Broadway show. For the next ten years he devoted himself to the theater, television, and the movies, including a picture made in 1957 with Frank Sinatra. His acting ability withstood the appraisal of the critics very well. In the late fifties he returned to the music business on a full-time basis but with a small band. Basically it was a show unit rather than a dance band and tailored for the lounges in the Nevada gambling casinos. When those casinos closed their lounges, converting them to bingo parlors, Sherwood remained in the Las Vegas area, putting together a full-size band for engagements in Las Vegas and Southern California as the occasion demanded. He died in January 1981, a victim of cancer.

NOBLE SISSLE

Started First Band Late twenties
Previous Band Affiliation Vaudeville units
Sidemen With Band Included Information limited but at one time his band included Sidney Bechet, Buster Bailey, and Tommy Ladnier, Charlie Parker
Vocalists With Band Included Best known was Lena Horne

Theme Song "Hello, Sweetheart, Hello"
Songs Written "Gypsy Blues," "Hello, Sweetheart, Hello," "Low Down Blues," "Characteristic Blues," "I Was Meant For You," and many Broadway show tunes. On most of his writing he collaborated with pianist Eubie Blake
Recording Affiliations Okeh, Victor

Sissle is much better known for his performances in Broadway shows and his appearances with Eubie Blake than he is as a bandleader. Nonetheless he did tour the country periodically with a dance band, and it was in that band that Lena Horne got her first break as a singer. The Sissle band played Billy Rose's Diamond Horseshoe in New York for a four-year period in the late thirties and early forties. During the early forties Sissle transferred his headquarters to the Los Angeles area and from there he toured the country for several years. He was still active as a bandleader during the early thirties, but eventually returned to Eubie Blake to team up once again for personal appearances.

FREDDIE SLACK

Started First Band 1941
Where West Coast
Previous Band Affiliations Jimmy Dorsey, Will Bradley/Ray McKinley
Vocalists With Band Included Ella Mae Morse
Theme Song "Strange Cargo"
Recording Affiliations Capitol

Slack was an accomplished pianist, identified with boogie-woogie, a style which he helped popularize. A native of Wisconsin, he broke into the band business when he joined Jimmy Dorsey in 1936. He was the pianist in the Bradley/McKinley band from 1939 to its demise in 1941. He was featured on their hit record of "Beat Me, Daddy, Eight To The Bar," a tribute to pianist Peck Kelley. Not much happened with Slack's own orchestra until Ella Mae Morse came in to do the vocals. When their Capitol recording of "Cow Cow Boogie" caught on, it made the band a hot attraction and did a great deal to put the newly formed Capitol Record Company in the black. Additional momentum was given to the band's popularity when they followed up with another hit titled "Mr. Five By Five." Early in 1945 Slack disbanded for over a year, reorganizing in mid-1946. In October of that year the band was reviewed by *Billboard* at Chicago's Band Box Theater as "a musically strong organization needing a strong novelty number or

Freddie Slack.

another hit record." Around the same time Slack and the orchestra worked in a Monogram picture called *High School Hero*. They had previously (1944) been in Universal's *Babes On Swing Street*. In the early fifties Slack gave up the band to concentrate on his arranging and to work on the West Coast as a night club headliner. Later he formed a small combo to work cocktail lounges, with only moderate success. In August 1965 he was found dead in his Hollywood apartment of undetermined causes.

Freddie Slack and his orchestra in a Universal picture in 1944.

PAUL SPECHT

Started First Band 1916
Where Detroit
Sidemen With Band Included Johnny O'Donnell, Russ Morgan, Harold Saliers, Don Lindley, Francis Smith, Frank Guarante, Chauncey Morehouse, Arthur Schutt, Harold Deppe, Joe Tarto, Hal Monquin, Arch Jones, Frank Quartell, Henry Wade, Roy Smeck, Charlie Spivak, Johnny Egan, Charlie Butterfield, Frank Kildert, Gil Detton, Billy Wolfe, Ted Noyes, Johnny Morris, Al Philburn, Ernie Warren, Foster Morehouse, Lou Calabrese, Jack Cressy, Bob Chester, Peter Van Steeden, Artie Shaw, Orville Knapp, and others
Theme Song "Evening Star," "Sweetheart Time"
Songs Written "Moonlight on the Ganges," "Who Takes Care of the Caretaker's Daughter?"
Recording Affiliations Columbia, Okeh

Paul Specht.

During the early and mid-twenties the Paul Specht orchestra was one of the best known in the business and the training ground for many who would later become the big musical names of the 1930s. Specht was a violinist, and the six-piece group which he started in 1916 made him a pioneer in a business which at that time was in its infancy. Within a few years he had enlarged the band

379

to twelve, many of them the all-star musicians of the period. He was also the first to have a "band within a band." His was a six-piece group called "The Georgians," initially made up of Guarante, Morgan, Morehouse, Schutt, Smith, and O'Donnell, which was featured not only on personal appearances but on records. In the early twenties radio was just beginning to develop and there are many who claim that Specht's was the first dance orchestra to be heard over the air waves. His broadcast was made over station WWJ in Detroit in late 1920s, and was a one-time appearance. It was also in Detroit that he, like other important leaders of the day, began to form additional units which he booked under his own name. As his popularity grew, partially from his success in later radio broadcasts, he moved on to Philadelphia and New York, eventually making his headquarters in the latter city. With an all-star orchestra he made at least one European tour, with somewhat disappointing results. Eventually he became discouraged with leading a band himself and gave it up to operate an agency booking other bands. At one time he had fourteen units working under his banner, all of them busily engaged. When the major agencies such as MCA took over the lion's share of the band business, he reduced his own booking activities to a minimum, eventually giving it up entirely. He died in New York in April 1954 at the age of fifty-nine.

Paul Specht and his orchestra at the Addison Hotel in Detroit in1923.

CHARLIE SPIVAK

Started First Band 1940
Where Washington, D.C.
Previous Band Affiliations Paul Specht, Ben Pollack, the Dorsey Brothers, Benny Goodman, Ray Noble, Bob Crosby, and Glenn Miller

Sidemen With Band Included Buddy Yeager, Les Elgart, Cyril Rommell, Ben Long, Bill Mustard, Nelson Riddle, Larry Elgart, Ben Lagasse, Don Raeffel, Roy Hammerslag, Hal Pennison, Buddy Reed, Kenny White, Jimmie Middleton, Andy Ricard, Bunny

Charlie Spivak.

Shawker, Bob Higgins, Dave Mann, Lee Knowles, Tris Haver, Peanuts Hucko, Charlie Russo, Francis Ludwig, Jerry Florian, Dave Tough, Dan Vannelli, Frank D'Annolfo, Paul Tanner, Jimmy Priddy, Willie Smith, Lionel Prounting, Alvin Stoller, Ralph Nichols, Herb Harper, Willie Forman, Sal Pace, Henry Haupt, Sid Caesar, Bill Mullens, Rusty Nichols, Ted Bergren, Bobby Rickey, Russ Montcalm, Paul Fredericks, Bunny Bardach, Al Kociuba, Abe Login, Jack Jacobson, Bob Carter, Harry Di Vito, Al Caiola, Dud Siscoe, Wayne Andre, Dick Bellerose, Leon Cox, Jimmy Dean, Bob MacGhee, Eddie Wasserman, Sal Collura, Jack Larson, George Rumanis, Don McLean, Tom Lozier, Dave Schultz, Vince Forrest, Tim Jordan, Bill Anthony, Ted Steele, Hal McCormick, Paul Perlman, LeRoy Anderson, Urbie Green, and others. Much of the arranging for the early band was done by Sonny Burke and Nelson Riddle

Vocalists With Band Included Gary Stevens, The Stardusters, June Hutton, Jimmy Saunders, Irene Daye, Tommy Mercer, Tommy Leonetti, Pat Collins, Eileen Rogers, Audrey Morris, Ann Lorraine, Peggy King
Sponsored Radio Shows "The Kate Smith Show," repeat appearances on Coca Cola's "Spotlight Bands"
Television With Band "Cavalcade of Bands"
Motion Pictures With Band *Pin Up Girl,* and *Follow The Girls*
Longest Engagement Pennsylvania Hotel
Theme Song "Star Dreams"
Recording Affiliations Columbia, Victor, Okeh, London, Design

Spivak's tag line was "The Man Who Plays The Sweetest Trumpet In The World" and as that tag line would indicate, he leaned toward the smoother style of music. He gave his vocalists featured billing and had some fine talent on the bandstand with him during the years. He had many years of experience with the top bands in the land before starting his own. He joined up with the first of these, Paul Specht, when he was only fifteen. It was Glenn Miller who gave him his tag line and the financial aid necessary to start his own band in 1940. The place was Washington, D.C. His first big engagement was at the Glen Island Casino, an ideal spot to launch a band, and the place where Miller first found success himself. Sid Caesar, who would later become one of television's top comedians, played saxophone briefly on that Glen Island engagement. The Glen Island air time paved the way for Spivak to move into the other top locations, including Frank Dailey's Meadowbrook, the Hollywood Palladium, and the Pennsylvania Hotel, where he played his longest engagement and went back year after year. The band's first record contract was with Okeh. The arrangements for those early recording dates were done by Nelson Riddle, who was also playing trombone in the band. As Spivak's record sales increased, so did his popularity for personal appearances. During the war years his band was featured regularly on the

At the Glen Island Casino in 1940. If you examine the sax section carefully you'll find Sid Caesar, who played with the band briefly.

One of Spivak's many appearances at the Pennsylvania Hotel, New York.

This rare photo shows Tommy and Jimmy Dorsey sitting in with Spivak at the Hollywood Palladium (about 1947).

"Coca Cola Parade Of Spotlight Bands"; and with Hollywood's interest in the big bands, Spivak joined the others on the Hollywood movie sets. During most of his years as a musician and bandleader he used the Atlantic seaboard as his base of operations, eventually establishing residence in Miami, Florida, during the 1950s. He kept active with a big band throughout the fifties and into the early sixties. In the early sixties, except for occasional tours with a full-size band, he worked with a small dance combination of seven pieces. The engagements he played with it included the Las Vegas clubs, usually the Fremont Hotel in downtown Las Vegas. In the early seventies he went into Ye Olde Fireplace, a club in Greenville, South Carolina, with a five-piece band and remained there until his health failed. He passed away on March 1, 1982, a victim of cancer.

DICK STABILE

Started First Band   1936
Where   New York City
Previous Band Affiliations   George Olsen, Ben Bernie
Sidemen With Band Included   Joe Sparta, Adrian Tei, Joe Stabile, Frank Fleming, Tony Gianelli, George Katz, Fred Pfeiffer, Chauncey Gray, Spencer Clark, Ray Tolan, Mike Poveromo, Geno Bono, Benny Bullardo, Jimmy Curry, Frank Gibson, Harry Walton, Harry Du Peer, Charlie Castaldo, Howard King, George Navarre, Bill De Mayo
Vocalists With Band Included   Billie Trask, Paula Kelly, Bert Shaw, Gracie Barrie, Paul

Warner, Shirley Gay, Jane Morgan, Jimmie Palmer

Sponsored Radio Shows "The Chesterfield Show," "The American Can Company Show"
Television With Band "The Dean Martin and Jerry Lewis Show"
Longest Engagement Ciro's Night Club in Hollywood, eight years
Theme Song "Blue Nocturne"
Songs Written "Blue Nocturne," "My Heart Has Found A Home Now," "Cloudburst," "Raindrops On The River," "That's How I Need You"
Recording Affiliations Victor, Dot, Capitol, Tops, Fraternity, MGM

Dick Stabile, who claims the world's record for hitting a high note on a saxophone, was born in Newark, New Jersey, in 1909 and began the study of saxophone during his school days in that city. His professional career began at the age of fifteen with theater bands. In 1926 he joined the George Olsen orchestra to play the musical comedy *Sunny* in New York City. In the spring of 1929 he joined the Ben Bernie orchestra to work with them until early 1936. With his own orchestra launched in April 1936, he played a few break-in dates in the Boston area before opening with it in Maria Kramer's Lincoln Hotel in New York. Following an extended engagement there he spent the next several years playing hotels and ballrooms throughout the country. In 1942 he entered military service, turning the band over to his wife, Gracie Barrie, who fronted it until he returned. Following World War II he quickly regained his earlier momentum although his musical style was now aimed slightly more towards the listener than the dancer. Eventually he settled on the West Coast, where he enjoyed his long engagement at Ciro's nightclub. It was during that time that he associated himself with Martin and Lewis as the arranger and conductor for their television show, spending nine years

Dick Stabile.

with them. He also made appearances with the two comedians in several motion pictures at Paramount Studios. When Martin and Lewis broke up, Stabile remained in Southern California where he was active with his band in the clubs of Las Vegas, the Newporter Inn, and with an engagement at the Cocoanut Grove which ran for a couple of years. In the early seventies he moved to New Orleans to become the house band at the Roosevelt Hotel (now the Fairmont). He was still there when a heart attack took his life on September 25th, 1980.

An early 1940s photo of Dick Stabile and his sax section: George Navarre, Bill De Mayo, Frank Gibson, Joe Stabile.

Dick Stabile and the band he fronted at the Coconut Grove in the mid 1960s.

BLUE STEELE

Started First Band   Mid-twenties
Where   Atlanta, Georgia
Sidemen With Band Included   Sam Goble, Ole Hoel, G. Morrison, Frank Martinez, Frank Krisher, John Langley, Kenny Sargent, Pete Schmidt, Sonny Clapp, Roger Sanford, Sol Lewis, Ted Delmarter, Marvin Long-fellow, Henry Cody, Pat Davis, Bob Nolan, Clyde Davis, Moe Goodman, George Marks, Irving Verette, Jesse James, Frank Myers, Ernie Winburn, Jack Echols, B. English, Galen Grubb, Red Rountree, Cookie Tran-tham, Ollie Warner, Ben Saxon, Arnell Schwartz
Vocalists With Band Included   Blue Steele,

Bob Nolan, George Marks, Kay Austin, Mabel Batson, Clyde Davis
Theme Song   "Coronado Memories"
Recording Affiliations   Victor

Steele built his early popularity as a band-leader in the Florida area. For several years he toured the South and Midwest with a band which was a combination of "sweet and swing." By the early thirties he had reached the peak of his popularity and after the mid-thirties that popularity declined to the point where he was only occasionally leading a band at the end of the decade. In the early forties he moved to Mexico City to concen-

Blue Steele and his orchestra.

trate his activities, usually with small combinations. Steele had a reputation as a very difficult man to work for, and with a hair-trigger temper that could be set off with the slightest provocation. The one thing that aggravated him the most was having band members quit to go with someone else. One sideman, knowing Steele's reputation, decided the safest way to turn in his resignation was to catch Steele in the bathroom while he was washing up. When he delivered his message Steele was in front of the mirror with his face covered with lather, and shaving. In nothing but his jockey shorts he chased the offending musician down the hotel stairs and through the lobby into the street. Other musicians, anxious to depart the Steele orchestra, had sometimes been less successful in making their escape and had ended up in physical combat with the bandleader.

CHARLIE STRAIGHT

Started First Band   About 1917
Where   Chicago
Sidemen With Band Included   Guy Carey, Wally Preissing, Frank Sylvano, Gene Caffarelli, Ike Williams, Bob Conselman, Randy Miller, Bob Strong, Frank Stoddard, Dale Skinner, Joe Gist, Don Morgan, Ralph Morris, Jack Davis, Johnny Jacobs, Bix Biederbecke
Songs Written   "Mocking Bird Rag"
Recording Affiliations   Paramount, Brunswick

Though hardly known outside the Midwestern area, Charlie Straight was one of Chicago's pioneer bandleaders and for several years one of its most popular. When MCA began to build its band empire in the mid-twenties, he was one of the first to sign and through its efforts he became a strong Midwestern attraction. During the late twenties Straight's music was aired frequently over Chicago stations and was available on records made for Brunswick. It was on these records that he claimed to have originated the singing song titles, later made famous by Kay Kyser and to a lesser degree by Sammy Kaye. Another of Straight's claims was that it was he who originated the style called "Swing," which would become so popular during the thirties.

Among the musical greats who worked with him during that period was Bix Beiderbecke, who stayed only briefly because of his inability to read the band's arrange-

Charley Straight, a big attraction in Chicago during the mid 1920s.

ments. Straight's band was seldom more than ten men but it was rated as an excellent dance band. Although the peak of his popularity was in the twenties he remained active as a leader until the late thirties. On September 21, 1940, he was killed when struck by a speeding car on the streets of Chicago.

BENNY STRONG

Started First Band 1938
Where Brown Hotel, Louisville, Kentucky
Television With Band A West Coast show on Channel 7, (1952), from the Trianon Ballroom in South Gate, California
Longest Engagement Stevens Hotel, Chicago
Theme Song "That Old Gang of Mine," "That Certain Party"
Recording Affiliations Capitol, Coral, Imperial, Heartbeat, Winit, Crescendo

Benny Strong, who built his reputation as "The Young Man Who Sings The Old Songs," began his career in show business in Chicago when scarcely in his teens. An opportunity to sing at a political rally earned him a job singing in a local theater. There he attracted the attention of Paul Ash, who took him under his wing and made him part of his show at the Oriental Theater. When his changing voice gave him some difficulty

Benny Strong.

Benny Strong and his orchestra at the Coconut Grove in 1943.

in singing on key he gave up singing to study drums and tap dancing, becoming especially proficient in the latter. The launching of his own band at the Brown Hotel in Louisville was successful and he stayed there for nearly three years. By that time he had established a musical style which, with the help of radio, had made him one of the most popular dance bandleaders in the Middle West. His career was interrupted by World War II. Trade papers made quite a story of the fact that Strong had spent a year recruiting sidemen who were draft-exempt by reason of being 4F, only to be drafted into the army himself. At the war's end he resumed as a leader, quickly regaining his momentum and position in the field. His musical style was strictly on the sweet side, but his organization was made up of talent capable of putting on its own floor show and this became a standard feature wherever they appeared. While not neglecting the currently popular tunes, it was the emphasis on the "oldies" which contributed most to his popularity. He appeared in at least one motion picture at Universal and was one of the pioneers in attempting to adapt television pickups to ballroom operation. In the late fifties he gave up bandleading to take over the management of a San Francisco radio station. In the early sixties he moved to the Hollywood area for another radio assignment but in the mid-sixties he once more became active as a bandleader, playing the local ballrooms. During the late 70s and through the mid-80s he was involved in radio with California stations. He passed away in 1991.

T

JACK TEAGARDEN

Started First Band 1939
Where New York City
Previous Band Affiliations R. J. Marin, Doc Ross, Al King, Ben Pollack, Red Nichols, Mal Hallett, Paul Whiteman
Sidemen With Band Included John Anderson, Art Miller, Clois Teagarden, Allen Reuss, Carl Garvin, Charlie Spivak, Lee Castle, Jose Guttierrez, Charlie McCamish, Mark Bennett, Ernie Caceres, Hub Lytle, Clint Garvin, Johnny Van Eps, Art St. John, Red Bohn, Alec Fila, Eddie Dudley, Jack Russin, Charlie Teagarden, Dave Tough, Frank Ryerson, Benny Pottle, John Fallstitch, Tom Gonsoulin, Sid Feller, Seymour Goldfinger, Joe Ferral, Jack Goldie, Joe Ferdinando, Larry Walsh, Nat Jaffe, Dan Perri, Arnold Fishkind, Ben Lagasse, Danny Polo, Paul Collins, Art Moore, Ernie Hughes, Truman Quigley, Tony Antonelli, Joe Reisman
Vocalists With Band Included Jean Arnold, Linda Keene, Kitty Kallen, Marianne Dunne, David Allen, Lynne Clark, Phyllis Lane, Sally Lang
Theme Song "I've Got A Right To Sing The Blues"
Recoding Affiliations Columbia, Brunswick, Variety, Decca

They called him Mr. T, Big T, Jackson T, Big Gate. Louis Armstrong called him the world's greatest jazz musician—a title which Teagarden said belonged to Armstrong. Another famous trombonist, Tommy Dorsey, was quoted as saying "I play pretty—Jackson Teagarden plays great." He was a modest, soft-spoken man, outwardly relaxed to the point that some described him as lazy. Probably he had no driving ambition to attain great financial success. Perhaps his theme song, more than that of any other bandleader, truly expressed his philosophy. He both sang and played the blues. No one else did it so well, for Jack Teagarden was a great musician. When he sang, his phrasing, like Armstrong's, was identical to that played on his instrument.

Teagarden was born in Vernon, Texas in 1905. His mother was a piano teacher and his father led the town band. It was his mother who taught him to read music and with whom he played background music for silent pictures in a local theater, using his first trombone, a Christmas gift from his father when he was seven years old. While he was still in grammar school he was invited to play in the high school orchestra, perhaps

390

Jack Teagarden and his orchestra in 1939: piano—John Anderson; bass—Art Miller; drums—Clois Teagarden; guitar—Allen Reus; trumpets—Karl Garvin, Charlie Spivak, Lee Castaldo; trombones—Jose Gutierrez, Charlie McCamish, Mark Bennet; saxophones—Ernie Caceres, Hub Lytle, Clint Garvin, Johnny Van Eps, Art St. John; vocalist—Linda Keene.

The Teagarden Band on a Spotlight Band Show in 1944: bass—Earl Strickland; drums—Frank Harrington; piano—Norma Teagarden; trumpets—Clair Jones, Ray Borden, Tex Williamson; trombones—Jim Barngrover, Wally Wells; saxophones—Gish Gilbertson, Vic Rossi, Joe Lenza, Joe Reisman; vocals—Sally Lang.

Backstage at the Golden Gate Theater in 1945. *Front row:* Bob Derry, Bert Noah, Charles Gilruth, Teagarden, Wally Wells, Charles Smith, Jack Lantz. *Back row:* Merton Smith, Dale Jolley, Bob Short, Jack Williams, Frank Harrington, Norma Teagarden, Mildred Shirley, Stew Pletcher, Jerry Redmond, Tex Williamson, Nyles Davis.

Teagarden's Royal Room Band doing an Armed Forces Radio Service Broadcast in Hollywood in 1952. With Teagarden are: drums—Ray Bauduc; clarinet—Jay St. John; trumpet—Charlie Teagarden; bass—Kas Malone; piano—Marvin Ash.

The two Teagardens and Ray Bauduc, Columbus, Ohio, 1953.

the first acknowledgment that his was no ordinary talent.

At the age of sixteen he took his first professional job with a four-piece group playing out of San Antonio, a group which included pianist Terry Shand. Then both he and Shand played with Peck Kelley in a band working the Houston-Galveston area. He then joined R. J. Marin's band for a Mexican tour; following which he went with Doc Ross and his band, working in the Texas area. With Ross he made a West Coast trip and finally a tour which took him into New York in 1927. The availability of record dates prompted Teagarden to remain in New York. His first New York job was with Al

King, playing the "Elizabeth Brice Show." In 1928 he joined Ben Pollack's band at the Park Central, taking over Glenn Miller's place. Miller stayed on as an arranger. It was while Teagarden was with Pollack that he and Miller wrote the words to "Basin Street Blues," for a 1929 recording which Teagarden made with Red Nichols. Neither he nor Miller received any credit for the lyrics on the sheet music.

After leaving Pollack in 1933 and playing briefly with Mal Hallett, he joined Paul Whiteman. For the next five years he was a featured member of the then very popular organization, and it was Whiteman who started calling him "Big T." He, with trumpet-playing brother Charlie and Frank Trumbauer were called the "Three T's" of the Whiteman band.

Although Teagarden's early band ventures included a lot of talented sidemen, he never attained the financial success which the band's musicianship deserved. One of the early jobs was Chicago's Blackhawk Restaurant, which had a reputation for building bands. Somehow it didn't come off for Teagarden. At the end of the first year he was reported to be nearly $50,000 in debt. Several reorganizations followed, a procedure which went on during the next several years. Despite the fact that the band did quite well on records and personal appearances, bad luck hounded him during his entire career as a leader of a big band. He was a great musician, not a great business man, and apparently he never found the right people to manage him. A good personal manager could well have made the difference needed for the success that the band deserved.

In 1947 he gave up his big band to join Louis Armstrong's All-Stars, remaining with Louie until 1951. Then he stepped out to form his own small group in Hollywood. The six-piece band with which he appeared at the Royal Room in 1952 included sister Norma on piano, brother Charlie on trumpet, Jay St. John on clarinet, Casper Malone on bass, and Ray Bauduc on drums. During the next twelve years the personnel changed several times, but he enjoyed greater success with the small combo than he had ever known with his big band.

During the early sixties those close to him knew his health was failing, even though he did his best to keep the fact to himself. From his Pompano Beach, Florida home he continued to go on the road to play the music he loved so much. His last engagement was in New Orleans at a Bourbon Street night-club called the "Dream Room," in January 1964. With only a few days of the engagement still remaining he took sick on the bandstand and went to his room in a nearby motel. The next day he was found dead on the floor, ending his long career at the age of fifty-eight.

CLAUDE THORNHILL

Started First Band 1940
Where New York City
Previous Band Affiliations Austin Wylie, Hal Kemp, Meyer Davis, Benny Goodman, Ray Noble, Artie Shaw, Freddy Martin
Sidemen With Band Included Bob Sprentall, Ralph Hardin, Joe Aguanno, Bob Jenney, T. Harris, Dale Brown, George Paulson, Bill Motley, Hammond Russen, John Nelson, Hal Tennyson, Al Harris, Harvey Cell, Judy Burke, Rusty Dedrick, Conrad Gozzo, Irving Fazola, Ted Goddard, Chuck Robinson, Gene Laman, Allen Hanlon, Nick Fatool, Jimmy Abato, Lester Merkin, Barry Galbraith, Billy Butterfield, Bud Smith, John Graas, Vince Jacobs, Danny Polo, Jack Ferrier, Marty Berman, Dave Tough, Randy Brooks, Buddy Dean, Irv Cottler, Jake Koven, Lee Konitz, Joe Shulman, Bill Barber. Arrangements were done by Thornhill himself, Andy Phillips, Gil Evans, Gerry Mulligan, and Ralph Aldridge

The Thornhill band in the postwar years.

Claude Thornhill.

Vocalists With Band Included Jane Essex, Dick Harding, Kay Doyle, Lillian Lane, Martha Wayne, Buddy Stewart, Fran Warren, "The Snowflakes," Maxine Sullivan, Terry Allen

Sponsored Radio Shows The "Judy 'N Jill 'N Johnny" show on Mutual during the '46-'47 season

Theme Song "Snowfall"

Recording Affiliations Vocalion, Okeh, Columbia, Decca, Camden

Thornhill was born in Terre Haute, Indiana and got his musical education at the Cincinnati Conservatory and the University of Kentucky. His mother was a choir director who hoped her son would become a classical musician. While still a teenager, he got his first experience as a professional musician working on one of the riverboats which plied the Mississippi. His first important job was with Austin Wylie in the Cleveland area, and he then went on to work with a series of name bandleaders, both as musician and arranger. The orchestra which he formed in 1940 had become quite popular by the time World War II had begun to simultaneously deplete the supply of available musicians and create a demand for their services. Thornhill wanted to participate actively in the defense of his country and in 1942 enlisted in the navy. Although he requested active duty, he ended up playing in Artie Shaw's service band and was soon directing his own navy band, a capacity in which he continued to serve until the war's end. When he was discharged from the navy in 1945, he reorganized his dance orchestra, having little difficulty in picking up where he had left off. His smoothly styled organization won several trade magazine polls in 1946 and 1947, with some assistance doubtless given by the fine vocals of Fran Warren. Throughout the fifties he was periodically active with a big band, continuing on into the early sixties. He was still very active in the music business when a series of heart attacks took his life in his Caldwell, New Jersey home on July 1, 1965.

AL TRACE

Started First Band 1933
Where Chicago
Vocalists With Band Included Toni Arden, Bob Vincent
Sponsored Radio Shows "It Pays To Be Ignorant"
Television With Band A local Chicago show which ran for twenty-six weeks in 1949
Theme Song "Sweet Words and Music,"
"Mairzy Doats," "You Call Everybody Darling"
Songs Written "You Call Everybody Darling," "If I'd Known You Were Comin' I'd Have Baked A Cake," "Brush Those Tears From Your Eyes," "Wishin'," and many many more, in total about 300.
Recording Affiliations Mercury, MGM, Columbia

Al Trace and his orchestra doing their "Silly Symphony" number at the Blackhawk Restaurant, Chicago, 1948.

Prior to launching his own band Trace had played drums with various small combos and also performed as a vocalist. Chicago in 1933 was a good place for a new band to get its start, with the World's Fair in progress, and Trace got himself booked into the Streets of Paris for the duration of the Fair. In the next few years he became a Chicago landmark, with a long run at the Blackhawk Restaurant and a three-year stay at the Sherman Hotel. His popularity was not restricted to the Chicago area for, with the renown given him by his many hit songs, he was also in big demand in New York City and on a national basis. Although the Trace musical style was a bit on the western side, he still played the best dining and dance locations repeatedly. His records, primarily with his own compositions, sold well and many of them were in the hit category throughout the forties and fifties. Eventually he gave up his bandleading career and moved to the West Coast, where he settled down to devote most of his efforts to promoting his songs. For awhile he also busied himself with a personal management agency. In the mid-seventies he moved to Scottsdale, Arizona to make his home and associated himself with bandleader Tommy Reed in the Southwest Booking Agency.

PAUL TREMAINE

Started First Band   Late twenties
Where   New York City
Theme Song   "Lonely Acres"
Sidemen With Band Included   Sonny Dunham, Archie Newell, Arnold Lehner, Jay Wade, L. Hussin, Cliff Harkness, John Baldwin, Andy Fonder, Jack Triphagen, Bob Tremaine, Charles Bagby, Eddie Kilanoski, Lester Cruman, Merlyn Shields, Eddie Orlando, Laurie Mitchinton, and others
Recording Affiliations   Victor, Columbia

Most of Tremaine's bandleading career was spent on the East Coast where he got his

Paul Tremaine and his orchestra.

start in the late twenties. His musical style was aimed at the dancers, usually well-arranged, and featured ensemble work both by the musicians and on vocal numbers in which all the bandsmen participated. That style, however, was not sufficiently distinc-tive to boost Tremaine into the bandleading big money bracket. In the mid-thirties he retired briefly, only to resume once again a year later and continue on into the early forties.

ORRIN TUCKER

Started First Band Early thirties (Had previously a small high school dance orchestra)
Where St. Louis
Previous Band Affiliations Tweet Hogan
Sidemen With Band Included Dick Robinson, Doc Morrison, Joe Strassburger, Morton Wells, Norbert Stammer, Will Flanders, Roy Cohan, Everett Ralston, George Sontag, Lorry Lee, Arnold Jensen, Phil Patton, Doc Essick, Elmo Hinson, George Liberace
Vocalists With Band Included Bonnie Baker, Gil Mershon, the Bodyguards, Jack Bartell, Eddie Rice, Lorraine Benson, Scotty Marsh
Theme Song "Drifting And Dreaming"
Recording Affiliations Vocalion, Columbia

Tucker's professional career as a bandleader began while he was still in college. By the time of the 1933 World's Fair he was already a strong attraction in the Chicago area. In 1936 he took his orchestra into the Marine Room of Chicago's Edgewater Beach Hotel for what was the first of several successful engagements. Here continuous air time added to Tucker's reputation.

It was during the Edgewater engagement that he was attracted by the singing style of Bonnie Baker, whose home town was also St. Louis. He brought her into the band, convinced that with the right material she could become a singing star. Early in 1939, while playing in the Cocoanut Grove in Los Angeles, they recorded "Oh Johnny" for Columbia, with Miss Baker featured on the novelty vocals. Within a few short months it was one of the hottest records in the nation, making the Tucker orchestra with Miss Baker a

Orrin Tucker, with the help of Wee Bonnie Baker, hit it big with "Oh Johnny" about 1939.

big national attraction. Other hit records followed, also a season on "Lucky Strike's Hit Parade" on the CBS network. Despite the success which resulted from "Oh Johnny," Tucker never again permitted a vocalist to be so prominently featured in his band. This is probably understandable since the publicity which Miss Baker received from the record reached the point where it was no longer "Orrin Tucker and His Orchestra, featuring Wee Bonnie Baker" but "Orrin Tucker —The Bandleader With Bonnie Baker."

In 1942 Tucker volunteered for service in the navy, and returned to front his orchestra when the war was over. The organization which he put together at that time was

Orrin Tucker's orchestra and glee club with Harriett Smith's Lovely Ladies at the Marine Room, Edgewater Beach Hotel, Chicago, in the late 1930s.

slightly larger than his prewar group, in keeping with the trend of the times towards larger bands. He soon once again had his career in full stride, playing the nation's top hotels and clubs for the next several years. Like others he attempted to break into television, doing a weekly "on location" show from the Hollywood Palladium for several months during 1955. In the mid-fifties he went into semiretirement to look after other business interests. About 1959 he picked up his saxophone again to resume as a bandleader, but with a group never larger than seven. He concentrated his activities in the Hollywood, Las Vegas, and Tahoe areas. These engagements carried him well into the seventies.

In 1975 he took over a ballroom on Hollywood's Sunset Boulevard, naming it "The Stardust Ballroom" after a very successful television special in which he had appeared some months earlier. With his own band on the stand five nights a week, he is currently doing very well with this new venture.

Bonnie Baker, whose record of "Oh Johnny" made her a big attraction.

Orrin Tucker and his orchestra at Elitch's Gardens, Denver, in 1946.

TOMMY TUCKER

Started FIrst Band   About 1928
Where   Midwest
Previous Band Affiliations   None
Vocalists With Band Included   Amy Arnell, Archie Berdahl, Ray Hawkins, Don Brown, Kerwin Summerville, and a trio, "The Voices Three"
Sponsored Radio Shows   "The Lucky Strike Show with Walter Winchell," "The George Jessel Show"
Theme Song   "I Love You"
Songs Written   "The Man Who Comes Around," "The Man Don't Come To Our House Anymore," "How Come, Baby?," "Stars Over The Campus," and "All Things Come To Those Who Wait"
Recording Affiliations   Vocalion, Okeh, Columbia

Tucker was born in Souris, North Dakota and studied music at the University of North Dakota. The dance band which he put together played a soft romantic style, a style which did not vary greatly during his career.

Tommy Tucker.

400

At the Syracuse Hotel, Syracuse, New York, in the late 1930s. The vocalist is Emily Lane.

The Tucker orchestra in the 1940s was a little larger in both brass and reed sections.

Radio listeners during the thirties and forties were accustomed to hearing his "Tommy Tucker Time" beamed to them from any one of the nation's top entertainment spots, although he concentrated his activities on the East Coast and in the Middle West. Several hit records, including "The Man Who Comes Around," contributed towards making him a very strong competitor to other bandleaders in the early and mid-forties.

Radio success had come to him earlier when he was chosen to be featured on the "Lucky Strike Show with Walter Winchell" in the early thirties. Tucker gave up his bandleading career in the mid-fifties to teach English in an Asbury Park high school. A more recent news story identified him as an assistant professor of music at Monmouth College in Longbranch, New Jersey. He passed away in the summer of 1989.

RUDY VALLEE

Started First Band   1928
Where   New York City
Previous Band Affiliations   College bands and free-lance work in New York City
Sidemen With Band Included   Jules De Vorzon, Manny Lowy, Hal Mathews, Joe Miller, Don Moore, Cliff Burwell, Charles Peterson, Harry Patent, Ray Tolan, George Morrow, Del Staigers, Harry Shilkret, Chuck Campbell, Sammy Feinsmith, Jimmy Catino, Bob Bowman, Sam Diehl, Phil Buatto, Al Evans, Frank Staffa, Frank Friselle, Mickey Bloom, Henry Cincione, Jimmy Hansen, Charlie Butterfield, Bud Webber, Sal Terini, Zelly Smirnoff, Walter Gross, Bud Sheppard, Sy Baker, Sal Gennett, Ralph Mendez, Red Stanley, Billie White, Bill Vorsacki, Elliot Daniels, Jerry Yeoman, Don Conlin, Cyril Smith, Eddie Waide, Al Newman, Morey Samuels, Ken Delaney, Jimmy Lytell, Eddie Kusby, Jack Mayhew, Mort Freedman, Warren Baker, Nick Pisani, Stan Wrightsman, Artie Bernstein, and others
Vocalists With Band Included   Vallee usually did vocals himself, occasionally used a vocal group on recording, and Alice Faye got her singing start with the Vallee band

Rudy Vallee and the famous megaphone.

Sponsored Radio Shows   "Blue White Diamond Show," "The Fleischman Yeast Show," "The Drene Shampoo Show"
Theme Song   "My Time Is Your Time"
Recording Affiliations   Harmony, Victor, Columbia, Bluebird, ARC

Rudy Vallee and his orchestra.

Born Hubert Pryor Vallee, he was one of the biggest radio personalities, but he reached that status as a musician and bandleader who saw the potential of radio and the advantages of being heard on it at every possible opportunity.

The heights to which he rose could be misleading in terms of effort involved. Success did not arrive overnight nor was it delivered on a silver platter. Vallee was one who knew what he wanted and was able to analyze his talents and shortcomings in a detached manner, even though the ego he displayed would seem to deny it. He drove himself to long hours of practice to master the saxophone, then worked his way through Yale, earning his college expenses as a musician. Before this he had spent a year at the University of Maine, and while he was there he was given the name "Rudy" because of his near-worship of another saxophonist, Rudy Wiedoeft.

He interrupted his work at Yale for a year in England, playing with a band at the London Savoy. Returning in the fall of 1925, he graduated from Yale in 1927. Recognizing that the big market for musicians was in New York, he went there in late 1927 and, armed with a scrapbook, a record player and his saxophone, he made the rounds of the booking offices daily, auditioning for work with the well-known bands of the day.

Early in 1928 he formed his own group, "The Connecticut Yankees," to go into the newly opened Heigh Ho Club. Soon a regular broadcast over station WABC started to get them public recognition. He became a vocalist when the violinist hired for this double duty did not meet the approval of the club's manager. Prevailing upon the station to permit him to announce the program, Vallee was as much surprised as anyone else when the fan mail started pouring in.

Other stations started to pick them up and they soon had a sponsor, Herbert's Blue-White Diamonds. This was the start of a long career in radio, movies, theaters, and eventually television. By the end of the roaring twenties he was one of America's highest paid entertainers. Most of those who witnessed the hysterical reaction of the bobby soxers to Frank Sinatra in the early forties were probably not aware that it had all happened once before for Rudy Vallee.

In the early thirties he began to deemphasize his role as a bandleader, in preference to other radio work, although he usually had a band under his own direction behind him. Eventually he became almost completely identified as a radio personality. During World War II, he entered the Coast Guard to direct a band of forty pieces, touring the nation for service and morale-building functions. He died quietly in his Hollywood home on July 3, 1986, at age 84.

GARWOOD VAN

Started First Band 1936
Where Los Angeles
Previous Band Affiliations Hal Grayson, Eddie Oliver, Victor Young, Lennie Hayton, studio bands
Vocalists With Band Included Maxine Conrad, Gail Storm
Longest Engagement Frontier Hotel, Las Vegas
Theme Song "Poinciana,' "Time To Dream"
Songs Written "Time To Dream"
Recording Affiliations Modern, also on Standard Transcriptions

Van's was basically a smooth-styled band, occasionally slightly swing-oriented, and described by reviewers as an excellent hotel band. For the most part he concentrated on hotel locations such as the St. Francis and Mark Hopkins in San Francisco, the Hotel Utah in Salt Lake City, the Chase in St. Louis, the Muehlebach in Kansas City, and the Statler chain throughout the Middle West and East Coast. In the Los Angeles area, which was his headquarters, he enjoyed long engagements at the Trocadero, Ciro's, and the Florentine Gardens. In the early forties he made his first appearance in Las Vegas as one of the earliest bands to play El Rancho, the Las Vegas location which pioneered the introduction of dance bands. During the next several years he made repeat engagements in that city and in

Garwood Van.

1952 went into the Frontier Hotel for a five-year stand. Two years later he came back to play the Thunderbird during which time he opened a record shop and music store in the Las Vegas area. This venture became so successful that he retired permanently from the music business in 1962.

JOE VENUTI

Started First Band Early thirties (Had previously assembled band under his own name for recording dates)
Where New York City
Previous Band Affiliations Jean Goldkette, Red Nichols, Frank Trumbauer, Roger Wolfe Kahn, Phil Napoleon, Paul Whiteman, plus recording with many other bands
Sidemen With Band Included Most of the greats from the Goldkette and Whiteman band as well as from the California Ramblers recorded with him and it's difficult to separate these from those who played with him on regular appearances. The latter included Toots Camarata, Tony Gianelli, Shuck Evans, Ernie Strickler, John Owens, Murray Williams, Bob Romeo, Elmer Beechler, Carl Orech, Joe White, Noah Kilgen, Buster Michaels, Jake Engel, Bob Stockwell, Glenn Rohlfing, Wayne Shonger, Charlie Spero, Clark Galehouse, Frank Victor, Mel Grant, George Horvath, Barrett Deems, Ernie Mathias, Bud Freeman, Arthur Schutt, and others
Vocalists With Band Included Smith Ballew, Scrappy Lambert, Dolores Reed, Slim Fortier, Ruth Lee, Kay Starr
Sponsored Radio Shows "Duffy's Tavern"
Theme Song "Last Night"
Recording Affiliations Okeh, Bluebird, Columbia, Decca

While never too successful with his periodic ventures as a bandleader, Venuti is without doubt one of the legends of the music business. Books could be written about his clowning and the humorous incidents involving those associated with him. He was never one to tolerate much criticism from his audience. Thus, some of these stories would be devoted to the many unorthodox methods he used to put those critics firmly in their places. He did the same with his sidemen when he felt they might be developing ambitions a little too rapidly, or when they did something he disapproved of. Whether it's

One of Kay Starr's first singing jobs was with Venuti's orchestra (1943).

At the Sheraton Townhouse with King Jackson and Red Nichols in the early 1960s.

Joe Venuti and one of the big bands he fronted with moderate success.

true or not, he was supposed to have punished one of his sidemen who insisted on tapping his foot to the music by nailing his shoes to the floor. Probably with the passage of time most of those stories have been exaggerated out of proportion. But there is no exaggeration to his status as a jazz man, for his position in the history books is secure. He was known as the first "hot violinist," a title he earned while playing with such bands as Goldkette, Roger Wolfe Kahn, Whiteman and Nichols. But his success as the leader of a big band was limited, probably because he never took the business seriously. In addition he preferred fronting a small combo which had greater flexibility and gave him a better chance to work with his violin. His career with a full-size band (twelve to fourteen) had several starts and restarts during the thirties and ended in the mid-forties. For the next several years he worked from a Hollywood base with a small combo, often a trio. Until television forced radio shows off the air, his old friend Bing Crosby often featured Venuti on his radio show with a meaty part written into the script for him. Eventually Venuti moved to Seattle. In the mid-seventies (and in the seventies himself) Venuti attended a jazz concert in Colorado Springs, and with his hot violin stole the show. He passed away on August 14, 1978.

W

JERRY WALD

Started First Band 1941
Where New York City
Sidemen With Band Included Information limited. At one time included Larry Elgart, Bob Dukoff, Les Robinson, Art Ryerson, Sid Weiss, with arrangements done by Ray Conniff and Jerry Gray
Sponsored Radio Shows "The Robert Q. Lewis Show"
Television With Band "The Kate Smith Show," "The Jackie Gleason Show"
Theme Song "Call Of The Wild"
Recording Affiliations Decca, Majestic, Columbia

Wald was a clarinetist who had a style somewhat similar to Artie Shaw's. The band that he launched in New York City in 1941 had its first important job at Child's Spanish Garden, and then a long run at the Lincoln Hotel. Throughout the forties he fronted a swing band, veering slightly toward the progressive jazz style in the late forties. In the early fifties he ran a club of his own in the Hollywood area, featuring a small musical combo under his own name. In late 1951 he put together another big band in the Los Angeles area to tour the country, and eventually settled down in New York City. During the balance of the fifties he fronted bands of varying sizes, and also kept busy in radio and television.

HERMAN WALDMAN

Started First Band Late twenties
Where Texas
Sidemen With Band Included Rex Preis, Bill Clemens, Ken Sweitzer, Jim Segars, Bob Harris, Tink Nauratal, Tom Blake, Vernon Mills, Barney Dodd, Reggie Kaughlin, Arnold Wadsworth, Jimmie Mann, Harry James
Recording Affiliations Brunswick, Bluebird

During the early thirties the Waldman orchestra was one of the most popular in the Southwest, working from a base in Dallas, Texas. They played the Baker and Adolphus Hotels, and also repeat engagements at the Peabody in Memphis and the Muehlebach in Kansas City. It was on a one-nighter in Beaumont, Texas that Harry James tried out with the group, and was hired for his first job with a travelling band. The popularity of the Waldman band did not survive beyond the thirties.

Jerry Wald.

Herman Waldman and his orchestra atop the Peabody Hotel, Memphis, Tennessee, 1934.

FATS WALLER

Started First Band 1932
Where New York City
Previous Band Affiliations Erskine Tate
Theme Song "Ain't Misbehavin' "
Songs Written "Ain't Misbehavin," "Honey-suckle Rose," "Keepin' Out Of Mischief Now," "Variety Stomp," "If It Ain't Love," "My Fate Is In Your Hands," "Stealin' Apples," "Lennox Avenue Blues," "Concentratin'," "Blue Turning Grey Over You," "Minor Drag," "Harlem Fuss," "St. Louis Shuffle," "Your Feet's Too Big," "Blue Black Bottom," "Black Raspberry Jam," "African Ripples," "The Jitterbug Waltz"
Recording Affiliations Columbia, Victor, Bluebird

Waller is best remembered for the music he composed and for his work as a pianist than as a bandleader. Nonetheless he did make some intermittent ventures into fronting a big band although each was of short duration. The first band under his own name was a six-piece group with which he played the New York City area and began a series of recordings with Victor which established him firmly as a recording star. In the late thirties he made a nationwide tour and spent several months in Europe with a band of his own. In late 1939 and 1940 he was leading a combo in New York which also played the Chicago and Milwaukee area and made theater tours. During 1941 and 1942 he was on tour with the big band and this was the last of his bandleading ventures. During 1943 he was again working as a single and writing scores for Broadway musicals. He also did a great deal of entertaining in service camps and once again made a trip to the West Coast. In December 1943 while en route to the East Coast from Los Angeles by train he was stricken with pneumonia and on December 15, died from a heart attack as the train pulled into Kansas City, Missouri.

FRED WARING

Started First Band About 1916
Where Pennsylvania
Sidemen With Band Included Tom Waring, Fred Buck, Jimmy Mullen, Poley McClintock, Fred Campbell, Jim Gilliland, Nelson Keller, Elton Cockerill, Si Sharp, Bill Townsend, George Culley, Will Morgan, Earl Gardner, Francis Foster, Clare Hanlon, Charley Henderson, Stewart Churchill, Wade Schlegel, Johnny "Scat" Davis, Gene Conklin, Virgil Davis, Murray Kelner, Lou Bonnies, Frank Zullo, Eddie Redel
Vocalists With Band Included Tom Waring, Frank Sylvano, The Lane Sisters (Rosemary, Priscilla, Lola)
Sponsored Radio Shows "The Old Gold Show," "The Chesterfield Supper Club," (early), "The Fred Waring Show"
Television With Band "The Fred Waring Show"

NBC photo release, September 21, 1938, when Waring was on NBC Red Network, sponsored by Grove's Bromo Quinine.

Waring's Pennsylvanians, Colonial Theater, Richmond, Virginia, September 8, 1924.

As an augmented show unit, Waring and his Pennsylvanians did the "Old Gold Hour" on radio.

Theme Song "Sleep"
Recording Affiliations Victor

Since this book is devoted to the dance bands, Waring's place in it is marginal, despite the tremendous success he enjoyed in theaters, radio, and television with his musical organization. His career was not very old before he abandoned dance appearances to become a show unit. His first musical group was a quartet of banjo players called "Waring's Banjatrazz." By the early twenties they had grown to a band of ten and sometimes twelve musicians, and grew

411

steadily from that point on. Waring's entry into radio was made with a broadcast over WWJ in Detroit in the early twenties. He had moved his headquarters from Philadelphia to Detroit, even though his band was now known as "Waring's Pennsylvanians." As radio began to hit its stride and bring the sound of live entertainment into the home, the interest in recorded music diminished. For several years record sales seriously declined. Smaller radio stations, unable to provide live entertainment, depended on recorded music. But some of the announcers who played the records did not identify the music as recorded: some even implied that the listener was hearing a live broadcast. In 1928 the Federal Radio Commission stepped into the picture and insisted that all broadcasters identify recorded music. A year later the first efforts to force broadcasters to pay royalties on the records they played was begun.

Waring took a very firm stand in this matter, and refused to make any records until a fair compensation arrangement with radio broadcasters was worked out and enforced. He maintained that position for several years before once again signing with a recording company. By the late twenties the popularity of Waring's Pennsylvanians had increased to the point where they were in demand for a European tour. His success from that point on is a very important part of America's musical history, although not in the dance band field. He passed away on July 29, 1984, at age 84.

CHICK WEBB

Started First Band 1926
Where New York City
Sidemen With Band Included Only partial list available. Included Bobby Stark, Benny Carter, Jimmy Harrison, Johnny Hodges, John Trueheart, Elmer Williams, Edgar Sampson, John Kirby, Weyman Carver, Sandy Williams, Taft Jordan, Don Kirkpatrick, Chauncey Haughton, Tommy Fulford, Reunald Jones, Claude Jones
Vocalists With Band Included Best known was Ella Fitzgerald
Theme Song "I May Be Wrong"
Recording Affiliations Decca, Okeh, Columbia

Gene Krupa, a great drummer himself, rated Webb as one of the greatest—the one who influenced all other drummers who were learning during the early thirties. He was born in Baltimore. It was said that his early inspiration came from watching military drummers in street parades. He began his own career by playing with small bands in his home city, and moved into New York in 1924. Two years later he started his own band, which included among its members Johnny Hodges, Bobby Stark, and Benny Carter. It was Duke Ellington who helped them get their first engagement at the Black Bottom Club in Manhattan. A few months later, again with Ellington's help, they moved to the Paddock Club on 50th Street. For the balance of the twenties the band worked in various clubs and dance pavilions around New York City. In the early thirties he was playing regularly at the Savoy Ballroom, the Roseland Ballroom, and made a tour with a "Hot Chocolates" revue. Webb was extremely popular at the Savoy, and Decca has preserved some of the music of that period on an album titled "Chick Webb —King Of The Savoy" (DL9223). In May 1937 Webb engaged the Benny Goodman band in a battle dance at the Savoy, drawing a crowd of nearly 5,000 people, most of whom thought the Webb band was the winner. Webb's remarkable drumming prowess was achieved despite a back injury sustained when he was a child, which left him permanently crippled. Only those close to him knew how much pain he suffered through-

The Chick Webb Orchestra in 1937. Ella Fitzgerald waves from the mike.

out his legendary career. That career came to an all-too-early end in 1939 when he died of tuberculosis at the age of thirty-seven. Ella Fitzgerald, who had become a star in her own right, as a result of her work with the band on recordings and radio broadcasts, took over leadership of the band and kept it going for nearly three years after Webb's death.

ANSON WEEKS

Started First Band   1924
Where   University of California Berkeley
Sidemen With Band Included   Enoch Pacheco, Pete Fylling, Abbey Brown, Russ Craze, Jimmy Walsh, Earl Morgan, Rene Moural, Kenneth Cole, Mark Girard, Don Hutton, Griff Williams, Ted Walters, Frank Hubbell, Frank Barton, Frank Saputo, Abbey Rasor, Leo Groman, Bill Moreing, Xavier Cugat, Henry Gilbert, Billy O'Brien, Al Burton, Neely Plumb, Phil Bodley, George Liberace, Bill Clifford, Gary Nottingham, Bob Saunders, Eddie Fitzpatrick, Neil Bondshu, and others. Several of these men were with him throughout most of his musical career
Vocalists With Band Included   Dale Evans, Kay St. Germaine, June Knight, Ben Gage,

Bob Crosby, Carl Ravazza, Tony Martin, Margie Dee
Tag Line   "Let's Go Dancin' With Anson"
Sponsored Radio Shows   "The Lucky Strike Show," "The Eddie Cantor Camel Show," the "Lady Esther Serenade," "The Florsheim Shoe Hour," "The M.J.B. Coffee Program," and "The Chamberlain's Lotion Show"
Longest Engagement   The Mark Hopkins Hotel — 1927 to 1934
Theme Song   "I'm Sorry, Dear," "I'm Writing You This Little Melody"
Recording Affiliations   Columbia, Brunswick, Decca, Fantasy

The two-beat style which Weeks featured throughout his forty year career as a band-

This was Anson Weeks' orchestra in Sacramento in 1924.

Anson Weeks, the Golden Gate's favorite maestro.

leader influenced virtually every other bandleader who ever came out of the San Francisco Bay area. It all began while he was attending the University of California at Berkeley. His first professional engagement was at the Hotel Oakland. It was followed by appearances in the Senator Hotel in Sacramento and at the Tahoe Tavern at Lake Tahoe. In 1927 he was booked into the Mark Hopkins Hotel in San Francisco, where he stayed for seven years. It was during that period that many of the future big names of the entertainment world worked with him, including some who became famous bandleaders and others who became famous radio, motion picture, and television stars. Air time from the Mark Hopkins, plus his record sales, made him sufficiently well known coast-to-coast so that he was able to go into the St. Regis Hotel in New York City in 1934 for another long run.

Then the Weeks orchestra appeared in such major hotels as the Waldorf-Astoria, the New York Roosevelt, the Boston Statler, Chicago's Edgewater Beach, College Inn, Palmer House, and the Aragon and Trianon

At the College Inn, Chicago, in 1936.

Ballrooms, the Cocoanut Grove and Biltmore Hotel in Los Angeles, the Muehlbach in Kansas City, the Chase Hotel in St. Louis, the Roosevelt in New Orleans, and every major amusement park in the country. The band also appeared in motion pictures for Paramount, Republic, and Monogram.

Early in 1941 while at the peak of his career, he was involved in a bus crash on a Midwestern highway in which he suffered a badly mangled right arm. For several years he underwent a series of operations which kept him virtually inactive, at a time when the music business was enjoying some of its best years. Eventually he gave up bandleading to try his hand at real estate and selling automobiles.

In the late fifties, unable to stay away from music, he reorganized with a small seven-piece orchestra, playing the same dance tempos which had made him famous. With this group he went into the Palace Hotel in San Francisco and eventually back to his old stand at the Mark Hopkins. In the mid-sixties he moved into the Sacramento Inn, where he finished out his career, still giving Northern Californians the kind of music that made them want to dance. Plagued with emphysema, he also suffered a heart attack and had to be increasingly absent from the bandstand. He died on February 7, 1969 at age seventy-two.

TED WEEMS

Started First Band 1923
Where Philadelphia
Previous Band Affiliations College dance orchestras

Sidemen With Band Included Art Weems, Norman Nugent, Paul Creedon, Walt Livingston, Francis Buggy, Charlie Gaylord, Dewey Bergman, Weston Vaughn, George Barth,

415

At the Meuhlebach Hotel in Kansas City in 1934.

Cecil Richardson, Dudley Fosdick, Mark Fisher, Parker Gibbs, Jack O'Brien, Louis Terman, Dusty Rhodes, Carl Agee, Charlie Stenroos, Thal Taylor, Bill Comfort, Bob Royce, Carl Workman, Merrill Connor, Pete Beilman, Ormand Downes, Art Jarrett, Country Washbourne, Red Ingle, Don Watt, Andy Secrist, Rosy McHargue, Jack Turner, Joe Rushton

Vocalists With Band Included Dusty Rhodes, Art Jarrett, Frank Munn, Country Washbourne, Parker Gibbs, Wes Vaughn, Mary Lee, Perry Como, and Marvel (Marilyn) Maxwell

Sponsored Radio Shows "Hildegarde's 'Beat The Band' Show," "The Fibber McGee and Molly Show"

Theme Song "Out Of The Night"

Recording Affiliations Victor, Bluebird, Columbia, Decca

Weems was born in Pennsylvania in 1901, attended high school in Philadelphia, and then enrolled at the University of Pennsylvania to study engineering. Somewhere along the line he had taken up the study of the trombone, and began playing in local college dance orchestras. Shortly after organizing his own band in 1923, he left

Ted Weems.

416

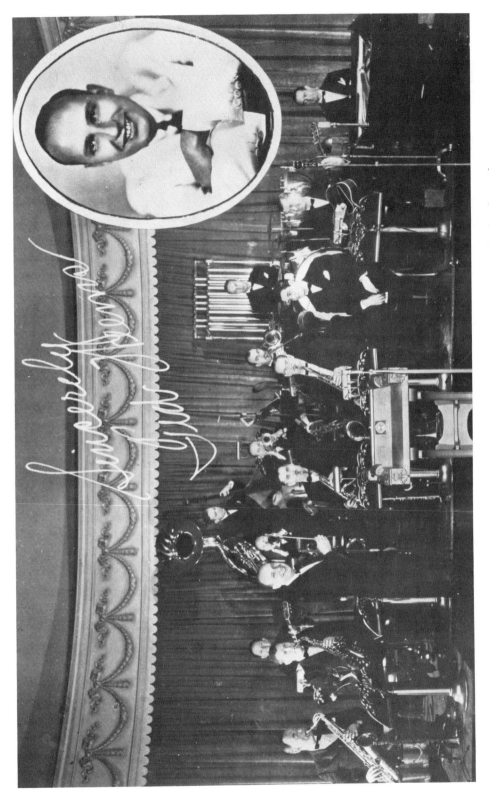

When this photo was taken in Chicago in 1936, Perry Como had been the band's male vocalist for almost three years.

417

The postwar Weems orchestra at the Strand Theater, New York.

Philadelphia to move into Chicago for better opportunities to be heard on radio. By 1926 he had become one of the first leaders to sign an exclusive contract with the fast-rising Music Corporation of America, and was well on his way as one of the Midwest's favorites. Coast-to-coast time made him a national attraction. In 1932 he got his first sponsored radio show and also made his first recording of "Heartaches" for RCA Victor. Nothing much happened with it; but when he switched to Decca a few years later, he once again recorded the song and this time it became a hit, topping the million-seller mark. By now he was a national attraction, enjoying popularity which continued unabated through the thirties. Major contributions to his success were made by the whistling of Elmo Tanner and the singing of Perry Como and Marvel Maxwell, who later changed her name to Marilyn when she left the band to try motion pictures. During World War II Weems conducted a band in the merchant marines, entering in 1942 and staying for the duration. His postwar activity as a dance bandleader was uneventful until 1947. Then a disc jockey in the South began plugging his old record of "Heartaches," making it a hit all over again. It quickly put Weems back into the national spotlight, where he remained for several years. In the late fifties he became a disc jockey himself, first in Memphis and later in Dallas. He still kept his hand in the band business, with occasional tours through the Midwest, becoming increasingly active in the early sixties. In March 1963, while on a tour of one-night stands, he was hospitalized in Tulsa, Oklahoma, with an attack of emphysema. Seven weeks later, on May 6, he died.

LAWRENCE WELK

Started First Band   About 1925
Where   North Dakota
Previous Band Affiliations   Lincoln Bold
Vocalists With Band Included   Gordon Maile, Frankie Sanders, Lois Best, Walter Bloom, Jules Herman, Mildred Stanley, Bob Paige, Jayne Walton, Jo Ann Hubbard, Bobby Beers, Joan Mowery, Roberta Lynn, Alice Lon
Television With Band   "The Lawrence Welk Show"
Theme Song   "Bubbles In The Wine"
Recording Affiliations   Gennett, Lyric, Vocalion, Okeh, Decca, Dot, Ranwood

Welk's long career really divides itself into two parts, and it is the first of these with which this book is concerned. When the "Lawrence Welk Show" first appeared on the ABC network as a national television show in 1955, there was a fairly large percentage of the younger generation who thought Welk was a relative newcomer both in show business and as a bandleader. Those who had celebrated a few more birthdays, however, knew that he had been around for a good many years, successfully leading a popular dance band.

Born and raised on a farm near Strasburg, North Dakota, he was brought up to believe that anything worth having could only be obtained by hard work. On a mail order accordion he practiced long hours in the evenings to develop sufficient skill to eventually play community dances and other social events in the area. At the age of twenty-one he left the farm to become a musician on a full-time basis. Soon he organized a small band, with which he began to tour the Dakotas, widening the scope of his operations as his reputation grew. His first radio broadcast was made in 1925, over station WNAX in Yankton, South Dakota. As a result, the band was featured daily on the station's program, providing them with an audience throughout the entire Central States region as well as a following which made them in demand for personal appearances in the entire area. That first band was called "Welk's Novelty Orchestra," and was transported from job to job in an old Graham-Paige sedan converted into a band bus.

In 1928 Welk was signed by Music Corporation of America, who took the band further east. The first billing by MCA was as "Lawrence Welk and His Hotsy-Totsy Orchestra." It was in Pittsburgh, Pennsylvania that some fan described Welk's music as "having a bubbly sound," thus inspiring the well known term, "Champagne Music."

For the next several years Welk roamed the Middle West, becoming one of its most popular territorial bands and gradually building the size of his orchestra as well

Lawrence Welk.

as his name value. He appeared many times as the relief band at the Trianon Ballroom in Chicago, and eventually became one of its headliners. The Trianon's air time did much for his musical stature, creating a demand for him at other major ballrooms and theaters. In the early forties he switched from Music Corporation of America to the Fredericks Brothers Agency, who handled him until they liquidated the agency in the late forties, releasing all the talent they had under contract. Shortly thereafter Welk placed himself under the management of Sam Lutz, with a "handshake contract" which became a very successful association that is still in effect.

Welk's first West Coast tour had been made in late 1945, and his first location appearance was in the Mural Room of the St. Francis Hotel in San Francisco. Following this engagement he went directly to the Los Angeles area for an appearance at the Ara-

Lawrence Welk and his Hotsy Totsy Orchestra.

Welk and his orchestra, still a small group in Yankton, South Dakota, 1933.

In 1936, the Welk Band had grown to eight men, plus Welk's own accordion. Yankton, South Dakota, was still headquarters, where they were heard regularly over station WNAX.

gon Ballroom, which enjoyed only moderate success. He returned to the coast again a few years later for an appearance at the Hollywood Palladium, with a band leaning towards the swing side, contrasting sharply with the smooth, sweet dance band he had been accustomed to fronting, which had often been described by his critics as being "Mickey Mouse." The Palladium appearance was disappointing, despite heavy publicity and promotion given it by both the ballroom and by Welk himself.

In 1951 he was back on the West Coast again, this time returning to the Aragon at Ocean Park, coming in for what was intended to be a six-weeks engagement. By this time television had replaced live radio as the entertainment medium in the home,

The Welk Band on the stand at the Hollywood Palladium in the 1960s.

and every bandleader was trying to break into it. Ballrooms were experimenting, attempting to adapt it to on-location pickups in the same manner as radio. The Aragon initiated a weekly show on a local television station which started out as a sustaining program. The following year it attracted local sponsors, and began to have a wide following in the Southern California area. Welk's Aragon contract was renewed over and over, but now for twelve-month periods instead of six weeks. Eventually there came a slowdown in the attendance and response to the television show. Conferences were held to decide whether to discontinue it or to try to add something new. Welk insisted that the answer was to give everyone just a little bit more, and to augment the size of the band as a step in that direction. Luckily he won his point. In the summer of 1955 the show was picked up by ABC for national coverage, under the sponsorship of Dodge Motor Cars.

If the band business had taken a vote in the early fifties to decide on the bandleader most likely to become a big success in television, Welk's name would have been far down the list. Yet while other bandleaders looked on and wondered what he was doing right that they had overlooked, he became the only bandleader to make a worthwhile place for himself as a television headliner. In 1971 ABC dropped the show but producer Don Fedderson quickly syndicated it, eventually creating a bigger network of stations carrying the show than it had previously. It was finally dropped at the end of the 1981-82 season after having been one of the most popular TV shows for thirty years.

PAUL WHITEMAN

Started First Band 1918
Where San Francisco, the Fairmont Hotel
Previous Band Affiliations None
Sidemen With Band Included (Practically all the greats and future greats of the twenties and thirties) . . . Henry Busse, Ferde Grofé, Mike Pingatore, Ross Gorman, Harry Reser, Frank Siegrist, Roy Matson, Jim Cassidy, Don Clark, Henry Lange, Wilbur Hall, Chester Hazlitt, Billy Murray, Charlie Strickfadden, Jack Fulton, Kurt Dieterle, Mischa Russell, Charles Gaylord, Matty

Malneck, Ray Turner, Nat Shilkret, Red Nichols, Vic d'Ippolito, Max Farley, Jimmy Dorsey, Charlie Margulis, Bob Mayhew, Tommy Dorsey, Boyce Cullen, Mike Trafficante, Rube Crozier, Tom Satterfield, Bill Challis, Bix Beiderbecke, Frankie Trumbauer, Hoagy Carmichael, Nye Mayhew, Jack Mayhew, Steve Brown, Roy Bargy, Izzy Friedman, Lennie Hayton, Bill Rank, Fud Livingston, Harry Goldfield, Andy Secrest, Bunny Berigan, Jack Teagarden, Charlie Teagarden, Casper Reardon, Benny Bonacio, Carl Kress, Art Ryerson, Frank Signorelli, Rudy Novak, Murray McEachran, Danny D'Andrea, Buddy Weed, Tony Romano, Artie Shapiro, Billy Butterfield, and many others

Vocalists With Band Included Charles Gaylord, Austin Young, The Rhythm Boys (Bing Crosby, Al Rinker, Harry Barris), Mildred Bailey, The King's Jesters, Red MacKenzie, Bob Lawrence, Jack Fulton, Johnny Mercer, Ken Darby, Joan Edwards, Mabel Todd, Dolly Mitchell, Ramona

Tag Line "The King of Jazz"

Sponsored Radio Shows "The Old Gold Cigarette Program," "The Kraft Music Hall" (when Al Jolson was star), "The Burns and Allen Show"

Motion Pictures With Band *The King Of Jazz, Strike Up The Band,* and *Rhapsody In Blue*

Theme Song "Rhapsody In Blue"

Recording Affiliations Victor, Columbia, Decca, Capitol and Signature

Although some might question his right to the title "King of Jazz," no one could deny the contribution he made to the causes of popular music and the welfare of the professional musician. Without Paul Whiteman, the history of the band business might have been altered substantially.

Born in Denver in 1890, he learned music from his father, an instructor who later taught many musicians who became famous. After playing with the San Francisco Symphony he started his first band in 1918 and played an engagement at the Fairmont

Paul Whiteman, King of Jazz, Rajah of Rhythm, and Monarch of Melody.

The "Three T's" of the Whiteman band, 1936: Frankie Trumbauer, Jack Teagarden, Charlie Teagarden.

The Paul Whiteman Orchestra in 1923.

Atlantic City, 1935. *Left to right:* The King's Men—Rad Robinson, John Dodson; tenor sax—Jack Cordaro; trombone—Bill Rank; vocals and violin—Bob Lawrence; The King's Men—Bud Lynn; trombone—Jack Teagarden; violin—Harry Struble; alto sax—Bennie Bonaccio; trombone—Hal Matthews; vocals—Durelle Alexander; vocals—Ken Darby; Paul Whiteman; piano and vocals—Ramona Davies; violin—Mischa Russell; alto sax—Frankie Trumbauer; drums—Larry Gomar; violin—Kurt Dieterle; piano—Roy Bargy; accordion—Vince Pirro; trumpet—Charlie Teagarden; banjo—Mike Pingitore; trumpet—Harry Goldfield; bass—Artie Miller; trumpet—Eddie Wade; vocals—Bob Hauser.

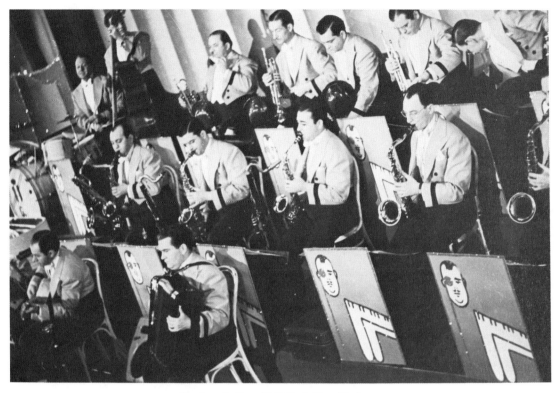

On stage in the mid 1940s in New York.

Hotel. The next year they went to Southern California, to play briefly in Santa Barbara, and then at the Alexandria Hotel in Los Angeles. By the end of 1920 they were in the Palais Royal in New York City for an engagement which many say was the real beginning of the "jazz age."

On February 12, 1924 after a tour of Europe, he staged a symphonic jazz concert at New York's Aeolian Hall, at that time the city's sanctuary of classical music. Special compositions were written for this concert by Victor Herbert and George Gershwin, whose "Rhapsody In Blue" was introduced that night with the composer at the piano, and went on to immortality. Music critics rated the concert an unqualified success, but financially it cost Whiteman a great deal of money.

By the end of the twenties Whiteman was the biggest name in the music business. He also had the biggest band (thirty-four), an all-star organization enjoying weekly incomes from a low of $150 to a high of $575. Such salaries were previously unheard of and did a great deal to improve the earnings level of sidemen in other bands from that time on. His personnel roster in the late twenties included, at one time or another, most of those who would become the famous leaders of the 1930s. He wanted the best and usually got them, even though he did not always permit them the freedom they needed to render their top performances.

Whiteman did not jump into radio as quickly as some of his fellow bandleaders. But by 1928 he was on the air for Old Gold cigarettes, and had "The Old Gold Orchestra" until he switched to Kraft Cheese sponsorship in 1933. In the meantime, he and the band had made *The King of Jazz* for Universal Pictures in 1930, and other motion pictures followed. In the early thirties the Whiteman band became more of a show unit than a dance orchestra, and only occasionally played dance engagements. The size of

The Whiteman orchestra on stage at the Paramount Theater, New York.

the band later decreased, but an on-the-stand photo made as late as 1938 still showed twenty-seven musicians and a vocalist.

In the next few years, Whiteman continued to be a dominant force in the business. In the mid-forties he was musical director for the Blue Radio Network, and dropped his "King of Jazz" title to become the "Dean of Modern American Music." When live radio programming declined and radio was taken over by the disc jockeys, Whiteman joined them for a brief fling as a

platter spinner on ABC. He also made a number of special appearances on television, and was Jackie Gleason's summer replacement in 1955, with a show which featured four guest dance bands on each weekly segment. In the early sixties he became active in the promotion of sports car racing in Florida and California. He died in a Doylestown, Pennsylvania hospital on December 29, 1967, the victim of a heart attack at age seventy-seven.

DICK WICKMAN

Started First Band 1941
Where Omaha, Nebraska
Television With Band A Midwestern Show in the late sixties originating from Lincoln, Nebraska for a local sponsor
Theme Song "I Want To Be Happy"
Recording Affiliations Produced records under his own label

Wickman's entry into the band business in 1941 was a short-lived venture, interrupted by military service the following year. After the war, he engaged in a business venture for a few years before resuming his musical

career. Then during the next several years he became a Midwestern favorite, playing the ballroom circuit in Nebraska, Iowa, and the Dakotas. Despite the difficulty most bandleaders experience in finding a place on television, the weekly half-hour show Wickman launched from a Lincoln, Nebraska station in 1965 had a three-year run. It was also seriously considered for syndication for other markets. Wickman was still busy with the band in the early seventies, but then took over leadership of the Jan Garber band until late 1987. He died of cancer on November 2, 1988, at age 72.

426

Dick Wickman and his orchestra in the studios of the KOLN-TV, Lincoln, Nebraska, in the mid 1960s.

HERB WIEDOFT

Started First Band   Early twenties
Where   Los Angeles
Sidemen With Band Included   Jess Stafford, Joe Nemoli, Gene Secrest, Larry Abbott, Fred Bibesheimer, Vincent Rose, Jose Sucedo, Guy Wiedoft, Adolph Wiedoft, Clyde Lucas, Dub Kirkpatrick, Gene Rose, Leon Lucas, Art Winters, Rudy Wiedoft
Vocalists With Band Included   Clyde Lucas, Dub Kirkpatrick, the Wiedoft Trio
Theme Song   "Cinderella Blues"
Recording Affiliations   Brunswick

Herb Wiedoft was a trumpet player. Although he would never become so well known as his saxophone-playing brother Rudy, he did establish himself firmly in the West Coast music picture as a result of a long run at the Cinderella Roof in Los Angeles. The reputation established there, plus the help of record sales made for Brunswick, enabled this band to make at least one successful eastern tour. Rudy Wiedoft had already left the band before that tour, and was established in New York as one of the nation's best known saxophonists. In May 1928 Herb Wiedoft was killed in an auto accident between Medford and Klamath Falls, Oregon, and trombonist Jess Stafford took over the leadership of the band. Stafford concentrated the band's activities in San Francisco for a three-year run at the Palace Hotel and several years as a theater band. The band was broken up when Stafford died of a heart attack in 1947.

GENE WILLIAMS

Started First Band   1950
Where   New York City
Previous Band Affiliations   Vocalist with Claude Thornhill
Sidemen With Band Included   Harry Weg-
breit, Jack Mootz, Don Josephs, Harry Di Vito, Dick Hoch, Sam Marowitz, Charlie O'Cain, Mickey Folus, Joe Reisman, Teddy Napoleon, Russ Saunders, Mel Zelnick
Arrangers For Band Included   Gil Evans,

Herb Wiedoft and his orchestra, 1924.

Hubie Wheeler, Chico O'Farrell, Joe Reisman
Vocalists With Band Included Gene Williams, Adele Castle

In its early stages Williams's band devoted its efforts to weekends and college dates, with the frequent personnel changes common under such unstable conditions. During that period the sound was a combination of numbers in the Thornhill style and also some bebop instrumentals. The band personnel listed above was put together in 1952 and began to gather momentum with engagements at such places as Glen Island Casino.

John S. Wilson reviewed them for *Downbeat* in 1952. He described the band as having established a style of its own, with little of the Thornhill influence remaining except for the lush sound created when the brass section blew into metal derbies. But on uptempo tunes, the brass section opened up and acquitted itself quite handily. Basically, however, it was a smooth band styled for dancing, with the emphasis on ensemble work rather than instrumental solos. Wilson's review commented that the Williams orchestra had reached a point where it was ready to capitalize on any of the unexpected breaks which usually contributed to launching a band into the big time. He went on to comment that there was nothing at all wrong with the band, but neither was there anything sufficiently outstanding about it to attract the necessary attention needed to sell records or the appearances and broadcasting necessary for a band's success. Since the band business in the 1950s was on the downgrade, the band's abilities were just not enough to prevent Williams' bandleading venture from being short-lived.

The Gene Williams Band.

GRIFF WILLIAMS

Started First Band   About 1933
Where   San Francisco
Previous Band Affiliations   Anson Weeks, also college bands
Sidemen With Band Included   Information limited. First band included Gene MacDonald, Horace Perazzi, Ray Anderson, Albert Arnold, Jack Buck, Paul Hare, Buddy Moreno, Walter Kelsey, Bob Logan, Warren Luce, and vocalist Coralee Scott. Williams was the pianist. Later in the thirties the band included Bill Clifford, Don Mulford, Walter King, Bob Kirk, and Lyle Gardner
Vocalists With Band Included   Coralee Scott, Buddy Moreno, Lois Lee, The Williams Trio
Theme Song   "Dream Music"
Songs Written   "Dream Music"
Recording Affiliations   Okeh, Varsity, Columbia

Griff Williams.

429

Griff Williams and his orchestra at Elitch's Gardens, Denver, in the late 1930s.

Williams was born in La Grande, Oregon and educated at Stanford University. For awhile during his college days he had a campus band of his own, but when he left college he joined Anson Weeks at the Mark Hopkins Hotel, to play second piano in the Weeks band. The first engagement with his own band was at the Edgewater Beach, a dine-and-dance spot in San Francisco where he opened on October 4, 1933. His musical style reflected the influence of his former boss and throughout his career he would front an orchestra styled for dancing, primarily a hotel band. After leaving the Edgewater he played other San Francisco locations before taking the band on a tour of hotels. In later years he returned periodically to play the Mark Hopkins Hotel where he had first worked with Weeks. Eventually he settled down in the Chicago area, where he played the Stevens Hotel for the first time in 1939. In the early forties he went into that very popular Chicago spot for a stay which lasted most of the war years. He remained active as a bandleader in the postwar years until 1953, when he virtually retired from the music business to associate himself with the Haywood Publishing Company, which put out a number of national business magazines. During that period he also made occasional appearances with his dance orchestra and in 1956 worked in a brief Chicago television series. In 1957 he was elected a vice president of the publishing company and became one of its directors. He died of a heart attack in Chicago in February, 1959.

The Austin Wylie Orchestra, Cleveland, in the mid 1920s.

AUSTIN WYLIE

Started First Band Early twenties
Where Cleveland, Ohio
Sidemen With Band Included Claude Thornhill, Spud Murphy, Tony Pastor, Artie Shaw, Clarence Hutchenrider, Joe Bishop, Billy Butterfield, Bill Stegmeyer, Vaughn Monroe, and many others
Vocalists With Band Included Helen O'Connell, Vaughn Monroe
Recording Affiliations Beltoba, Vocalion

Most of Wylie's bandleading career was spent in the Cleveland area. From the beginning of his career and throughout the twenties he worked at only one location, the Golden Pheasant. Perhaps he is best noted for the number of important musicians who worked in his band and who would later become bandleaders themselves. He remained active throughout the thirties in the Middle West. He gave up his band to manage the Artie Shaw band for a couple of years in the early forties. Then he reorganized again, but this bandleading venture was brief. He gave up music to go into other business ventures in the Cleveland area.

Z

SI ZENTNER

Started First Band   1957
Where   Los Angeles, California
Previous Band Affiliations   Abe Lyman,
Les Brown, Harry James, Jimmy Dorsey
Sidemen With Band Included   Bernie Fleis-
cher, Lanny Morgan, Don Davidson, Bob
Hardaway, John Lowe, Dick Hurwitz, Jules
Chaiken, Tom Scott, Vern Guertin, Bobby
Pring, Bob Edmundson, Don Nelligan, Bob
Florence, Lyle Ritz, Mel Lewis. This was
Zentner's first band; subsequent personnel
not available
Theme Song   "Up A Lazy River"
Recording Affiliations   Liberty, Bel Canto,
Victor

At a time when most everyone else was
holding postmortems for the big bands, Si
Zentner decided that someone should fight
back to prove there was still life in the business. In 1957 he launched a big band of his
own, and undertook the uphill battle to
achieve some of the successes enjoyed by
bandleaders in the thirties and forties. His
musical background was solid. In addition
to working with the name bands listed
above, he had worked as a staff musician
at MGM, and was constantly on call by all
the major studios in the Hollywood area.
With his wife Frances as personal manager,

Si Zentner.

the band took off on road tours, to play in-
terminable strings of one-nighters in country clubs, on college dates, and in the few
ballrooms still remaining. In January 1959

they played their first date at the Hollywood Palladium. This weekend booking did so well that they were brought back for several repeats. Favorable reviews, including strong support by *Downbeat*, began to make the future of the band look brighter. Recordings made for the Bel Canto label began to get some support from the public, probably as a result of Zentner's personally romancing the disc jockeys. In 1960 the break he was seeking came. His record of "Lazy River," made on the Liberty label, became a hit, bringing with it a wave of prosperity which carried into the mid-sixties and earned him a contract with RCA. In 1965 he went into the Tropicana Hotel in Las Vegas for an engagement publicized as the beginning of the hotel's big band policy. He stayed on to make Las Vegas his home and become the Tropicana's musical director. Like other bandleaders who went that route he became virtually submerged in the Las Vegas scene, continuing his position as musical director until the early seventies. At present, news stories indicate that Zentner is in Atlantic City, attempting to make a place for the big band sound in the casinos which are preparing to open in that city.

They Also Served

In the preceding pages those bandleaders whose efforts made major contributions to the big band era either during its formative years, its peak periods, or in their attempts to keep it alive in its declining years, have been profiled in varying degrees of detail. They were not the only ones who contributed. There are doubtless others who were also deserving of in-depth coverage but the sources available at this time do not provide sufficient information. During those years which many have described as "America's brightest entertainment period" there were bands everywhere—not only in the heavily populated areas but in the smaller communities as well. In addition to those we have included in our "big band" coverage there were hundreds of small 4-, 5-, and 6-piece combos doing an excellent job of providing dance music in clubs across the nation, some of them even appearing as theater attractions, but their story is deserving of a whole other book.

In the earlier years New York City was the base for the music business with almost all of its music publishers located there and with a large percentage of the early recordings made in that city. A well-known band in the early twenties was the *Weidemeyer Brothers*, who competed with Vincent Lopez and Paul Whiteman for the prime locations. There was *Ben Selvin*, whose activities consisted of more recordings than personal appearances and who may well have recorded more numbers than any other bandleader who ever lived. Brian Rust's Discography

gives him over 50 pages of listings. *Sam Lanin* would run him a close second, and both recorded under various pseudonymns. There was *Gene Kardos*, whose activities were primarily radio and recording, and although few will remember *Nathan Glantz*, he too was a very active New York recording bandleader. There were *Meyer Davis* and *Lester Lanin*, both heading up society band empires of their own, and a long list of other society leaders who will be found in the alphabetic listing towards the end of this chapter.

Henny Youngman had a band in the early twenties at Atlantic City and among the popular bands in the Boston area about that time was *Jimmy Gallagher* and His Checker Inn Orchestra. The early thirties found *Bill Gove and His Continentals* popular in the Boston area, the only band ever known to have featured four accordions.

Chicago was always a major city in the band business, in fact the biggest agency for dance bands originated in Chicago— Music Corporation Of America. During the twenties there were probably more black bands working in Chicago than in any other city. They included *Lottie Hightower's Nighthawks, Doc Cook's Doctors Of Syncopation, Hugh C. Swift's Band, Elger's Creole Band, Jimmy Wade's Syncopaters, Ma Rainey's Jazz Band, Sammy Stewart's Band, Al Wynn*, and *Erskine Tate* among others. *Art Benson* was a popular Chicago area leader and the *Benson Brothers Orchestra* had a number of bands playing under their name. And there was *Jules Hurbuveaux, Paul Ash, Zez Confrey, Don Bestor, Carl Fenton, Earl Hoffman, Ross Reynolds,* and the *Egyptian Serenaders*.

But the entire Middle West was always a very productive dance band market and the bands were there to serve them. In the Kansas City area *George E. Lee* competed with *Benny Moten* and the other names of the day. There was a band on the road directed by *Blanche Calloway*, whose major claim to fame was that she was the sister of another famous Calloway. *Cecil Scott* and *His Salt and Pepper Shakers* played throughout the area and from Denver came a black bandleader named *Leo Davis*, who at one time billed himself as the black Guy Lombardo. Working out of Omaha were *Ted Adams, Art Bronson, Preston Love, Art Randall, Frank Hodek*, and headquartering in nearby Beatrice, Nebraska, was *Fred Gerwick*, whose drummer was a handsome lad named Spangler Arlington Brough, better known later as *Robert Taylor*. Other Nebraska bands included *Emerson-Hudson, Eddie Jungebluth, Leo Pieper*, and *Jimmy Barnett*. Also identified with that section of the Midwest were *Cliff Perrine, Carl Bean, Wilson Humber*, and *Lee Williams*. *Hal Wasson* was a popular Midwest orchestra, even though his base was in Texas. From Milford, Kansas, *Steve Love* built up a following with a daily broadcast from Doctor Brinkley's 50,000-watt radio station which permitted him to tour the neighboring states with success.

Salt Lake City had its *Jerry Jones*, who ran Jerry Jones' Rendezvous, and *Larry Kent*. A few miles away in Helena, Montana, *Dick Whittinghill* was playing the local dance circuit and a local theater with a band which he gave up to join the Pied Pipers. After World War II Whittinghill became one of the most highly paid disc jockeys in Southern California.

The West Coast always produced a lot of bands even though most of them went somewhere else to cash in on it. Seattle had its *Jackie Souders* and *Vic Meyers*, the lat- ter the lieutenant-governor of the state for several years. In Portland, *Cole McElroy* dominated the scene for several years, not only with his band, but as the operator of a ballroom. From out of San Francisco came a long string of bands including *Tom Coakley*, who turned his band over to vocalist *Carl Ravazza* to become a successful lawyer and later a district judge, *Eddie Fitzpatrick, Gary Nottingham, Neal Bondshu, Leon Mojica, Merle Carlson, Buddy Maleville, Bob Saunders, Jimmy Davis, Ran Wilde*, and strictly for the local scene, *John Wolohan* whose son *Maury Wolohan* carries on the tradition, *Sid Hoff*, and *Wally Heider*. The Southern California list included *Georgie Stoll, Sterling Young, Ken Baker, Eddie Oliver, Malcolm Beelby, Johnny Richards* (whose brother was bandleader Chuck Cabot), *Marvin Dale*, and *Everett Hoaglund*, who moved to Mexico City in the early forties and found business so good for his band that he stayed there.

But that's not all of them . . . far from it. Throughout the years of big band popularity there was *Barclay Allen, Bob Alexander, LeRoy Anderson, Johnny Archer, Murray Arnold, Zinn Arthur*, and *Mickey Alpert*, who was playing the Cocoanut Grove in Boston when it was destroyed by fire in November, 1942, and who lost some of his band members in the fire.

There were *Will Back, Dick Barrie, Alex Bartha, Charlie Baum, Les Baxter, Leon Belasco, Denny Beckner, Don Bigelow, Gus Bivona, Jerry Delaine, Archie Bleyer, Bert Block, Walter Bloom, Earl Bostic, Charlie Boulangar, Mario Braggiotti, Lou Bring, Frank and Milt Britton, Bernie Burns, Willie Bryant*.

There were *Floyd Campbell, Del Campo, Pupi Campo* (Jack Paar Show), *Del Casino, Reggie Childs, Buddy Clarke, Tom Clines, Jolly Coburn, Russ Columbo, Emil Coleman, Christopher Columbus, Irving Cottle, Ben Cutler*, and *Bob Cross, Chris Cross, Dale Cross*, and *Milton Cross*, which may prompt our readers to ask if the real *Cross* will please stand up.

Bobby Day, Duke Daly, Eli Dantzig, Peter Dean, George De Carl, Buddy De Franco, Eddie De Lange, Jack Denny, Emery Deutsch, Lou Diamond, Saxie Dowell, George Duffy, Mike Durso, and Dick Dildine, a West Coast bandleader who had the heartbreaking experience of scattering his musical library all the way across the Nevada desert when the door of the trailer in which he was transporting it came open.

There were Roy Eldridge, Baron Elliott, the Elliott Brothers, Don Ellis, and Val Ernie.

There were Happy Felton, Max Fisher, Jacques Fry, Buddy Franklin, Larry Funk, and Herbie Fields, who took his own life because he felt he had accomplished all in life that was worthwhile.

Al Gayle, Glenn Garr, Dick Gasparre, Tom Gerun, Eddie Grady, Henry Gallagher, Terry Gibbs, Lud Gluskin, and King Guion.

There were George Haefely, Cass Hagen, Sleepy Hall, Johnny Hamp and the Kentucky Kardinals, Edgar Hayes, Ray Heatherton, Will Hauser, Tal Henry, Skitch Henderson, Teddy Hill, Buddy Heisey, Carl Hoff, Le Roy Holmes, Ernie Holst, Lloyd Huntley, Frankie Hyle, and Jack Hylton, the first English leader to be permitted to bring his own band to the United States.

There were Sonny Kendis, Jules Klein, and Dick Kuhn.

Lloyd La Brie, Howard Lally, Peter Lance, Howard Lanin, Milton Larkin, Eddie Le Baron, Bob Lee, Phil Levant, Enoch Light And His Light Brigade, and Little Jack Little.

Matty Malneck, Richard Maltby, Dick Mansfield, Joe Marsala, Jack Marshard, Nye Mayhew, Jack McClean, Bill McCune, Bobby Meeker, Paul Meeker, and Ruby Newman.

There were Will Oakland, Sy Oliver, and Al Overend.

Louis Panico, George Paxton, Caesar Petrillo, (brother of the one-time A.F. of M. president), and Roger Pryor.

There were George Rank, Floyd Ray, Houston Ray, Peyson Rey, Don Reid, Gene Rodemich, Adrian Rollini, Dick Rock, Dick Rogers, Luigi Romanell, Ernie Rudy, Carl Schrieber, Chick Scoggins, Marvin Scott, Terry Shand, Milt Shaw, Merlin Sheets, Seymour Simons, Ralph Slade, Beardsley Smith, Le Roy Smith, Harold Stern, Royce Stoener, Ted Straeter, Bob Sylvester, Earl Spencer, Joseph Sudy, and Nick Stuart, who alternated between fronting a dance band and working in motion pictures.

There were Elmo Tanner, Dan Terry, Henry Theis, George Towne, Anthony Trini, Frankie Trumbauer, and Pinky Tomlin, better known as a vocalist and a composer of such hit tunes as "The Object Of My Affections," and "What's The Reason I'm Not Pleasin' You."

There were Peter Van Steeden, who among other things was featured on the Fred Allen Show, Wheeler Wadsworth, Jimmy Walsh, Marek Weber, Jack Wendover, Billy Williams, Cootie Williams, Wayne Wills, Barry Wood, Frank Wooley, Julian Woodworth, Harry Yerkes and Bob Zurke.

That should be the X,Y,Z, of it but it isn't!

There were all-girl bands in addition to Ina Ray Hutton and they included Phil Spitalny, D'Artega, Ada Leonard, and out in Lincoln, Nebraska, Boots And Her Buddies.

There were bandleaders who gave it up to become successful agents, including Harold Oxley, Bill Black, Bill Fredericks, Lyle Thayer, Hal Howard, Art Rowley, and Don Mulford.

There was Ted Mack, who led a fine dance band in the early thirties but gave it up to join the staff of "Major Bowes' Amateur Hour" and eventually head up the program himself.

There were Cecil Golly and his "Music By Golly," George Liberace and his "Music By George," Emerson Gill—"Music With A Thrill," "Music Of The Times" by Don Grimes, "Music Sweet As Sugar Cane" by Hal Strain.

There were Hawaiian-styled bands including Ray Kinney, Lani McIntyre, and

Johnny Pineapple. There were Latin bands indicating the Cugat influence including *Carlos Molina, Miguelito Valdes, Perez Prado,* and *Noro Morales.* And who could forget the Cuban bandleader *Desi Arnaz,* who went on to become the co-owner of one of television's biggest production companies.

Yes, there were even more. At the height of the big band era *Downbeat* magazine listed, on a weekly basis, the itineraries of some 600 dance orchestras. Many of them operated only briefly, some were only local attractions, many were semi-names, and there were those who rose to become the biggest attractions in the business. Whether or not they achieved fame they provided the training ground for musicians who went on to play with bigger names. Some were the minor leagues where the talent for the major leagues was developed. Without those musical minor leagues the musical major leagues can hardly be expected to continue beyond where its current participants, the same ones who were active during the height of the big band era, retire from active participation.

One who speaks of the "music of the big bands" is not referring only to a period when the size of musical organizations numbered twelve or more musicians but to a type of music, a well-defined sound. That was the sound of the big band era, a sound to which very little has been added in recent years in the way of new compositions, but which still survives even though most of last year's hit tunes are already forgotten. It has been a popular conception that the younger generation of the last two decades has looked with scorn upon the music of the big band era. Perhaps a good percentage of them did but there was another percentage who loved it, some of them treating it as a "new discovery." Most of those bands still going on tour were staffed with young musicians, many recruited from colleges where courses in big band music were taught. All over the nation high school students have been collecting the arrangements of Basie, Ellington, Goodman, Shaw, James, Dorsey, and Miller, forming a band to play them, mostly for kicks but also to play available jobs when they could get them.

As the '80s draw to a close the days of the travelling bands are virtually a thing of the past. Most of those who still go on tour are "ghost bands"—bands booked under the name of a departed leader and using the original library but fronted by someone probably never identified with the leader whose name is advertised. A few legends from the big band era still travel but recruit all or most of their sidemen locally, for in each major city there are new bands made up of skilled, well-rehearsed musicians playing fine arrangements of the old standards interspersed with what they find usable in newer compositions. Most of those local bands have a following in their own area which gets them one or two dates weekly, usually private functions.

During the big band era two basic ingredients built a band to "name" status. Nothing was more important than records. A big hit record could convert a struggling band into an overnight sensation. The big bands no longer get any support from the record industry; a bandleader who wants to make a record must finance it himself. Part of the reason record companies turned away from the big bands was the action of the A.F. of M. under James C. Petrillo in calling two prolonged recording strikes during a ten-year period in the '40s.

The other band-building ingredient was radio, both local and national. A new band got on local radio and then graduated to network. Every night from 9:00 until midnight bands were picked up from on-the-stand remote locations and broadcast coast-to-coast. Eventually those broadcasts made a new west coast band (or vice versa) sufficiently well-known to book into New York and play a string of lucrative one-nighters enroute. Now there is no network radio, no remote broadcasts, and radio stations have found more profitable ways of filling their time—a state of affairs not likely to change.

And so the big band sound is likely to stay alive indefinitely, but it will be played by local and "territory" bands.

PHOTO CREDITS

We would like to thank all those who kindly supplied photographs for use in this book.

Page 2, upper, Paul Mertz, lower, Ernie Mathias; p. 3, Charlie Agnew; p. 4, Van Alexander; p. 5, Ray Anthony; p. 6, Jack Lomas; p. 7, Ray Anthony; p. 9, Louis Armstrong; p. 10, Photo Files; p. 11, Frank Driggs; p. 12, Don Haynes; p. 13, Karl Hubenthal; p. 14, Gus Arnheim; p. 15 upper, Ted Krise, lower, Manny Stein; pp. 16-20, Jack Lomas; p. 22, Frank Driggs; p. 23, MCA; p. 24 upper, Barney McDevitt, lower, Wally Heider; p. 25 upper, Murray Williams, lower, Gene's Photo & Rock Shop; pp. 26, 27 upper, MCA, lower, Arsene Studios; p. 29 upper Tony Barron, lower, p. 30, William Morris Agency; p. 31, Frank Driggs; p. 32 upper Jack Lomas, lower, Gene's Photo & Rock Shop; p. 33, Joe Reisman; p. 34, Don Haynes; p. 35, Tex Beneke; p. 36, Tom Sheils; p. 37, Riley Gaynor; p. 38, Wally Heider; p. 39 upper, Murray Williams, lower, p. 40, Memo Bernabei; p. 41, Ward Archer; p. 42, Jack Lomas; p. 43 Dick Stabile; p. 44, Frank Bettencourt; p. 45, Jack Lomas; p. 47 Frank Driggs; pp. 48-50, Jack Lomas; p. 51, Les Brown; p. 52 upper, Don Kramer, lower, p. 53 upper left, Jack Lomas, lower left, right, Butch Stone; p. 54 left, Don Kramer, right, Les Brown; p. 55 upper, Betty Lanigan and NBC; p. 56, Riley Gaynor; p. 57 Butch Stone; p. 60, Ted Krise; p. 61, lower, Jack Lomas; p. 62, Barney McDevitt; p. 63 upper, Murray Williams, lower, Gene's Photo & Rock Shop; p. 66, Chuck Cabot; p. 67, Joe Rushton; p. 68 lower, Jack Lomas; pp. 69-70, Frankie Carle; p. 71 upper, Bill Block, lower, Orchestra's Inc.; p. 72, Wally Heider; p. 73 upper, Frank Driggs, lower, MCA; p. 75, Cato Mann; p. 76 upper, Johnny Catron, lower, Carmen Cavallero; p. 77, Jack Lomas; p. 78 upper, MCA; p. 79, Bill Clifford; p. 80, Larry Clinton; p. 81 upper, Frank Driggs, lower, Jack Lomas; p. 83 left, William Morris Agency, right, Del Courtney; p. 84, Frank Driggs; p. 86 upper, Manny Stein; lower, MCA; pp. 87, 88, Gene's Photo Rock Shop; p. 89 upper, Elitch's Gardens; lower, Disneyland; p. 90 upper, Mutual Broadcasting System, lower, MCA; p. 91, Jack Lomas; pp. 92-93 Mick Cummins; p. 95, Joe Reisman; p. 97, Al Donahue; p. 98 lower, Joe Reisman; pp. 99-100, MCA; p. 101, Jack Lomas; p. 102 upper, Charlie Teagarden, lower, Gene's Photo & Rock Shop; p. 103 upper, Coliseum Ballroom; p. 104, Jack Lomas; p. 105, Dick Whittinghill; p. 106 upper, Barney McDevitt, lower, Wally Heider/Duncan Scheidt; p. 107, Johnny Catron; p. 109, Jack Lomas; pp. 110, 111 upper, Peter Duchin; p. 114 upper, Hollywood Palladium, lower, Jack Lomas; p. 115, Columbia Records; p. 116, Jack Lomas; pp. 117, 118, Frank Driggs; p. 119, Columbia Records; p. 120, President Nixon and the White House; p. 121 upper, Ralph Portnor; p. 122 upper, Skinnay Ennis, lower, Bob Hope Office; p. 123, Eddie Kusby; p. 124, Jack Everette; p. 127, Shep Fields; p. 128 lower, Jerry Kadovitz; pp. 129-131, Muzzy Marcellino, p. 132 upper, Ralph Flanagan, lower, Hollywood Palladium; p. 133 upper, Arsene Studio, lower, Jack Lomas; p. 135 upper, Basil Fomeen, lower, p. 136, Chuck Foster; p. 137, Memo Bernabei; p. 138 upper, Paul Weirick, lower, Freddie Large; p. 139 upper, Memo Bernabei, lower, Seymour Weiss; p. 142, Jean Goldkette; pp. 143, 145, Paul Mertz; p. 147, Walter Dougherty; p. 148, Jack Lomas; p. 149, Gene's Photo & Rock Shop; p. 150, Joe Rushton, p. 151, Wally Heider/Rex Stevens; p. 152 upper, Jack Lomas; p. 153, Claude Gordon; p. 154 upper, Elitch's Gardens; p. 155, Walter Dougherty; p. 156, Ted Krise; p. 157, Elitch's Gardens; p. 158, Joe Reisman; p. 159 upper, MCA, lower, Barney McDevitt; p. 160, Gene's Photo & Rock Shop; pp. 162, 163 upper, MCA, lower, Irving Archer Studios; p. 165 upper, Jack Lomas, lower, Frankie Carle; p. 166, Henry Jaworski; p. 167, Joe Glaser; p. 168 upper, Arsene Studio, lower, Joe Glaser; p. 170 upper left, Walter Dougherty, upper right, MCA, lower, Irving Verret; pp. 172, 173, Jack Lomas; p. 175, upper, Dave Jacobs; lower, Jack Lomas; p. 176, Charlie Higgins; p. 177 upper, G.A.C., lower, Ernie Hecksher; p. 178, MCA; p. 179, Horace Heidt; p. 180, Ronnie Kemper; p. 181, Joe Rushton; p. 183 upper, Rex Stewart, lower, Jack Lomas; p. 185 lower, Elitch's Gardens; p. 186, Lenny Herman; pp. 187-190, Walter Yoder; p. 191, Arsene Studio; p. 192, Ray Hoback; pp. 193, 194, Jack Lomas; p. 196, Frank Driggs; p. 197, Arsene Studio; p. 198, Harold Jovien; p. 199 upper, Paul Mertz, lower, Frank Driggs; p. 200, MCA; p. 201 upper, Eddy Howard, lower, Gene's Photo & Rock Shop; p. 202, Jack Lomas; p. 203, Max Herman; p. 204, Jack Lomas; p. 205, Harry James; p. 206 upper, Fred Monte, lower, MCA; p. 207, Jack Lomas; pp. 208, 209, Harry James; p. 210, Pee Wee Monte; p. 211, Art Jarrett; pp. 212, 213, Wally

Heider; pp. 214, 215 Henry Jerome; p. 216, Freddy Martin; p. 217, Anson Weeks; pp. 218, 219 upper, Walter Yoder; p. 221, Jack Lomas; p. 222, MCA; p. 223 upper, Ronnie Kemper, lower, Jack Lomas; p. 225 upper, Ralph Portnor; lower, Perry Botkin; p. 227 lower, Jack Lomas; pp. 228, 229 lower, Bud Dant; p. 231 upper, Butch Oblak, lower, Elitch's Gardens; p. 232, Joe Kayser; p. 235, John Scott Trotter; p. 236 upper, Jack Lomas; p. 236 lower, William Morris Agency; p. 238, Mart Kenney; p. 239 upper, G.A.C., lower, Barney McDevitt; p. 240, Gene Howard; p. 241 upper, Stan Kenton, lower, Gene's Photo & Rock Shop; p. 242, Al King; pp. 243, 244 lower, 245, Jack Lomas; p. 246 upper, Frank Driggs, lower, Paul Mertz; p. 247, Freddy Martin; p. 248 upper, MCA, lower, Ed Burke; p. 249, 250 upper, Gene Krupa, lower left, MCA, lower right, Pee Wee Monte; p. 251 upper, Bob Strahl; p. 252 upper, Gene's Photo & Rock Shop, lower, Barney McDevitt; p. 253 upper, Gene's Photo & Rock Shop, lower, Roc Hillman; p. 254, Jack Lomas; p. 256, Arsene Studio; p. 257, Harlan Leonard; p. 258, Jack Lomas; p. 259 upper, Sammy Blank, lower, 3M Company; pp. 260, 261 upper, Jack Lomas, lower, p. 263, Guy Lombardo; p. 264, G.A.C.; p. 265 upper, Jack Lomas, lower, G.A.C; p. 266, MCA; p. 267 upper, Vincent Lopez, lower, Red Nichols; p. 269, William Morris Agency; p. 270, Arsene Studio; p. 271 upper, MCA, lower, p. 272, Rose Lyman; p. 273, G.A.C.; p. 274, Elitch's Garden's; p. 275, G.A.C.; p. 276 upper, Billy McDonald; p. 277, G.A.C.; p. 278, Arsene Studio; p. 279, Paul Weirick; p. 280 upper, Ray McKinley, lower, Wally Heider; p. 281, Paul Mertz; p. 282, Joe Rushton; pp. 283, 284, Jack Lomas; p. 285 upper, MCA; pp. 286, 287, 288 upper, Freddy Martin, lower, MCA; p. 289, Arsene Studio; p. 290, Billy May; p. 291, Jack Lomas; p. 292, Paramount Pictures; p. 294, Paul Tanner; p. 295 upper, Don Haynes, lower, Willie Schwartz; p. 296, Tom Sheils; p. 297, Joe Reisman; p. 299 upper, Ward Archer, lower, Frank Driggs; p. 301, Vaughn Monroe; p. 302, G.A.C.; p. 303, Buddy Moreno; pp. 304, 305 upper, Russ Morgan, lower, Gene's Photo & Rock Shop; p. 307 upper, Jerry Kadovitz, lower left, G.A.C., lower right, Buddy Morrow; p. 309, Jack Lomas; p. 310, Paul Neighbors; p. 311 upper, Ozzie Nelson, lower, Jack Lomas; p. 312, Howard Bruno; p. 314 upper, Red Nichols, lower, Joe Rushton; pp. 315, 316, Red Nichols; p. 317 upper, MCA, lower, Gene's Photo & Rock Shop; p. 318, MCA; p. 319, Jack Lomas; p. 320 upper, Manny Stein, lower, Gene's Photo & Rock Shop; p. 321, MCA; p. 322, Jack Lomas; pp.

324, 325, Ted Krise; p. 326 upper, Frank Driggs, lower, G.A.C.; p. 327, Jack Lomas; pp. 328, 329, Will Osborne; pp. 330, 331, Harry Owens; p. 334 upper, Joe Glaser, lower, Jimmy Palmer; p. 336 upper, Joey Starr, Phoenix, lower, G.A.C.; p. 337 upper, Gene's Photo & Rock Shop, lower, Barney McDevitt; p. 338, MCA; p. 339 upper, Memo Bernabei, lower, Jean Gordon; p. 341, Eddie Sheffert; p. 342, upper left, MCA, upper right, Johnnie Kolberg, lower, Teddy Phillips; pp. 343, 344, Jack Lomas; p. 345, Walter Yoder; p. 347, Teddy Powell; p. 348, MCA; p. 349, Hal Pruden; p. 350, Pee Wee Monte; p. 351, Jack Lomas; p. 352 upper, Paul Mertz; p. 353, Jack Lomas; p. 355, Tommy Reed; p. 356 upper, Arsene Studio, lower, Joe Reichman; p. 358, Leo Reisman; p. 359 upper, Alvino Rey, lower, Hollywood Palladium; p. 360, Jack Lomas; p. 362, Arsene Studios; p. 365 upper, Paul Mertz, lower, Paul Weirick; p. 366 upper, Gene's Photo & Rock Shop, lower, Harry Owens; p. 367, Jack Russell; p. 368, Ted Fio-Rito; p. 370, Hollywood Palladium; p. 371 upper left, Jack Lomas, Upper right, Chuck Cecil; p. 373, Jack Lomas; p. 374, Artie Shaw; p. 375, Hugh Turner; p. 376, Gil Harris; p. 377, Evan Aiken; p. 378, Jack Lomas; p. 379 upper, Wally Heider, lower, Paul Specht; p. 380, Frank Driggs; p. 381, MCA; p. 382 upper, Charlie Spivak, lower, Wally Heider; p. 383, Charlie Spivak; p. 384, 385, Dick Stabile; p. 386, Jack Lomas; p. 387, Karl Kramer; p. 388 upper, MCA, lower, Benny Strong; p. 391 upper, Jack Lomas, lower, Joe Reisman; p. 392 upper, Hal Wasson; lower, p. 393, Charlie Teagarden; p. 395 upper, Arsene Studio, lower, G.A.C.; p. 396, Al Trace; p. 397, Jack Lomas; p. 398, MCA; p. 399 upper, Roc Hillman, lower, MCA; p. 400 upper, Elitch's Gardens, lower, p. 401 upper, Jack Lomas; lower, Arsene Studio; p. 403, Rudy Vallee; p. 404, Jack Lomas; p. 405, Joe Glaser; p. 406 upper, Ernie Mathias, lower, Red Nichols; p. 407, Jack Lomas/John Stanier; p. 409 upper, Jack Lomas, lower, Herman Waldman; p. 411 upper, Ted Krise, lower, Jack Lomas; p. 413, John Stanier; pp. 414 upper, 415, Anson Weeks; p. 416 upper, Joe Rushton; p. 417, Jack Lomas; p. 418, Arsene Studio; pp. 419-421, Lawrence Welk; p. 422, Hollywood Palladium; p. 423 lower, Charlie Teagarden; p. 424 upper, Ted Krise, lower, Charlie Teagarden; p. 425, Arsene Studio; p. 426, Jack Lomas; p. 428, Bill Stafford;, p. 429 upper, Joe Reisman, lower, MCA; p. 430, Bill Clifford; p. 431, Freddy Martin; p. 432, Si Zentner.

Index

440

Dedrick, Art, 300
Dedrick, Rusty, 394
Dee, John, 277
Dee, Margie, 413
Deems, Barrett, 406
Defenbach, Moe, 358
De Franco, Buddy, 29, 350
De Haven, Gloria, 284, 370
De Julius, Rudy, 23
De Kay, George, 254
Delaney, Al, 49
Delaney, Ken, 403
DeLange, Eddie, 202
de Laurence, Larry, 165
Dell, Al, 291
Dell, Helen, 284
Dell, Herbie, 77
Del Lampe Orchestra, 244
Delmarter, Ted, 386
De Lory, Wendell, 173, 372
De Luca, Neil, 243
Deluce, Augustine, 22
De Mayo, Bill, 383; photos, 385
DeMill, Pete, 58
DeNicola, Tony, 205
Dennis, Denny, 45, 154
Dennis, Stan, photos, 156
Denny, Carl, 277
Dent, Laforet, 269
Dentino, Mario, photos, 95
DeParis, Wilbur, 72, 298
De Paul, Gene, 370
DePaul, Joe, 211
Depew, Art, 205
Deppe, Harold, 379
Deppe, Lois, 195, 196
Derry, Bob, photos, 392
Derwin, Hal, 96
De Santos, Pete, photos, 314
de Simone, Tony, 284
Desmond, Johnny, 248
De Soto, John, 346
Dessel, Barney, 51
Deters, Bassie, 51
Detorly, Wendell, 217
Detton, Gil, 379
Deutsch, Adolph, photos, 225
de Vito, Al, 290
De Vito, Buddy, 206
De Vol, Frank, 178
De Vorzon, Jules, 403
De Witt, Allen, 192, 370
Dey, Georgia, 237
Diamant, Shanty, 291
Diamond, Harold, 257
Diamond, Jack, 243
Diaz, Horace, 1, 23; photos, 2
Diaz, Vince, 205
De Bari, Vince, 139, 162; photos, 139
De Carlo, Tom, 248
Dick, Guy, 247
Dickenson, Vic, 29, 72, 200
Dickerson, Carroll, 8, 195, 196
Dickson, Dick, photos, 2

Dickson, Ross, 286
Diehl, Al, 300
Diehl, Bill, 92; photos, 93
Diehl, Sam, 403
Dieterle, Kurt, 422; photos, 424
Digiaro, Dino, 300
Dillard, John, 173, 194
Dillon, Buss, 288
Dillon, Jimmy, 284
Dilly, Bert, photos, 274
Dimaio, Nick, 51
De Maio, Dick, 361
de Martino, Frank, 264
Dinkin, Irv, 279; photos, 280
d'Ippolito, Vic, 255, 264, 423
De Prima, Frank, 298
Dirvin, William, 245
Divan, Ernie, 18, 23
DiVito, Harry 51, 381, 427
Dixie Ramblers, photos, 341
Dixon, Dick, 1
Dixon, Joe, photos, 104
Dixon, Morris, 255
Dodd, Barney, 408
Dodds, Baby, 324; photos, 325
Dodds, Johnny, 324; photos, 325
Dodson, John; photos, 424
Doe, Dudley, 214
Doerr, Clyde, 192
Doggett, Bill, 298, 300; photos, 299
Dohrman, Harold, 243
Dolan, Red, 264
Domenick, Rocque, 77
Dominick, Bob, 77, 347, 364
Dombach, Fred, 284
Donahue, Al, 5, 96; photos, 97
Donahue, Norman, 139
Donahue, Sam, 58, 98-99, 103, 205,
    248, 290; photos, 98
Donna and her Don Juans, 178;
    photos, 179
Dooley, Phil, 173
Dorham, Kenny, 113
Dorris, Red, 238
Dorsey, George, 47; photos, 72
Dorsey, Jimmy, 5, 21, 33, 51, 64, 67,
    80, 99-101, 103, 105, 108, 125, 141,
    142, 173, 224, 255, 264, 278, 279,
    292, 293, 313, 348; photos, 99, 100,
    101, 102, 106, 383
Dorsey, Tommy, 20, 33, 38, 64, 67, 73,
    80, 99, 100, 101, 103-108, 142, 173,
    207, 249, 255, 278, 279, 292, 293,
    306, 308, 348, 361, 369; photos, 103,
    104, 106, 107, 383
Dotson, Dotty, 83, 1135; photos, 83
Doty, Mike, 38, 173, 318
Dougherty, Chink, 154
Dougherty, Ed, 336
Douglas, Jack, 364
Douglas, Mark, 51
Douglas, Steve, 192
Dover, Jane, 173, 202
Dover, Jayne, 38

Dowell, Saxie, 233, 234; photos, 235
Downe Sisters, 298
Downes, Ormand, 416
Downing, Rex, 82
Dowski, Charlie, 214
Doxaras, Russell, 352
Doyle, Kay, 394
Doyle, Johnny, 164
Drellinger, Art, 372
Drewes, Herman, 242
Drugan, Seymour, 61
Druzinsky, Meyer, 290
Duane, Ted, 370
Duchene, Miguel, 284
Duchin, Eddy, 110, 228, 357; photos,
    108-109
Duchin, Peter, 110, 109; photos, 110,
    111
Dudley, Eddie, 390
Duel, Dean, 254
Duffy, Al, 363
Dufresne, Wilfred, 361
Dugan, Mary, 80
Dugat, Ross, 166
Duhe, Lawrence, 324
Duke Blue Devils, 51; photos, 52
Duke, Marilyn, 300
Dukoff, Bob, 202, 408
Dulany, Howard, 94, 248
Dumont, Jack, 318
Duncan, Marin Orchestra, 278
Dunham, Sonny, 54, 110-112, 154,
    156, 397; photos, 111, 112, 156
Dunlap, Richard, 22
Dunn, Grace, 225
Dunne, Marianne, 390
Dunning, George, 251
Du Peer, Harry, 383
Dupont, Rolly, 194
Duran, Larry, 61, 251
Durand, Paul, 352
Durham, Allen, 84, 198, 245
Durham, Clyde, 84
Durham, Eddie, 30, 269, 333, 370
Durso, Mike, 298
Duryea, Andre, 84
Duro, Fred, 164
Dutray, Honore, 324; photos, 325
Dutton, Kenny, 51
Duvivier, George, photos, 299

E

Eager, Allen, 361
Eaton, Benny, 286
Eberhardt, Elmer, 290
Eberle, Ray, 292
Eberly, Bob, 99, 100; photos, 99, 100,
    101, 294
Echols, Jack, 386
Echolstone, Bill, 247
Eckert, Fred, 94
Eckstine, Billy, 113, 141, 195

450

187, 188
Marcasie, Lou, 192; photos, 192
Marcellino, Muzzy, 129, 131, 284; photos, 130, 131, 285
Marchard, Jack, 300
Marcus, Billy, 311
Margolin, Jack, 94
Margulis, Charlie, 194, 233, 298, 374, 423
Mariano, Mario, 77
Marin, R. J., 390, 393
Marineau, Al, 254
Market, Steve, 372
Markowitz, Abe, 164
Markowitz, Irv, 361
Markowitz, Kaspar, 161
Marks, George, 386
Marlow, Mack, 372
Marmarosa, Dodo, 350
Maro, Julio, 334
Marowitz, Sam, 205, 361, 427
Marquis, Rosalind, 273
Marr, Frank L., 76
Marsala, Joe, 38, 361, 362
Marsh, Franklyn, 323
Marsh, Scotty, 398
Marshall, Billy, 98
Marshall, Dave, 247, 326
Marshall, Doc, 278
Marshall, Jack, 290
Marshall, Kaiser, 182
Marshall, Mary, 78
Marshall, Wendell, photos, 118
Marshard, Jack, 300
Martel, John, 51, 358
Marterie, Ralph, 285-286; photos, 285
Martin, Bob, 361
Martin, Carrol, 217
Martin, Claire, 233
Martin, Dean, 384
Martin, Freddy, 69, 129, 214, 242, 247, 286-287; photos, 286, 287, 288
Martin, Jack, 251
Martin, Joe, 217, 355, 370
Martin, Louis, 94
Martin, Skip, 23
Martin, Slim, 270
Martin, Tony, 413
Martinez, Frank, 386
Martinez, Ray, 205
Martini, Mike, 164
Martino, Sundi, 206
Marvin, Dolores, 336
Marvin, Eugenie, 243
Marvin, Johnny, 224
Marx, Chico, 345
Masefield, Happy, 49
Maser, Dave, 336
Masingill, O. B., 98; photos, 98
Mason, Herb, 318
Mason, Paul, 267
Mason, Sully, 251
Massi, Vince, 372
Massingill, Bill, 205

Masters, Art, 374
Masters, Frankie, 152, 288; photos, 288, 289
Masters Voices, 288
Mastran, Hal, 313
Mastren, Al, 77, 321
Mastren, Carmen, 103, 164, 300, 347; photos, 104
Math, Louis, 184
Mathews, Dave, 99, 146, 205, 277, 343, 347
Mathews, George, 298
Mathews, Hal, 403
Mathews, Jay, 288
Mathias, Ernie, 1, 139, 202, 221, 264, 313, 325, 355, 357, 364, 406; photos, 2, 139, 314
Matlock, Matty, 38, 86, 221, 242, 343
Matson, Roy, 422
Matta, George, 300
Matteson, Don, 99
Matthews, Bob, 98
Matthews, Hal, photos, 424
Matzer, Jimmy, photos, 95
Maule, Abe, 166
Maus, Carl, 372
Mauver, Walter, 129
Maxfield, Harry, 298
Maxon, Charles, 202
Maxon, Chuck, 51
Maxon, Roy, 214
Maxted, Billy, 313
Maxwell, Jimmy, 372
Maxwell, Marvel (Marilyn), 364, 416, 418
Maxwell, Norman, 192
May, Billy, 26, 33, 99, 153, 277, 292, 313, 363, 403, 423; photos, 291, 294
Mayhew, Bob, 233
Mayhew, Gus, photos, 235
Mayhew, Jack, 233
Mayhew, Nye, 423
Mayhew, Russ, 311
Mays, George, 247
Mazza, George, 194
McAfee, Johnny, 205, 317
McCahn, Lloyd, 192
McCall, Mary Ann, 23, 186, 361
McCamish, Charles, 248, 372, 390; photos, 391
McCarthy, Charlie, 319
McCarthy, Pat, 66, 346
McCauley, Frank, photos, 139
McClintock, Poley, 410
McCongo, Leo, 224
McConville, Leo, 255, 363
McCormick, Hal, 381
McCosh, Ray, 313
McCoy, Clyde, 129, 273; photos, 273, 274, 275
McCoy, Paul, 66, 277
McCoy, Stanley, 273
McDonald, Billy, 274-277; photos, 276
McDonald, Everett, 205

McDonough, Dick, 313
McEachern, Murray, 146, 154, 423; photos, 156
McFarland Twins, The, 277; photos, 276
McGarity, Lou, 335
McGarvey, Red, 77, 318, 321
McGee, Johnny, 194
McGhee, Howard, 113
McGovern, Don, photos, 93
McGowan, Jack, 358
McGreery, Lewis, 205
McGuire, Larry, 205
McHargue, Rosie, 282, 416
McIntyre, Hal, 277, 292; photos, 277, 278, 294
McKay, Ernie, 278; photos, 278
McKay, Marion, 278; photos, 279
McKay, Stewart, 51
McKee, Stacy, 51
McKeenan, Harry, 286
McKeever, Johnny, 164
McKehan, Harry, photos, 2
McKendrick, Mike, photos, 10
McKenna, Marty, 229
McKeown, Harry, 1
McKinley, Ray, 278-281, 369, 378; photos, 280
McKinney, Andrew, 364
McKinney, Bill, 281
McKinney, Ed, 326, 335
McKinney, Ray, 21, 99
McKinney's Cotton Pickers, 72, 144, 202, 281-282, 353; photos, 281
McKnight, Paul, 85
McKusick, Hal, 51, 350, 358
McLaughlin, Everet, 162
McLean, Don, 381
McLean, Hal, 82
McLean, John, 47
McLure, Don, 92
McManus, Jeanne, 277
McManus, Larry, 153
McMickle, Dale, 292; photos, 294
McMillan, Dutch, 51
McMillen, Jimmy, 92
McMullen, Jimmy, photos, 93
McMurray, Ruth, 202
McNeary, Ray, 85
McNeil, Charles, 217
McNeil, Ed, 245
McPartland, Jimmy, 21, 225, 255, 282, 323, 343, 358; photos, 282
McQuater, Tommy, 4
McRae, Teddy, photos, 68
McReynolds, Bob, 184, 358
McShann, Jay, 283
McVea, Jack, 167, 256
Meely, Phil, 270
Meisel, Ken, 98
Melachrino, George, 4
Melnick, Mitch, photos, 251
Melton, James, 85, 363
Mendell, Johnny, 202
Mendelsen, Art, 277

455

458

Powers, Al, 139; photos, 139
Prager, Carl, 357
Prano, Lou, 285
Pratt, Jimmy, 358
Preis, Rex, 221, 408
Preissing, Wally, 387
Prentiss, Bud, 273
Preston, Walter, 142
Price, Bob, 23, 186; photos, 188
Price, Charlie, 129, 358
Price, Jesse, 256
Price, Ruth, 206
Priddy, Jim, 292, 381; photos, 294
Prima, Frank O, photos, 299
Prima, Louis, 348; photos, 348
Prime, Harry, 129, 132, 198
Prince, Gene, 245
Prince, Henry, 198
Prince, Joe, 366
Pring, Bobby, 432
Pritchard, Bill, 288, 335
Pritikin, Arnold, 290
Privin, Bernie, 18, 23, 374
Procope, Russell, 47, 115, 182, 321; photos, 118
Prospero, Nick, 248
Prouting, Lionel, 77, 381
Pruden, Hal, 135, 349; photos, 349
Pugh, Raymond, 357
Pullen, Don, 22
Pumiglio, Pete, 21, 194, 214, 372
Purce, Ernest, photos, 299
Purcell, Jack, 202
Purtill, Maurice, 103, 292, 321; photos, 294
Purvis, Jack, 21, 233
Pyar, Coon, 51
Pzine, Benny, photos, 68

Q

Quadbach, Al, 262
Quadling, Lew, 222; photos, 223
Quartell, Frank, 217, 343, 379
Quartell, Joe, 290
Quealey, Chelsea, 57, 139, 217; photos, 363
Quenge, Andrew, 357
Quenger, Art, 357
Quenzer, Artie, 1
Quenzler, Bill, 66
Quicksell, Howdy, 142; photos, 143
Quigley, Truman, 390

R

Radcliffe, Fred, 47
Rader, Don, 125
Raderman, Harry, 257
Raderman, Lou, 194
Radio Rascals, 173
Radlach, Carl, 92

Rae, June, 313
Raeburn, Boyd, 95, 125, 350-351, 364; photos, 350, 351
Raeffel, Don, 380
Raff, Vince, 243
Raglin, Junior, 84
Raines, Gray, 78
Rains, Gary, 335
Ralston, Art, 154; photos, 156
Ralston, Everett, 398
Ralton, Bert, 192
Ramos, Juan, 192; photos, 192
Rand, Carl, 51
Randall, Jess, 247
Randall, Judy, 139
Randall, Slatz, 233
Randle, Paul, 47
Rando, Doc, 242
Randolph, Irving, 245
Randolph, Lester, 352
Randolph, Z. T., photos, 10
Rang, Bunny, 184
Rank, Bill, 142, 374, 423; photos, 143, 424
Rapfogel, Ben, 164
Rapp, Barney, 338, 351; photos, 352
Raskin, Milt, 58, 103, 347, 358
Raskind, Sil, 153
Rasmus, Frank, 369
Rasor, Abbey, 413
Ratiner, Angie, 161
Rausch, Billy, 154; photos, 155, 156
Ravazza, Carl, 352-353, 413; photos, 352
Ray, Forrest, 192; photos, 192
Ray, Huston, 23
Ray, Lea, 169
Ray, Leonard, 202
Ray, Rita, 153
Rayman, Morris, 370
Raymond, Dick, 4
Raymond, Don, 243, 247
Raymond, Harold, 361
Raymond, Joe, 224
Reardon, Casper, 423
Reardon, Tim, 139
Reasinger, Clyde, 98
Redd, Ernie, 340
Redd, Johnny, 340
Redding, Marian, 313
Redel, Eddie, 410
Redman, Don, 144, 182, 183, 202, 281, 282, 353-354; photos, 353
Redmond, Glenn, photos, 274
Redmond, Jerry, photos, 392
Reed, Buddy, 380
Reed, Dolores, 406
Reed, Ernie, 166
Reed, John, 22
Reed, Marion, 251
Reed, Oscar, 221
Reed, Tommy, 354, 397; photos, 354, 355
Reese, Gail, 292

Reese, Lloyd, 198
Rehmus, Elmer, 286
Reichman, Joe, 355; photos, 356
Reid, Don, 39, 243
Reid, Dorothy, 361
Reid, Neal, 186, 187; photos, 188
Reinhart, Rudy, 164
Reino, Frank, 264
Reis, Happy, 247
Reisman, Joe, 33, 98, 99, 154, 288, 390, 427, 428; photos, 95, 98, 297, 391
Reisman, Leo, 48, 108, 351-358; photos, 357, 358
Reitz, Oscar, 229
Remley, Frank, 169
Renzulli, Mike, 1; photos, 2
Reo, Tom, 347, 364
Reser, Harry, 247, 255, 282, 422
Reus, Allen, 38, 51, 390; photos, 391
Rey, Alvino, 178, 179, 242, 358; photos, 179, 359, 360
Reynolds, Bill, 77
Reynolds, Blake, 374
Reynolds, Dick, 257
Reynolds, John, 77
Reynolds, Tommy, 361
Rhea, Donald, 129
Rhoads, Bill, 251
Rhodes, Dusty, 129, 416
Rhodes, Joe, 139
Rhodes, Todd, 281
Rhythm Boys, The, 423
Rhythmaires, 77
Ribble, Ben, 355
Ricard, Andy, 380
Ricci, Paul, 38, 173, 194, 304
Rice, Eddie, 398
Rice, Floyd, 325
Rice, Marcia, 17
Rich, Buddy, 72, 103, 177, 205, 361-363, 374; photos, 107, 362
Rich, Freddy, 33, 211, 212, 362
Rich, Mickey, 361
Richards, Ann, 238
Richards, Billy, photos, 299
Richards, Johnny, 363-364
Richards, Judy, 237, 304
Richards, Lynn, 206
Richards, Newton, 85
Richards, Ralph, 192
Richards, Sally, 361
Richardson, Bob, 357
Richardson, Cecil, 416
Richardson, Dick, 98
Richardson, Jerome, 195
Richardson, Rodney, 256
Richman, Jack, 154
Richmond, June, 99, 246
Richter, Paul, 211
Rickenbach, Paul, 264
Rickey, Bobby, 381
Ricolson, Joe, 82
Riddle, Nelson, 380, 381

Other titles of interest

BENNY: King of Swing
Introduction by Stanley Baron
208 pp., 250 photos
80289-9 $14.95

THE ESSENTIAL JAZZ RECORDS
Volume I: From Ragtime to Swing
Max Harrison, Charles Fox
and Eric Thacker
605 pp.
80326-7 $14.95

GLENN MILLER & HIS
ORCHESTRA
George T. Simon
Introduction by Bing Crosby
473 pp., over 130 photos
80129-9 $12.95

JACK TEAGARDEN
Jay Smith and Len Guttridge
208 pp., 18 photos
80322-4 $9.95

JAZZ MASTERS OF THE 20s
Richard Hadlock
255 pp., 12 photos
80328-3 $11.95

JAZZ MASTERS OF THE 30s
Rex Stewart
283 pp., 13 photos
80159-0 $11.95

MUSIC IS MY MISTRESS
Edward Kennedy Ellington
522 pp., 112 photos
80033-0 $14.95

THE RELUCTANT ART
Five Studies in the
Growth of Jazz
Expanded Edition
Benny Green
208 pp.
80441-7 $11.95

STOMPING THE BLUES
Albert Murray
272 pp., 127 illus.
80362-3 $13.95

WHO'S WHO OF JAZZ
Storyville to Swing Street
John Chilton
362 pp., 97 photos
80243-0 $13.95

THE WONDERFUL ERA
OF THE GREAT
DANCE BANDS
Leo Walker
316 pp., over 400 photos
80379-8 $18.95

THE WORLD OF
COUNT BASIE
Stanley Dance
399 pp., 48 photos
80245-7 $14.95

THE WORLD OF
DUKE ELLINGTON
Stanley Dance
311 pp., 65 photos
80136-1 $12.95

THE WORLD OF SWING
Stanley Dance
436 pp., 88 photos
80103-5 $10.95

JAZZ MASTERS OF THE 40s
Ira Gitler
298 pp., 14 photos
80224-4 $12.95

JAZZ MASTERS OF THE 50s
Joe Goldberg
246 pp., 8 photos
80197-3 $11.95

SWING OUT
Great Negro Dance Bands
Gene Fernett
New foreword by
Dan Morgenstern
176 pp., 152 illus.
80501-4 $14.95

Available at your bookstore

OR ORDER DIRECTLY FROM

DA CAPO PRESS

1-800-321-0050